Accounting—
By Principle or Design?

Accounting—
By Principle or Design?

AHMED RIAHI-BELKAOUI

 PRAEGER

Westport, Connecticut
London

Library of Congress Cataloging-in-Publication Data

Riahi-Belkaoui, Ahmed, 1943–
    Accounting—by principle or design? / Ahmed Riahi-Belkaoui.
      p. cm.
    Includes bibliographical references and index.
    ISBN 1–56720–553–4 (alk. paper)
    1. Accounting. 2. Income accounting. 3. Corporations—Accounting. 4. Smoothing
(Statistics) 5. Fraud. I. Title.
    HF5635.R455   2003
    657—dc21   2002030332

British Library Cataloguing in Publication Data is available.

Library of Congress Catalog Card Number: 2002030332
ISBN: 1–56720–553–4

First published in 2003

Praeger Publishers, 88 Post Road West, Westport, CT 06881
An imprint of Greenwood Publishing Group, Inc.
www.praeger.com

Printed in the United States of America

The paper used in this book complies with the
Permanent Paper Standard issued by the National
Information Standards Organization (Z39.48–1984).

10 9 8 7 6 5 4 3 2 1

To Dimitra

Contents

Preface

Basically, an interested and inquisitive observer from outside the accounting establishment who examines the accounting discipline and the accounting process and output may be easily tempted to see more of various deliberate attempts to choose accounting techniques and solutions that fit a preestablished goal and picture to be conveyed as representative constructions of realities, a phenomenon that I label as "designed accounting," rather than a choice of principle-based techniques and solutions, a phenomenon that I label as "principled accounting." Aspects of this designed accounting include:

1. Income smoothing as choices of accounting techniques aimed at affecting the variance of earnings (Chapter 1).
2. Earnings management as choices of accounting techniques aimed at affecting the level of earnings (Chapter 2).
3. "Big bath" and creative accounting as choices of techniques to reduce the current level of earnings in favor of increasing the future level of earnings and to engage in various forms of "window dressing" (Chapter 3).
4. Fraud in accounting as deliberate attempts to present a false picture of reality (Chapter 4).
5. Slack in accounting as the tendency to refrain from using all of the resources available to the firm in the form of organizational slack or budgetary slack (Chapter 5).

This book should be of interest to preparers and users of accounting information and should be used in graduate courses covering the current crisis in accounting.

Many people helped in the development of this book. I received considerable assistance from the University of Illinois at Chicago, especially Ewa Thomaszewski and Maninder Bhuller. I also thank the staff at Praeger for their continuous and intelligent support.

Chapter 1

Income Smoothing

INTRODUCTION

Income smoothing is a clear form of designed accounting. It is a deliberate attempt by management to show stable earnings by reaching the variations in earnings fluctuations and securing an acceptable earnings growth. The complexity of the phenomenon warrants examination of its nature, history, the motivations behind its construction, smoothing dimensions, and variables used, as well as the objects of smoothing. Because it may take different forms depending on different contextual confirmations, income smoothing may have different impacts that also warrant examination. All of these issues are discussed in this chapter.

ACCOUNTING POLICY AND CHANGES

Firms need to make choices among the different accounting methods in recording transactions and preparing their financial statements. These choices, as dictated by generally accepted accounting principles, represent the accounting policies of the firm. They are best defined by the Accounting Principles Board (APB) in its Opinion 22, *Disclosure of Acceding Polices* (April 1972), paragraph 6:

The *accounting policies* of a reporting entity are the specific accounting principles and the methods of applying those principles that are judged by the management of the entity to be the most appropriate in the circumstances to present fairly financial position, changes in financial position, and results of operations in accordance with generally accepted accounting principles and that accordingly have been adopted for preparing the financial statements.

Firms also make accounting changes as part of their accounting policies. The general belief is that firms make accounting changes to mask performance problems. The accounting literature explains the changes in accounting principles and estimates in terms of management's desire to reach definite objectives such as income smoothing[1] or the reduction of agency costs associated with a violation of debt covenants. A summary of existing research results suggests that as the tightness of debt covenant increases, firms are more likely to loosen the tightness of covenant restrictions through appropriate accounting changes.[2] In fact, two studies that examined the accounting changes of (1) successful and unsuccessful firms[3] and (2) firms facing or experiencing bond rating changes[4] provide some evidence consistent with the assertion that managers can modify income through judicious accounting changes.

Accounting regulators have tried to limit management's ability to use accounting changes to increase or decrease net income. Since 1970, APB No. 20 has stipulated that accounting changes should be accounted for as a cumulative effect change, requiring the reporting in the comparative income statements of the cumulative effect of change in the net income of the period of the change as well as the disclosure in the notes of the effect of adopting the new accounting principle on income before extraordinary income and net income (and on related per share amounts) of the period change. Similarly, the Securities and Exchange Commission's (SEC) accounting Release No. 177 required that accounting changes be made to more preferable accounting methods, using reasonable business judgment in the choice. While both pronouncements act as a control mechanism, they do not eliminate management's ability to increase and/or decrease income through accounting changes. SEC Chairman Arthur Levitt contended that public companies have used six accounting practices to manage corporate earnings:

1. overstatement of restructuring changes to clean up the balance sheet;
2. classification of a significant portion of the price of an acquired entity as in-process research and development so that the amount can be written off as a onetime charge;
3. creation of large liabilities for future expenses (recorded as part of the accounting for an acquisition) to protect future earnings;
4. use of unrealistic assumptions to estimate liabilities for items such as sales returns, loan losses, and warranty costs so that the overaccrual can be reversed to improve earnings during a subsequent period;
5. intentional inclusion of errors in the company's books and justifying the failure to correct the errors by arguing materiality; and
6. recognition of revenue before the earnings process is complete.[5]

INCOME SMOOTHING HYPOTHESIS

Nature of Income Smoothing

Income smoothing may be viewed as the deliberate normalization of income in order to reach a desired trend or level. As far back as 1953, Heyworth observed "more of the accounting techniques which may be applied to affect the assignment of net income successive accounting periods . . . for smoothing or leveling the amplitude of periodic net income fluctuations."[6] What followed were arguments made by Monsen and Downs[7] and Gordon[8] that corporate managers may be motivated to smooth their own income security, with the assumption that stability in income and rate of growth will be preferred over higher average income streams with greater variability. More specifically, Gordon theorized on income smoothing as follows:

Proposition 1: The criterion that a corporate management uses in selecting among accounting principles is the maximization of its utility or welfare.

Proposition 2: The utility of management increases with (1) its job security, (2) the level and rate of growth in the management's income, and (3) the level and rate of growth in the corporation's size.

Proposition 3: The achievement of the management goals stated in Proposition 2 is dependent in part on the satisfaction of stockholders with the corporation's performance; that is, other things being equal, the happier the stockholders, the greater the job security, income, and so on of the management.

Proposition 4: Stockholders' satisfaction with a corporation increases with the average rate of growth in the corporation's income (or the average rate of return on its capital) and the stability of its income. This proposition is as readily verified as Proposition 2. Theorem: Given that the above four propositions are accepted or found to be true, it follows that management would, within the limits of its power, that is, the latitude allowed by accounting rules, (1) smooth reported income and (2) smooth the rate of growth in income. By "smooth the rate of growth in income" we mean the following: if the rate of growth is high, accounting practices that reduce it should be adopted, and vice versa.[9]

The best definition of income smoothing was provided by Beidleman as follows:

Smoothing of reported earnings may be deemed as the intentional dampening or fluctuations about some level of earnings that is currently considered to be normal for a firm. In this sense smoothing represents an attempt on the part of the firm's management to reduce abnormal variations in earnings to the extent allowed under sound accounting and management principles.[10]

Given the above definition, what needs to be explicated are the motivation of smoothing, the dimensions of smoothing, and the instruments of smoothing.

History of Income Smoothing

Most of the literature on income smoothing attributes the origin of the concept to one of the three works by Gordon et al.,[11] Hepworth,[12] and White.[13] However, an article by Buckmaster[14] on income smoothing in accounting and business literature prior to 1954 identifies up to thirty-four works from 1893 to 1953 that contain some kind of reference to the smoothing properties of an accounting method or to an accounting practice used in such a way as to dampen the fluctuations of reported income. The article reports on pages that focus on the balance sheet and secret reserves that result in the reduction of the volatility of income time-series and those that examined the last in, first out (LIFO) base-stock inventory debate as it related to income smoothing.

Secret reserves were created by management in order to "avoid the distribution of firm assets as dividends, by creating a contra asset account or a liability or by failing to record assets and/or writing them off as expenses or directly to surplus (retained earnings)."[15] The secret reserves can also be created by the recording of unusually large amounts of depreciation in good years,[16] the write-down of assets,[17] the classification of extraordinary losses as extraordinary depreciation,[18] the use of flexibility in the capitalize/expense decisions for plant and equipment related costs,[19] the charging of large amounts of capital expenditures to expenses in periods of high profits,[20] the practice of overly excessive repairs in good years and inadequate repairs in bad years,[21] and the making of excessive provisions for bad debt and valuing inventories at below cost.[22]

Base-stock inventory was also used for smoothing purposes and dampening of business cycles. As Warshaw explains:

The leveling of inventory gains and losses, with the comparative stability of yearly profits which this method brings about . . . exerts a subconscious effect upon business policy which is very desirable. Prices of manufacturing articles are kept in more proper relation to prices of raw material. The management is not elated by apparent profits or depressed by apparent losses. Such elation and depression are responsible for most business follies. The normal stock inventory automatically creates a reserve that strengthens the basis for credit, gives stability, and makes expansion safe. Moreover, it has the great advantage of being a concrete suggestion for mitigating the security of business cycles.[23]

Warshaw's arguments were later supported by Davis[24] and Cotter.[25] Cotter mentioned the smoothing properties of LIFO and the advantages of (a) dampening the business cycles, (b) avoiding overexpansion of credit, (c) avoiding demands for excessive dividends, and (d) better information for pricing decisions.[26]

Motivations of Smoothing

As early as 1953 Heyworth claimed that motivations behind smoothing include the improvements of relations with creditors, investors, and workers, as well as dampening of business cycles through psychological processes.[27] Gordon proposed that:

1. The criterion that a corporate management uses in selecting among accounting principles is to maximize its utility or welfare.
2. The same utility is a function of job security, the level and rate of growth of salary, and the level and growth rate in the firm's size.
3. Satisfaction of shareholders with the corporation's performance enhances the status and rewards of managers.
4. The same satisfaction depends on the rate of growth and stability of the firm's income.[28]

These propositions culminate in the need to smooth as explained in the following theorem:

Given that the above four propositions are accepted or found to be true, it follows that a management should, within the limits of its power, i.e., the latitude allowed by accounting rules, (1) smooth reported income and (2) smooth the rate of growth in income. By smoothing the rate of growth in income we mean the following: If the rate of growth is high, accounting practices which reduce it should be adopted and vice-versa.[29]

Beidelman considers two reasons for management to smooth reported earnings.[30] The first argument rests on the assumption that a stable earnings stream is capable of supporting a higher level of dividends than a more variable earnings stream, having a favorable effect on the value of the firm's shares as overall riskiness of the firm is reduced. He states:

To the extent that the observed variability about a trend of reported earnings influences investors' subjective expectations for possible outcomes of future earnings and dividends, management might be able favorably to influence the value of the firm's shares by smoothing earnings.[31]

The second argument attributes to smoothing the ability to counter the cyclical nature of reported earnings and likely reduce the correlation of a firm's expected returns with returns on the market portfolio. He states:

To the degree that auto-normalization of earnings is successful, and that the reduced covariance of returns with the market is recognized by investors and incorporated into their evaluation process, smoothing will have added beneficial effects in share values.[32]

It results from the need felt by management to neutralize environmental uncertainty and dampen the wide fluctuations in the operating performance of the firm subject to an intermittent cycle of good and bad times. To do so, management may resort to organizational slack behavior,[33] budgetary slack behavior,[34] or risk-avoiding behavior.[35] Each of these behaviors necessitates decisions affecting the incurrence and /or allocation of discretionary expenses (costs) that result in income smoothing.

In addition to these behaviors intended to neutralize environmental uncertainty, it is possible to identify organizational characterizations that differentiate firms in their extent of smoothing. For example, Kamin and Ronen[36] examined the effects of the separation of ownership and control on income smoothing, under the hypothesis that management-controlled firms are more likely to be engaged in smoothing as a manifestation of managerial discretion and budgetary slack. Their results confirmed that income smoothing is higher among management-controlled firms with high barriers to entry.

Management was also assigned to circumvent news of the constraints of generally accepted accounting principles by attempting to smooth income numbers so as to convey their expectations of future cash flows, enhancing in the process the apparent reliability of predictions based on the observed smoothed series of numbers.[37] Three constraints are presumed to lead managers to smooth:

1. the competitive market mechanisms, which reduce the options available to management;

2. the management compensation scheme, which is linked directly to the firm's performance; and

3. the threat of management displacement.

This smoothing is not limited to high-level management and external accounting; it is also presumed to be used by lower-level management and internal accounting in the form of organizational slack and slack budgeting.[38]

Types of Smoothing

An early definition of income smoothing states that it "moderates year-to-year fluctuations in income by shifting earnings from peak years to less successful periods."[39] A more recent definition of income smoothing sees the phenomenon as "the process of manipulating the time profile of earnings or earnings reports to make the reported income less variable, while not increasing reported earnings over the long run."[40] Both definitions seem to imply that there is only one form of income smoothing used to dampen fluctuations of earnings toward an expected level of earnings. Of the studies that distinguished between potentially different types of smoothing, the article by Eckel[41] provides the more exhaustive classification of the different types of smooth income statements. The first distinction is made between an intentional or designed smoothing and a natural smoothing. The second distinction is to classify the intentional or designed smoothing with either an artificial smoothing or a real smoothing. These various types of smoothing are explicated next.

Intentional or designed smoothing refers specifically to the deliberate designing choices made to dampen earnings fluctuations around a desired level. Therefore, intentional or designed smoothing is essentially an accounting smoothing that uses the existing flexibility in generally accepted accounting principles and the choices and combinations available to smooth income. It is therefore essentially a form of the designed accounting that is the objective of this book.

Natural smoothing, unlike designed smoothing, is a natural product of the income-generating process, rather than the result of actions taken by management. Eckel gives the following example: "For example, one would expect the income generating process of public utilities to be such that income streams would be naturally smooth."[42]

Designed smoothing may be accomplished by either artificial or real smoothing. Artificial smoothing is the result of resorting to accounting manipulations to smooth income. As stated by Eckel:

These manipulations do not represent underlying economic events or affect cash flows, but shift costs and/or revenues from one period to another. For example, a firm would increase or decrease reported income smoothing by changing its actuarial assumptions concerning pension costs.[43]

Finally, real smoothing involves the deliberate choice and timing of transactions that can affect cash flows and control underlying choices of purchasing, hiring production, investment, sales, capital budgeting, research and development, advertising, and other decisions. It is basically a choice of business conduct to deliberately alter the cash flows of a corporation toward dampening earnings fluctuations. It can be either an attempt to control economic events or an attempt to construct economic events with the intention of affecting cash flows and smooth earnings. The actions taken by management in real smoothing are intended to alter the firm's production and/or investment decisions at year-end based on the knowledge of how the firm has performed up to that time of the year.[44]

The Smoothing Object

Basically, the smoothing object should be based on the most visible and used financial indication, which is the profit. Because income smoothing is not a visible phenomenon, the literature speculates on various expressions of profit as the most likely object of smoothing. These expressions include (1) net income-based indicators generally before extraordinary items and before or after tax, (2) earnings per share-based indicators generally before extraordinary gains and losses and adjusted for stock splits and dividends. The researchers choose net income- or earnings per share-based indicators as the object of smoothing because of the belief that management's long-term concern is with the net income, and users have a kind of functional fixation on the bottom figure, whether it is income or earnings per share. This is simplistic reasoning, as management may find it necessary and practical to smooth sales, and fixed sales commitments have only the flexibility of smoothing expenses. Similarly, a firm with good control on its expenses may find it more practical to smooth its sales revenues.

The Dimensions of Smoothing

The dimensions of smoothing are basically the means used to accomplish the smoothing of income numbers. Dascher and Malcolm distinguished between real smoothing and artificial smoothing as follows:

Real smoothing refers to the actual transaction that is undertaken or not undertaken on the basis of its smoothing effect on income, whereas artificial smoothing refers to accounting procedures which are implemented to shift costs and/or revenues from one period to another.[45]

These types of smoothing may be indistinguishable. For example, the amount of reported expenses may be lower or higher than in previous periods because of either deliberate actions on the level of the expenses (real smoothing) or the reporting methods (artificial smoothing). For both types, an operational test proposed is to fit a curve to a stream of income calculated two ways, excluding a possible manipulative variable and including it.[46]

Artificial smoothing was also considered by Copeland and defined as follows:

Income smoothing involves the repetitive selection of accounting measurement or reporting rules in a particular pattern, the effect of which is to report the stream of income with a smaller variation from trend than would otherwise have appeared.[47]

Besides real and artificial smoothing, other dimensions of smoothing were considered in the literature. A popular classification adds a third smoothing dimension, namely, classificatory smoothing. Barnes et al. distinguished between three smoothing dimensions as follows:

1. *Smoothing through events' occurrence and/or recognition.* Management can time actual transactions so that their effects on reported income would tend to dampen its variations over time. Mostly, the planned timing of events' occurrences (e.g., research and development) would be a function of the accounting rules governing the accounting recognition of the events.

2. *Smoothing through allocation over time.* Given the occurrence and the recognition of an event, management has more discretionary control over the determination over the periods to be affected by the events' quantification.

3. *Smoothing through classification (hence, classifactory smoothing).* When income statement statistics other than net income (net of all revenues and expenses) are the

object of smoothing, management can classify intraincome statement items to reduce variations over time in that statistic.[48]

Basically, real smoothing corresponded to the smoothing through events' occurrence and/or recognition, while artificial smoothing corresponded to the smoothing through the allocation over time.

The Smoothing Variables

The smoothing devices or instruments are the variables used to smooth the chosen performance indicator. Copeland suggested the following five conditions as necessary for a smoothing instrument:

A. Once used, it must not commit the firm to any particular future action.
B. It must be based upon the exercise of professional judgment and be considered within the domain of "generally accepted accounting principles."
C. It must lead to material shifts relative to year-to-year differences in income.
D. It must not require a "real" transaction with second parties, but only a reclassification of internal account balances.
E. It must be used, singularly or in conjunction with other practices, over consecutive periods of time.[49]

Beidelman suggested two different and less restrictive criteria:

1. It must permit management to reduce the variability in reported earnings as it strives to achieve its long-run earnings (growth) objective.
2. Once used, it should not commit the firm to any particular action.[50]

Examples of smoothing instruments used include:

1. Switch from accelerated to straight-line depreciation[51]
2. Choice of cost or equity method[52]
3. Pension costs[53]
4. Dividend income[54]
5. Gains and losses on sale of securities[55]
6. Investment tax credit[56]

RESEARCH FINDINGS ON INCOME SMOOTHING

Sector and Country Analysis

It is possible to identify organizational characterizations, sector classifications, and country classifications that differentiate among different firms in their extent of smoothing.

1. With respect to the organizational characterizations, Kamin and Ronen[57] examined the effects of the separation of ownership and control on income smoothing under the hypothesis that management-controlled firms are more likely to be engaged in smoothing as a manifestation of managerial discretion and budgetary slack. Their results confirmed that a majority of the firms examined behave as if they were smoothers, and a particularly strong majority is included among management-controlled firms with high barriers to entry.

2. With respect to sectorial classifications, Belkaoui and Picur[58] tested the effects of a dual economy on income-smoothing behavior. The main hypothesis was that a higher degree of smoothing of income numbers will be exhibited by firms in the periphery sector than firms in the core sector as a reaction to differences in the opportunity structures, experiences, and environmental uncertainty. Their results indicated that a majority of U.S. firms may be resorting to income smoothing, with a higher number included among firms in the periphery sector. However, using an income variability method of analysis, those results could not be replicated using a U.S. sample[59] or a Canadian sample.[60] In a Finnish context, Kinnunen et al.[61] found that one-sector firms may have more opportunities and more predisposition to income-smoothing behavior than firms operating in the more peripheral sector of the Finnish economy. The following explanation is provided for the Finnish results:

As an explanation for these findings, it can be argued that compared with the periphery sector, Finnish accounting rules provide the sector firms more opportunities to exploit certain earnings management instruments (such as accounting for depreciation of fixed assets, untaxed reserves, pension liabilities, exchange losses and R&D [research and development] costs). Furthermore, because these firms sell their products in highly competitive international markets, and are very much dependent on those markets, they presumably face a higher degree of environmental uncertainty than firms in the periphery sector. Therefore, the core sector firms are more apt to use income smoothing in the conventional sense.[62]

3. With regard to country classifications excluding the United States, the evidence shows a certain degree of income smoothing in Japan,[63] the United Kingdom,[64] Canada,[65] France,[66] and Singapore.[67]

Job Security and Anticipatory Smoothing

The general idea behind income smoothing is that the manager may take actions that increase reported income when income is low and take actions that decrease reported income when income is high. This is possible through either the flexibility allowed within generally accepted accounting principles or deliberate changes in operations. We may ask about the motivations of managers engaged in income smoothing. Fudenberg and Tirole[68] analytically show that income smoothing to increase job security arises in equilibrium if the following assumptions hold:

1. Managers enjoy nonmonetary private benefits (incumbency rents) from running the firm.
2. The firm is not committed to long-term incentive contract, which results in managers' dismissal in case of poor performance.
3. This is information decay in the sense that current earnings are more important than previous earnings in management's performance evaluation.

Because of these assumptions, managers in good times save for bad times. In other words:

First, when current earnings are relatively low, but expected future earnings are relatively high, managers will make accounting choices that increase current period discretionary accruals. In effect, managers in this setting are "borrowing" earnings from the future. Second, when current earnings are relatively high, but expected future earnings are relatively low, managers will make accounting choices that decrease current year discretionary accruals. Managers are effectively "saving" current earnings for possible use in the future.[69]

DeFond and Park[70] investigated the intuition derived from the Fudenberg-Tirole model by examining the effects of current relative premanaged earnings and expected future relative earnings on the behavior of discretionary accruals. Their evidence suggests that when current earnings are "poor," and expected future earnings are "good," managers "borrow" earnings from the future for use in the current period. Conversely, when current earnings are "good" and expected future earnings are "poor," managers "save" current earnings for possible use in the future. These findings that managers of firms experiencing poor (good) performance in the current period and expecting good (poor) performance in the next period choose income-increasing (income-decreasing) discretionary accruals in order to reduce the threat of being dismissed did not directly examine the link between job security and income smoothing. Accordingly, Ahmed et al.[71] hypothesized that the extent of income smoothing varies directly with managers' job security concern as proxied by the degree of competition in a firm's product markets, product durability, and capital-intensity. Basically, the argument is that managers of firms in more competitive industries, durable goods industries, and capital-intensive businesses are likely to have greater job security concerns than managers of other firms and therefore are more likely to engage in a greater extent of income smoothing. The results were consistent with the predictions. Using a different methodology, Elgers et al.[72] were able to provide results indicating that patterns in measured discretionary accruals and relative earnings performance are consistent with the theory that managers smooth earnings based on both current-year results and expected next-year results, a phenomenon better labeled as "anticipatory income smoothing."

Stockholders' Wealth and Income Smoothing

The only literature in income smoothing maintained and/or established a positive relationship between income smoothing and shareholders' wealth. The statements and/or findings are as follows:

1. Stockholder satisfaction is bound to increase with the rate of growth in a firm's income and the stability of its income.[73]
2. The possibility that analysts may become more enthusiastic about self-smoothers increases the interest in the firm's market shares and may have a favorable effect on share value and cost of capital.[74]
3. Income variability may be shown to be significantly correlated with both overall and systematic risk measures.[75]
4. Smoothing may imply a direct, cause-effect relationship between earnings fluctuations and market risk.[76]
5. By allowing management to select alternative accounting techniques, owners can capitalize upon managers' expertise.[77]
6. Smooth income reduces the probability of financial ratio covenants' leading to a reduction in the cost of default and renegotiation.[78]
7. Smooth income reduces the probability of financial ratio covenants' leading to a reduction in the cost of default and renegotiation.[79]
8. Firms that do not smooth have higher unexpected returns from earnings surprises than firms that smooth income.[80]
9. Institutional investors avoid firms that exhibit large variations in earnings. A smoother income stream is preferred.[81]

Other analyses of the impact of income smoothing on stockholders' wealth were more market-based. Nichelson et al.[82] found lower returns, lower risk, and larger firm sizes for smoothing firms. Wang and Williams[83] found that firms with a smooth income series were less risky and had a market response four times as large as that for the other firms. This favorable impact of smoothing is evaluated as follows:

Contrary to the widespread view that managers engage in income smoothing to increase their own welfare at the expense of stockholders, this study documents consistent evidence indicating that accounting income smoothing can be beneficial to the firm's stockholders and prospective investors. Specifically, the analysis demonstrated that income smoothing may enhance the informational value of earnings and reduce the riskiness of the firm.[84]

Chaney et al.[85] presents evidence that managers smooth income around their arrangements of the firm's permanent earnings. Income smoothing becomes a long-term strategy to communicate a firm's permanent earnings using discretionary accruals to remove (or offset) a portion of the transitory component of reported earnings. The evidence shows that (1) if the current year's income before discretionary accruals is lower than last year's reported earnings, discretionary accruals will be positive and (2) if the current year's income before discretionary accruals is already higher than last year's reported earnings, discretionary accruals will be negative. They conclude as follows:

We suggest that smoothing income around the managers' assessment of the firm's permanent earnings enhances the market's perception of the firm whose earnings are being managed. When firms consistently manage earnings to present a smooth pattern of profits to market participants, they avoid the dips in earnings (and related reputation effects) that may follow periods of over-reported earnings. We hypothesize and present evidence that earnings response coefficients, which reflect the relation between unexpected earnings and market returns, as well as the perceived reliability of reported earnings, are higher for firms that engage consistently in income smoothing.[86]

Finally, Chaney and Lewis[87] investigated income smoothing and underperformance in initial public offerings. They found a positive association between a proxy for income smoothing and firm performance, in the sense that (1) firms that perform well tend to report earnings with less variability relative to cash from operations compared to other firms and (2) the earnings response coefficient is greater for firms that are able to smooth earnings relative to cash flows. The result is interpreted as being totally consistent with the hypothesis that the market is better able to assess the information content of earnings for firms with smoother earnings.

NOTES

1. A. Belkaoui, *Accounting and Public Policy* (Westport, CT: Quorum Books, 1995).

2. A. Christie, "Aggregation of Test Statistics: On Evaluation of the Evidence as Contracting and Size Hypotheses," *Journal of Accounting and Economics* 12 (1990).

3. S. Lilien, M. Mellman, and V. Pastena, "Accounting Changes: Successful or Unsuccessful Firms," *The Accounting Review* (October 1988), pp. 642–651.

4. A. Belkaoui, "The Effect of Bond Ratings on Accounting Changes," Working Paper, University of Illinois at Chicago, 2002.

5. "SEC Chairman Discusses Earnings Management," *Deloitte & Touche Review* (October 12, 1998), p. 1.

6. S.R. Heyworth, "Smoothing Periodic Income," *The Accounting Review* (January 1953), p. 32.

7. R.J. Monsen and A. Downs, "A Theory of Large Managerial Firms," *The Journal of Political Economy* (June 1965).

8. M.J. Gordon, "Postulates, Principles, and Research in Accounting," *The Accounting Review* (April 1964), pp. 251–263.

9. Ibid., pp. 261–262.

10. C.R. Beidleman, "Income Smoothing: The Role of Management," *The Accounting Review* (October 1973), p. 653.

11. M.J. Gordon, B.M. Horwitz, and P.T. Meyers, "Accounting Measurement and Normal Growth of the Firm," in R. Jaedicke, Y. Ijiri, and O. Nielsen (eds.), *Research in Accounting Measurement* (Evanston, IL: American Accounting Association, 1966), pp. 221–231.

12. Hepworth, "Smoothing Periodic Income," pp. 32–39.

13. G. White, "Discretionary Accounting Disclosures and Income Normalization," *Journal of Accounting Research* (Autumn 1970), pp. 260–273.

14. D. Buckmaster, "Income Smoothing in Accounting and Business Literature Prior to 1954," *The Accounting Historian's Journal* (December 1992), pp. 147–173.

15. Ibid., p. 155.

16. E. Matheson, *The Depreciation of Factories, Mines and Industrial Undertaking and Their Valuation* (London: E. and F.N. Spon, 1910; reprint, New York: Arno Press, 1976), p. 44.

17. J.P. Joplin, "Secret Reserves," *Journal of Accountancy* (December 1910), pp. 407–417.

18. A.B. Grunder and D.R. Becker, "The Straight-Line Depreciation Accounting Practice of Telephone Companies in the United States," in *International Congress on Accounting* (New York: International Congress, 1930), pp. 351–403.

19. L.R. Dicksee, *Depreciation, Reserves, and Reserve Funds* (London: Gee & Co., 1903).

20. J.F. Johnson and E.S. Meade, "Editorial: Maintenance Expenses and Concealment of Earnings," *Journal of Accountancy* (March 1906), pp. 410–412.

21. Ibid.

22. Joplin, "Secret Reserves."

23. H.T. Warshaw, "Inventory Valuation and the Business Cycle," *Harvard Business Review* (October 1924), pp. 27–34.

24. A.R. Davis, "Inventory Valuation and Business Profits: The Case for a Cost or Market Basis," *N.A.C.A. Bulletin* (December 1937), pp. 400–409.

25. A. Cotter, *Fool's Profits* (New York: Barwin's Publishing, 1940).

26. Ibid.

27. Heyworth, "Smoothing Periodic Income," p. 34.

28. Gordon, "Postulates, Principles, and Research in Accounting," pp. 251–263.

29. Ibid.

30. Beidleman, "Income Smoothing," pp. 658–667.

31. Ibid., p. 654.

32. Ibid.

33. R.M. Cyert and J.G. March, *A Behavioral Theory of the Firm* (Englewood Cliffs, NJ: Prentice-Hall, 1963).

34. M. Schiff and A.Y. Levin, "Where Traditional Budgeting Fails," *Financial Executive* (May 1968), pp. 57–62.

35. J.D. Thompson, *Organizations in Action* (New York: McGraw-Hill, 1967).

36. J.Y. Kamin and J. Ronen, "The Smoothing of Income Numbers: Some Empirical

Evidence in Systematic Differences among Management-Controlled and Owner-Controlled Firms," *Accounting, Organizations and Society* 3, 2 (1978), pp. 141–153.

37. A. Barnea, J. Ronen, and S. Sadan, "Classificatory Smoothing of Income with Extraordinary Items," *The Accounting Review* (January 1976), pp. 110–122.

38. A. Belkaoui, *Behavioral Accounting* (Westport, CT: Greenwood Press, 1989).

39. R. Copeland, "Income Smoothing," *Empirical Research in Accounting: Selected Studies*, suppl. to *Journal of Accounting Research* 6 (1968), p. 101.

40. D. Fudenberg and J. Tirole, "A Theory of Income and Dividend Smoothing Based on Incumbency Rents," *Journal of Political Economy* 1 (1995), pp. 75–93.

41. N. Eckel, "The Income Smoothing Hypothesis Revisited," *Abacus* 17 (June 1981), pp. 28–40.

42. Ibid., p. 28.

43. Ibid., p. 29.

44. R.A. Lamber, "Income Smoothing as Rational Equilibrium Behavior," *The Accounting Review* 59 (October 1984), p. 606.

45. P.E. Dascher and R.E. Malcolm, "A Note on Income Smoothing in the Chemical Industry," *Journal of Accounting Research* (Autumn 1970), pp. 253–254.

46. M.J. Gordon, "Discussions of the Effects of Alternative Accounting Rules for Nonsubsidiary Investments," *Empirical Research in Accounting: Selected Studies*, suppl. to *Journal of Accounting Research* 4 (1966), p. 223.

47. Copeland, "Income Smoothing," 6, p. 101.

48. Barnea, Ronen, and Sadan, "Classificatory Smoothing of Income with Extraordinary Items," p. 111.

49. Copeland, "Income Smoothing," p. 102.

50. Beidleman, "Income Smoothing," p. 658.

51. T.R. Archibald, "The Return to Straight-Line Depreciation: An Analysis of a Change in Accounting Method," *Empirical Research in Accounting: Selected Studies*, suppl. to *Journal of Accounting Research* 5 (1967), pp. 164–180.

52. R.M. Barefield, and E.E. Comiskey, "The Smoothing Hypothesis: An Alternative Test," *The Accounting Review* (April 1972), pp. 291–298.

53. Beidleman, "Income Smoothing," pp. 653–667.

54. Copeland, "Income Smoothing," pp. 101–116.

55. N. Dopuch and D. Drake, "The Effect of Alternative Accounting Rules for Nonsubsidiary Investments," *Empirical Research in Accounting: Selected Studies* (1966), pp. 192–219.

56. Gordon, Horwitz, and Meyers, "Accounting Measurement and Normal Growth of the Firm," pp. 220–223.

57. Kamin and Ronen, "The Smoothing of Income Numbers," pp. 141–153.

58. A. Belkaoui and R.D. Picur, "The Smoothing of Income Numbers: Some Empirical Evidence on the Systematic Differences between Core and Periphery Industrial Sectors," *Journal of Business Finance & Accounting*, 11, 4 (Winter 1984), pp. 527–545.

59. W.D. Albrecht, and F.M. Richardson, "Income Smoothing by Economic Sector," *Journal of Business Finance & Accounting* 17, 5 (Winter 1990), pp. 713–730.

60. G. Breton and Jean Piere Chenail, "Une Etude Emperique du Lissage des Benefices dansles Enterprises Canadiennes," *Comptabilite, Controle, Audit* (March 1997), pp. 53–68.

61. J. Kinnunen, E. Kasanen, and J. Nisleanen, "Earnings Management and the Eco-

nomy Sector Hypothesis: Empirical Evidence on a Converse Relationship in the Finnish Case," *Journal of Business Finance and Accounting* (June 1995), pp. 497–520.

62. Ibid., p. 498.

63. H. Genay, "Assessing the Condition of Japanese Banks: How Informative Are Accounting Earnings?" *Economic Perspectives* 22, 4 (1998), pp. 12–34; M. Sheikkoleslami, "The Impact of Foreign Stock Exchange Listing on Income Smoothing: Evidence from Japanese Firms," *International Journal of Management* 11, 2 (1994), pp. 737–742.

64. R.E. Bragshaw and A.E.K. Elchni, "The Smoothing Hypothesis and the Role of Exchange Differences," *Journal of Business Finance and Accounting* 16, 5 (1989), pp. 621–633; V. Beattie, S. Brown, D. Ewers, B. John, S. Manson, S. Thomas, and M. Turner, "Extraordinary Items and Income Smoothing: A Positive Accounting Approach," *Journal of Business Finance and Accounting* 21, 6 (1994), pp. 791–811.

65. S.M. Saudagaran and J.F. Sepe, "Replication of Moses Income Smoothing Tests with Canadian and U.K. Data, A Note," *Journal of Business Finance and Accounting* 23, 8 (1996), pp. 1219–1222; Breton and Chenail, "Une Etude Empirique," p. 54.

66. S. Chalayer, "Le Lissage des Resultats: Elements Enqlicatifs Avances des la Literature," *Comptabilite, Controle, Audit*, 2, 1 (1995), pp. 89–104.

67. N. Ashani, H.C. Koh, S.L. Tan, and W.H. Wang, "Factors Affecting Income Smoothing among Listed Companies in Singapore," *Accounting and Business Research*, 24, 96 (1994), pp. 291–301.

68. K. Fudenberg and J. Tirole, "A Theory of Income and Dividend Smoothing Based on Incumbency Results," *Journal of Political Economy*, 103 (1995), pp. 75–93.

69. M.L. DeFond and C.W. Park, "Smoothing Income in Anticipation of Future Earnings," *Journal of Accounting and Economics* 23 (1997), p. 1116.

70. Ibid., pp. 115–139.

71. A.S. Ahmed, G.J. Lobo, and J. Zhou, "Job Security and Income Smoothing: An Empirical Test of the Fudenberg and Tirole (1995) Model," Working Paper, Syracuse University, October 2000.

72. P.T. Elgers, R.J. Pfeiffer Jr., and S.L. Porter, "Anticipatory Income Smoothing: A Re-Examination," Working Paper, University of Massachusetts, February 2000.

73. Gordon, "Postulates, Principles and Research in Accounting," p. 262.

74. Beidleman, "Income Smoothing," p. 655.

75. B. Lev and S. Kunitzky, "On the Association between Smoothing Measures and the Risk of Common Stock," *The Accounting Review* (April 1974), p. 268.

76. O.D. Moses, "Income Smoothing and Incentives: Empirical Tests Using Accounting Changes," *The Accounting Review* (April 1987), p. 366.

77. J.S. Demski, J.M. Patell, and M.A. Wolfson, "Decentralized Choice of Monitoring Systems," *The Accounting Review* 59 (1984), pp. 16–34.

78. B. Trueman and S. Titman, "An Explanation for Accounting Income Smoothing," *Journal of Accounting Research* (Supplement, 1988), pp. 127–139.

79. Beattie et al., "Extraordinary Items and Income Smoothing," pp. 791–811.

80. G.G. Booth, J. Kallanki, and T. Martikainem, "Post Announcement Drift and Income Smoothing; Finnish Evidence," *Journal of Business Finance and Accounting* 23 (1996), pp. 1197–1211.

81. S.G. Badrinath, D. Gay, and J.P. Kale, "Patterns of Institutional Investment, Prudence and the Managerial 'Safety Net' Hypothesis," *Journal of Risk and Insurance* 56 (1989), pp. 605–629.

82. S.E. Nichelson, J. Jordan-Wagner, and C.W. Wroton, "A Market Based Analysis

of Income Smoothing," *Journal of Business Finance and Accounting* 22, 8 (1995), pp. 1179–1193.

83. Z. Wang and T.H. Williams, "Accounting Income Smoothing and Stockholder Wealth," *Journal of Applied Business Research* 10, 3 (1994), pp. 96–104.

84. Ibid., p. 102.

85. P.K. Chaney, D.C. Jeter, and C.M. Lewis, "The Use of Accruals in Income Smoothing: A Permanent Earnings Hypothesis," *Advances in Quantitative Analysis of Finance and Accounting* 6 (1998), pp. 103–135.

86. Ibid., p. 131.

87. P.K. Chaney and C.M. Lewis, "Income Smoothing and Underperformance in Initial Public Offerings," *Journal of Corporate Finance* 4 (1998), pp. 1–29.

SELECTED REFERENCES

Albrecht, W.D., and F.M. Richardson. "Income Smoothing by Economic Sector." *Journal of Business Finance & Accounting* 17, 5 (Winter 1990), pp. 713–730.

American Institute of Certified Public Accountants (AICPA). *Report of the Study Group on the Objectives of Financial Statements.* New York: AICPA, October 1973.

Amihud, Y., J. Kamin, and J. Ronen. "Managerialism and Ownerism in Risk-Return Preferences." Ross Institute of Accounting Research (R.I.A.R.) Working Paper 95-4, New York University, 1975.

Archibald, T.R. "The Return to Straight-Line Depreciation: An Analysis of a Change in Accounting Method." *Empirical Research in Accounting: Selected Studies*, suppl. to *Journal of Accounting Research* 5 (1967), pp. 161–180.

Barefield, R.M., and E.E. Comiskey. "The Smoothing Hypothesis: An Alternative Test." *The Accounting Review* (April 1972), pp. 291–298.

Barnes, A., J. Ronen, and S. Sadan. "Classificatory Smoothing of Income with Extraordinary Items." *The Accounting Review* (January 1976), pp. 110–122.

———. "The Implementation of Accounting Objectives—An Application to Extraordinary Items." *The Accounting Review* (January 1975), pp. 58–68.

Baumol, W.J. *Business Behavior, Value and Growth.* New York: Macmillan, 1959.

Beidleman, C.R. "Income Smoothing: The Role of Management." *The Accounting Review* (October 1973), pp. 653–667.

Belkaoui, A., and R.D. Picur. "The Smoothing of Income Numbers: Some Empirical Evidence on the Systematic Differences between Core and Periphery Industrial Sectors." *Journal of Business Finance & Accounting* 11, 4 (Winter 1984), pp. 527–545.

Bernard, V.L., and R.S. Stober. "The Nature and Amount of Information Reflected in Cash Flows and Accruals." *The Accounting Review* (October 1989), pp. 624–652.

Copeland, R., "Income Smoothing." *Empirical Research in Accounting: Selected Studies*, suppl. to *Journal of Accounting Research* 6 (1968), pp. 101–116.

Copeland, R., and R. Licastro. "A Note on Income Smoothing." *The Accounting Review* (July 1968), pp. 540–545.

Copeland, R., and J. Wojdak. "Income Manipulation and the Purchase Pooling Choice." *Journal of Accounting Research* (Autumn 1969), pp. 188–195.

Cushing, B.E. "An Empirical Study of Changes in Accounting Policy." *Journal of Accounting Research* (Autumn 1969), pp. 196–203.

Cyert, R.M., and J.G. March. *A Behavioral Theory of the Firm.* Englewood Cliffs, NJ: Prentice-Hall, 1963.

Dascher, P.E., and R.E. Malcolm. "A Note on Income Smoothing in the Chemical Industry." *Journal of Accounting Research* (Autumn 1970), pp. 253–259.

Eckel, N. "The Income Smoothing Hypothesis Revisited." *Abacus* 17 (June 1981), pp. 28–40.

Gordon, M.J. "Postulates, Principles and Research in Accounting." *The Accounting Review* (April 1964), pp. 251–263.

Gordon, M.J., B.M. Horwitz, and P.T. Meyers. "Accounting Measurement and Normal Growth of the Firm." In R. Jaedicke, Y. Ijiri, and O. Nielsen (eds.), *Research in Accounting Measurement.* Evanston, IL: American Accounting Association, 1966, pp. 221–231.

Hepworth, S.R. "Smoothing Periodic Income." *The Accounting Review* (January 1953), pp. 32–39.

Horwitz, B.N. "Comments on Income Smoothing: A Review by J. Ronen, S. Sadan and C. Snow." *Accounting Journal* (Spring 1977), pp. 27–29.

Imhoff, E.A., Jr. "Income Smoothing—A Case for Doubt." *Accounting Journal* (Spring 1977), pp. 85–101.

———. "Income Smoothing: An Analysis of Critical Issues." *Quarterly Review of Economics and Business* (Autumn 1981), pp. 23–42.

Jeter, D.C., and P.K. Chancy. "An Empirical Investigation of Factors Affecting the Earnings Association Coefficient." *Journal of Business Finance & Accounting* 19, 6 (November 1992), pp. 839–863.

Jordan-Wagner, J., and C.W. Wootton. "An Analysis of Earnings in Oil Related Industries." *Petroleum Accounting and Financial Management Journal* (Spring 1993), pp. 110–123.

Lamber, R.A. "Income Smoothing as Rational Equilibrium Behavior." *The Accounting Review* 59 (October 1984), pp. 604–618.

Lev, B., and S. Kunitzky. "On the Association between Smoothing Measures and the Risk of Common Stock." *The Accounting Review* (April 1974), pp. 259–270.

Mason, R.D., and D.A. Lind. *Statistical Techniques in Business and Economics,* 8th ed. Homewood, IL: Irwin, 1993, pp. 136–137.

Moses, O.D. "Income Smoothing and Incentives: Empirical Tests Using Accounting Changes." *The Accounting Review* (April 1987), pp. 358–377.

O'Hanlon, J. "The Relationship in Time between Annual Accounting Returns and Annual Stock Market Returns in the UK." *Journal of Business Finance & Accounting* 18, 3 (April 1991), pp. 305–314.

Ronen, J., and S. Sadan. "Classificatory Smoothing: Alternative Income Models." *Journal of Accounting Research* (Spring 1975), pp. 133–149.

———. *Smoothing Income Numbers, Objectives, Means, and Implications.* Reading, MA: Addison Wesley, 1981.

Strong, N. "Modelling Abnormal Returns: A Review Article." *Journal of Business Finance & Accounting* 19, 4 (June 1992), pp. 531–553.

Thorne, D. "The Information Content of the Trend between Historic Cost Earnings and Current Cost Earnings (United States of America)." *Journal of Business Finance & Accounting* 18, 3 (April 1991), pp. 289–303.

Trueman, B., and S. Titman. "An Explanation for Accounting Income Smoothing." *Journal of Accounting Research* (Supplement, 1988), pp. 127–139.

Zmijewski, M.E., and R.L. Hagerman. "An Income Strategy Approach to the Positive
     Theory of Accounting Standard Setting/Choice." *Journal of Accounting and Eco-
     nomics* (August 1981), pp. 129–149.

Appendix 1A. Accrual Accounting and Cash Accounting: Relative Merits of Derived Accounting Indicator Numbers

One of the dominant characteristics in early views of the purpose of financial statements is the stewardship function. Under this view, management is entrusted with control of the financial resources provided by capital suppliers. Accordingly, the purpose of financial statements is to report to the concerned parties so as to facilitate the evaluation of management's stewardship. To accomplish this objective, the reporting system favored and deemed essentially superior to others is the accrual system. Simply, the accrual basis of accounting refers to a form of record keeping that, in addition to recording transactions resulting from the receipt and disbursement of cash, records the amounts that it owes others and that others owe it (Gross, 1972). At the core of this system is the matching of revenues and expenses (Paton and Littleton, 1940). The interest in the accrual method generated a search of the "best" accrual method in general and the "ideal income" in particular (Paton, 1922 [1962]; Canning, 1929; Alexander, 1950). For a long time, this accounting paradigm governed the evaluation of accounting alternatives and the asset valuation and income determination proposals (Edwards and Bell, 1961; Chambers, 1966; Sterling, 1970). The approach was, however, constantly challenged by cash-flow accounting. The cash-flow basis of accounting has been correctly defined as the recording not only of the cash receipts and disbursements of the period (the cash basis of accounting) but also the future cash flows owed to or by the firm as a result of selling and transferring title to certain goods (the accrual basis of accounting (Hicks, 1980)). The challenge by cash-flow accounting is more evident in some of the questioning of the importance and efficacy of accrual accounting and a shift toward cash-flow approaches in security analysis (Hawkins and Campbell, 1978).

The question about the superiority of accrual accounting over cash-flow accounting is central to the determination of the objectives and the nature of financial reporting. Consensus on criteria of superiority may be difficult to attain given the diversity of users and interests. What may be more practical to examine are the relative merits of derived accounting numbers from both accrual and cash-flow accounting. Thus, the main objective of this appendix is to examine empirically the relative merits of derived performance indicator numbers from both accrual and cash-flow accounting in terms of both the persistence and the variability of such numbers.

In the first section of this appendix, the conceptual differences and the controversy between accrual accounting and cash-flow accounting are examined. This is followed by a discussion of the sample design. The third section then examines the impact of the choice of either cash flow or accrual on accounting indicator numbers in terms of their persistence and variability. The final section presents a brief summary and conclusion.

ISSUE: ACCRUAL VERSUS CASH ACCOUNTING

As stated earlier, accrual accounting is deemed a superior system to facilitate the evaluation of management's stewardship and is essential to the matching of revenues and expenses so that efforts and accomplishments are properly aligned. The efficacy of the accrual system has been, however, questioned. Thomas (1969, 1974) stated that all allocations are arbitrary and incorrigible and recommended the minimization of such allocations. Hawkins and Campbell (1978) reported a shift in security analysis from earnings-oriented valuation approaches to cash flow-oriented approaches. Many decision usefulness theorists advocated cash-flow accounting based on the investor's desires to predict cash flows (Staubus, 1961, 1971; American Accounting Association [AAA], 1969; American Institute of Certified Public Accountants [AICPA], 1973; Revsine, 1973). Finally, various authors recommended that financial statements be based upon a cash-flow orientation because of limitations in accrual accounting (Lawson, 1971, 1973; Lee, 1972a, 1972b; Stern, 1972; Ashton, 1976; Climo, 1976; Ijiri, 1978, 1979). Most of these authors feel that the problems of asset valuation and income determination are so formidable that another accounting system should be derived and propose the inclusion of comprehensive cash-flow statements in companies' annual reports. More recently Lee (1981) described how cash-flow accounting and net realizable value accounting can be brought together in a series of articulating statements that provide more relevant information for the report user about cash and cash management than can be given by either system on its own.[1]

Cash-flow accounting is viewed by supporters as superior to conventional accrual accounting. Lawson (1971) argues that his system of cash-flow accounting provides an analytical framework for linking past, present, and future financial performance. Lee (1972a) argues that investors could see from the projected cash flows both the ability of the company to pay its way in the future and also its planned financial policy. Ashton (1976, p. 75) maintains that a "price/discounted flow" ratio would be a more reliable investment indicator than the present "price/earnings" ratio because of the numerous arbitrary allocations used to compute the earnings per share. Ijiri (1979, p. 57) argues for the development of cash-flow accounting to correct the gap in practice between the way in which an investment decision is made (generally based on cash flows) and the ways that the results are evaluated (generally based on earnings). Finally, various authors are expressing doubt with regard to the relevance and utility of accrual accounting information for investors who are concerned mainly with decision making (Edey, 1963; Lawson, 1971; Lee, 1971, 1972b).

Objectives

Given the issue of accrual versus cash accounting, the main objective in this appendix is to evaluate the relative merits of accounting indicators derived from either an accrual accounting system or a cash-flow accounting system. The accounting indicators derived from an accrual accounting system included both a balance sheet-oriented number and an income statement-oriented number. The indicators also had two basic characteristics. First, they are computed as per share numbers, and second, they are ratios whose dominator is the market price of a share. The first characteristic is used to ensure comparability between the indicators and the companies. The second characteristic is used to ensure that the indicator reflects both accounting-based performance and market-based numbers. A second argument for dividing the accounting-based datum by the market price of a share reflects the belief that the accounting datum should be evaluated in terms of the impact on its relationships to the market price. The implied hypothesis is that of the accounting data derived from either an accrual accounting system or a cash-flow accounting system. The one most favored by the market and/or reflected in the market price will show less variability and a higher persistence than the other numbers. The rationale is that the nature of the association between the derived accounting numbers and the behavior of security prices indicates which method the market perceives to be the most related to the information used in setting equilibrium prices. The method that produces accounting numbers having the association with security prices, with the least variability and the highest persistence, is the most consistent with the information that results in an efficient determination of security prices. But as pointed out by Beaver and Dukes (1972, p. 321), the evidence on the nature of the association is also essential regardless of the efficiency of the market. It is an important factor in any accounting policy regardless of the nature of the policymakers' views about other issues, including market efficiency.

The cash flow per share/stock price of security i for time period t, is defined as:

$$CFP_{i,t} = \frac{CFO_{i,t}/CSO_{i,t}}{P_{i,t}}$$

where

$P_{i,t}$ = price of security i at the end of period t adjusted for capital changes such as stock splits and stock dividends.

$CFO_{i,t}$ = cash flows from operations calculated by adjusting net income for noncash charges (credits) and for changes in the current accounts exclusive of changes in the firm's cash position, of firm i in period t (Compustat variable No. 10).

$CSO_{i,t}$ = common shares outstanding of firm i in period t (Compustat variable No. 25).

The common equity per share/stock price of security i for time period t is defined as:

$$CEP_{i,t} = \frac{CE_{i,t}/CSO_{i,t}}{P_{i,t}}$$

where

$CE_{i,t}$ = common equity of company i at the end of period t. Common equity (Compustat variable No. 11) represents common stock plus retained earnings, capital surplus, self-insurance reserves, and capital stock premium.

The earnings per share/stock price of security i for time period t, is defined as:

$$EPSP_{i,t} = \frac{EPS_{i,t}}{P_{i,t}}$$

where

$EPS_{i,t}$ = Earnings per share (primary), excluding extraordinary items, of company i for period t.

EPS (Compustat variable No. 58) represents the primary earnings per share figure as reported by the company.

Each of these numbers, $CFP_{i,t}$, $CEP_{i,t}$, and $EPSP_{i,t}$, represents numbers that are derived from either an accrual or a cash-flow accounting system and related to the stock price and whose merits will be evaluated in terms of variability and persistence. They represent semiaccounting indices of rate of return derived from either an accrual or a cash-flow accounting system (Barley and Levy, 1979, p. 307).

The Sample Design

The study employs both accounting and market data. Market data were retrieved from the Center for Research in Security Prices (CRSP) tape developed at the University of Chicago, while accounting data were retrieved from the Compustat tape.

Two criteria were used for the selection of companies to be included in the sample. First, its accounting and market data were available on both the Compustat and the CRSP tape for a period of nineteen years beginning in 1959 and ending in 1977. This criterion was necessary to allow for the computation of each of the semiaccounting indices of rate of return. Second, the company must figure in the *Fortune* magazine's list of the 500 largest American companies.

This criterion was adopted to limit the size and profitability differences, which may affect the results of the study. Of these companies, sixty-six met the sampling requirement. A list of these companies appears in Table 1A.1.

The three semiaccounting indices of rate of return were used for a comparison of the relative merits of accrual and cash accounting.

a. A cash-flow per share/stock price ratio was used to represent the cash accounting-derived semiaccounting index of rate of return.

b. A common equity per share/stock price ratio was used to represent the accrual accounting-derived and balance sheet-oriented semiaccounting index of rate of return.

c. An earnings per share/stock price ratio was used to represent the accrual accounting-derived and income statement-oriented semiaccounting index of rate of return.

Results

Variability of the Derived Accounting Indicator Numbers

The three accounting indicators, namely, the cash flow per share/stock price (CFP), the common equity per share/stock price (CEP), and the earnings per share/stock price (EPSP), were computed for the sixty-six companies for the years 1959 to 1977. The means, standard deviation, and coefficients of variation of these numbers are presented in Table 1A.1. In addition, this table includes a ranking of the coefficients of variations of the derived accounting indicator numbers.

An examination of Table 1A.1 shows a definite difference in the variability of these numbers. The variability of the EPSP numbers exceeds the variability of the CEP and CFP numbers. More precisely, the coefficients of variation of the EPSP's numbers are higher than those of the CEP numbers in forty-two cases or those of the CFP numbers in forty-five. The coefficients of variation of the CFP numbers were higher than those of the CEP numbers in forty-four cases. Those differences are, in most cases, considerable (see Table 1A.1).

For those cases where the variability of CEP and CFP numbers exceeds those of the EPSP numbers, the differences for more than 50 percent of the cases are rather small and do not indicate any specific pattern. The variability of the EPSP numbers, as measured by their coefficients of variation, ranges from a high of 4.723 for Allegheny Airlines to a low of 0.19 for Philip Morris Inc. The variability of the CEP numbers ranges from a high of 1.84 for General Motors to a low of 0.18 for Phillips Petroleum. Finally, the variability of the CFP numbers ranges from a high of 1.31 for Lockheed to a low of 0.19 for Phillips Petroleum.

Next, the relationship between the distributions of the coefficients of variation of EPSP, CEP, and CFP was examined by computing Spearman's rank order correlation coefficient between these distributions. The computed correlation between the coefficients of variation of CEP and EPSP is equal to .5 ($t_s = 4.6$) which is significant at $= .001$. Finally, the computed correlation coefficient

Table 1A.1
CEP, EPSP, and CFP's Means, Standard Deviations, and Coefficients of Variation for the Sample Companies, 1959–1977

Company	CEP_i Mean	Standard Deviation	Coefficient of Variation	$EPSP_i$ Mean	Standard Deviation	Coefficient of Variation	Ranking	CFP_i Mean	Standard Deviation	Coefficient of Variation	Ranking
1. General Motors Corp.	0.000528	0.000976	1.848484849	0.088996	0.038450	0.43204189	37	0.000129	0.000052	0.403100775	38
2. Lockheed Corp.	0.001338	0.001665	1.244394619	0.097106	0.21719	2.236628015	2	0.000390	0.000514	1.317948718	25
3. EXTRA Corp.	0.000560	0.000616	1.1	0.083259	0.104938	1.260380259	5	0.000342	0.000278	0.812865497	5
4. Honeywell Inc.	0.000546	0.000533	0.976190476	0.057101	0.043605	0.763646871	9	0.000183	0.000203	1.109289618	2
5. Cities Service Co.	0.001095	0.000163	0.879452055	0.097346	0.028520	0.292975572	59	0.000229	0.000063	0.27551917	57
6. Allegheny Airlines Inc.	0.000888	0.000696	0.783783784	0.050166	0.206859	4.12349	1	0.000421	0.000375	0.890736342	4
7. NCR Corp.	0.000670	0.000453	0.676119403	0.052659	0.063827	1.212081506	6	0.000184	0.000148	0.804347826	6
8. McDonnell Douglas Corp.	0.000851	0.000575	0.675675676	0.121786	0.069912	0.574056131	16	0.000180	0.000106	0.588888889	12
9. General Tire & Rubber Co.	0.001018	0.000655	0.643418468	0.125968	0.078580	0.623809221	12	0.000808	0.000116	0.557692308	15
10. Uniroyal Inc.	0.001388	0.000866	0.623919308	0.094273	0.053926	0.57201956	17	0.000261	0.000158	0.605363985	71
11. General Dynamics Corp.	0.000965	0.000593	0.614507772	0.078956	0.164421	2.08243832	3	0.000208	0.000186	0.894230769	3
12. FMC Corp.	0.000654	0.000393	0.600917431	0.057844	0.052524	0.597923592	14	0.000162	0.000101	0.62345679	9
13. Westinghouse Electric Corp.	0.000786	0.000467	0.594147583	0.072075	0.044888	0.6227956	13	0.000130	0.000099	0.761538462	7
14. RCA Corp.	0.000439	0.000260	0.592255125	0.062512	0.031864	0.509726133	28	0.000159	0.000110	0.691823899	8
15. VSI Corp.	0.000733	0.000422	0.575716235	0.103011	0.067321	0.653532147	10	0.000170	0.000090	0.529411765	18
16. Texaco Inc.	0.000713	0.000374	0.52454418	0.096196	0.052297	0.543650464	21	0.000156	0.000081	0.519230769	19
17. Owens-Illinois Inc.	0.000762	0.000388	0.509186352	0.079463	0.038722	0.487295974	31	0.000144	0.000074	0.513888889	22
18. IBM Corp.	0.000181	0.000091	0.502762431	0.032806	0.017787	0.542187405	23	0.000066	0.000030	0.454545455	25
19. Textron Inc.	0.000603	0.000297	0.492537313	0.098990	0.044234	0.446853218	35	0.000177	0.000078	0.440677966	89
20. TRW Inc.	0.000421	0.000203	0.482185273	0.084327	0.046748	0.554363743	19	0.000170	0.000094	0.552941176	16
21. Republic Steel Corp.	0.001923	0.000924	0.48049922	0.123040	0.094391	0.767157022	8	0.000255	0.000137	0.537254902	17
22. Atlantic Richfield Co.	0.000739	0.000352	0.47631935	0.072849	0.026904	0.369311864	49	0.000185	0.000051	0.275675676	56
23. Celanese Corp.	0.000810	0.000376	0.464197531	0.091250	0.050207	0.5502136	20	0.000279	0.000159	0.569892473	14
24. Utah Power & Light	0.000724	0.000332	0.458563356	0.079384	0.033082	0.4167338	40	0.000137	0.000050	0.364963504	46
25. Coca-Cola Co.	0.000177	0.000080	0.451977401	0.037553	0.014116	0.375895401	47	0.000049	0.000017	0.346938776	48
26. Minnesota Mining & Mfg. Co.	0.000185	0.000083	0.448648649	0.034273	0.013230	0.386018148	45	0.000048	0.000021	0.4375	31
27. Warner-Lambert Co.	0.000262	0.000111	0.423664122	0.047978	0.014925	0.31108	54	0.000059	0.000019	0.322033898	50
28. Republic of Texas Corp.	0.000620	0.000262	0.422580645	0.079088	0.042522	0.5376542	26	0.000065	0.000031	0.476923077	24
29. Ford Motor Co.	0.000947	0.000393	0.418162619	0.116545	0.062840	0.53919087	24	0.000190	0.000086	0.452631579	27
30. Philip Morris Inc.	0.000440	0.000181	0.411363636	0.071162	0.014109	0.198265928	67	0.000091	0.000021	0.230769231	61

#	Company										
31.	American Shores Co.	0.001382	0.000565	0.408827786	0.109488	0.058236	0.5318939	27	0.000250	0.000126	0.504	83
32.	Owens-Corning Fiberglass Corp.	0.000423	0.000172	0.406619385	0.048238	0.023777	0.4929101	30	0.000086	0.000039	0.453448372	26
33.	Johnson & Johnson	0.000246	0.000099	0.402439024	0.031981	0.009834	0.307495075	56	0.000047	0.000016	0.340425532	49
34.	Aluminium Co. of America	0.000779	0.000311	0.399229818	0.644410	0.034966	0.542866815	22	0.000153	0.000068	0.4444	28
35.	Gulf Oil Corp.	0.000923	0.000366	0.396533044	0.109213	0.058743	0.537875528	25	0.000203	0.000105	0.517241379	20
36.	Greyhound Corp.	0.000494	0.000177	0.393858478	0.090411	0.032712	0.361814381	50	0.000152	0.000065	0.427631579	33
37.	Raytheon Corp.	0.000665	0.000256	0.384962406	0.026635	0.027031	0.352723951	51	0.000140	0.000055	0.391857143	40
38.	Champion Intl. Corp.	0.000805	0.000307	0.38136646	0.095903	0.061573	0.642034139	11	0.000197	0.000120	0.609137056	10
39.	American Home Products Corp.	0.000110	0.000041	0.372727273	0.039494	0.009948	0.251886362	64	0.000045	0.000011	0.2444444	59
40.	Getty Oil Co.	0.000966	0.000360	0.372670807	0.087845	0.026303	0.299425124	58	0.000153	0.000034	0.2222222	62
41.	General Electric Co.	0.000306	0.000114	0.37254902	0.047901	0.020719	0.432537943	36	0.000078	0.000033	0.423076923	32
42.	Emerson Electric Co.	0.000266	0.000096	0.360902256	0.046987	0.013029	0.2772894	63	0.000063	0.000017	0.26984127	51
43.	Allied Chemical Corp.	0.000735	0.000265	0.360544218	0.078056	0.030755	0.474723276	33	0.000184	0.000071	0.385869565	44
44.	National Steel Corp.	0.001202	0.000424	0.352745424	0.101600	0.050885	0.500836614	29	0.000212	0.000086	0.405660377	37
45.	Upjohn Co.	0.000270	0.000093	0.344444444	0.043755	0.014220	0.3249914	53	0.000057	0.000086	0.350877193	47
46.	Union Oil Co. of California	0.000831	0.000284	0.341756919	0.099550	0.040527	0.4071019	42	0.000286	0.000116	0.405594406	38
47.	U.S. Steel Inc.	0.001470	0.000497	0.338095238	0.101321	0.059112	0.5834131	15	0.000231	0.000090	0.38961039	43
48.	Standard Oil Co. (California)	0.000870	0.000290	0.33333333	0.104958	0.045292	0.431524991	38	0.000170	0.000069	0.405882353	36
49.	Bethlehem Steel Corp.	0.001423	0.000467	0.328179902	0.077385	0.145041	1.874277961	4	0.000218	0.000127	0.582568807	13
50.	Borden Inc.	0.000628	0.000206	0.328015478	0.073927	0.029890	0.404317773	43	0.000120	0.000049	0.408335333	36
51.	Armco Inc.	0.001201	0.000393	0.32641196	0.105100	0.050815	0.483491912	32	0.000208	0.000086	0.413461538	34
52.	Bowater Corp. Ltd. Adr.	0.00115	0.000367	0.319130435	0.088466	0.068530	0.7746478	7	0.000238	0.000123	0.516806723	1
53.	Shell Oil Co.	0.000718	0.000226	0.314763231	0.087232	0.039576	0.45368672	34	0.000188	0.000070	0.372540426	44
54.	Standard Oil Co. (Ohio)	0.000691	0.000217	0.314037627	0.064283	0.021525	0.334847471	52	0.000125	0.000055	0.44	30
55.	R.J. Reynolds Inds.	0.000477	0.000145	0.303983229	0.092009	0.028431	0.30900238	55	0.000120	0.000047	0.591666667	41
56.	Tenneco Inc.	0.000601	0.000174	0.289517471	0.091933	0.034854	0.378876654	46	0.000215	0.000065	0.502325581	55
57.	Inland Steel Co.	0.001064	0.000300	0.281954887	0.102078	0.041250	0.404102745	44	0.000202	0.000065	0.32178218	53
58.	Georgia-Pacific Corp.	0.000362	0.000100	0.276243094	0.555220	0.020491	0.371079319	48	0.000113	0.000033	0.292055398	50
59.	Standard Oil Co. (Indiana)	0.000930	0.000251	0.269892473	0.089009	0.025605	0.287667539	60	0.000199	0.000043	0.216080402	64
60.	Dow Chemical	0.000367	0.000094	0.256113079	0.056794	0.024162	0.4254322	39	0.000116	0.000020	0.336206897	50
61.	Colgate-Palmolive Co.	0.000489	0.000119	0.243357583	0.060901	0.013485	0.221424936	66	0.000092	0.000020	0.217511504	63
62.	American Brands Inc.	0.000589	0.000135	0.229202307	0.101381	0.028532	0.281433405	62	0.000131	0.000048	0.366412214	45
63.	Kraft Inc.	0.000594	0.000132	0.22222222	0.075648	0.021650	0.286193951	60	0.000115	0.000027	0.234782601	60
64.	Caterpillar Tractor Co.	0.000365	0.000073	0.2	0.062712	0.015501	0.247177574	65	0.000096	0.000020	0.208333333	65
65.	International Paper Co.	0.000665	0.000130	0.195488722	0.070480	0.028830	0.409052213	41	0.000135	0.000043	0.318518519	53
66.	Phillips Petroleum Co.	0.000667	0.000121	0.181409295	0.070019	0.021111	0.301503878	57	0.000146	0.000028	0.191780822	66

between the coefficients of variation of CEP and CFP is equal to .57 ($t_s = 5.65$), which is also significant. Thus, it may be concluded that in spite of the differences in the variability of EPSP, CEP, and CFP numbers, there is some correlation between them. The main question created by these results refers to the possible reason(s) that the variability of income statement-oriented and accrual accounting-based numbers (EPSP) exceeds for a large number of firms in the sample those of the cash accounting-based numbers (CFP) and the balance sheet-oriented and accrual accounting-based numbers (CEP).

One reason may stem from the fact that EPSP numbers are based on accounting data, which are a likelier object of discretionary accounting income smoothing, as defined by Gordon (1964) and others, and of the smoothing process inherent in the very definition of accounting income (Barley and Levy, 1979). It may be stated first that the income smoothing is easier and more dramatic with income figures than balance sheet and cash-flow accounting data, and second, that managers may have a greater incentive in smoothing income figures given the stronger links between accounting income and the firm's reward structure (Barley and Levy, 1979, p. 314). As a result, the market is efficiently reflecting a "true" income figure different from the "reported" one, which may explain the variability of income statement-oriented and accrual accounting-based numbers.

A second reason may be that the market, very much aware of the smoothing process affecting income figures, is attaching more importance to the balance sheet position first and the cash flow second. The superiority of the balance sheet over cash-flow data may be due to a selective market response due either to the higher familiarity with balance sheet data than cash-flow data or basically to a balance sheet fixation and a stronger interest in the financial position of the firms.

PERSISTENCY OF DERIVED ACCOUNTING INDICATOR NUMBERS

The persistency of the derived accounting indicator numbers was determined by examining the median rank correlation between the accounting indicator number in the year of formation and the same number in subsequent years.[2] Tables 1A.2, 1A.3, and 1A.4 show consecutively the rank correlation of all the sample companies' CEP, CFP, and EPSP with the CEP, CFP, and EPSP in subsequent years. The median correlation of each column is reported at the bottom of the tables.

The median correlation of the CEP numbers shown in Table 1A.2 decreases from .918 in the first year after formation to .250 in the fourteenth year after formation. Five years after formation the median correlation is .629, while ten years after formation the median is .385.

The median correlation of the CFP numbers shown in Table 1A.3 decreases from .835 in the first year after formation to .281 in the fourteenth year after

Table 1A.2
Rank Correlations of All the Sample Companies' CEPs with CEPs in Subsequent Years

Base Year	Years Following Base Year													
	1	2	3	4	5	6	7	8	9	10	11	12	13	14
1959	0.825	0.733	0.670	0.592	0.431	0.468	0.304	0.288	0.207	0.310	0.726	0.244	0.257	0.106
1960	0.878	0.801	0.720	0.632	0.599	-.443	0.374	0.329	0.457	0.385	0.364	0.350	0.182	0.215
1961	0.920	0.808	0.722	0.687	0.495	0.433	0.383	0.467	0.386	0.368	0.335	0.122	0.196	0.250
1962	0.916	0.856	0.834	0.658	0.579	0.536	0.539	0.475	0.492	0.451	0.175	0.242	0.296	0.371
1963	0.941	0.836	0.672	0.607	0.578	0.607	0.566	0.560	0.522	0.298	0.364	0.398	0.491	0.576
1964	0.858	0.702	0.652	0.630	0.665	0.637	0.611	0.567	0.352	0.465	0.482	0.559	0.584	
1965	0.894	0.839	0.782	0.737	0.655	0.681	0.665	0.322	0.334	0.375	0.462	0.558		
1966	0.936	0.925	0.813	0.723	0.729	0.735	0.372	0.419	0.465	0.552	0.649			
1967	0.952	0.863	0.784	0.769	0.780	0.457	0.506	0.536	0.615	0.635				
1968	0.909	0.855	0.825	0.812	0.506	0.507	0.542	0.622	0.650					
1969	0.945	0.893	0.879	0.671	0.602	0.657	0.714	0.655						
1970	0.946	0.907	0.752	0.644	0.683	0.743	0.656							
1971	0.946	0.731	0.536	0.615	0.695	0.705								
1972	0.806	0.521	0.596	0.681	0.688									
1973	0.492	0.531	0.618	0.512										
1974	0.962	0.927	0.636											
1975	0.958	0.691												
1976	0.833													
1977														
Median Correlation	.918	.836	.721	.658	.629	.607	.541	.475	.461	.385	.364	.350	.276	.250

Table 1A.3
Rank Correlations of All the Sample Companies' CFPs with CFPs in Subsequent Years

Base Year	Years Following Base Year													
	1	2	3	4	5	6	7	8	9	10	11	12	13	14
1959	0.811	0.808	0.668	0.530	0.288	0.488	0.409	0.379	0.302	0.486	0.466	0.299	0.302	0.223
1960	0.675	0.627	0.655	0.367	0.465	0.429	0.377	0.214	0.496	0.494	0.146	0.187	0.196	0.271
1961	0.690	0.513	0.321	0.618	0.516	0.541	0.437	0.514	0.464	0.367	0.348	0.220	0.273	0.281
1962	0.829	0.666	0.807	0.677	0.583	0.428	0.599	0.621	0.435	0.450	0.315	0.420	0.380	0.478
1963	0.867	0.713	0.564	0.452	0.233	0.522	0.529	0.387	0.428	0.436	0.550	0.466	0.562	0.688
1964	0.642	0.508	0.328	0.190	0.403	0.453	0.350	0.399	0.388	0.561	0.564	0.557	0.477	
1965	0.912	0.815	0.674	0.786	0.734	0.580	0.610	0.397	0.486	0.467	0.530	0.383		
1966	0.861	0.780	0.793	0.716	0.550	0.628	0.373	0.426	0.375	0.448	0.350			
1967	0.767	0.742	0.651	0.594	0.631	0.352	0.369	0.338	0.408	0.307				
1968	0.763	0.643	0.674	0.206	0.415	0.383	0.370	0.432	0.130					
1969	0.868	0.567	0.600	0.300	0.366	0.345	0.424	0.383						
1970	0.520	0.509	0.203	0.371	0.342	0.368	0.347							
1971	0.924	0.794	0.746	0.779	0.783	0.368								
1972	0.841	0.765	0.780	0.800	0.438									
1973	0.895	0.808	0.888	0.600										
1974	0.909	0.905	0.665											
1975	0.929	0.482												
1976	0.673													
1977														
Median Correlation	.835	.713	.667	.600	.452	.429	.393	.397	.418	.450	.408	.383	.341	.181

Table 1A.4
Rank Correlations of All the Sample Companies' EPSPs with EPSPs in Subsequent Years

Base Year	Years Following Base Year													
	1	2	3	4	5	6	7	8	9	10	11	12	13	14
1959	0.574	0.545	0.394	0.327	0.257	0.377	0.296	0.148	0.200	0.428	0.208	0.292	0.181	0.179
1960	0.576	0.360	0.262	0.306	0.474	0.358	-0.018	0.161	0.425	0.263	0.282	0.235	0.136	-0.020
1961	0.536	0.366	0.537	0.583	0.439	0.409	0.375	0.473	0.005	0.456	0.307	0.165	0.133	0.260
1962	0.900	0.738	0.655	0.504	0.342	0.291	0.168	-0.243	0.442	0.376	0.331	0.205	0.273	0.324
1963	0.812	0.790	0.570	0.380	0.384	0.172	-0.278	0.492	0.500	0.481	0.349	0.391	0.444	0.182
1964	0.819	0.710	0.424	0.549	0.407	-0.349	0.450	0.588	0.546	0.473	0.369	0.391	0.012	
1965	0.880	0.567	0.664	0.612	-0.163	0.492	0.599	0.532	0.420	0.329	0.424	0.165		
1966	0.602	0.790	0.689	-0.141	0.540	0.715	0.507	0.412	0.271	0.292	-0.009			
1967	0.626	0.441	-0.059	0.498	0.446	0.215	0.296	0.424	0.250	-0.232				
1968	0.685	-0.111	0.651	0.693	0.479	0.384	0.371	0.274	-0.172					
1969	0.016	0.537	0.592	0.350	0.530	0.153	0.136	-0.141						
1970	-0.107	-0.171	-0.265	-0.363	-0.261	-0.291	0.051							
1971	0.752	0.447	0.239	0.487	0.386	-0.091								
1972	0.717	0.554	0.463	0.492	0.127									
1973	0.820	0.653	0.779	0.395										
1974	0.666	0.698	0.266											
1975	0.840	0.091												
1976	0.490													
1977														
Median Correlation	.666	.545	.500	.487	.385	.215	.296	.412	.395	.376	.319	.235	.158	.182

29

formation. Five years after formation the median correlation is .452, while ten years after formation the median is .281.

The median correlation of the EPSP numbers shown in Table 1A.4 decreases from .666 in the first year to .182 in the fourteenth year. Five years after formation the median correlation is .385, while ten years after formation the median is .182.

The results show a good persistency in the CEP and CFP numbers and a low persistency in the EPSP numbers. Again the main question refers to the possible reason(s) that the persistencies of the balance sheet-oriented and accrual accounting-based number (CEP) and the cash-flow accounting-based number (CFP) exceed that of the income statement-oriented and accrual accounting-based number (EPSP). The two reasons given for the variability results may apply to the persistence results, namely, the income smoothing distortion hypothesis and the selective market response hypothesis.

SUMMARY AND CONCLUSIONS

The purpose of this study was to evaluate the relative merits of accounting indicators derived from either an income statement based on accrual accounting, a balance sheet based on accrual accounting, or cash-flow accounting. The hypothesis is that the number most favored by the market and/or reflected in the market price will show less variability and a higher persistence than the other numbers. The balance sheet-oriented number and accrual accounting-based number showed a lower variability and a higher persistence than the cash-flow accounting-based number and the income statement-oriented and accrual accounting-based number. The phenomenon was attributed to both an income smoothing distortion hypothesis and a selective market response hypothesis.

One implication of these results is that the financial position of a firm is deemed more indicative of a firm's potential by the market than either cash flows or income statement numbers. A second implication for standard-setting bodies is to consider the fundamental measurement process as being the measurement of the attributes of assets and liabilities and changes in them rather than the matching process (Belkaoui, 1981, p. 83). In short, the evidence argues for an asset/liability view of earnings rather than either a revenue/expense view or the cash-flow view.

NOTES

1. Lee also showed that the Fisherian financial statement is cash flow-based, which tends to support the contention of Whittington that Fisher was the father of cash-flow accounting (Lee, 1979, p. 327; Whittington, 1977, p. 202).

2. A similar approach was used by Beaver and Morse (1978).

REFERENCES

Alexander, S. (1950). *Five Monographs on Business Income*. New York: Study Group on Business Income, AICPA.

American Accounting Association. (1969). Committee on External Reporting, *An Evaluation of External Reporting Practices*. A Report of the 1966–68 Committee on External Reporting. *The Accounting Review* (Supplement), pp. 79–123.

American Institute of Certified Public Accountants. (1973). Study Group on the *Objectives of Financial Statements*. New York: American Institute of Certified Public Accountants.

Ashton, R. (1976). "Cash Flow Accounting: A Review and Critique." *Journal of Business Finance and Accounting* (Winter), pp. 63–81.

Barley, B., and H. Levy. (1979). "On the Variability of Accounting Income Numbers." *Journal of Accounting Research* (Autumn), pp. 305–315.

Beaver, W., and D. Morse. (1978). "What Determines Price—Earnings Ratios?" *Financial Analysts Journal* (July–August), pp. 65–76.

Beaver, W.H., and R.E. Dukes. (1972). "Interperiod Tax Allocation, Earnings Expectations, and the Behavior of Security Prices." *The Accounting Review* (April), pp. 320–332.

Belkaoui, A. (1981). *Accounting Theory*. San Diego: Harcourt Brace Jovanovich.

Canning, J. (1929). *The Economics of Accountancy*. New York: The Ronald Press.

Chambers, R. (1966). *Accounting, Evaluation and Economic Behavior*. Englewood Cliffs, NJ: Prentice-Hall.

Climo, T.A. (1976). "Cash Flow Statements for Investors." *Journal of Business Finance and Accounting* (Autumn), pp. 3–16.

Edey, H.C. (1963). "Accounting Principles and Business Reality." *Accountancy* (November), pp. 998–1002; (December), pp. 1083–1088.

Edwards, E., and P. Bell. (1961). *The Theory and Measurement of Business Income*. Berkeley: University of California Press.

Financial Accounting Standards Board. (1976). "Tentative Conclusions on Objectives of Financial Statements of Business Enterprises." Stamford, CT: FASB.

———. (1978). *Statement of Financial Accounting Concepts No. 1*. Stamford, CT: FASB.

Gordon, M.J. (1964). "Postulates, Principles and Research in Accounting." *The Accounting Review* (April), pp. 221–263.

Gross, M.J., Jr. (1972). *Financial and Accounting Guide for Nonprofit Organizations*. New York: The Ronald Press.

Hawkins, D., and W. Campbell. (1978). *Equity Valuation: Models, Analysis and Implications*. New York: Financial Executives Institute.

Hicks, B.E. (1980). "The Cash Flow Basis of Accounting." Working Paper No. 13. Sudbury, Ontario: Laurentian University.

Ijiri, Y. (1978). "Cash Flow Accounting and Its Structure." *Journal of Accounting, Auditing and Finance* (Summer), pp. 331–348.

———. (1979). "A Simple System of Cash Flow Accounting," In R. Sterling and A.L. Thomas (eds.), *Accounting for a Simplified Firm Owning Depreciable Assets*. Houston, TX: Scholars Book Co., pp. 57–71.

Lawson, G.H. (1971). "Cash-Flow Accounting I & II." *Accountant* (October 28 and November 4), pp. 20–31.

————. (1973). "Some Arguments for Cash-Flow Accounting." *Certified Accountant* (April–May), pp. 15–21.

Lee, T.A. (1971). "Goodwill—An Example of Will-o-the-Wisp Accounting." *Accounting and Business Research* (Autumn), pp. 318–328.

————. (1972a). "A Case for Cash Flow Reporting." *Journal of Business Finance* 3, pp. 27–36.

————. (1972b). "The Relevance of Accounting Information Including Cash Flows." *The Accountant's Magazine* (January), pp. 122–132.

————. (1979). "The Contribution of Fisher to Cash Flow Accounting." *Journal of Business Finance and Accounting* (Autumn), pp. 321–330.

————. (1981). "Reporting Cash Flows and Net Realizable Values." *Accounting and Business Research* (Spring), pp. 163–170.

Paton, W. (1962). *Accounting Theory*. Chicago: Accounting Studies Press. Originally published in 1922.

Paton, W., and A. Littleton. (1940). *An Introduction to Corporate Accounting Standards*. Columbus, OH: American Accounting Association.

Revsine, L. (1973). *Replacement Cost Accounting*. Englewood Cliffs, NJ: Prentice-Hall.

Staubus, G. (1961). *A Theory of Accounting to Investors*. Berkeley: University of California Press.

————. (1971). "The Relevance of Cash Flows." In R.R. Sterling (ed.), *Asset Valuation*. Houston, TX: Scholars Book Co.

Sterling, R. (1970). *Theory of the Measurement of Enterprise Income*. Lawrence: University of Kansas Press.

————. (1974). "Earnings per Share Is a Poor Indicator of Performance." *Omega* 5, pp. 11–32.

Stern, J. (1972). "Let's Abandon Earnings per Share." *Barron's* (December 18), p. 2.

Thomas, A.L. (1969). *The Allocation Problem in Financial Accounting Theory*. Studies in Accounting Research No. 3. Sarasota, FL: American Accounting Association.

————. (1974). *The Allocation Problem: Part Two*. Studies in Accounting Research No. 9. Sarasota, FL: American Accounting Association.

Whittington, G. (1977). "Accounting and Economics." In *Current Issues in Accounting*. B. Carsberg and T. Hope (eds.). New York: Philip Allan.

Appendix 1.B. The Smoothing of Income Numbers: Some Empirical Evidence on the Systematic Differences between Core and Periphery Industrial Sectors

INTRODUCTION

While the subject of income smoothing was discussed and tested previously (Gordon, 1964; Gordon, Horwitz, and Meyers, 1966; Archibald, 1967; Copeland, 1968; Copeland and Licastro, 1968; Cushing, 1969; Dasher and Malcolm,

Source: A. Belkaoui and R.D. Picur, "The Smoothing of Income Numbers: Some Empirical Evidence on the Systematic Differences between Core and Periphery Sectors," *Journal of Business Finance and Accounting* (Winter 1984), pp. 527–546. Reprinted with permission.

1970; White, 1970; Barefield and Comiskey, 1972; Beidleman, 1973; Barnea, Ronen, and Sadan, 1976; Kamin and Ronen, 1978; Ronen, 1981), the effects of the dual economy on income smoothing was never tested specifically and separately.[1] Accordingly, this study attempts to discover whether managers do in fact behave as if they engage in goal-directed determination of the cues and signals conveyed to users of financial statements through income numbers and whether this behavior differs between managers in the core (cs) and managers in the periphery (ps) sectors.

INCOME SMOOTHING: RELATED RESEARCH

Income smoothing may be defined as either the intentional or deliberate dampening of fluctuations about some level of earnings that is currently considered to be normal for a firm (Beidleman, 1973; Barnea et al., 1976, p. 143).

The various empirical studies in income smoothing assumed various smoothing objects (i.e., operating income or ordinary income), various smoothing instruments (i.e., operating expenses, ordinary expenses, or extraordinary items), and various smoothing dimensions (either accounting smoothing or "real" smoothing) (Kamin and Ronen, 1978, p. 144). Accounting smoothing affects income through accounting dimensions, namely, smoothing through events' occurrence and/or recognition, smoothing through allocation over time, and smoothing through classification (Barnea et al., 1976, p. 11). Real smoothing affects income through the deliberate or intentional changing of the operating decisions and their timing.

Various motivations for smoothing are given in the literature, such as:

1. to enhance the reliability of prediction based on the observed smoothed series of accounting numbers along a trend considered best or normal by management (Barnea et al., 1976),
2. to gain tax advantages and to improve relations with creditors, employees, and investors (Hepworth, 1953),
3. to reduce the uncertainty resulting from the fluctuations of income numbers in general and reducing systematic risk in particular by reducing the covariance of the firm's returns with the market returns (Beidleman, 1973, p. 654; Lev and Kunitzky, 1974).

These reasons for motivation result from the need felt by management to neutralize environmental uncertainty and dampen the wide fluctuations in the operating performance of the firm subject to an intermittent cycle of good and bad times. To do so, management may resort to organizational slack behavior (Cyert and March, 1963), budgetary slack behavior (Schiff and Lewin, 1968), or risk-avoiding behavior (Thompson, 1967). Each of these behaviors necessitates decisions affecting the incurrence and/or allocation of discretionary expenses (costs), which result in income smoothing.

In addition to these behaviors intended to neutralize environmental uncertainty, it is possible to identify *organizational characterizations* that differentiate among different firms in their extent of smoothing. Kamin and Ronen (1978) examined the effects of the separation of ownership and control on income smoothing under the hypothesis that management-controlled firms are more likely to be engaged in smoothing as a manifestation of managerial discretion and budgetary slack. Their results confirmed that a majority of the firms examined behave as if they were smoothers, and a particularly strong majority is included among management-controlled firms with high barriers to entry. Other organizational characterizations may exist that differentiate among different firms along the dimension of the attempt to smooth. One such characterization derived from theories of economic dualism divides the industrial structure into two distinct sectors—the *core* and the *periphery* sectors.

STRATIFICATION IN A DUAL ECONOMY AND INCOME SMOOTHING

Models of sectorial economic differentiation derived from theories of economic dualism include various perspectives such as theories of dual economy, labor markets, and labor force segmentation (Cain, 1976). Common to all of these perspectives is the proposal of a division of the industrial structure of the economy into two distinct sectors (at least in the two-sector model) consisting of the *core* and *periphery* sectors. These models, however, differ in their definition and conceptualization of these sectors.

In the dual labor market and labor force segmentation perspective, the sectors are defined in terms of the characteristics of labor markets and worker behavior (cf. Harrison, 1974; Spilerman, 1982). For example, Piori (1977, p. 93) defines the two sectors as follows:

The central tenet of the analysis . . . is that the role of employment and of the disposition of manpower in the perpetuation of poverty is best understood in terms of a dual labor market. One sector of that market, which I have termed elsewhere the primary market, offers jobs which possess several of the following traits; high wages, good working conditions, employment stability and job security, equity and due process in the administration of work rules, and chances for advancement. The other, or secondary sector, has jobs which, relative to those in the primary sector, are decidedly less attractive. They tend to involve low wages, poor working conditions, considerable variability in employment, harsh and often arbitrary discipline, and little opportunity to advance. The poor are confined to the secondary labor market. The elimination of poverty requires that they gain access to primary employment.

In the dual economy perspective, the sectorial classification derives from the nature of modern industrial capitalism (Beck and Horan, 1978). More precisely, the sectorial classification resulted from the creation during the late nineteenth and early twentieth centuries of a core industrial sector dominated by large oligopolistic corporations (Baran and Sweezy, 1966). What remained, characterized by smaller firms and a less competitive environment, is considered the periphery sector (Averitt, 1968). For example, Bluestone et al. (1973, pp. 28–29) characterizes the two sectors as follows:

The core economy includes those industries that comprise the muscle of American economic and political power. . . . Entrenched in durable manufacturing, the construction trades and, to a lesser extent, the extraction industries, the firms in the core economy are noted for high productivity, high profits, intensive utilization of capital, high incidence of monopoly elements, and a high degree of unionization. What follows normally from such characteristics are high wages. The automobile, steel, rubber, aluminum, aerospace, and petroleum industries are ranking members of this part of the economy. Workers who are able to secure employment in these industries are, in most cases, assured of relatively higher wages and better than average working conditions and fringe benefits.

Beyond the fringes of the core economy lie a set of industries that lack almost all of the advantages normally found in center firms. Concentrated in agriculture, nondurable manufacturing, retail trade, and sub-professional series, the peripheral industries are noted for their small firm size, labor intensity, low profits, low productivity, intensive product market competition, lack of unionization, and low wages. Unlike core sector industries the periphery lacks the assets, size and political power to take advantage of economies of scale or to spend large sums on research and development.

Theories of dual economy suggest that these sectorial differences have important implications for the opportunity structures and environments faced by individual firms. Firms in the periphery sector face a more restricted opportunity structure and a higher degree of environmental uncertainty than firms in the core sector.

The environmental uncertainty is more evident with regard to the market for labor. The core sector is characterized by high productivity, nonpoverty wages, and employment stability, while the periphery sector is characterized by relatively low average and marginal productivity, low wages, and employment instability. The core sector uses its market power and high degree of profitability to hire and train the best workers and maintain nonpoverty wage levels without seriously eroding their profit margin. In fact, Beck and Horan examined the importance of industrial sectors as hypothesized by the dual economy literature on the process of earnings determination and found substantively and statistically significant differences in the labor force composition and economic status between core and periphery industrial sectors (Beck and Horan, 1978, p. 704). A direct result of this situation is that turnover in the core sector is likely more expensive and less attractive than in the periphery sector. As stated by Harrison:

Secondary (periphery) employers have several reasons for placing a value on turnover, in sharp contrast to their fellows in the primary market. They can, as a rule, neither afford nor do their technologies require them to invest heavily in "specific training." Instead, they tend to rely on the "general training" (e.g., literacy, basic arithmetic) provided socially. With minimal investment in their current labor force, and given the ready availability of substitute labor outside the firm, such employers are at the very least indifferent to the rate of turnover. (Harrison, 1974, p. 280)

Given this evidence on the differences in labor composition, economic status of employees, low turnover, higher wages, and unionized labor force, the firms in the core industry face less uncertainty in their labor management than firms in the periphery industry. Firms in the periphery industry have more opportunity and more predisposition to smooth both their operating flows (e.g., through their labor management) and reported income measures than firms in the core sector. In other words, the two economic sectors rely on their differential ability to maximize profits through the structuring of their labor processes (Hodson and Kaufman, 1982, p. 729).

The test, used also by Kamin and Ronen (1978), consists of observing the behavior of these smoothing variables: (1) operating expenses (OPEX) not inducted in cost of sales, (2) ordinary expenses (OREX), and (3) operating expenses plus ordinary expenses (OPEX + OREX), vis-à-vis the behavior of two objects of smoothing, (1) operating income (OP) and (2) ordinary income (OR).

It is assumed that management knows the future streams of inflows and outflows and their time distinction and has determined what should be the normal trend of OP and OR. To determine their normal trend, two expectation models are used here, namely, a time trend model and a market trend model.

1. *The Time Trend.* Two models will be used.

(a) The series of smoothed variables OP and OR and of smoothing variables OPEX, OREX, and OPEX + OREX were detrended in a time regression over a maximum span of twenty years, 1958 to 1977 as per the equations below.

$$Y_{ijt} = \alpha_{ij} + \beta_{ijt} + \varepsilon_{ijt}, \qquad\qquad i = 1,2,3,4,5 \quad t = 1958, \ldots 1977, (1)$$

where

$i = 1$ for OP, $i = 2$ for OR, $i = 3$ for OPEX, $i = 4$ for OREX and $i = 5$ for OPEX + OREX.

Y_{ijt} = observed OP, OR, OPEX, OREX, OPEX + OREX for firm j in year t.

(b) The first differences in OPEX, OREX and OPEX + OREX were detrended in a time regression as per equation (2) below.

$$\Delta Y_{ijt} = \delta'_{ij} + Y'_{ijt}, \qquad\qquad i = 1,2,3 \quad t = 1958, \ldots 1977 (2)$$

where

$i = 1$ for OPEX, 2 for OREX and 3 for OPEX + OREX

2. *The Market Trend*

The first differences in OP, OR, OPEX, OREX, and OPEX + OREX were regressed on a macroindex of first differences measured, respectively, as the mean observed first differences of OP, OR, OPEX, OREX, and OPEX + OREX as per equation (3) below.

$$\Delta Y_{ijt} = \alpha'_{ij} + \beta'_{ij}M_{it} + \varepsilon'_{ijt} \qquad\qquad i = 1,2,3,4,5 \quad t = 1958, \ldots 1977 \text{ (3)}$$

where

i = 1 for OP, 2 for OR, 3 for OPEX, 4 for OREX, and 5 for OPEX + OREX

M_{it} = Sample mean index of OP, OR, OPEX, OREX, and OPEX + OREX

where

$$M_{it} = \frac{1}{N}\sum_{i=1}^{N}\Delta Y_{ijt}, \text{ N being the sample size}$$

TEST CRITERION

Similarly to Kamin and Ronen (1978), the test criterion was based on the correlation coefficient between the deviations of the smoothing objects and the deviations of the smoothing variables. A positive correlation is consistent with a smoothing behavior.

Then for each subsample classified with respect to core or periphery variables as well as for the complete sample, we test if the correlation coefficients are significantly positive using a binomial test. The statistic Z_p is computed to test the null hypothesis that r is distributed symmetrically about $\bar{r} = 0$ using the alternative hypothesis $\bar{r} > 0$. Z_p is the standard normal statistic

$$Z_p = \frac{\chi \neq 0.5n - 0.5n}{0.5n} \qquad\qquad \text{(Siegel, 1956, p. 41)}$$

where

χ = small frequency

n = number of observations

A concentration of a highly positive correlation within the 0.01 level of significance would indicate that it is sensible to use the magnitude of the association in addition to its sign (Kamin and Ronen, 1978, p. 156). This was not possible in this study due to the differences in the number of observations used for each firm in the sample. This number varied between a minimum of ten years and a

maximum of twenty years. Data for the firms in the periphery sector were un-
derstandably less available than for the firms in the core sector.

Instead of testing the magnitude of the association, the present authors tested
the differences in smoothing behavior. A χ^2 text uses only the proportions of
smoothers in each group to indicate different proportions of smoothers.

$$\chi^2 = \sum_{t=1}^{2} \frac{(\chi_i - n_i\theta)^2}{n_i\theta(1 - \theta)}$$

where

χ_i = number of firms that indicate a smoothing behavior in group i
n_i = total number of firms in group i

THE DATA SAMPLE AND THE CLASSIFICATION OF FIRMS INTO CORE AND PERIPHERY SECTORS

To detect the differences in smoothing behavior between firms in the core
sector and firms in the periphery sector, it was necessary to determine the distinction between core and periphery economic sectors and to classify the sample
in these two main groups.

The data included 171 U.S. firms from forty-two industries (see the Appendix). The classification into core and periphery sectors was based on Beck and
Horan's (1978) classification. Beck and Horan relied on Bluestone et al.'s (1973)
analyses, as quoted above, and allocated to the core sector those industries that
exhibit high levels of capital intensity, unionization, large assets, high profit
margins, product diversification, and market concentration. These include mining, construction, durable and nondurable manufacturing, transportation, communications, utilities, wholesale trade, finance, professional services, and public
administration. Industries were assigned to the periphery sector because of their
small firm size, seasonal and other variations in product supply and demand,
labor intensity, weak unionization, and low assets. These include agriculture,
portions of durable and nondurable manufacturing, retail trade, business and
repair, and personal and entertainment services. This classification into a core
and a periphery group resulted in 114 firms in the core sector and 57 firms in
the periphery sector, chosen on the basis of availability of data for the period
of the analysis.[2]

RESULTS AND DISCUSSION

An overall summary of the results is shown in Table 1B.1. This shows the
significant differences in the extent to which firms in the periphery sector and
the core sector may be smoothing income. Under the time expectation model

Table 1B.1
Overall Summary of Results

Smoothing Object	Smoothing Variables	Income Trend	"Smoothing"					
			Core Firms	%	Periphery Firms	%	Differences	
OP	OPEX	Time (1)	57	68	33	82	S*[1]	
		Market	56	71	35	83	S*	
		Time (2)	57	70	35	81	NS[2]	
OR	OPEX	Time (1)	54	64	28	76	S*	
		Market	45	59	24	62	S**[3]	
		Time (2)	46	57	26	65	NS	
OR	OREX	Time (1)	55	59	28	74	S*	
		Market	51	58	23	62	NS	
		Time (2)	47	55	22	56	NS	
OR	OREX +	Time (1)	60	61	36	78	S**	
	OPEX	Market	50	57	28	72	S*	
		Time (2)	50	56	28	68	NS	

Notes:
1. S* = Significant at 0.10 level and indicates that the results are consistent in the greater smoothing.
2. NS = Not significant.
3. S** = Significant at 0.05 level and indicates that the results are consistent with greater smoothing by periphery firms than core firms.

No. 1 and the market model, all the differences, with one exception, are significant. Under the time expectation model No. 2, based on first differences, all the differences are not significant. Two points are noteworthy. First, where the differences are not significant, the proportion of smoothers in the periphery sector is still higher than in the core sector. Second, while most of the significant differences are at $\alpha = 0.10$, the difference resulting from a smoothing of ordinary income with operating and ordinary expenses under the first time expectation model and the difference resulting from smoothing ordinary income with ordinary expenses under the market model were significant at $\alpha = 0.05$.

The extent of smoothing in each sector is shown in Tables 1B.2–1B.13 and is indicated by Z_p. With no exceptions, the extent of smoothing for the periphery sector was significant. It was significant in seven out of the twelve cases for the core sector. These points are noteworthy. First, for the periphery sector, the extent of smoothing was significant at a higher level of confidence for the smoothing of operating income with operating expense under each of the three

Table 1B.2

Smoothing of Operating Income with Operating Expenses (Time Expectation Model No. 1)

	Core Sector $r > 0$ $r > 0$ Z_p			Periphery Sector $r > 0$ $r > 0$ Z_p			Control Effect X^2
No. of firms	57	27	-2.83*	33	7	-4.26*	2.229**
%	(68)	(32)		(82)	(17)		
r	0.51			0.60			

Notes:
*Significant at 0.05; **significant at 0.10.
$r > 0$ indicates positive correlation coefficients (consistent with smoothing).
r is the mean of the distribution of the correlation coefficients.

Table 1B.3

Smoothing of Operating Income with Operating Expenses ("Market" Income Expectation Model)

	Core Sector $r > 0$ $r < 0$ Z_p			Periphery Sector $r > 0$ $r < 0$ Z_p			Control Effect X^2
No. of firms	56	23	-3.71*	35	7	-4.47*	1.659**
%	(71)	(29)		(83)	(17)		
r	0.38			0.48			

Notes:
*Significant at 0.05; **significant at 0.10.
$r > 0$ indicates positive correlation coefficients (consistent with smoothing).
r is the mean of the distribution of the correlation coefficients.

Table 1B.4

Smoothing of Operating Income with Operating Expenses (Time Expectation Model No. 2)

	Core Sector $r>0\ r<0\ Z_p$			Periphery Sector $r>0\ \ r<0\ \ Z_p$			Control Effect X^2
No. of firms	57	25	- 3.53*	33	8	- 3.96*	1.484
%	(70)	(30)		(81)	(19)		
r	0.38			0.52			

Notes:
*Significant at 0.05.
$r > 0$ indicates positive correlation coefficients (consistent with smoothing).
r is the mean of the distribution of the correlation coefficients.

Table 1B.5

Smoothing of Ordinary Income with Operating Expenses (Time Expectation Model No. 1)

	Core Sector $r>0\ r<0\ Z_p$			Periphery Sector $r>0\ \ r<0\ \ Z_p$			Control Effect X^2
No. of firms	54	30	2.618*	28	9	-2.96*	2.204**
%	(64)	(36)		(76)	(24)		
r	0.41			0.49			

Notes:
*Significant at 0.05; **significant at 0.10.
$r > 0$ indicates positive correlation coefficients (consistent with smoothing).
r is the mean of the distribution of the correlation coefficients.

Table 1B.6

Smoothing of Operating Income with Operating Expenses ("Market" Income Expectation Model)

	Core Sector $r > 0 \ r < 0 \ Z_p$			Periphery Sector $r > 0 \ \ r < 0 \ Z_p$			Control Effect X^2
No. of firms	45	31	- 1.605*	24	15	-1.60*	3.799*
%	(59)	(41)		(62)	(38)		
r	0.31			0.49			

Notes:

*Significant at 0.05.

$r > 0$ indicates positive correlation coefficients (consistent with smoothing).

r is the mean of the distribution of the correlation coefficients.

Table 1B.7

Smoothing of Operating Income with Operating Expenses (Time Expectation Model No. 2)

	Core Sector $r > 0 \ r < 0 \ Z_p$			Periphery Sector $r > 0 \ \ r < 0 \ Z_p$			Control Effect X^2
No. of firms	46	34	- 1.34*	26	14	-2.055*	0.351
%	(57)	(42)		(65)	(35)		
r	0.30			0.49			

Notes:

*Significant at 0.05.

$r > 0$ indicates positive correlation coefficients (consistent with smoothing).

r is the mean of the distribution of the correlation coefficients.

Table 1B.8
Smoothing of Ordinary Income with Operating Expenses (Time Expectation Model No. 1)

	Core Sector $r>0$ $r<0$ Z_p			Periphery Sector $r>0$ $r<0$ Z_p			Control Effect X^2
No. of firms	55	38	-1.762*	28	10	-7.08*	1.871*
%	(59)	(41)		(74)	(26)		
r	0.41			0.44			

Notes:
*Significant at 0.05.
$r > 0$ indicates positive correlation coefficients (consistent with smoothing).
r is the mean of the distribution of the correlation coefficients.

Table 1B.9
Smoothing of Ordinary Income with Operating Expenses ("Market" Income Expectation Model)

	Core Sector $r>0$ $r<0$ Z_p			Periphery Sector $r>0$ $r<0$ Z_p			Control Effect X^2
No. of firms	51	37	1.49	23	14	-1.64*	0.056**
%	(58)	(42)		(62)	(38)		
r	0.36			0.42			

Notes:
*Significant at 0.05; **significant at 0.10.
$r > 0$ indicates positive correlation coefficients (consistent with smoothing).
r is the mean of the distribution of the correlation coefficients.

Table 1B.10
Smoothing of Ordinary Income with Operating Expenses (Time Expectation Model No. 2)

	Core Sector $r > 0$	$r < 0$	Z_p	Periphery Sector $r > 0$	$r < 0$	Z_p	Control Effect X^2
No. of firms	47	39	0.863	22	17	- 0.960	0.0001
%	(55)	(45)		(56)	(44)		
r	0.38			0.43			

Notes:
*Significant at 0.05.
$r > 0$ indicates positive correlation coefficients (consistent with smoothing).
r is the mean of the distribution of the correlation coefficients.

Table 1B.11
Smoothing of Operating Income with Operating Expenses (Time Expectation Model No. 1)

	Core Sector $r > 0$	$r < 0$	Z_p	Periphery Sector $r > 0$	$r < 0$	Z_p	Control Effect X^2
No. of firms	60	39	- 2.11*	32	9	- 3.75*	3.179*
%	(61)	(39)		(78)	(22)		
r	0.41			0.49			

Notes:
*Significant at 0.05.
$r > 0$ indicates positive correlation coefficients (consistent with smoothing).
r is the mean of the distribution of the correlation coefficients.

44

Table 1B.12
Smoothing of Ordinary Income with Ordinary and Operating Expenses ("Market" Income Expectation Model)

	Core Sector $r > 0$ $r < 0$ Z_p			Periphery Sector $r > 0$ $r < 0$ Z_p			Control Effect X^2
No. of firms	50	38	- 1.27	28	11	- 2.88*	1.964*
%	(57)	(43)		(72)	(28)		
r	0.30			0.39			

Notes:
*Significant at 0.05.
$r > 0$ indicates positive correlation coefficients (consistent with smoothing).
r is the mean of the distribution of the correlation coefficients.

Table 1B.13
Smoothing of Operating Income with Ordinary and Operating Expenses (Time Expectation Model No. 2)

	Core Sector $r > 0$ $r < 0$ Z_p			Periphery Sector $r > 0$ $r < 0$ Z_p			Control Effect X^2
No. of firms	50	39	- 1.165	28	13	- 2.488*	1.248
%	(56)	(44)		(68)	(32)		
r	0.33			0.48			

Notes:
*Significant at 0.05.
$r > 0$ indicates positive correlation coefficients (consistent with smoothing).
r is the mean of the distribution of the correlation coefficients.

expectation models. Second, for both the core and periphery sectors the extent of smoothing was always significant under the first time expectation model. Third, the insignificant results in the core sector were mainly under the market income expectation and the second time expectation models.

What appears worth noting from the findings is that first, both core and periphery sectors lead in terms of proportion of smoothers and extent of smoothing. Second, in attempting to smooth income, managers in both sectors are more inclined to look for a "normal" time trend as a guide rather than a market trend or a first difference trend. With respect to the first identified finding, it may be advanced that the motivation to smooth is higher for managers in the periphery sector, who have to face a more restricted opportunity structure and a higher degree of environmental uncertainty than firms in the core sector. With respect to the second identified finding, it may be advanced that what management considers the normal trend of OP and OR is the easy to conceive and to compute time trend rather than the market trend or the first differences trend.

CONCLUSION

This study has tested the effects of a dual economy on income smoothing behavior. The main hypothesis was that a higher degree of smoothing of income numbers is exhibited by firms in the periphery sector than firms in the core sector as a reaction to differences in opportunity structures, experiences, and environmental uncertainty. The results indicate that a majority of the firms may be resorting to income smoothing, with a higher number included among firms in the periphery sector. These results add to other attempts to identify organizational characteristics that differentiate between firms in their extent of smoothing (Kamin and Ronen, 1978). Future research looking into the impact of other organizational characteristics of firms that have a propensity to smooth may be helpful to users of accounting numbers.

APPENDIX: SAMPLE

Agriculture, Forestry, Fisheries

American Agronomics	3735
New Hall Land and Farm	651427

Mining

Metal Mining

Amax Inc.	023127
Cyprus Mines Corp.	232813
Standard Metals	853615
Inco Ltd-Cl B Conv	453258
Cleveland-Cliffs Iron Co.	186000

Coal Mining

West Moreland Coal Co.	960878
Piston Co.	725701
McIntyre Mines Ltd.	581283
General Exploration	369784
Woods Petroleum Corp.	980140

Crude Petroleum and Natural Gas

American Petrofina	028861
Dome Petroleum Ltd.	257093
Getty Oil Co.	634280
Ranger Oil (Canada) Ltd.	752805

Nonmetal Mining and Quarrying

Arundel Corp.	043177
Florida Rock Inds.	341140
Pebble Beach Corp.	705090
Freeport Minerals Co.	356715

Construction

Morisson-Knudsen	286438
Great Lakes Dredge and Dock Co.	390604
Centex Corp.	156312
U.S. Home Corp.	912061

Durable Manufacturing

Lumber and Wood Products

Barclay Industries	067374
Boise Cascade Corp.	097383
Louisiana Pacific	546347
Pope and Talbot Inc.	732827

Furniture and Fixtures

Aberdeen Mfg. Co.	003068
Kirsh Co.	497656
Simmons Co.	828709
Weiman Co. Inc.	948662

Stone, Clay and Glass Products

Corning Glass Works	219327
Libbey-Owens Ford Co.	530000
Midland Glass Co.	597521

Glen Gery Corp.	377568
Lenox Inc.	526264
Metal Industries	
Kaiser Steel Corp.	483098
Hofmann Industries Inc.	434560
Inland Steel Co.	457470
Bethlehem Steel Co.	087509
Cyclops Corp.	232525
Machinery (except electrical)	
Binks Mfg. Co.	090527
Ingersoll-Rand Co.	456866
Torin Corp.	891067
Parker-Hannifin Corp.	701094
Electrical Machinery, Equipment, Supplies	
North American Philips Corp.	657045
Westinghouse Electric Corp.	960402
General Electric Co.	369604
Sperry Rand Corp.	848355
Transportation Equipment	
Winnebago Industries	974637
ACF Inds.	000800
Pittsburgh Forgings Co.	725106
Rohr Industries	775422
Timken Co.	887389
Professional and Photo Equipment	
Cavitron Corp.	149645
Polaroid Corp.	731095
Visual Graphics	928438
American Sterilizer Co.	030087
Ordinance	
R.E.D.M. Corp.	749482
General Recreation	370594
Remington Arms Co.	759574
Raymond Industries Inc.	754713
Miscellaneous Durable Manufacturing	
American Technical Industries	030141
Bally Manufacturing Corp.	058732

Compudyne Corp.	204795
Hillenbrand Industries	431573
Jostens Inc.	481088

Nondurable Manufacturing

Food and Kindred Products

Beatrice Foods Co.	074077
General Mills Co.	370334
Pillsbury Co.	721510
Carnation Co.	143483

Tobacco Manufacturing

American Brands Inc.	024703
Philip Morris Inc.	718167
Reynolds (R.J.) Industries	761753
U.S. Tobacco Inc.	912775
BAYUK Cigars Inc.	073239

Textile Mill Products

West Point-Pepperell	955465
Riegel Textile Corp.	766481
Graniteville Co.	387478
Belden Hemingwey	077491
Collins & Aikrnan Corp.	194828

Apparel and Other Fabricated Textiles

Puritan Fashions Corp.	746316
Levi Strauss and Co.	527364
Fairfield-Noble Corp.	304621
Wilson Brothers	972091

Paper and Allied Products

American Israeli Paper Mills	027069
Technical Tape Inc.	878504
Domtar Inc.	257561
International Paper Co.	460146

Printing, Publishing and Allied Products

Simplicity Pattern Co.	828879
Western Publishing	959265
Knight-Ridder Newspapers Inc.	499040
Affiliated Publications	008261
Times Mirror Co.	887360

Chemical and Allied Products

American Cynamic Co.	025321
Celanese Corp.	150843
Dow Chemical	260543
Diamond Shamrock Corp.	252741

Rubber and Miscellaneous Plastic Products

Rubbermaid Inc.	781088
Armstrong Rubber	042465
Mohawk Rubber	608302
Firestone Tire and Rubber Co.	318315
Aegis Corp.	007603

Leather and Leather Products

Seton Co.	817814
Jaclyn Inc.	469772
U.S. Shoe Corp.	912605
Interco Inc.	458506
Barry (RG)	068797

Transportation

Railroads and Railway Express Services

Burlington Northern Inc.	121897
IC Industries Inc.	449268
Soo Line Railroad	835716
Santa Fe Industries	802020
Saint Louis–San Francisco Railways	791808

Trucking Services

Arkansas Best Corp.	040789
Smith's Transfer	832407
Golden Cycle Corp.	380892
Tri-State Motor Transit	895691
CW Transport Inc.	126693

Water Transportation

Seatrain Lines	812557
Sea Containers	811369
Overseas Shipping Group	690368

Air Transportation

Ozark Airlines Inc.	692515
Frontiers Airlines Inc.	359064

Piedmont Airlines Inc.	720101
Southwest Airlines	844741
Capitol International Airways	140627
Petroleum and Gas Pipelines	
Bay State Gas	072612
Mountain Fuel Supply Co.	624029
Texas Oil and Gas Co.	882593
United Energy Resources	910210
Services Incidental to Transportation	
WTC Inc.	929340
Canal-Randolph Corp.	137051

Communications

Radio Broadcasting and Television	
Metromedia Inc.	591690
CBS Inc.	124845
Reeves Telecomp Corp.	759650
Sonderling Broadcasting Corp.	835427
American Broadcasting	024735
Telephone (Wire and Radio)	
General Telephone and Electronics	371028
Continental Telephone Corp.	212093
Bell Telephone of Canada	078149
American Telephone and Telegraph	030177
Mid-Continent Telephone	595390
Telegraph (Wire and Radio)	
Western Union Corp.	959805

Utility and Sanitary Services

Electric Light and Power	
Arizona Public Service Co.	040555
Wholesale Trade	
Ketchum and Co.	492620
Lloyd's Electronics	539434
Retail Trade	
Fay's Drug Co.	313035
House of Fabrics Inc.	441758
House of Vision Inc.	441726

Walgreen Co.	031422
Servomation Corp.	817715
Finance, Insurance, and Real Estate	
Wells Fargo Mtg. and Equity T.R.	949752
Mony Mortgage Investors	615339
Tri-South Mortgage Inv.	895580
Business and Repair Services	
American Consumer Industries	025231
Ryder System Inc.	783549
Allright Auto-Parks Inc.	019879
Nielsen (A.C.) Co. Cl.	654098
Personal Services	
Family Record Plan Inc.	307045
Service Corporation International	817565
Block H & R Inc.	093671
Seligman and Latz Inc.	816323
IFS Industries Inc.	449510
Entertainment and Recreation Services	
American International Pictures	026877
San Juan Racing Assoc.	798407
Metro-Goldwyn-Mayer Inc.	591605
Disney (Walt) Productions	254687
Harrah's	413615
Public Administration	
Stone and Webster Inc.	861572
Baker (Michael) Corp.	057149

NOTES

1. A new monograph on income smoothing (Ronen, 1981) and the new and active interest in the "positive" theory of accounting bear witness to the relevance and the timeliness of the income-smoothing paradigm and the urgent need for answers and solutions.

2. Since the firms in the core/periphery sectors are likely to differ significantly in size, both parametric and nonparametric tests were done to test for differences in sizes. The differences were significant at the 0.10 level for the period of analysis. The differences were not, however, restricted to size. Significant differences were found in terms of levels of capital intensity, unionization, profit margin, product differentiation, and market concentration (Beck and Horan, 1978).

REFERENCES

Archibald, T.R. "The Return to Straight-Line Depreciation: An Analysis of a Change in Accounting Method," *Empirical Research in Accounting: Selected Studies*, suppl. to *Journal of Accounting Research* 5 (1967), pp. 161–180.

Averitt, R.T. *The Dual Economy: The Dynamics of American Industry Structure.* New York: Horton, 1968.

Baran, P.A., and P.N. Sweezy. *Monopoly Capital.* New York: Monthly Review Press, 1966.

Barefield, R.M., and E.E. Comiskey. "The Smoothing Hypothesis: An Alternative Test." *The Accounting Review* (April 1972), pp. 291–298.

Barnea, A., J. Ronen, and S. Sadan. "Classificatory Smoothing of Income with Extraordinary Items." *The Accounting Review* (January 1976), pp. 110–122.

Beck, E.M., and P.M. Horan. "The Structure of American Capitalism and Status Attainment Research: A Reassessment of Contemporary Stratification Theory." Unpublished Paper, Department of Sociology, University of Georgia, Athens, 1978.

Beck, E.M., P.M. Horan, and C.M. Tolbert II. "Stratification in a Dual Economy: A Sectorial Mode of Earnings Determination." *American Sociological Review* (October 1978), pp. 704–720.

Beidleman, C.R. "Income Smoothing: The Role of Management." *The Accounting Review* (October 1973), pp. 653–667.

Bluestone, B.W., N. Murphy, and M. Stevenson. *Low Wages and the Working Poor.* Ann Arbor: Institute of Labor and Industrial Relations, University of Michigan, 1973.

Cain, G.G. "The Challenge of Segmented Labor Market Theories to Orthodox Theory." *Journal of Economic Literature* 14 (1976), pp. 1215–1257.

Copeland, R. "Income Smoothing." *Empirical Research in Accounting: Selected Studies*, suppl. to *Journal of Accounting Research* 6 (1968), pp. 101–116.

Copeland, R., and R. Licastro. "A Note on Income Smoothing." *The Accounting Review* (July 1968), pp. 540–546.

Cushing, B.E. "An Empirical Study of Changes in Accounting Policy."*Journal of Accounting Research* (Autumn 1969), pp. 196–203.

Cyert, R.N., and J.G. March. *A Behavioral Theory of the Firm.* Englewood Cliffs, NJ: Prentice Hall, 1963.

Dasher, B.E., and R.E. Malcom. "A Note on Income Smoothing in the Chemical Industry." *Journal of Accounting Research* (Autumn 1970), pp. 253–259.

Gordon, M.J. "Postulates, Principles and Research in Accounting." *The Accounting Review* (April 1964), pp. 251–263.

Gordon, M.J., B.N. Horwitz, and E.T. Meyers. "Accounting Measurements and Normal Growth of the Firm." In R. Jaedicke, Y. Ijiri, and O. Nielson (eds.), *Research and Accounting Measurement.* Evanston, IL: American Accounting Association, 1966, pp. 221–231.

Harrison, B. "The Theory of the Dual Economy." In B. Silverman and M. Yanovitch (eds.), *The Worker in "Post Industrial" Capitalism.* New York: Free Press, 1974, pp. 269–271.

Hepworth, S.R. "Smoothing Periodic Income." *The Accounting Review* (January 1953), pp. 32–39.

Hodson, R., and R.L. Kaufman. "Economic Dualism: A Critical Review." *American Sociological Review* (December 1982), pp. 727–739.

Kamin, J.Y., and J. Ronen. "The Smoothing of Income Numbers: Some Empirical Evidence on Systematic Differences among Management-Controlled and Owner-Controlled Firms." *Accounting, Organizations and Society* 3 (1978), pp. 141–153.

Lev, B., and S. Kunitzky. "On the Association between Smoothing Reasons and the Risk of Common Stock." *The Accounting Review* (April 1974), pp. 259–270.

Piori, M. "The Dual Labor Market: Theory and Implications." In D.M. Gordon (ed.), *Problems in Political Economy: An Urban Perspective*. Lexington, MA: Heath, 1977, pp. 257–270.

Ronen, J. *Smoothing Income Numbers, Objectives, Means and Implications*. Reading, MA: Addison-Wesley, 1981.

Ronen, J., and S. Sadan. *Smoothing Income Numbers: Objectives, Reasons and Implications*. Reading, MA: Addison-Wesley, 1981.

Schiff, M., and A.N. Lewin. "Where Traditional Budgeting Fails." *Financial Executive* (May 1968), pp. 57–62.

Siegel, S. *Nonparametric Statistics for the Behavioral Sciences*. New York: McGraw-Hill, 1956.

Spilerman, S. "Careers, Labor Market Structure, and Socioeconomic Achievement." *American Journal of Sociology* 93 (1982), pp. 645–665.

Thompson, J.D. *Organizations in Action*. New York: McGraw-Hill, 1967.

White, C.E. "Discretionary Accounting Decisions and Income Normalization." *Journal of Accounting Research* (Autumn 1970), pp. 260–273.

Appendix 1C: Anticipatory Smoothing and the Investment Opportunity Set: An Empirical Test of the Fudenberg and Tirole (1955) Model

1. INTRODUCTION

It is both an empirical and anecdotal fact that managers make discretionary accounting choices that "smooth" reported earnings around some predetermined target (e.g., Ronen and Sadan, 1981; Hand, 1989; Gaver et al., 1995; Chaney et al., 1998; Defond and Park, 1997; Subramanyam, 1996). Analytical results by Fudenberg and Tirole (1995) propose that concern about job security creates an incentive for managers to smooth earnings in consideration of both current and future relative performance. Defond and Park (1997) find support for this job security and anticipatory income smoothing theory. They find that managers facing poor (good) current earnings and expecting good (poor) future earnings resort to income-increasing (income-decreasing) accruals. Their results, although consistent with the Fudenberg and Tirole (1995) thesis, do not constitute a direct test of the link between job security and income smoothing. A more direct test was provided by Ahmed et al. (2000), who hypothesized that the extent of smoothing would vary directly with managers' job security concerns as proxied by the degree of competition in firms' product markets, product durality, and capital intensity. Their results show that managers of firms in more competitive industries and durable goods engage to a greater extent in income smoothing. The results on the relations between income smoothing and capital intensity are mixed. While their attempt and results are compatible with various calls for further research to explain how business factors affect accruals, they fail to provide an integrative explanation of the link between job security and anticipatory income smoothing. The results are silent on firms' meeting different levels on each of the economic attributes. For example, what is the motivation for smoothing in firms that are highly competitive, with low capital intensity, and coming from nondurable goods industries? Given the high number of economic characteristics espoused by firms and the high number of levels of these characteristics possible, quite a number of possible links between job security and income smoothing can be found without being helpful for an understanding of the phenomenon. This study, instead, suggests a more integrative approach by looking at a variable depicting a general economic situation that is itself a composite number of economic characteristics that can be indicative of employment situation in general and job security concerns in particular and that can be linked to anticipatory income smoothing. The economic variable deemed to fit these requirements is the investment opportunity set or growth opportunities. We argue that managers of firms with lower growth opportunities as measured by the investment opportunity set are likely to have greater job security concerns than managers of other firms. A greater extent of income motivating is expected from managers of such firms.

The empirical analysis is based on a sample of 8,632 firm-year observations selected from the Compustat database. For comparative purposes, we used the same methodology for the measurement of accruals and the estimation of discretionary accruals used in previous research. Basically, the measurement of accruals was based on both the traditional balance sheet approach and the alternative cash-flow approach proposed by Collins and Hribar (1999). The estimation of the discretionary accruals relied on two different models: the modified Jones model and the Kang and Sivaramakrishnan (1995) model.

The results of the study show that managers of firms with lower investment opportunity sets engage to a greater extent in income smoothing. In other words, the evidence suggests that when current earnings are "poor" and expected future earnings are "good," managers of firms with lower growth opportunities "borrow" earnings from the future for use in the current period. Conversely, when current earnings are "good" and expected earnings are "poor," the same managers "save" current earnings for possible use in the future. The results hold after controlling for size, leverage, and prior-period discretionary accruals. The study provides a more direct and integrative examination of the link between job security concern and income smoothing. The investment opportunity set

(IOS), rather than separate and disparate economic characteristics, is shown to be related to anticipatory income smoothing.

The appendix is organized as follows: Section 2 presents the hypothesis on the association between the IOS and job security. Section 3 presents the research design. Section 4 covers the results. The summary and conclusions are presented in Section 5.

2. THE ASSOCIATION BETWEEN THE INVESTMENT OPPORTUNITY SET AND JOB SECURITY

2.1. The Investment Opportunity Set

A firm comprises assets-in-place and future investment options or growth opportunities. The lower the proportion of firm value represented by assets-in-place, the higher the growth opportunities. Myers (1977) described these potential investment opportunities as call options, whose values depend on the likelihood that management will exercise them. Like call options, these growth opportunities represent real value to the firm (Kester, 1984). Growth options include such discretionary expenditures as capacity expansion projects, new project introductions, acquisitions of other firms, investment in brand name through advertising, and even maintenance and replacement of existing assets (Mason and Merton, 1985). A significant portion of the market value of equity is accounted for by growth opportunities (Kester, 1984; Pindyck, 1988).

2.2. Hypothesis

The IOS of a firm may be viewed as a crucial characteristic of the firm with profound influence on the way that the firm is viewed by managers, owners, investors, and creditors (Kallapur and Trombley, 2001). It has been shown theoretically to be a crucial determinant of the risk characteristics of the firm (Miles, 1986), a result confirmed empirically by Riahi-Belkaoui (1999) after controlling for multinational diversification. Similarly, Kallapur and Trombley (1999) showed strong association between some investment opportunity set proxy variables and realized growth.

Smith and Watts (1992) argue that managers of firms with relatively more growth opportunities are likely to be allowed more decision-making discretion because managers have better information about the investment opportunities than the firms' stockholders. As a result, Smith and Watts (1992) predict that growth firms are more likely to use incentive compensation schemes that tie management compensation to measures of firm performance (such as accounting earnings or stock price). The evidence indicates that growth firms are more likely to use stock-option plans (Smith and Watts, 1992) but is inconclusive with respect to which firms are more likely to use bonus plans (Gaver and Gaver,

1993). In addition, Gaver and Gaver (1993)[1] find that growth firms pay significantly higher levels of cash compensation to their executives.

The fact that IOS is related to the risk characteristics of the firm (Miles, 1986;
Riahi-Belkaoui, 1999), to the realized growth of the firm (Adam and Goyal,
1999; Kallapur and Trombley, 1999), and to a greater use of incentive
compensation (Smith and Watts, 1992; Gaver and Gaver, 1993; Baber et al.,
1996) indicates a greater job reward and job security associated with growth
opportunities.[2] Therefore, in conformity with the Fudenberg and Tirole (1995)
model of association between job security and income smoothing, our hypothesis
relates IOS to the extent of smoothing as follows:

H_0: *The extent of income smoothing is negatively related to the level of
IOS.*

3. RESEARCH DESIGN

For purposes of comparability with and replication of previous work, the
research design is essentially based on previous published research. The empirical methodology, described in Section 3.1, is based on Defond and Park (1997),
Ahmed et al. (2000), and Elgers et al. (2000). The methods used to estimate
discretionary accruals is described in Section 3.2. Section 3.3 discusses the
measurement of a proxy for IOS.

3.1. Methodology

Following the methodology of Defond and Park (1997), Ahmed et al. (2000),
and Elgers et al. (2000), we classify firm-year observations into three groups:
(1) firm-years in which the current relative performance is good while the expected future relative performance is poor; (2) firm-years in which the current
relative performance is poor while the expected future relative performance is
good; and (3) firm-years in which the current relative performance and the expected future relative performance are both either poor or good. The focus is
on groups 1 and 2, where income smoothing is expected. Current relative performance is considered good when current premanaged earnings are above the
sample median earnings by year and industry. It is considered bad when current
premanaged earnings are below the sample median by year and industry. Expected future relative performance is considered good when expected earnings
are above the sample median, by year and industry. It is bad when the expected
earnings are below the sample median by year. Group 1 is expected to have
negative mean and median discretionary accruals in conformity with the theory
predicting that managers will have an incentive to manage earnings upward.

Using discretionary accruals as the measure of extent of smoothing and a
proxy for IOS and based on our expectations that the extent of smoothing is
negatively related to the level of IOS in periods of low current/high future

performance and positively related to the level of IOS in periods of high current/ low future performance, the pooled regression takes the following form:

$$DACC_{it} = \beta_o + \beta_1 IOS_{it} + \beta_2 LEV_{it} + \beta_3 SIZE_{it} + \beta_4 DACC_{it-1} + \varepsilon_{it} \tag{1}$$

where

$DACC_{it}$ = discretionary accruals for firm i in year t

IOS_{it} = level of firm's IOS in year t

$SIZE_{it}$ = size of firm i in year t measured as log of total assets

LEV_{it} = leverage of firm i in year t

$DACC_{it-1}$ = discretionary accruals for firms in year $t - 1$

Discussion of the measurement of all these variables is presented below. Following earlier research, control variables included leverage and size as in Becker et al. (1998) and prior discretionary accruals as in Ahmed et al. (2000).

3.2. Measurement of Premanaged Earnings and Discretionary Accruals

Premanaged earnings in a given year are measured by the reported (asset-scaled) earnings before extraordinary items less discretionary accruals.

The estimation of discretionary accruals follows the approach of (1) using alternative ways of estimating discretionary accruals: the modified Jones model (1991) and the Kang and Sivaramakrishnan model (1995) and (2) using two alternative measures of accruals: the traditional balance sheet approach and the cash-flow approach proposed by Collins and Hribar (1999).

Total accruals, as based on the balance sheet approach, are as follows:

$$TAAC_{it} = (\Delta CA_{it} - \Delta CL_{it} - \Delta Cash_{it} + \Delta STDEBT_{it} - DEPTN_{it}) \tag{2}$$

where

ΔCA_i = change in current assets during period t (Compustat No. 4)

ΔCL_{it} = change in current liabilities during period t (Compustat No. 5)

$\Delta STDEBT_{it}$ = change in the current maturities of long-term debt and other short-term debt included in current liabilities during period t (Compustat No. 34)

$DEPTN_{it}$ = depreciation and amortization expense during period t (Compustat No. 14)

Based on the findings that studies relying on the traditional balance sheet approach to the measurement of total accruals suffer from potential contamination from measurement errors in the total accruals, Collins and Hubar (1999) suggested a straightforward approach that computes total accruals as the difference between net income and operating cash flow (taken from the cash-flow statement).

Discretionary accruals are also computed using a variant of the Jones (1991) model. The model captures regularities over time in the relations among total accruals, assets, and changes in revenues of a given firm:

$$TACC_{it} = \alpha_1(1/TA_{it-1}) + \alpha_2[(\Delta REV_{it} - \Delta REC_{it})/TA_{it-1}] \qquad (3)$$
$$+ \alpha_3(PPE_{it}/TA_{it-1}) + \varepsilon_{it}$$

where $TACC_{it}$ is total accruals calculated as in equation (2), TA_{it-1} is total assets, $\Delta REV_{it} - \Delta REC_{it}$ is the change in cash-basis revenue, and PPE_{it} is gross property, plant, and equipment. Discretionary accruals from the modified Jones model are the residuals from the regression in equation (3).

An alternative approach to the measurement of discretionary accruals is proposed by Kang and Sivaramakrishnan (1995). Their model estimates managed accruals using the level, rather than the change, of current assets and current liabilities. It is expressed as follows:

$$ACCB_{it} = \Phi_0 + \Phi_1 + (\delta_1 REV_{it}) + (\delta_2 EXP_{it}) + \Phi_3(\delta_3 PPE_{it}) + \varepsilon_{it} \qquad (4)$$

$ACCB_{it}$ = the balance of noncash current assets (net of tax receivables) less current liabilities (net of tax payables) for firm i at the end of year y, divided by total assets for firm i at the end of year $t - 1$. The parameters δ_1, δ_2, and δ_3 are the previous year's turnover ratios, which leads to the measurement of (1) the current period's receivables as a product of the previous year's receivables-to-sale ratio (δ_1) and the current period's sales (REV_t) and (2) the current period net current assets as the product of the previous year's net current assets-to-expense ratio (δ_2) times the current period's expenses (EXP_t).

3.3. Estimation of IOS

Because the IOS is not observable, there has not been a consensus on an appropriate proxy variable (Kallapur and Trombley, 1999). Similar to Smith and Watts (1992) and Gaver and Gaver (1993), we use a corporate measure of IOS that is designed to reduce classification error in this variable. Specifically, we use a common factor analysis of three variables to construct an index of the IOS of each firm. The three variables are market-to-book assets (MASS), market-to-book equity (MVE), and the earnings price ratio (EP). These variables are designed as follows:

1. MASS = [Assets—Total equity + Shares outstanding * Share closing price]/Assets
2. MVE = [Shares outstanding * Share closing price]/Total common equity
3. EP = [Primary EPS before extraordinary items]/Share closing price

4. RESULTS

This section covers a presentation and a discussion of the results of the empirical analysis. The sample selection criterion and a discussion of the descriptive statistics are presented in section 4.1. The results of income smoothing are discussed in section 4.2. Finally, the results of the regressions relating IOS to the extent of income smoothing are discussed in section 4.3.

4.1. Data

The sample selection criteria are the same as those reported in Elgers et al. (2000), as they constitute an improvement on those reported in Defond and Park (1997). The sample is chosen from the 152,883 firm-years in the 1998 S&P Compustat PC—this database of active and research companies having a CUSIP identifier and an SIC code. The main selection criteria are as follows:

1. Firms are chosen from industries with at least twenty members in each year.
2. Firms are eliminated due to missing data from both the I/B/E/S and Compustat databases.
3. The extremes of 1 percent of firm-years based on scaled discretionary accruals, non-discretionary accruals, operating cash flows, and IOS as well as firm-years having less than $1 million in assets were eliminated.
4. All financial institutions and unclassified firms (SIC between 5999 and 7000 and SIC = 9999) were excluded.
5. Finally, all non-December fiscal-year-end-firm-years are excluded.[3]

The final sample contains 8,632 firm-years. Table 1C.1 represents the results of the common factor analysis of the three measures of the IOS for the sample of firms. The estimated communalities of the individual measures of the investment opportunity set are shown in panel A (see Hartman, 1976).[4] The eigenvalues of the reduced correlation matrix of the three individual measures of IOS are shown in panel B. It has been suggested that the number of factors needed to approximate the original correlations among the individual measures is equal to the number of summed eigenvalues needed to exceed the sum of the communalities. In this study, the first eigenvalue exceeds the sum of the three comunalities. It appears that one common factor explains the intercorrelations among the three individual measures.

In panel C, the correlations between the common factor and the three individual measures of the IOS indicate, as expected, a positive correlation with MASS and MVE and a negative correlation with EP. It strongly suggests that the factor captures the underlying construct common to the three measures. The descriptive statistics of the common factor are presented in panel D.

Table 1C.2 reports the descriptive statistics for the sample of firm-years used

Table 1C.1
Selected Statistics Related to a Common Factor Analysis of Three Measures of the Investment Opportunity Set (IOS)

Panel A: Estimated communalities of three IOS measures[a]

MASS[b]	MVE[c]	EP[d]
0.294	0.141	0.065

Panel B: Eigenvalues of the reduced correlation matrix of three IOS measures

1	2	3
0.831	0.267	0.052

Panel C: Correlation between the common factor and three IOS measures

MASS	MVE	EP
0.789	0.622	−0.385

Panel D: Descriptive statistics of the common factor extracted from three IOS measures

Maximum	5.236	Third quartile	2.215	Median	1.123
First quartile	0.521	Minimum	0.229	Mean	0.080

Notes:
a. Communalities are equivalent to the squared multiple correlations obtained from regressing each of the IOS measures on the other two measures.
b. The ratio of the market value of the firm to the book value of assets. The market value of the firm is computed as the book value of liabilities plus the market value of common shares.
c. The ratio of the market value of common shares to the book value of common shares.
d. The ratio of primary earnings per share before extraordinary items to closing price per share.

in the study. Both total accruals and discretionary accruals are shown under both the balance sheet approach and the cash-flow approach. The total accruals have a mean (median) of − 0.031 (0.082) under the balance sheet approach (TACC1) and a mean (median) of − 0.042 (0.091) under the cash-flow approach (TACC2). Similarly, the discretionary accruals have a mean (median) of − 0.002 (0.050) under the balance sheet approach (DACC1) and a mean (median) of −0.004 (0.001) under the cash-flow approach (DACC2). The differences between DACC1 and DACC2 appear to justify the use of both of these accrual measurement methods to test the sensitivity of the results of the impact of IOS on anticipatory income smoothing.

Table 1C.2 also reports descriptive statistics on return on assets (EB), leverage (LEV) and size (SIZE). The mean (median) is 0.071 (0.052) for return on assets (EB), 0.515 (0.301) for leverage (LEV), and 3,125 (5,230) for size (SIZE).

Table 1C.2
Descriptive Statistics (n = 8,632, 1979–1996)

Variable	Mean	σ	Lower Quartile	Median	Upper Quartile
TACC1	-0.021	-0.082	-0.071	-0.032	-0.026
TACC2	-0.042	0.091	-0.085	-0.036	0.018
DACC1	-0.002	0.050	-0.032	-0.003	0.036
DACC2	-0.004	0.001	-0.041	0.000	0.041
EBI	0.071	0.052	0.037	0.051	0.096
LEV	0.515	0.301	0.381	0.539	0.632
SIZE	3,125	5,230	252	863	2,893

Note: Variables are defined as follows:

TACC1 = Total accruals using the balance sheet approach ($\Delta CA_{it} - \Delta CL_{it} - \Delta Cash_{it} + \Delta STDEBT_{it} - DEPTN_{it}/TA_{it-1}$)

TACC2 = Total accruals using the cash-flow approach

DACC1 = Discretionary accruals based on the modified Jones model and TACC1

DACC2 = Discretionary accruals based on the modified Jones model and TACC2

EB = Earnings before extraordinary items, deflated by total assets at the beginning of the year

SIZE = Total assets ($millions)

4.2. Evidence in Anticipatory Smoothing

Anticipatory smoothing evidence has been reported in Defond and Park (1997), Ahmed et al. (2000), and Elgers et al. (2000). Table 1C.3 provided results replicating prior evidence on anticipatory smoothing. As in previous studies, Table 1C.3 partitions the discretionary accruals results (based on the modified Jones model) on the basis of "poor" and "good" relative performance, on one hand, and "poor" and "good" expected future relative performance, on the other hand. Current relative performance is classified as poor (good) when current premanaged earnings (earnings before discretionary accruals) are below (above) the sample median earnings by year and by industry. Current premanaged earnings are measured by subtracting the Jones model discretionary accrual estimate from reported earnings. Expected future relative performance is classified as poor (good) when next year's premanaged earnings (earnings before discretionary accrual) are below (above) the sample median by year and industry. Expected earnings are measured by the next period's forecast earnings taken from the I/B/E/S database.

Table 1C.3
Discretionary Accruals Partitioned by Current Relative Performance and Expected Relative Performance[a]

Current Relative Performance[b]

Expected Future Relative Performance[c]		"Poor" (Current premanaged earnings below sample median earnings, by year and industry)		"Good" (Current premanaged earnings above sample median earnings, by year and industry)		Total	
"Poor" (Expected earnings below the sample median, by year and industry)	Mean	(i)	0.001 *** (d)	(ii)	-0.051 ***		-0.003 ***
	Median		0.0039 ***		-0.038 ***		-0.001 ***
	% positive		52.39 % ***		10.15% ***		46.31% ***
	N		2772		1342		4114
"Good" (Expected earnings above the sample median, by year and industry)	Mean	(iii)	0.058 ***	(iii)	-0.002 ***	0.02	0.02 ***
	Median		0.041 ***		-0.013 ***		0.00 ***
	% positive		85.21% ***		31.12%		51.16 ***
	N		1485		3032		4517
Total	Mean		0.036 ***		-0.029 ***		-0.001
	Median		0.017 ***		-0.016 ***		0.000
	% positive		85.21% ***		36.12 ***		50.31%
	N		4257		4374		8631

Notes:

a. Discretionary accruals are from the modified Jones model using the balance sheet approach.

b. Current relative performance is classified as poor (good) when current premanaged earnings (earnings before discretionary accruals) are below (above) the sample median earnings, by year and industry.

c. Expected future relative performance is classified as poor (good) when next period's premanaged earnings (earnings before discretionary accruals) are below (above) the sample median by year and industry.

d. ***Significantly different from 0 at less than the 0.01 level (two-tailed). Significance levels for means refer to t-tests; for medians refer to Wilcox on sign-rank tests, and for percentage positive refer to proportions.

The anticipatory smoothing hypothesis developed in Defond and Park (1997) predicts earnings management via discretionary accruals in the second and third cell of the classification matrix in Table 1C.2. The discretionary accruals are expected to be negative in the second cell as managers are expected to "save" current earnings for possible use in the future. The discretionary accruals are expected to be positive in the third cell, as managers are expected to "borrow" earnings from the future for use in the current period. The results of the replication correspond closely to those reported in Defond and Park (1997), Ahmed et al. (2000), and Elgers et al. (2000). When current performance is good and future performance is expected to be poor, the average and median discretionary accruals are -0.051 and -0.038, respectively. The prediction of anticipatory smoothing hypothesis is supported, with only 10.15 percent of 1,342 observations in cell (3) positive. Managers are assumed to be making income-decreasing discretionary accruals to reduce the threat of dismissal due to poor performance in the future.

When current performance is poor and future performance is expected to be good, the average and median discretionary accruals are 0.058 and 0.039, respectively. The predictions of the anticipatory smoothing hypothesis are again supported, with 85.21 percent of the 1,485 observations in cell (3) positive. Managers are assumed to be making income-increasing accruals to reduce the threat of dismissal due to poor performance in the current period.

4.3. Regression Results

The replication reported in Table 1C.3 corresponds closely to the anticipatory smoothing evidence reported in Defond and Park (1997), Ahmed et al. (2000), and Elgers et al. (2000). They do not, however, provide a direct test of the link between job security and income smoothing. A direct test, proposed in this study, is to evaluate the impact of the level of IOS on the extent of smoothing as the level of IOS is related to job security. The regression results reported in this section indicate that the extent of income smoothing varies with managers' job security concerns as proxied by the level of IOS. The results of the regression on equation (1) are reported in section 4.3.1 for the good current performance/poor future performance observations and in section 4.3.2 for the poor current performance/good future performance observations. To test the sensitivity of the results to the estimation procedure used, the results are presented using (1) the modified Jones model and the Kang and Sivaramakrishnan model for the estimation of discretionary accruals and (b) the traditional balance sheet and cash-flow approaches for the computation of total accruals.

4.3.1. Results for the Good Current Performance/Poor Future Performance Partition

The hypothesis is that the extent of income smoothing is negatively related to the level of IOS. The expectation is that when current earnings are "good" and expected earnings are "poor," the managers will "save" current earnings for possible use in the future, resulting in the use of negative disclosure accruals in the current period. As the level of IOS increases, the concern for job decreases, and therefore the discretionary accruals will be less negative. As a result, we predict the coefficient on IOS, the proxy for job security concern, to be positive.

Table 1C.4 reports the regression results for discretionary accruals from the modified Jones model (panel A) and from the Kang and Sivaramakrishnan model (panel B), using both the balance sheet and cash-flow approaches for computing total accruals. The significant negative intercept in the four cases confirms the anticipatory smoothing evidence reported in Table 1C.3. In addition, the IOS variable has a positive and significant coefficient as hypothesized. It shows that the anticipatory smoothing associated with good current performance/poor future performance increases as the level of IOS decreases. As expected and as found in prior research by Defond and Park (1997) and Ahmed et al. (2000), discretionary accruals are positively related to size and negatively related to leverage and size.

The regression results for the Kang and Sivaramakrishnan model using both the balance sheet and cash-flow approaches to the computation of total accruals are similar to the results provided by the modified Jones model.

4.3.2 Results for the Poor Current Performance/Good Future Performance Partition

The managers in this group of firms are expected to use positive disclosure accruals in the current period. As the level of IOS increases, the concern for the job decreases, and therefore the discretionary accruals will be less positive. As a result, we predict the coefficient on IOS, the proxy for job security, to be negative.

Table 1C.5 reports the regression results for discretionary accruals from the modified Jones model (panel A) and from the Kang and Sivaramakrishnan model (panel B), using both the balance sheet and cash-flow approaches for computing total accruals. The significant positive intercept in the four cases confirms the anticipatory smoothing evidence reported in Table 1C.3. In addition, the IOS variable has a negative and significant coefficient as hypothesized. It shows that the anticipatory smoothing evidence associated with poor current performance/ good future performance increases as the level of IOS decreases. As expected, the results on leverage, size, and prior disclosure accruals are similar to the findings reported for the other groups in section 4.3.2. The results for the Kang and Sivaramakrishnan model are also consistent with the results from the modified Jones model.

5. SUMMARY AND CONCLUSIONS

Fudenberg and Tirole (1995) propose that concern about job security creates an incentive for managers to smooth earnings. Consistent with their model,

Table 1C.4

Regression Results for the Good Current Performance/Poor Future Performance Partition Model: $DACC_{it} = \beta_0 + \beta_1 IOS_{it} + \beta_2 LEV_{it} + \beta_3 SIZE_{it} + \beta_4 DACCLG_{it} + \varepsilon_{it}$

Panel A: Discretionary Accruals estimated with the Modified Jones Model

	Dependent Variable = DACC1 (Balance Sheet Approach)	Dependent Variable = DACC2 (Cash-Flow Approach)
Intercept (-)	-0.13 (-7.61)	-0.13 (5.32)
IOS (+)	+0.19 (4.61)	-0.32 (6.01)
LEV (-)	-0.03 (6.23)	-0.05 (-10.32)
SIZE (?)	0.02 (6.32)	0.02 (7.32)
DACCLG (-)	-0.01 (-0.31)	-0.02 (-0.15)
R-sq	11.42%	16.31%

Panel B: Discretionary Accruals Estimated with the Kang and Sivaramakrishnan Model

	Dependent Variable = DACC1 (Balance Sheet Approach)	Dependent Variable = DACC2 (Cash-Flow Approach)
Intercept (-)	-0.12 (-8.67)	-0.36 (-10.96)
IOS (+)	0.20 (7.35)	-0.32 (9.50)
LEV (-)	-0.13 (-10.15)	-0.15 (15.16)
SIZE (?)	0.01 (16.32)	0.01 (13.25)
DACCLG(-)	-0.13 (8.15)	-0.08 (-3.98)
R-sq	20.16%	85.13%
N		

Table 1C.5

Regression Results for the Poor Current Performance/Good Future Performance Partition Model: $DACC_{it} = \beta_0 + \beta_1 IOS_{it} + \beta_2 LEV_{it} + \beta_3 SIZE_{it} + \beta_4 DACCLG_{it} + \varepsilon_{it}$

Panel A: Discretionary Accruals Estimated with the Modified Jones Model

	Dependent Variable = DACC1 (Balance Sheet Approach)	Dependent Variable = DACC2 (Cash-Flow Approach)
Intercept (+)	0.15	0.16
	(6.23)	(6.45)
IOS (−)	−0.06	−0.09
	(4.82)	(−6.15)
LEV (−)	−0.04	−0.05
	(8.50)	(6.13)
SIZE (?)	−0.002	−0.002
	(−2.12)	(8.13)
DACCLG (−)	0.01	0.08
	(0.16)	(3.98)
R-sq	3.2%	5.6%
N		

Panel B: Discretionary Accruals Estimated with the Kang and Sivaramakrishnan Model

	Dependent Variable = DACC1 (Balance Sheet Approach)	Dependent Variable = DACC2 (Cash-Flow Approach)
Intercept (+)	0.23	0.26
	(6.37)	(9.53)
IOS (−)	−0.63	−0.14
	(−8.15)	(−5.25)
LEV (−)	−0.07	−0.08
	(−6.16)	(−8.32)
SIZE (?)	−0.004	−0.007
DACCLG (−)	−0.04	−0.02
	(−2.13)	(−0.31)
R-sq	6.5%	7.32%
N		

67

Defond and Park (1997) show that managers smooth earnings in consideration of both current and future relative performance. To provide a more direct evidence of anticipatory smoothing and job security, this study hypothesizes that the extent of smoothing, as measured by four different measures of discretionary accruals, varies with managers' job security concerns as proxied by the level of the investment opportunity set or growth opportunities. More explicitly, the extent of smoothing is expected to be negatively related to the level of IOS in periods of low current/high future performance and positively related to the level of IOS in periods of high current/low future performance. The empirical results confirmed our predictions.

NOTES

1. Studies that explicitly model endogeneity between IOS and compensation type find different results. Holthausen et al. (1995) find a preference for accounting-based incentive corporations, which incorporate long-term targets.

2. Results on the impact of IOS on financial and dividend policies may also be used to support the job security hypothesis. First, firms with a high level of firm value represented by IOS rather than assets in place tend to use less debt in their capital structure (Smith and Watts, 1992; Gaver and Gaver, 1993; Skinner, 1993; Gul, 1999). Second, Smith and Watts (1992), Gaver and Gaver (1993), and Gul (1999) find a strong negative relation between dividend yield and IOS.

3. This last criterion was motivated by the reasoning that when all industry members do not share the same fiscal year, management may find it difficult to identify the median firm, as it would require comparisons of industry members across many months of the year. Support for this position is provided by Murphy (1998), Byrd et al. (1998), and Elgers et al. (2000).

4. Communalities are equivalent to the squared multiple correlations obtained from regressing each of the investment opportunity set measures on the other two measures.

REFERENCES

Adam, T., and V. Goyal. 1999. The Investment Opportunity Set and Its Proxy Variables: Theory and Evidence. Working Paper, Hong Kong University of Science and Technology.

Ahmed, A.S., G.J. Lobo, and J. Zhou. 2000. Job Security and Income Smoothing: An Empirical Test of the Fudenberg and Triole (1995) Model. Working Paper, Syracause University.

Baber, W., S. Janakiaraman, and S. Kang. 1996. Investment Opportunities and the Structure of Executive Compensation. *Journal of Accounting and Economics* 3: 297–318.

Becker, C., M. Defond, J. Jiambalvo, and K.R. Subramanyam. 1998. The Effect of Audit Quality on Earnings Management. *Contemporary Accounting Research* 15 (Spring): 1–2.

Byrd, J., M. Johnson, and S. Porter. 1998. Discretion in Financial Reporting: The Voluntary Disclosure of Compensation Peer Groups in Proxy Statement Performance Graphs. *Contemporary Accounting Research* 15: 25–52.

Chaney, P.K., D.C. Jeter, and C.N. Lewis. 1998. The Use of Accruals in Income Smoothing: A Permanent Hypothesis. *Advances in Quantitative Analysis of Finance and Accounting* 6: 103–135.

Collins, D., and P. Hribar. 1999. Errors in Estimating Accruals: Implications for Empirical Research. Working Paper, University of Iowa.

Defond, M.L., and C.W. Park. 1997. Smoothing Income in Anticipation of Future Earnings. *Journal of Accounting and Economics* 23: 115–139.

Elgers, P.T, R.J. Pfeiffer Jr., and S.L. Porter. 2000. Anticipatory Smoothing: A Reexamination. Working Paper, University of Massachusetts.

Fudenberg, K., and J. Tirole. 1995. A Theory of Income and Dividend Smoothing Based on Incumbency Rents. *Journal of Political Economy* 103: 75–93.

Gaver, J., K. Gaver, and J. Austin. 1995. Additional Evidence on Bonus Plans and Income Management. *Journal of Accounting and Economics* 19 (February): 3–28.

Gaver, J.J., and K.M. Gaver. 1993. Additional Evidence on the Association between the Investment Opportunity Set and Corporate Financing, Dividend, and Compensation Policies. *Journal of Accounting and Economics* 16: 125–140.

Gul, F. 1999. Growth Opportunities, Capital Structure and Dividend Policies in Japan. *Journal of Corporate Finance* 5: 141–168.

Hand, J. 1989. Did Firms Undertake Debt—Equity Swaps for an Accounting Paper Profit or True Financial Gain? *The Accounting Review* 64 (October): 587–623.

Hartman, H.H. 1976. *Modern Factor Analysis*, 3rd ed. Chicago: University of Chicago Press.

Holthausen, R., D. Larcker, and R. Sloan. 1995. Business Unit Innovation and the Structure of Executive Compensation. *Journal of Accounting and Economics* 19: 279–314.

Jones, J. 1991. Earnings Management during Import Relief Investigations. *Journal of Accounting Research* 29: 193–228.

Kallapur, S., and M.A. Trombley. 1999. The Association between Investment Opportunities Set Proxies and Realized Growth. *Journal of Business Finance and Accounting* 26: 505–519.

Kallapur, S., and M.A. Trombley. 2001. The Investment Opportunity Set Determinants, Consequences and Measurement. *Managerial Finance* 27: 3–15.

Kang, S., and K. Sivaramakrishnan. 1995. Issues in Testing Earnings Management and an Instrumental Variable Approach. *Journal of Accounting Research* 33 (Autumn): 353–367.

Kester, W.C. 1984. Todays Options for Tomorrow's Growth. *Harvard Business Review* 62 (2): 153–160.

Mason, S.P., and R.C. Merton. 1985. The Role of Contingent Claims Analysis in Corporate Finance. In E.I. Altman, ed., *Recent Advances in Corporate Finance*. Homewood, IL: Irwin, 7–45.

Miles, J. 1986. Growth Options and the Real Determinants of Systematic Risk. *Journal of Business Finance and Accounting* 13: 95–105.

Murphy, K. 1998. Executive Compensation. Working Paper, Marshall School of Business, Los Angeles.

Myers, S. 1977. Determinants of Corporate Borrowing. *Journal of Financial Economics* 5: 147–177.

Pindyck, R. 1988. Irreversible Investment Capacity Choice, and the Value of the Firm. *American Economic Review* 78: 969–985.

Riahi-Belkaoui, A. 1999. The Association between Systematic Risk and Multinationality: A Growth Opportunities Perspective. *Global Business and Finance Review* (Fall): 1–10.

Ronen, J., and S. Sadan. 1981. *Smoothing Income Numbers: Objectives, Means and Implications.* Reading, MA: Addison-Wesley.

Skinner, D.J. 1993. Asset Structure, Financing Policy and Accounting Choice: Preliminary Evidence. *Journal of Accounting and Economics* 16: 407–446.

Smith, C.W., and R.L. Watts. 1992. The Investment Opportunity Set and Corporate Financing, Dividend Compensation Policies. *Journal of Financial Economics* 32: 263–292.

Subramanyam, K.R. 1996. The Pricing of Discretionary Accruals. *Journal of Accounting and Economics* 22: 249–281.

Chapter 2

Earnings Management

INTRODUCTION

Managers have the flexibility of choosing between the alternative ways to account for transactions as well as choosing between options within the same accounting treatment. This flexibility, which is intended to allow managers to adapt to economic circumstances and portray the correct economic consequences of transactions, can also be used to affect the level of earnings at any particular time with the objective of securing gains for management and the stakeholders. This is the essence of earnings management, which is the ability to "manipulate" the choices available and make the right choices that can achieve a desired level of income. It is another flagrant example of designed accounting, which is the object of this chapter.

NATURE OF EARNINGS MANAGEMENT

Conceptual Definitions of Earnings Management

Various definitions have been offered to explain earnings management as a special form of "designed" rather than "principled" accounting. Schipper sees earnings management as a purposeful intervention in the external reporting process with the intent of obtaining some private gain.[1] This is assumed to be possible through either a selection of accounting methods within Generally Accepted Accounting Principles (GAAP) or application of given methods in particular ways.[2] Schipper also views earnings management from either an economic (or true) income perspective or an informational perspective. The true income perspective assumes (1) the existence of a true economic income that is distributed by a deliberate earnings management and/or by measurement errors embedded in accounting rules and (2) noisy unmanaged earnings acquire through earnings management new properties in terms of amount, bias, or variance. The informational perspective assumes (1) that earnings are one of the signals used for decisions and judgments and (2) that managers have private information that they can use when they choose elements within GAAP under different sets of contracts that determine their conversation and behavior.[3]

The information perspective in better explicated in the following definitions:

Earnings management occurs when managers use judgement in financial reporting and in structuring transactions to alter financial reports to either mislead some stakeholders about the underlying economic performance of the company or to influence contractual outcomes that depend on reported accounting numbers.[4]

This definition of Healy and Wahlen focuses on the exercise of judgment in financial reports to (1) either mislead the stakeholders who do not or cannot do earnings management and (2) make financial reports more informative to users. There is therefore a good and bad side to earnings management; the bad side is the cost created by the misallocation of resources, and the good side is made up of the potential improvements in management's credible communication of private information to external stakeholders, improving resource allocation decisions.[5]

Earnings Management as Accrual Management

Basically, the operational definition of earnings management is the potential use of accrual management with the intent of obtaining some private gain. The following relationships are central to an understanding of earnings management as accrual management.

1. Total accruals = Reported net income − Cash flows from operations
2. Total accruals = Nondiscretionary accruals + Discretionary accruals

The general approach for estimating discretionary accruals is to regress total accruals on variables that are proxies for normal accruals. Unexpected accruals or discretionary accruals are considered to be the unexplained (the residual) components of total accruals.

In addition to the use of unexpected accruals and discretionary accruals as a proxy for earnings management, many studies provided evidence on which specific accruals or accounting methods are used for earnings management. Examples of specific accruals proven to be used for earnings management include:

1. Depreciation estimates and bad debt provisions surrounding initial public offers[6]
2. Loan loss reserves of banks[7] and claim loss reserves of insurers[8]
3. Deferred tax valuation allowances[9]

ACCRUALS MODELS

Discretionary accruals models involve first the computation of total accruals. Therefore, total accruals models are presented first, followed by discretionary accruals models.

Total Accruals Models

Two models are generally used for the computation of accruals: the balance sheet approach and the cash-flow approach.

The balance sheet approach for the computation of total accruals (TA) is as follows:

$$TA_t = \Delta CA_t - \Delta Cash_t - \Delta CL_t + \Delta DCL_t - DEP_t$$

where ΔCA_t is the change in the current assets in year t (Compustat No. 4); $\Delta Cash_t$ is the change in cash and cash equivalent in year t (Compustat No. 1); ΔCL_t is the change in current liabilities in the year t (Compustat No. 5); ΔDCL_t is the change in debt included in current liabilities in the year t (Compustat No. 34); and DEP_t is the depreciation and amortization expense in year t (Compustat No. 14). Based on the findings that studies relying on the traditional balance sheet approach to the measurement of total accruals suffer from potential contamination from measurement of total accruals, Collins and Hribar[10] suggested a straightforward approach that computes total accruals as the difference between net income and operating cash-flow (taken from the cash-flow statement).

Discretionary Accruals Models

Six competing discretionary accruals models are considered in the literature. They are as follows:

The DeAngelo Model

The discretionary portion of accruals in the DeAngelo model[11] is the difference between total accruals in the event year t scaled by total assets (A_{t-1}) and nondiscretionary accruals (NDA_t). The measure of nondiscretionary accruals (NDA_t) rests on last period's total accruals (TA_{t-1}) scaled by lagged total assets (A_{t-2}). In other words:

$$NDA_t = TA_{t-1}/A_{t-2}$$

The Healy Model

In the Healy model[12] the nondiscretionary accruals (NDA_t) are the mean of total accruals TA_t scaled by lagged total assets (A_{t-1}) from the estimation period. In other words:

$$NDA_t = 1/n\Sigma_y(TA_y / A_{y-1})$$

where NDA_t is nondiscretionary accruals in the year t scaled by lagged total assets; n is the number of years in the estimation period; and γ is a year subscript for years $(t-n, t-n+1, \ldots, t-1)$ included in the estimation period. The discretionary portion is the difference between the total accruals in the event year scaled by A_{t-1} and NDA_t. The main difference between the DeAngelo model and the Healy model is that NDA follows a random walk process in the DeAngelo model and a mean reverting process in the Healy model.

The Jones Model[13]

The main objective of the Jones model is to control for the effect of changes in the firm's circumstances on nondiscretionary accruals. The nondiscretionary accruals in the event year are expressed as follows:

$$NDA_t = \alpha_1(1/A_{t-1}) + \alpha_2(\Delta REV_t/A_{t-1}) + \alpha_3(PPE_t/A_{t-1})$$

where NDA_t is the nondiscretionary accruals in the year t scaled by lagged total assets; ΔREV_t is the revenue in the year t less revenues in year $t-1$; PPE_t is gross property plant and equipment at the end of the year t; A_{t-1} is total assets at the end of the year $t-1$; and $\alpha_1, \alpha_2, \alpha_3$ are the firm-specific parameters.

The estimate of the firm-specific parameters is obtained by using the following model in the estimation period:

$$TA_t/A_{t-1} = \alpha_1(1/A_{t-1}) + \alpha_2(\Delta REV_t/A_{t-1}) + \alpha_3(PPE_t/A_{t-1}) + E_t$$

where α_1, α_2, and α_3 represent the OLS estimates of α_1, α_2, and α_3. The residual E_t represents the firm-specific discretionary portion of the total accruals.

The variations of the Jones model include:

1. A model that expands the Jones model by adding lagged total accruals and lagged stock returns as two additional explanatory variables.[14]
2. A model that replaces "changes in sales" in the Jones model by "change in cash sales."[15]

The Modified Jones Model

In order to eliminate the conjectured tending of the Jones model to measure discretionary accruals with error when discretion is exercised over revenue recognition, the modified model estimates nondiscretionary accruals during the event period (i.e., during periods in which earnings management is hypothesized) as follows:

$$NDA_t = \alpha_1(1/A_{t-1}) + \alpha_2[(\Delta REV_t - \Delta REC_t)/A_{t-1}] + \alpha_3(PPE_t/A_{t-1})$$

where ΔREC_t is net receivables in year t less net receivables in year $t-1$, and other variables are as in the previous equation.

The estimates of α_1, α_2, and α_3 and nondiscretionary accruals are obtained from the original Jones model, not from the modified model, during the estimation period (in which no systematic earnings management is hypothesized). The difference between the two models is explicated as follows:

Revenues are adjusted for the change in receivables in the event period. The original Jones model implicitly assumes that discretion is not exercised over revenue in either the estimation period or the event period. The modified version of the Jones model implicitly assumes that all changes in the credit sales in the event period result from earnings management. This is based on the reasoning that it is easier to manage earnings by exercising discretion over the recognition of revenue on credit sales than to manage earnings by exercising discretion over the recognition of revenue on cash sales. If this modification is successful, then the estimate of earnings management should no longer be biased toward zero in samples where earnings management has taken place through the management of revenues.[16]

The Industry Model

The industry model relaxes the assumption that nondiscretionary accruals are constant over time. Rather than attempting a modeling of the determinants of nondiscretionary accruals directly, the industry model assumes that the variations in the determinants of nondiscretionary accruals are common across firms in the same industry. The model is expressed as follows:

$$NDA_t = \beta_1 + \beta_2 median;(TA_t/A_{t-1})$$

where NDA_t is measured by the Jones model and median; TA_t/A_{t-1} is the median value of total accruals in year t scaled by lagged total assets for all non-sample firms in the same two-digit standard industrial classification (SIC) industry (industry j). The firm-specific parameters β_1 and β_2 are obtained from an ordinary least squares regression in the observation in the estimation period. The ability of the industry model to mitigate measurement error in discretionary accruals hinges critically on the following two factors:

First, the industry removes variation in nondiscretionary accruals that is common across firms in the same industry. If changes in nondiscretionary accruals largely reflect responses to changes in firm-specific circumstances, then the industry model will not extract all nondiscretionary accruals from the discretionary accrual proxy. Second, the industry removes variation in discretionary accruals that is correlated across firms in the same industry, potentially causing problem 2. The severity of this problem depends on the extent to which the earnings management stimulus is correlated across firms in the same industry.[17]

The Kang and Sivaramakrishnan Model

The Kang and Sivaramakrishnan model[18] relies on an alternative approach that (1) estimates managed accruals using the level rather than change of current assets and current liabilities, (2) includes cost of goods sold as well as other expenses, and (3) does not require the regression to be uncontaminated. The model is expressed as follows:

$$AB_{i,t} = \phi_0 + \phi_1[\delta_{1,i}REV_{i,t}] + \phi_2[\delta_{2,i}EXP_{i,t}] + \phi_3[\delta_{3,i}GPPE_{i,t}] + u_{i,t}$$

where

$AB_{i,t}$ = accrual balance
        = $AR_{i,t} + INV_{i,t} + OCA_{i,t} - CL_{i,t} - DEP_{i,t}$

$AR_{i,t}$ = receivables, excluding tax refunds

$INV_{i,t}$ = inventory

$OCA_{i,t}$ = current assets other than cash, receivables, and inventory

$CL_{i,t}$ = current liabilities excluding taxes and current maturities of long-term debt

$DEP_{i,t}$ = depreciation and amortization

$REV_{i,t}$ = net sales revenues

$EXP_{i,t}$ = operating expenses (cost of goods sold, selling, and administrative expenses before depreciation)

$GPPE_{i,t}$ = gross property plant and equipment

$NTA_{i,t}$ = net total assets

$$\delta_{1,i} = \frac{AR_{i,t} - 1}{REV_{i,t} - 1}$$

$$\delta_{2,i} = \frac{NV_{i,t-1} + OCA_{i,t-1} - CL_{i,t-1}}{EXP_{i,t-1}}$$

$$\delta_{3,i} = \frac{DEP_{i,t} - 1}{GPPE_{i,t-1}}$$

The parameters and δ_1, δ_2, and δ_3 are turnover ratios that accommodate firm-specificity and compensate for the fact that the equation is estimated from a pooled sample.

DETECTION OF EARNINGS MANAGEMENT

Financial reporting allows a distinction between best performing firms and poorly performing firms and better and more efficient resource allocation and financial analysis by stakeholders. The U.S. accounting standards permit managers to exercise judgment in financial reporting, allowing them to provide not only timely and credible information but also relevant information under alternative standards. The situation creates opportunities, however, for "earnings management," in which managers select reporting methods and estimates that do not reflect the firm's true economic picture. This led the chairman of the Securities and Exchange Commission (SEC), Arthur Levitt, to warn about the threat to the credibility of financial reporting created by abuses of "big bath" restructuring charges, premature revenue recognition, "cookie jar" reserves, and write-offs of purchases in process R&D.[19] A good definition of earnings management follows:

Earnings Management occurs when managers use judgement in financial reporting and in structuring transactions to alter financial reports to either mislead some stakeholders about the underlying economic performance of the company or to influence contractual outcomes that depend on reporting accounting numbers.[20]

The detection of earnings management can be accomplished by:[21]

1. The use of simple analytical procedures that can reveal unusual relationships and significant changes in financial statement item relationships.
2. The use of sophisticated models to assess the risk of earnings manipulation such as the use of artificial neural network technology to assess fraud.[22]
3. The use of a profit model that can yield an earnings manipulation index as a linear combination of financial variables to be converted to a "profitability manipulation."

The third technique is of interest to international accounting and can best be illustrated by the Beneish profit model.[23] With the objective of differentiating between GAAP violators and control firms, Beneish uses a number of variables to proxy for (1) the *probability of detection* of the violation by the market through distortions in the financial statements and (2) *incentive/ability* to violate GAAP.

The six financial statement variables designed to capture distortions in financial statement data to assess the probability of detection are:[24]

1. Day's sales in receivables index—measuring whether changes in receivables are in time with changes in sales.
2. Gross margin index—assessing whether gross margins have deteriorated, a negative signal about a firm's prospects.
3. Asset quality index—measuring changes in the risk of assets realization, with an increase to be interpreted as indicating an increased propensity to capitalize and therefore defer costs.

4. Depreciation index—measuring the change in the rate of depreciation.

5. SG&A index—measuring sales general and administrative expense (SG&A) relative to sales with a disproportionate increase in SG&A relative to sales to be considered as a negative signal suggesting loss of managerial cost control or unusual sales effort.

6. Total accruals to total assets—measuring the extent to which earnings are cash-based, with high increases in noncash working capital to reflect possible manipulation.

These variables are defined in Figure 2.1.

The five variables intended to measure a firm's incentives/ability to violate GAAP are:[25]

1. Capital structure, as the incentives to violate GAAP increase with leverage.

2. Prior market performance, as the incentives to violate GAAP increase with declining stock prices.

3. Time listed, as firms may violate GAAP and manipulate earnings at the time of initially going public or shortly thereafter.

4. Sales growth, as high-growth firms may have an incentive to dispel the impression that their growth is decelerating following a stock price drop at the release of bad news.

5. Prior positive accruals decisions, as incentives to violate GAAP may increase if managers attempt to avoid accrual reversals or cannot increase earnings.

The five proxies are operationalized by six variables: leverage, abnormal return, time listed, sales growth index, declining cash sales dummy, and positive accruals dummy. They are defined in Figure 2.1.

The earnings manipulation index, proposed by Beneish probit analysis, is expressed as the following linear combination:

Manipulation Index $= -2.224 + 0.221*$ (Day's Sales in Receivables Index)

$+0.102*$ (Gross Margin Index) $+ 0.007*$ (Assets Quality Index)

$+0.062*$ (Depreciation Index) $+ 0.198*$ (SG&A Index)

$-2.415*$ (Total Accruals to Total Assets) $+ 0.040*$ (Sales Growth Index)

$-0.684*$ (Abnormal Return) $- 0.001*$ (Time Listed)

$+0.587*$ (Leverage Index) $+ 0.421*$ (Positive Accrual Dummy)

$-0.413*$ (Declining Cash Sales Dummy)

The probability of manipulation is then computed by looking up the manipulation index in a standard normal distribution table, where $F(x)$ is the cumulative area under the standard normal distribution. That is:

Probability of earnings manipulation $= F$ (Manipulation Index).

Figure 2.1
Variables Used in the Beneish (1997) Probit Model

Variable	Definition	Hypothesized Relationship with Dependent Variable
Days Sales in Receivables Index	$$\dfrac{\dfrac{Receivables_t[2]}{Sales_t[12]}}{\dfrac{Receivables_{t-1}[2]}{Sales_{t-1}[12]}}$$	$+$
Gross Margin Index	$$\dfrac{\dfrac{Sales_{t-1}[12] - COGS_{t-1}[41]}{Sales_{t-1}[12]}}{\dfrac{Sales_{t-1}[12] - COGS_{t-1}[41]}{Sales_{t-1}[12]}}$$	$+$
Asset Quality Index	$$\dfrac{(1 - \dfrac{CurrentAssets_t[4] + PPE_t[8]}{TotalAssets_t[6]})}{(1 - \dfrac{CurrentAssets_{t-1}[4] + PPE_{t-1}[8]}{TotalAssets_{t-1}[6]})}$$	$+$
Depreciation Index	$$\dfrac{\dfrac{Depreciation_{t-1}[14-65]}{Depreciation_{t-1}[14-65+PPE_{t-1}[8]}}{\dfrac{Depreciation_t[14-65]}{Depreciation_t[14-65+PPE_t[8]}}$$	$+$
SG&A Index	$$\dfrac{\dfrac{SG\&AExpense_t[189]}{Sales_t[2]}}{\dfrac{SG\&AExpense_{t-1}[189]}{Sales_{t-1}[2]}}$$	$+$

Figure 2.1 (continued)

Variable	Definition	Hypothesized Relationship with Dependent Variable
Total Accruals to Total Assets	$$\frac{\left[\begin{array}{l}(\Delta CurrentAss_t[4] - \Delta Cash_t[1] \\ (\Delta CurrentLiab._t[5] - \Delta Short-termdebt_t[34] - \\ Deprec.\&Amort_t[14] - DefferedtaxonEarnings[50] + \\ EquityinEarnings[55]\end{array}\right]}{TotalAssets_t[6]}$$	?
Sales Growth Index	$Sales_t[12]/Sales_{t-1}[12]$	+
Abnormal Return	Size-adjusted return for a 12-month period ending on the month prior to release of the financial statements. Computed by subtracting from the firm's buy-and-hold return the buy-and-hold return on size-matched, value-weighted portfolio of the firms.	-
Time Listed	Distance in months between the fiscal year-end and the date the company was first listed on either the New York, American, or NASDAQ exchange.	-
Leverage	$$\frac{LTD_{t-1}[9] + CurrentLiabilities_{t-1}[5]}{TotalAssets_{t-1}[6]}$$	+
Positive Accruals Dummy	1 if total accruals were positive in the current and prior year; 0 otherwise.	+
Declining Sales Dummy	1 if cash sales in the current year were lower than in the previous year; 0 otherwise. $CashSales_t = Sales_t - (\Delta Receivables_t)$	?

Annual Compustat data items are provided in brackets.
Δ means the change in the account from previous year.
t refers to the year of interest.

Beneish derives cutoff values based on different relative costs of Type I versus Type II errors. A Type I error occurs when a GAAP violator is incorrectly classified as a control firm. Conversely, a Type II error occurs when a control firm is incorrectly classified as a GAAP violator.

The Beneish model relies on various cutoff values that can delineate different levels of risk of earnings manipulation. A cutoff value of 11.72 percent results in only 45 percent of GAAP violators being correctly classified as violators and only 3.6 percent of the control firms being correctly classified as violators. A cutoff value of 5.99 percent results in 67 percent of GAAP violators being correctly classified and 13.5 percent of control firms being incorrectly classified as violators. A cutoff value of 4.3 percent results in 76 percent of GAAP violators being correctly classified and 20.4 percent of control firms being incorrectly classified as violators. Finally, a cutoff value of 2.94 percent results in 83 percent of GAAP violators being correctly classified as violators and 28.6 percent of control firms being incorrectly classified as violators. Selection of the appropriate cutoff depends on different decision makers and different levels of risk.

THE MISPRICING OF DISCRETIONARY ACCRUALS

There is sufficient evidence showing that investors do correctly use available information in forecasting future earnings performance.[26] It reflects investors' naive fixation on reported earnings, rather than earnings ability to summarize value-relevant information. Most analysts would argue that since investors tend to "fixate" on reported earnings, examining the accrual and the cash-flow components of current earnings can be used to detect mispriced securities. The reasoning is that accrual and cash-flow components of earnings have different implications for the assessment of future earnings. Accordingly, Sloan[27] investigated whether stock prices reflect information about future earnings contained in the accrual and cash-flow components of current earnings. The persistence of earnings performance was found to depend on the relative magnitudes of the cash and accrual components of earnings.

However, stock prices acted as if investors failed to identify correctly the different properties of the two components of earnings. The market erroneously overestimates the persistence of the accruals component of accrual earnings while underestimating the persistence of the cash-flow component. Accruals also exhibit negative serial correlation or mean reversion tendencies. The end result is that the market responds as if surprised when seemingly predictable earnings reversal occurs in the following year. Similarly, Subramanyam[28] finds that abnormal accruals are positively related to future profitability. Xie[29] provides more evidence on the issue, estimating abnormal accruals after controlling for major unusual accruals and nonarticulation events (i.e., mergers, acquisitions, and divestitures), and found that this refined measure of abnormal accruals, which isolates managerial discretion, is still overpriced. These results are consistent with DeFond and Park's[30] conclusion that the market overprices abnormal accruals because investors underanticipate the future reversal of these accruals.

ISSUES IN EARNINGS MANAGEMENT

1. It is very easy to suspect that earnings management is intended to meet expectations of financial analysts or management (represented by public forecasts of earnings). In fact, there is evidence of (1) managers' taking actions to manage earnings upward to avoid reporting earnings lower than an analyst's forecast,[31] (2) financial analysts' stock recommendation (e.g., buy, hold, and sell) as a good predictor of earnings management,[32] (3) firms in danger of falling short of a management earnings forecast using unexpected accruals to manage earnings upward,[33] and (4) firms with a high percentage of institutional ownership typically not cutting research and development spending to avoid a decline in reported earnings.[34]

2. There are good reasons to suspect that earnings management is intended to influence short-term price performance in various ways.

1. There is evidence of negative unexpected accruals (income-decreasing) prior to management buyout.[35]
2. There is evidence of positive (income-increasing) unexpected accruals prior to seasoned equity offering,[36] initial public offers,[37] and stock-financed acquisitions.[38] A reversal of unexpected accruals seems to follow initial public offers and stock-financed acquisitions.

3. Earnings management is due and can persist because of asymmetric information, a condition caused by management's knowing information that they are not willing to disclose. The persistence is due to blocked communication where managers cannot communicate all their private information unless the principal contractually precommits not to use the information against the managers. Incentives for managers to reveal their private information truthfully, created by blocked communication, becomes a key for earnings management.

4. Earnings management takes place in the context of a feasible reporting set and a given set of contracts that determine sharing rules among stakeholders. Both contract sets are endogenous to the earnings management question. As the environment conditions change, both the reporting and contractual sets change, also leading to different forms of earnings management over time. For example, in environmental conditions where accounting data are used in compensation contracts, there is a strong incentive for managers to manage the data used in contracts. As a result the contracting use leads to an internal or stewardship incentive for earnings management.[39]

5. Corporate strategies for earnings management follow one or more of three approaches: (1) choosing from the flexible options available within GAAP, (2)

relying on the subjective estimates and application choices available within the options, and (3) using asset acquisitions and dispositions and the timing for reporting them.[40] Note here that the choices made within GAAP constitute earnings management, while choices made outside GAAP constitute fraud. The court may be the one to decide in some cases whether some management reporting actions that are taken outside the bounds of GAAP are fraud or earnings management.[41]

6. The earnings game—or, more precisely, the quarterly earnings report game—may be a major reason for earnings management.[42] Management is tempted to issue an earnings report that satisfies Wall Street's expectations more than it reflects financial reality. DeGeorge et al.[43] found that quarterly earnings reports that meet analysts' expectations exactly or exceed them by just a penny per share happen more frequently than would be likely in a random statistical distribution, while reports that miss by just a penny occur far less frequently.

7. Earnings management is a result of attempts to exceed thresholds.[44] The three thresholds of importance to executives are:

1. "to report positive profits, that is, report earnings that are above zero;
2. to sustain recent performance, that is, make at least last year's earnings; and
3. to meet analysts' expectations, particularly the analysts' consumer earnings forecast."[45]

Empirical explorations identified earnings management to exceed each of the three thresholds, with the positive profit threshold predominating.[46]

8. Earnings management may originate as a result of meeting covenants of implicit compensation contracts. Evidence for this thesis takes the following forms:

1. Divisional managers for a large multinational firm are likely to defer income when the earnings target in their bonus plan will not be met and when they are entitled to the maximum bonuses permitted under the plan.[47]
2. Firms with caps on bonuses are more likely to report accruals that defer income when that cap is reached than firms that have comparable performance but no bonus cap.[48]
3. During a proxy contest, incumbent managers exercised accounting discretion to improve reported earnings.[49]
4. Chief executive officers (CEOs) in their final years in office reduced R&D spending, presumably to increase reported earnings.[50]

9. Earnings management arises from the threat of two forms of regulation: industry-specific regulation and antitrust regulation. The banking and insurance industries are good examples of the existence of regulatory monitoring that is tied to accounting data. As stated by Healy and Wahlen:

Banking regulations require that banks satisfy certain capital adequacy requirements that are written in terms of accounting numbers. Insurance regulations require that insurers meet conditions for minimum financial health. Utilities have historically been rate-regulated and permitted to earn only a normal return in their invested assets. It is frequently asserted that such regulations create incentives to manage the income statement and the balance sheet variables of interest to regulators.[51]

There is, in fact, a lot of evidence supporting the above hypothesis. For example:

1. Banks that are close to minimum capital requirements tend to overstate loan loss provisions, understate loan write-offs, and recognize abnormal gains on securities portfolios.[52]
2. Financially weak property casualty insurers that risk regulatory attention tend to understate claim loss reserves[53] and engage in reinsurance transactions.[54]

10. Because of the need for government subsidies or protection as well as the fear of antitrust investigations or other political consequences, managers may resort to earnings management. A lot of evidence supports this hypothesis. For example:

1. Firms under investigation for antitrust violations reported income-decreasing abnormal accruals in the investigation years.[55]
2. Firms in industries seeking import-relief tend to defer income in the year of application.[56]
3. Firms in the cable television industry tend to defer earnings during the period of congressional scrutiny.[57]
4. Firms subject to price controls will adjust their discretionary accounting accruals downward to reduce net income and to increase the likelihood of approval of the requested price increase.[58]
5. The magnitude of the discretionary component of the postretirement obligation is negatively associated with the extent of the external regulations and auditor quality.[59]
6. More unionized firms are more likely to use immediate recognition of Statement of Financial Accounting Standards No. 106 on Employer's Accounting for Postretirement Benefits Other than Pensions, which is consistent with incentives to reduce labor negotiation costs.[60]

11. Firm valuation is generally assumed to be one of the targets of earnings management. Various analytical models have tried to explicate that relationship. Gigler[61] considers the case of the firm whose trade-off, when determining which income figure to disclose, is between the cost of acquiring new capital and the cost of competition. An overstatement of disclosed income will occur if the reduced cost of capital were higher than the increased cost of competition. The credibility of the disclosed income is possible because the firm incurs a propri-

etary cost by misrepresenting income. Chaney and Lewis[62] are concerned with an explanation for why corporate offices manage the disclosure of accounting information. They show that earnings management affects firm value when value-maximizing managers and investors are asymmetrically informed. Eilifsen et al.[63] add to the previous two models by showing that if taxable income were linked to accounting income, there will exist an automatic safeguard against manipulation of earnings, a claim also made by Johansson and Ostman.[64]

CONCLUSION

Earnings management is a deliberate choice of specific accounting techniques or options intended to secure a given level of earnings and some private gains. This chapter explicated the nature of earnings management from both a conceptual and operational viewpoint, described the different accruals models used in the literature to estimate discretionary or unexpected accruals, presented a model for the detection of earnings management, and discussed various issues, theoretical and empirical, on the form of designed accounting.

NOTES

1. K. Schipper, "Earnings Management," *Accounting Horizons* (December 1989), p. 92.

2. Ibid., p. 93.

3. Ibid.

4. P.N. Healy and J.N. Wahlen, "A Review of the Earnings Management Literature and Its Implications for Standard Setting," *Accounting Horizons* 4 (1999), p. 368.

5. Ibid, p. 369.

6. S.H. Toeh, T.J. Wong, and G. Rao, "All Accruals during Initial Public Offerings Opportunistic?" *Review of Accounting Studies* 3 (1998), pp. 173–208.

7. C. Liu, S. Ryan, and J. Wahlen, "Differential Valuation Implications of Loan Across Banks and Fiscal Quarters," *The Accounting Review* (January 1997), pp. 133–146.

8. K.R. Petroni, "Optimistic Reporting in the Property Casualty Insurance Industry," *Journal of Accounting and Economics* 18 (1994), pp. 157–179.

9. G. Visvanathan, "Deferred Tax Valuation Allowances and Earnings Management," *Accrual of Financial Statement Analysis* 3 (1998), pp. 6–15.

10. D.W. Collins and S.P. Hribar, "Errors in Estimating Accruals; Implications for Empirical Research," Working paper, University of Iowa, 1999.

11. L. DeAngelo, "Accounting Numbers as Market Valuation Substitutes: A Study of Management Buyouts of Public Shareholders," *The Accounting Review* 62, 3, pp. 431–453.

12. P.M. Healey, "The Effects of Bonus Schemes in Accounting Decisions," *Journal of Accounting and Economics* 7 (1989), pp. 85–107.

13. J. Jones, "Earnings Management during Import Relief Investigations," *Journal of Accounting Research* 29 (1991), pp. 193–228.

14. R.D. Beneish, "Detecting GAAP Violations: Implications for Assessing Earnings

Management among Firms with Extreme Financial Performance," *Journal of Accounting and Public Policy* 16 (1997), pp. 271–309.

15. R.D. Beneish, "Discussion of All Accruals during the Initial Public Offerings Opportunistic?" *Review of Accounting Studies* 3 (1998), pp. 209–221.

16. P.M. Dechow, R.G. Sloan, and A.P. Sweeney, "Detecting Earnings Management," *The Accounting Review* 70 (1995), p. 199.

17. Ibid., p. 42.

18. S.-H. Kang and K. Sivaramakrishnan, "Issues in Testing Earnings Management and an Instrumental Variable Approach," *Journal of Accounting Research* 33 (1995), pp. 353–366.

19. From Chairman Levitt's remarks in speech entitled "The Numbers Game," delivered at New York University on September 28, 1998.

20. Healy and Wahlen, "A Review of Earnings Management Literature," p. 368.

21. C.I. Wiedman, "Instructional Case: Detecting Earnings Manipulation," *Issues in Accounting Education* 14, 1 (February 1999), pp. 157–158.

22. B.P. Green and J.H. Choi, "Assessing the Risk of Management Fraud through Neural Network Technology," *Auditing: A Journal of Practice and Theory* 16 (1997), pp. 14–28.

23. Beneish, "Detecting GAAP Violations," pp. 271–309.

24. Wiedman, "Instructional Case: Detecting Earnings Manipulation," p. 160.

25. Ibid., p. 161.

26. J. On and S. Penman, "Financial Statement Analysis and the Prediction of Stock Returns," *Journal of Accounting and Economics* 11 (1989), pp. 159–330; V. Bernard and J. Thomas, "Evidence That Stock Prices Do Not Fully Reflect the Implications of Current Earnings for Future Earnings," *Journal of Accounting and Economics* 13 (1990), pp. 305–340; L.A. Maines and J.R. Hand, "Individuals' Perceptions and Misperceptions of the Time Series Properties of Quarterly Earnings," *The Accounting Review* (July 1996), pp. 317–336.

27. R.G. Sloan, "The Stock Prices Fully Reflect Information in Accruals and Cash Flows about Future Earnings," *The Accounting Review* 3 (1996), pp. 289–315.

28. K.R. Subramanyam, "The Pricing of Discretionary Accruals," *Journal of Accounting and Economics* 12 (1996), pp. 149–282.

29. H. Xie, "The Mispricing of Abnormal Accruals," *The Accounting Review* 76 (2001), pp. 357–373.

30. M.L. DeFond and C.W. Park, "The Reversal of Abnormal Accruals and the Market Valuation of Earnings Surprises," *The Accounting Review* (July 2001), pp. 145–176.

31. D., Burgstahler and M. Eames, "Management of Earnings and Analyst Forecasts," Working paper, University of Washington, 1998.

32. J. Abarbanell and R. Lehavy, "Can Stock Recommendations Predict Earnings Management and Analyst's Earnings Forecast Errors?" Working paper, University of California at Berkeley, 1998.

33. R. Kaznik, "On the Association between Voluntary Disclosure and Earnings Management," *Journal of Accounting Research* 37 (1999), pp. 57–82.

34. B. Bushee, "The Influence of Institutional Investors on Myopic R&D Investment Behavior," *The Accounting Review* 3 (1998), pp. 305–333.

35. S. Perry and T. Williams, "Earnings Management Preceding Management Buyout Offers," *Journal of Accounting and Economics* 15 (1992), pp. 157–179.

36. S.H. Teoh, I. Welch, and T.J. Wong, "Earnings Management and the Long-Term

Market Performance of Initial Public Offerings," *Journal of Finance* (December 1998), pp. 1935–1974.

37. S.H. Teoh, I. Welch, and T.J. Wong, "Earnings Management and the Post Issue Performance of Seasoned Equity Offerings," *Journal of Financial Economics* (October 1998), pp. 63–99; S.H. Teoh, I. Welch, T.J. Wong, and G. Rao, "Are Accruals during Initial Public Offerings Opportunistic?" *Review of Accounting Studies* 3 (2000), pp. 175–208.

38. M. Erickson and S.W. Wang, "Earnings Management by Acquiring Firms in Stock for Stock Mergers," *Journal of Accounting and Economics* 97 (April 1999), pp. 149–176.

39. R. Dye, "Earnings Management in an Overlapping Generations Model," *Journal of Accounting Research* 26 (1998), pp. 195–235.

40. P.R. Brown, "Earnings Management: A Subtle (and Troublesome) Twist to Earnings Quality," *The Journal of Financial Statement and Analysis* (Winter 1999), p. 62.

41. Ibid.

42. H. Collingwood, "The Earnings Game," *Harvard Business Review* (June 2001), pp. 65–74.

43. F. DeGeorge, J. Patel, and R. Zeckhauser, "Earnings Management to Exceed Thresholds," *Journal of Business* 72 (1999), pp. 1–33.

44. Ibid.

45. Ibid.

46. Ibid.

47. F.A. Guidry, A. Leone, and S. Rock, "Earnings-based Bonus Plans and Earnings Management by Business Unit Managers," *Journal of Accounting and Economics* 26 (1999), pp. 113–142.

48. R. Holhausen, D. Larker, and R. Sloan, "Annual Bonus Schemes and the Manipulation of Earnings," *Journal of Accounting and Economics* 19 (1995), pp. 29–74.

49. L.E. DeAngelo, "Managerial Competition, Information Costs, and Corporate Governance: The Use of Accounting Performance Measures in Proxy Contests," *Journal of Accounting and Economics* 10 (1988), pp. 3–36.

50. P. Dechow and R.G. Sloan, "Executive Incentives and the Horizon Problem: An Empirical Investigation," *Journal of Accounting and Economics* 14 (1991), pp. 51–89.

51. P.M. Healy and J.M. Wahlen, "A Review of the Earnings Management Literature and Its Implications for Standard Setting," *Accounting Horizons* 4 (1999), pp. 365–383.

52. S. Moyer, "Capital Adequacy Ratio Regulations and Accounting Choices in Commercial Banks," *Journal of Accounting and Economics* 12 (1990), pp. 123–154; M. Scholes, G.P. Wilson, and M. Wolfson, "Tax Planning, Regulatory Capital Planning, and Financial Reporting Strategy for Commercial Banks," *Review of Financial Studies* 3 (1990), pp. 625–650; A. Beatty, S. Chamberlain, and J. Magliolo, "Managing Financial Reports of Commercial Banks: The Influence of Taxes, Regulatory Capital and Earnings," *Journal of Accounting Research* 33 (1995), pp. 231–261; J. Collins, D. Shackelford, and J. Wahlen, "Bank Differences in the Coordination of Regulatory Capital, Earnings and Taxes," *Journal of Accounting Research* 2 (1995), pp. 263–291.

53. K.R. Petroni, "Optimistic Reporting in the Property Casualty Insurance Industry," *Journal of Accounting and Economics* 15 (1992), pp. 485–508.

54. R. Adiel, "Reinsurance and the Management of Regulatory Ratios and Taxes in the Property-Casualty Insurance Industry," *Journal of Accounting and Economics* 22, 1–3 (1996), pp. 207–240.

55. S. Cahan, "The Effect of Anti-Trust Investigations on Discretionary Accruals: A Refined Test of the Political Cost Hypothesis," *The Accounting Review* 67 (1992), pp. 77–95; S. Makar and P. Alam, "Earnings Management and Antitrust Investigations: Political Costs over Business Cycles," *Journal of Business Finance and Accounting* 5 (1998), pp. 701–720.

56. J.J. Jones, "Earnings Management during Import Relief Investigations," *Journal of Accounting Research* 29 (1991), pp. 193–228.

57. K.G. Key, "Political Cost Incentives for Earnings Management in the Cable Television Industry," *Journal of Accounting and Economics* 3 (1997), pp. 309–337.

58. S. Lim and Z. Matolcsy, "Earnings Management of Firms Subject to Produce Price Controls," *Accounting and Finance* 39 (1999), pp. 131–150.

59. S. Asthana, "The Impact of Regulatory and Audit Environment on Managers' Discretionary Accounting Choices: The Case of SFAS No. 196," *Accounting for the Public Interest* 1 (2001), pp. 23–96.

60. J. D'Souza, J. Jacob, and K. Ramesh, "The Use of Accounting Flexibility to Reduce Labor Renegotiation Costs and Manage Earnings," *Journal of Accounting and Economics* 30 (2001), pp. 187–208.

61. F. Gigler, "Self-Enforcing Voluntary Disclosures," *Journal of Accounting Research* 32 (1994), pp. 224–40.

62. P.K. Chaney and C.M. Lewis, "Earnings Management and Firm Valuation under Asymmetric Information," *Journal of Corporate Finance* 1 (1995), pp. 319–345.

63. A. Eilifsen, K.H. Knivsfla, and F. Saettem, "Earnings Manipulation: Cost of Capital versus Tax," *The European Accounting Review* 8 (1999), pp. 481–491.

64. S.E. Johansson and L. Ostman, *Accounting Theory—Integrating Behavior and Measurement* (London: Pitman, 1995), p. 201.

SELECTED REFERENCES

Adiel, R. "Reinsurance and the Management of Regulatory Ratios and Taxes in the Property-Casualty Insurance Industry." *Journal of Accounting and Economics* 22, 1–3 (1996), pp. 207–240.

Ayers, B.C. "Deferred Tax Accounting under SFAS No. 109: An Empirical Investigation of Its Incremental Value-Relevance Relative to APB No. 11." *The Accounting Review* 73, 2 (1998), pp. 195–212.

Beatty, A., S. Chamberlain, and J. Magliolo. "Managing Financial Reports of Commercial Banks: The Influence of Taxes, Regulatory Capital and Earnings." *Journal of Accounting Research* 33, 2 (1995), pp. 231–261.

Beaver, W., C. Eger, S. Ryan, and M. Wolfson. "Financial Reporting, Supplemental Disclosures and Bank Share Prices." *Journal of Accounting Research* (Autumn 1989), pp. 157–178.

Beneish, M.D. "Detecting GAAP Violation: Implications for Assessing Earnings Management among Firms with Extreme Financial Performance." *Journal of Accounting and Public Policy* 16 (1997), pp. 271–309.

———. "Discussion of: Are Accruals during Initial Public Offerings Opportunistic?" *Review of Accounting Studies* 3 (1998), pp. 209–221.

Burgstahler, D., and I. Dichev. "Earnings Management to Avoid Earnings Decreases and Losses." *Journal of Accounting and Economics* 24 (1997), pp. 99–126.

————. "Incentives to Manage Earnings to Avoid Earnings Decreases and Losses: Evidence from Quarterly Earnings." Working paper, University of Washington, 1998.

Burgstahler, D., and M. Eames. "Management of Earnings and Analysts' Forecasts." Working paper, University of Washington, 1998.

Bushee, B. "The Influence of Institutional Investors on Myopic R&D Investment Behavior." *The Accounting Review* 73, 3 (1998), pp. 305–333.

Cahan, S. "The Effect of Antitrust Investigations on Discretionary Accruals: A Refined Test of the Political Cost Hypothesis." *The Accounting Review* 67 (1992), pp. 77–95.

Collins, J., D. Shackelford, and J. Wahlen. "Bank Differences in the Coordination of Regulatory Capital, Earnings and Taxes." *Journal of Accounting Research* 33, 2 (1995), pp. 263–291.

DeAngelo, L.E. "Managerial Competition, Information Costs, and Corporate Governance: The Use of Accounting Performance Measures in Proxy Contests." *Journal of Accounting and Economics* 10 (1988), pp. 3–36.

DeAngelo, L.E., H. DeAngelo, and D. Skinner. "Accounting Choices of Troubled Companies." *Journal of Accounting and Economics* 17 (January 1994), pp. 113–143.

Dechow, P. "Accounting Earnings and Cash Flows as Measure of Firm Performance: The Role of Accounting Accruals." *Journal of Accounting and Economics* 18, 1 (1994), pp. 3–40.

Dechow, P., and R.G. Sloan. "Executive Incentives and the Horizon Problem: An Empirical Investigation." *Journal of Accounting and Economics* 14 (1991), pp. 51–89.

Dechow, P., R.G. Sloan, and A.P. Sweeney. "Causes and Consequences of Earnings Manipulation: An Analysis of Firms Subject to Enforcement Actions by the SEC." *Contemporary Accounting Research* 13, 1 (1996), pp. 1–36.

Defeo, V., R. Lamber, and D. Larcker. "The Executive Compensation Effects of Equity-for-Debt Swaps." *The Accounting Review* 54 (1989), pp. 201–227.

DeFond, M.L., and J. Jiambalvo. "Debt Covenant Effects and the Manipulation of Accruals." *Journal of Accounting and Economics* 17 (January), pp. 145–176.

Degeorge, F., J. Patel, and R. Zeckhauser. "Earnings Management to Exceed Thresholds." Working paper, Boston University, 1998.

Dye, R. "Earnings Management in an Overlapping Generations Model." *Journal of Accounting Research* 6 (1988), pp. 195–235.

Erickson, M., and S-W. Wang. "Earnings Management by Acquiring Firms in Stock for Stock Mergers." *Journal of Accounting and Economics* 27 (April 1999), pp. 149–176.

Foster, G. "Briloff and the Capital Market." *Journal of Accounting Research* 17 (Spring), pp. 262–274.

Gaver, J., K. Gaver, and J. Austin. "Additional Evidence on Bonus Plans and Income Management." *Journal of Accounting and Economics* 18 (1995), pp. 3–28.

Guay, W.A., S.P. Kothari, and R.L. Watts. "A Market-Based Evaluation of Discretionary Accrual Models." *Journal of Accounting Research* 34 (Supplement, 1996), pp. 83–105.

Healy, P.M., and E. Engel. "Discretionary Behavior with Respect to Allowances for Loan Losses and the Behavior of Security Prices." *Journal of Accounting and Economics* 22 (1996), pp. 177–206.

Healy, P.M., and M. McNichols. "The Characteristics and Valuation of Loss Reserves of Property-Casualty Insurers." Working paper, Stanford University, 1998.

Healy, P.M., and J.M. Wahlen, "A Review of the Earnings Management Literature and Its Implications for Standard Setting." *Accounting Horizons* 4 (1999), pp. 365–384.

Appendix 2A. Earnings Cycles and the Pricing of Securities

INTRODUCTION

Accounting research since the late 1960s has provided ample evidence of the significant effects of accounting earnings disclosures on firms' security prices (Bernard, 1987, 1989; Lev, 1989). Earnings appear to affect equity prices, even though the effect is in most cases small. However, given the constant criticism levied at earnings because of their historical cost emphasis or because they may be subject to earnings management, research has focused on the incremental value-relevance of cash flows and on the effects of managerial discretion (i.e., discretionary accruals) on the pricing of earnings (Bowen et al., 1987; Dechow, 1994; Riahi-Belkaoui, 2000). The interesting finding from this research is the evidence of the pricing of discretionary accruals, showing that even though opportunistic and value-irrelevant, the discretionary accruals are still priced by the market (Subramanyam, 1996). Whether it is the informativeness of earnings or the informativeness of its components (i.e., cash flows, discretionary accruals, and nondiscretionary accruals), most return-earnings regression studies have restricted themselves to a mere examination of the market pricing of a complete earnings cycle, that is to say, a chain of events with an impact of earnings power that lies in the past (AICPA, 1973; Cramer and Sorter, 1973). This is in conformity with objective No. 8 of the Trueblood Report, which states:

An objective [of financial statements] is to provide a statement of periodic earnings useful for predicting, comparing and evaluating enterprise earnings power. The net result of completed earnings cycles and enterprise activities resulting in recognizable progress toward completion of incomplete cycles should be reported. (AICPA, 1973)

For an earnings cycle to be defined as complete, three conditions should be fulfilled: (1) a realized sacrifice (an actual or high disbursement of cash); (2) a related realized benefit (an actual or probable receipt of cash); and (3) no further related substantive effort (AICPA, 1973, p. 9). In addition, the seventh objective distinguishes between a complete earnings cycle, an incomplete earnings cycle (a chain of events that has commenced but is not yet complete), and a prospective cycle (a chain of events that lies wholly in the future). For example, an earnings cycle is defined as incomplete when (1) a realized sacrifice or a benefit has occurred, but the related benefit or sacrifice has not been realized, (2) both sacrifice and benefit are not realized, or (3) the effort has not taken place (AICPA, 1973, p. 29).

It follows that the returns-earnings regression model, generally used in the accounting literature, suffers from a misspecification due to the absence of the effects of both incomplete and prospective earnings cycles.

Accordingly, this appendix empirically examined the pricing of the three components of earnings cycles: complete, incomplete, and prospective. Evidence on this issue could improve our understanding of the manner in which the capital markets process publicly available earnings and its components (cash flows, discretionary accruals, and nondiscretionary accruals) as a measure of the complete earnings cycle and other information that can act as surrogate measures of the incomplete and prospective earnings cycles. Evidence on this issue could also provide some insights into the economic incentives for discretionary accounting choice and disclosure of the results of incomplete and prospective earnings cycles.

The empirical analysis is conducted on a sample of 21,974 firm-years for 2,853 firms during 1978–1998. Discretionary accruals are obtained by decomposing total accruals into discretionary and nondiscretionary components using four models. The results of the complete earnings cycle are measured by cash flows, discretionary accruals, and nondiscretionary accruals. The results of the incomplete earnings cycle are measured by the ratio of gross margin over sales multiplied by inventory. The rationale is that, assuming the ratio of gross margin over sales to stay constant, multiplying it by inventory yields an approximate measure of the *unrealized holding gains and losses*. The results of the prospective earnings cycle are measured by the income growth for a year multiplied by income of the same year. The rationale is that a firm expects to achieve at least the same rate of income growth as in the preceding year. The results of the study show that the market attaches value to a complete earnings cycle and its components, as well as to the results of incomplete and prospective cycles.

RESEARCH DESIGN

The Model

The model relates stock returns to the results of the complete, incomplete, and prospective earnings cycle. It is estimated as follows:

$$ASR_{it} = \alpha_0 + \alpha_1 OCF_{it} + \alpha_2 NDACC_{it} + \alpha_3 DACC_{it} + URHGL_{it} + ING_{it}$$

where:

ASR_{it} = Annual stock returns for firm i and year t

OCF_{it} = Operating cash flows for firm i and year t

$NDACC_{it}$ = Nondiscretionary accruals for firm i and year t

$DACC_{it}$ = Discretionary accruals for firm i and year t

$URHGL_{it}$ = Results of the incomplete earnings cycle for firm i and year t

ING_{it} = Results of the prospective earnings cycle for firm i and year t

Annual stock returns (ASR) are measured as compounded monthly stock returns for a twelve-month period ending three months after the end of the fiscal year of the firm. Operating cash flows (OCF) are defined in Compustat No. 308.[1] All other variables are defined next.

Sample

Financial data to construct a sample of firms are obtained from the 1978 S&P Compustat, the Center for Research in Security Prices (CRSP). Both financial institutions (SIC 1999 to 7000) and observations with change in year-end are excluded. The nature of some tests required that the sample be restricted to those firms with a minimum of five consecutive years of data on all necessary variables. The available sample includes 22,532 firm-years. An elimination of observations on operating cash flows, nondiscretionary accruals, and discretionary accruals that are more than three standard deviations from their respective means resulted in a loss of 558 observations (2.47 percent of the sample). The final sample consists of 21,974 firm-years representing 2,853 firms during 1978–1998. The results with the outliers included are qualitatively unchanged.

Measurement of the Results of the Complete Earnings Cycle

The results of the complete earnings cycle are measured by net income. Following prior research in earnings management, net income (NI) can be decomposed as follows:

$$NI = OCF + DACC + NDACC \tag{1}$$

where

OCF = Operating cash flows

DACC = Discretionary accruals

NDACC = Nondiscretionary accruals

The estimation of discretionary accruals follows the approach based on using two alternative ways of estimating them—the modified Jones model (Dechow et al., 1995) and the Kang and Sivaramakrishnan model (1995)—and using two alternative measures of accruals—the traditional balance sheet approach and the cash-flow approach proposed by Collins and Hribar (1999). Total accruals, as based on the traditional balance sheet approach, are as follows:

$$TACC_{it} = (\Delta CA_{it} - \Delta CL_{it} - \Delta Cash + \Delta STDEBT_{it} - DEPTN_{it}) \tag{2}$$

where:

ΔCA_{it} = Change in current assets during period t (Compustat No. 4)

ΔCL_{it} = Change in current liabilities during period t (Compustat No. 5)

$\Delta Cash_{it}$ = Change in cash and cash equivalents during period t (Compustat No. 4)

$\Delta STDEBT_{it}$ = Change in the current maturities of long-term debt and other short-term debt included in current liabilities during period t (Compustat No. 34)

$DEPTN_{it}$ = Depreciation and amortization expense during period t (Compustat No. 14)

Based on the findings that studies relying on the traditional balance sheet approach to the measurement of total accruals suffer from potential contamination from measurement error in the total accruals, Collins and Hribar (1999) suggested a straightforward approach that computes total accruals as the difference between net income and operating cash flow (taken from the cash-flow statement).

Discretionary accruals are also computed using a variant of the Jones (1991) model. The model captures regularities over time for a given firm in the relations among total accruals, assets, and changes in revenues.

$$TACC_{it} = \alpha_1(1/TA_{i,t-1}) + \alpha_2 (\Delta REV_{it} - \Delta REC_{it})/TA + \alpha_3 PPE_{it}/TA_{i,t-1} + \varepsilon_{it} \tag{3}$$

where $TACC_{it}$ is total accruals calculated as in equation (2), A_{it-1} is total assets, $(\Delta REV_{it} - \Delta REC_{it})$ is the change in cash-basis revenue, PPE_{it} is gross property, plant, and equipment, and α_i is firm-specific parameters. Discretionary accruals from the modified Jones model are the residuals from the regression in equation (3). An alternative approach to the measurement of discretionary accruals is proposed by Kang and Sivaramakrishnan (1995). Their model estimates managed accruals using level, rather than change of current assets and current liabilities. It is expressed as follows:

$$ACCB_{it} = \Phi_0 + \Phi_1(\delta_1 REV_{it}) + \Phi_2(\delta_2 EXP_{it}) + \Phi_3(\delta_3 PPE_{it}) + \varepsilon_{it} \tag{4}$$

where:

$ACCB_{it}$ = The balance of noncash current assets (net of tax receivables) less current liabilities (net of tax payables) for firm i at the end of year t, divided by total assets for firm i at the end of year $t - 1$

EXP_{it} = The total pretax operating expense before depreciation and interest, for firm i at the end of year t, divided by total assets for firm i at the end of year $t-1$

The parameters δ_1, δ_2, and δ_3 are the previous year's turnover ratios, which lead to the measurement of (1) the current period's receivables as a product of the previous year's receivables-to-sales ratio (δ_1) and current period sales (REV_t) and (2) current period net current assets as the product of the previous year's net current asset-to-expense ratio (δ_2) times current period expenses (EXV_t).

Measurement of the Results of the Incomplete Earnings Cycle

The results of the incomplete earnings cycle stem from the decision not to liquidate ending inventory at the end of the period. If the decision were to liquidate/sell the ending inventory at the end of the period, the results of the incomplete earnings cycle would be equal to the unrealized holding gains and losses (Hanna, 1974; Chambers, 1975; Sterling, 1975). Therefore, the results of the incomplete earnings cycle represent the gains and losses that would accrue to the firm in the future when it sells its inventory (Drake and Dopuch, 1965; Barton 1974). Assuming the gross margin over sales stays constant, the results of the incomplete earnings cycle (or unrealized holding gains and losses) would be equal to gross margin over sales times the ending inventory. The variable will be denoted as $URHGL_{it}$ (to correspond to unrealized holding gains and losses).

Results of the Prospective Earnings Cycle

The prospective earnings cycle stems from the management decision to choose a rate of income growth. The most rational decision is to maintain or to increase the present rate of income growth. If the decision is to at least maintain the same rate of income growth, then the results of the prospective earnings cycle for a coming year $t+1$ is equal to the income of the year t times the growth of income from year $t-1$ to year t. This variable is referred to as ING.

Descriptive Statistics

Table 2A.1 represents descriptive statistics about the main variables used in the study. Over 80 percent of the firms included in the sample exhibit positive net income and operating cash flows, showing a slight bias toward profitable firms. Discretionary and nondiscretionary accruals are computed under four different models: (1) model 1 relies on the balance sheet approach for the computation of total accruals and the modified Jones model for the estimation of discretionary accruals; (2) model 2 relies on the balance sheet approach for the computation of total accruals and the Kang and Sivaramakrishnan model for the

Table 2A.1
Descriptive Statistics

Variable *	Mean	Std. Dev.	Median	Maximum	Minimum	% Positive
Returns (ASR)	0.175	0.518	0.097	23.11	-0.751	66
Net Income (NI)	0.064	0.091	0.051	0.753	-0.683	86
Operating Cash Flow (OCF)	0.081	0.110	0.091	0.816	-0.713	81
Discretionary Accruals 1 (DACC1)	-0.0041	0.115	-0.0011	0.864	-0.815	46
Nondiscretionary Accruals 1 (NDACC1)	-0.0220	0.0861	-0.0411	0.741	-0.682	31
Discretionary Accruals 2 (DACC2)	-0.0039	0.110	-0.0018	0.789	-0.613	45
Nondiscretionary Accruals 2 (NDACC2)	-0.0187	0.0713	-0.0391	-0.852	-0.652	33
Discretionary Accruals 3 (DACC3)	-0.0042	0.126	-0.0017	0.823	-0.728	45
Nondiscretionary Accruals 3 (NDACC3)	-0.0196	0.0812	-0.0362	0.723	-0.678	32
Discretionary Accruals 4 (DACC4)	-0.0036	0.132	-0.0018	0.759	-0.723	44
Nondiscretionary Accruals 4 (NDACC4)	-0.0175	0.0759	-0.0352	0.826	-0.625	33
Incomplete Earnings Cycle (UHGL)	0.032	0.081	0.026	0.323	-0.382	86
Prospective Earnings Cycle (ING)	0.078	0.095	0.057	0.826	-0.683	87

Notes: The original sample consists of 22,532 firm-years during the period 1978–1998 for which a minimum of five consecutive years of data is available. Observations that are more than three standard deviations from the mean for operating cash flows, nondiscretionary accruals, and discretionary accruals are excluded. This results in a loss of 558 observations, reducing the final sample to 21,924 firm-years.

*All variables are scaled by lagged total assets.

estimation of discretionary accruals; (3) model 3 relies on the cash-flow approach to the determination of total accruals and the cross-sectional modified Jones model for the estimation of discretionary accruals; and (4) model 4 relies on the cash-flow approach to the determinants of total accruals and the Kang and Sivaramakrishnan model for the estimation of discretionary accruals. Under the four models, both the nondiscretionary accruals and discretionary accruals have negative means and medians and are positive for fewer than 46 percent of the firms for discretionary accruals and for fewer than 33 percent of the firms for nondiscretionary accruals. The results of the incomplete earnings cycle and the prospective cycles show again that over 80 percent of the firms were expecting positive unrealized holding gains and losses and future income. This occurs by construction, given the positive bias toward profitability in the sample.

EARNINGS CYCLES AND STOCK RETURNS

To assess the pricing of the results of earnings cycles, returns are regressed on the level of earnings components as measures of the results of complete earnings cycles and on measures of incomplete and prospective earnings cycles. The level of earnings as the result of complete earnings is decomposed into its three component parts: operating cash flows, nondiscretionary accruals, and discretionary accruals.[2]

Table 2A.2 presents the results of the regression of returns on measures of complete, incomplete, and prospective earnings cycles. Four models are used for the computation of discretionary accruals, as explained in the preceding sections. The coefficients on OCF, NDACC, DACC, UGHL, and ING are significant at the 0.01 level. The incremental content of the incomplete and prospective earnings cycles are on the order of an incremental R^2 higher than 1.40 percent.

The results indicate that each of the components of the earnings cycle has a significant weight in each of the four models. However, the weights attached to the components of the incomplete and prospective earnings cycle are lower than the weights attached to the components of the complete earnings cycle. These results may be due to the surrogate measures used for measuring the results of incomplete and prospective earnings cycles. In summary, these results reveal (1) that discretionary accruals have information content and (2) that both results of incomplete and prospective earnings cycles have incremental information content and improve earnings' ability to explain market returns. This evidence is consistent with the market's attaching value to the results of incomplete and prospective earnings cycles, even though they are not explicitly included in accounting reports.

Table 2A.2
Regression of Returns Earnings Components and Results of Incomplete and Prospective Cycles Using Alternative Accruals Expectations Models

Description	Intercept	OCF	NDACC	DACC	UHGL	ING	Adj. R²%	Incr. R²%
1. Model 1	0.125	1.32	1.02	1.01	0.78	1.12	8.69	1.42%
	(20.325)	(26.15)	(15.13)	(15.23)	(7.32)	(6.32)		(6.78)
2. Model 2	0.135	1.31	1.01	0.98	0.62	1.11	8.52	1.41%
	(20.355)	(28.13)	(15.21)	(15.61)	(7.51)	(6.51)		(6.32)
3. Model 3	0.121	1.33	1.03	0.96	0.63	1.32	8.31	1.43%
	(20.526)	(26.15)	(15.72)	(15.22)	(7.52)	(6.13)		(6.51)
4. Model 4	0.12	1.31	1.07	0.97	0.61	1.15	8.21	1.44%
	(20.612)	(26.14)	(15.33)	(15.33)	(7.37)	(6.15)		(6.72)

Notes: The original sample consists of 22,532 firm-years during the period 1978–1998 for which a minimum of five consecutive years of data is available. Observations that are more than three standard deviations from the mean for operating cash flows, nondiscretionary accruals, and discretionary accruals are excluded. This results in a loss of 558 observations, reducing the final sample to n = 21,974 firm-years.

The dependent variable in all models is cumulative stock returns over a twelve-month period ending three months after the fiscal year-end. The independent variables are operating cash flows (OCF), nondiscretionary accruals (NCDACC), discretionary accruals (DACC), and results of the incomplete earnings cycle (UHGL) and the prospective earnings cycle (ING). All variables are scaled by lagged total assets. The four models differ in the estimation of discretionary accruals. Model 1 relies on the balance sheet approach for the computation of total accruals and the modified Jones model for the estimation of discretionary accruals. Model 2 relies on the balance sheet approach and the Kang and Sivaramakrishnan model. Model 3 relies on the cash-flow approach to the determination of total accruals and the modified Jones model for the estimation of discretionary accruals. Model 4 relies on the cash-flow approach and the Kang and Sivaramakrishnan model.

Figures in parentheses denote t statistics (except for incremental R-square) based on the heteroskedasticity-consistent covariance matrix (White, 1980) using a two-tailed test. Incremental R-square refers to the increase in explanatory power with the inclusion of the results of both incomplete and prospective earnings cycles. A t-statistic of 2.59 implies a significance level of 0.01 using a two-tailed test.

SUMMARY AND CONCLUSION

This appendix shows that in addition to the results of complete earnings cycles, the results of both incomplete and prospective earnings cycles are priced by the stock market. This result is consistent with the pricing of relevant information by an efficient market. There is evidence of information content of incomplete and prospective earnings cycles that improves the relevance of earnings. The results show also that although discretionary accruals are priced by an inefficient market, the information content of both incomplete and prospective earnings cycles points to the efficiency of the market looking beyond the pricing of opportunistic earnings manipulation in the pricing of future earnings.

NOTES

1. For firms that had not adopted the cash flow format, operating cash flow (OCF) is determined as follows: OCF = fund (#110) − Δ current assets (#4) + Δ current liabilities (#5) + Δ cash (#1) − Δ current portion of long-term debt (#34) if available.

2. The use of earnings levels rather than earnings changes is supported theoretically and empirically (Easton and Harris, 1991; Kothari, 1992; Ohlson and Shroff, 1992).

REFERENCES

American Institute of Certified Public Accountants. 1973. *Objectives of Financial Statements*. New York: AICPA.

Barton, A.D. 1974. Expectations and achievements in income theory. *The Accounting Review* (October): 664–681.

Bernard, V. 1987. Cross-sectional dependence and problems in inference in market-based accounting research. *Journal of Accounting Research* (Spring): 1–48.

Bowen, R.D., D. Burgstahler, and L. Daley. 1987. The incremental information content of accrual versus cash flows. *The Accounting Review* (October): 723–747.

Chambers, R.J. 1975. NOD, COG, and PUPU: See how inflation teases. *Journal of Accounting* (February): 56–62.

Cheng, C.S., C. Liu, and T. Schaefer. 1996. Earnings permanence and the incremental information content of cash flows from operations. *Journal of Accounting Research* (Spring): 173–181.

Collins, D., and P. Hribar. 1999. Errors in estimating accruals: Implications for empirical research. Working paper, University of Iowa.

Cramer, J.J., Jr., and G.H. Sorter. 1973. *Objectives of Financial Statements: Selected Papers*, Vol. 2. New York: AICPA, 1973.

Dechow, P. 1994. Accounting earnings and cash flow as measures of firm performance: The role of accounting accruals. *Journal of Accounting and Economics* 17: 3–42.

Dechow, P., R. Sloan, and A. Sweeney. 1995. Detecting earnings management. *The Accounting Review* 70: 193–226.

Drake, D.F., and N. Dopuch. 1965. On the case of dichotomizing income. *Journal of Accounting Research* (Fall): 192–205.

Easton, P.D., and T.S. Harris. 1991. Earnings as an explanatory variable for returns. *Journal of Accounting Research* 29: 19–36.

Hanna, J.R. 1974. *Accounting Income Models: An Application and Evaluation.* Special Study No. 8. Toronto: Society of Management Accountants.

Jones, J. 1991. Earnings management during import relief investigations. *Journal of Accounting Research* (Fall): 193–228.

Kang, S., and K. Sivaramakrishnan. 1995. Issues in testing earnings management and an instrumental variable approach. *Journal of Accounting Research* 33: 353–367.

Kothari, S.P. 1992. Price earnings regressions in the presence of prices leading earnings: Implications for earnings coefficients. *Journal of Accounting and Economics* 15: 173–202.

Lev, B. 1989. On the usefulness of earnings and earnings research: Lessons and directions from two decades of empirical research. *Journal of Accounting Research* (suppl.): 153–192.

Ohlson, J., and P. Shroff. 1992. Changes versus levels in earnings as explanatory variables for returns: Some theoretical considerations. *Journal of Accounting and Research* 30: 210–226.

Riahi-Belkaoui, A. 2000. The value relevance of earnings, cash flows, multinationality, and corporate reputation as assessed by security markets. *Advances in Quantitative Analysis of Finance and Accounting* 8: 45–59.

Sterling, R.R. 1975. Relevant financial reporting in an age of price changes. *Journal of Accounting* (August): 42–51.

Subramanyam, K.R. 1996. The pricing of discretionary accruals. *Journal of Accounting Research* 22: 249–281.

White, H. 1980. A heteroskedasticity-consistent covariance matrix estimator and a direct test for heteroskedasticity. *Econometrica* 48: 817–838.

Appendix 2B. The Impact of Multinationality on the Informativeness of Earnings and Accounting Choices

INTRODUCTION

This appendix reports the results of an investigation in how the degree of multinationality affects the informativeness of accounting and the accounting choices of managers. Three theories of multinationality link multinationality to investment value, predicting either a higher or lower value (Morck and Yeung, 1991, 1992; Mishra and Gobelli, 1998). They are the internalization theory, the imperfect world capital markets theory, and the managerial objectives theory.

The internalization theory maintains that direct foreign investment occurs when a firm can increase its value by internationalizing markets for certain of its intangibles (Rugman, 1980, 1981).

The imperfect world capital markets theory maintains that because of the imperfect world markets, multinational firms offer shareholders international di-

Source: A. Riahi-Belkaoui and R.D. Picur, "The Impact of Multinationality on the Informativeness of Earnings and Accounting Choices," *Managerial Finance* 27, 2 (2001), pp. 82–94. Reprinted with the permission of the editor.

versification opportunities, which as a result enhance their share prices (Agmon and Lessard, 1977).

Finally, the managerial objectives theory predicts that the existence of divergence of objectives between managers and shareholders, with top management favoring international diversification, may reduce the value of multinationals relative to uninationals.

The three theories are silent on the role of earnings in the relationship between multinationality and investment value. Earnings are known to be informative in explaining stock returns. Therefore, the first hypothesis predicts the informativeness of earnings in explaining stock returns and varies systematically with the level of multinationality in the corporation.

The second hypothesis derives from the managerial objectives theory and postulates that managers' accounting choices are systematically related to the level of multinationality. The managerial objectives theory recognizes divergence of objectives between management and shareholders of multinational firms regarding the merits of international diversification. Accordingly, contracts must be written, often containing accounting-based constraints, to restrict managers' value-changing behavior when multinationality is high. These same accounting-based constraints may lead managers to exploit the latitude available in accepted accounting procedures to alleviate the same constraints. Therefore, for multinational firms the magnitude of discretionary accounting accrual adjustment is positively related to the level of multinationality.

The results of this study, using U.S multinational firms, shows (1) that the level of multinationality is positively associated with the informativeness of accounting earnings and (2) that the magnitude of discretionary accounting accrual adjustments is significantly higher when the level of multinationality is high. These results are robust in the presence of endogenous and exogenous determinants of accounting choices and earnings' explanatory power for returns, including firm size, systematic risk, growth opportunities, and the variability and persistence of accounting earnings.

MULTINATIONALITY, CONTRACTS, AND ACCOUNTING

The Impact of Multinationality on the Informativeness of Earnings

Both the internalization theory and the imperfect capital markets theory predict a positive association between multinationality and firm value.

The internalization theory maintains that foreign direct investment will cause the increase of the market value of the firm relative to its accounting value only if the firm can internalize markets for certain of its intangibles.[1] Examples of these firm-specific intangible assets include production skills, managerial skills, patent, marketing abilities, consumer goodwill, research and development, advertising spending, managerial incentives alignment, and corporate reputation, to name a few (Morck and Yeung, 1991; Mishra and Gobelli, 1998). These information-based proprietary intangible assets cannot be copied or exchanged at arm's length but can only be transferred to subsidiaries, thereby internationalizing the markets for such assets. As a result the market value of a multinational firm possessing these intangibles and engaging in foreign direct investment is directly proportional to the firm's degree of multinationality.

The imperfect capital markets theory suggests that investors, with institutional constraints on international capital flows and the information asymmetries that exist in global capital markets, invest in multinational firms to gain from the international diversification opportunities provided by these multinational firms.[2] This direct valuation of multinational firms by investors as a means of diversifying their portfolios internationally is assumed to enhance the share prices of multinational firms, independently of the information-based proprietary intangible assets possessed by these firms.

Accounting research has, however, consistently showed earning's explanatory power for returns, without explicitly examining the contingent role of multinationality. What has appeared in the international business literature with regard to the association between firm value and multinationality may be an association between earnings and firm value that is more pronounced with increased multinationality (Bodnar and Weintrop, 1997). This argumentation leads to the first testable hypothesis: *The informativeness of accounting earnings as an explanatory variable for returns is systematically related to the level of multinationality.*

The Impact of Multinationality on the Behavior of Discretionary Accounting Accruals

The managerial objectives theory rests on the assumption of the differences of motives between management and shareholders. The complexity of the multinational firm and the resulting difficulty for shareholders in monitoring management's decisions allow management to act in their self-interest. They may favor international diversification because it reduces firm-specific risk. The situation is assumed to potentially reduce the market value of multinational firms (Morck and Yeung, 1991). It can be predicted that when multinationality is high, incentives arise for managers to pursue non-value-maximization behavior. The situation calls for the writing of contracts, often containing accounting-based constraints, to monitor managers' decisions. Most likely, managers will exploit the latitude offered in available accepted accounting techniques to manage these constraints in their own interest. Their accounting choices, as reflected by the behavior of the discretionary portion of total accruals, are a positive function of the level of multinationality. These arguments lead to the second hypothesis: *The magnitude of adjustments in managers' accounting choices is systematically related to the level of multinationality.*

Other Considerations Affecting Accounting Choices

Based on contracting theory and economic theories of the political process that governs managers' incentives in the selection and reporting of accounting numbers, other endogenous and exogenous determinants of accounting choices and earnings' explanatory power for returns are also examined. They include six additional factors: firm size, systematic risk, leverage, growth opportunities, earnings variability, and earnings persistence (Warfield et al., 1995).

SAMPLE SELECTION AND DATA

Multinationality was measured as foreign sales over total sales for the most international 100 American manufacturing and service firms. *Forbes* publishes every year a list of the most international 100 American manufacturing and service firms. To be included in the sample, a firm must meet the following selection criteria:

1. The firm must be included in *Forbes'* most international 100 American manufacturing and service firms from 1994 to 1998.
2. Annual earnings-per-share and dividends are available from Standard and Poor's Compustat primary, secondary, tertiary and full coverage database.
3. Data necessary to compute stock returns (including dividends) are available from Standard and Poor's Computstat price, dividends and earnings database. Both price per share and earnings per share were adjusted for stock splits and stock dividends.
4. Annual data necessary to compute discretionary accruals are available from Standard and Poor's Compustat primary, secondary, tertiary and full coverage database.

The complete sample consists of 404 firm-year observations for the first hypothesis and 368 firm-year observations for the second hypothesis.

Descriptive statistics and correlation analysis of the data used in both hypotheses are shown in Tables 2B.1 and 2B.2.

INFORMATIVENESS OF EARNINGS CONDITIONAL ON MULTINATIONALITY

Multinationality as a Determinant of Earnings' Explanatory Power

Table 2B.3 presents the correlation between earnings and returns (column 3) and the earnings coefficients (column 4) for the different ranges of multinationality measured as foreign sales over total sales. The correlation between returns and earnings is positive and significantly greater than zero for the total sample with a level of multinationality ranging from 0 to 75 percent and for each of the other multinationality ranges. These correlations range from a minimum of

0.42 for the 0–25 percent level of multinationality to a high of 0.65 for the 50–75 percent level of multinationality. In addition, the Pearson (Spearman) correlation between the level of multinationality (column 1) and the correlation between earnings and returns (column 3) for the three multinationality levels equals 0.67 (0.75), which is significantly greater than zero at the 0.05 level. The evidence from this first test points to multinationality as a determinant of the informativeness of earnings.

The second test of the informativeness of earnings conditional on multinationality levels examines the cross-sectional variation of the earnings coefficient conditional on multinationality. The following pooled cross-sectional regression model, with a multinationality interaction term, is used:

$$(R_{i,t}) = \alpha_0 + \alpha_1 \cdot E_{i,t}/P_{i,t-1} + \alpha_2 \cdot E_{i,t} \cdot MULTY_i/P_{i,t-1} + \varepsilon_{i,t}$$

where $(R_{i,t})$ is the return of firm i for annual period t, extending from nine months prior to fiscal year-end through three months after fiscal year-end, $E_{i,t}$ is earnings-per-share, $P_{i,t-1}$ is the price-per-share at the end of period $t-1$, and $MULTY_i$ is the level of multinationality as measured by foreign sales over total sales for the year. The joint relation between earnings and multinationality is measured by α_2, showing the extent to which the informativeness of earnings is affected by the level of multinationality. The regression results in Table 2B.4 indicate that the informativeness is affected by the level of multinationality as both the regression coefficient (0.575) and the earnings-multinationality coefficient (0.865) are both significantly greater than zero at the 0.0001 level.

Given that the results in Table 2B.3 imply nonlinearity with the data, the same regression was run separately for each of the three categories of multinationality levels in the table, thereby not imposing a constant residual assumption across multinationality categories. The earnings coefficients from these regressions, reported in column 4 of Table 2B.3, imply a monotonic increase in the regression coefficients. The increase of these coefficients from 0.57 for the 0–25 range of multinationality to 0.71 for the 50–75 range of multinationality verifies the results of hypothesis 1 in Table 2B.4.

Multinationality and Other Determinants of Earnings' Explanatory Power

As stated previously, additional considerations are recognized regarding both the informativeness of earnings and managerial incentives determining accounting choices. These considerations, in addition to multinationality, include firm size, systematic risk, leverage, growth opportunities, earnings variability, and earnings persistence. Accordingly, the following pooled cross-sectional regression model is formulated:

Table 2B.1
Summary for the Variables in Section 4

Panel A: Descriptive Statistics

Variable	Mean	Standard deviation	Median	First quartile	Third quartile
Stock return ($R_{i,t}$)	0.0952	0.0552	0.0897	0.0602	0.1286
Accounting earning ($E_{i,t} / P_{i,t-1}$)	0.0570	0.0854	0.0649	0.0369	0.0847
Earnings interacted with:					
a. Multinationality ($E_{i,t} . MULTY_i / P_{i,t-1}$)	0.0193	0.0514	0.0189	0.0081	0.0332
b. Size ($E_{i,t} . SIZE_i / P_{i,t-1}$)	0.5309	0.6125	0.5689	0.3171	0.7832
c. Growth opportunities ($E_{i,t} . GROWTH_i / P_{i,t-1}$)	0.0881	0.2349	0.0508	0.0331	0.0774
d. Systematic risk ($E_{i,t} . RISK_i / P_{i,t-1}$)	0.0072	0.0134	0.0028	0.0008	0.0083
e. Leverage ($E_{i,t} . DEBT_i / P_{i,t-1}$)	0.0087	0.0119	0.0072	0.0023	0.0139
f. Earnings variability ($E_{i,t} . VAR_i / P_{i,t-1}$)	0.1269	0.099	0.1028	0.0601	0.1653
g. Earnings persistence ($E_{i,t} . PERS_i / P_{i,t-1}$)	-0.0082	0.1686	-0.0010	-0.0018	0.0005

Panel B: Pearson correlation matrix (using variables from Panel A)

Variable	E	MULTY	SIZE	GROWTH	RISK	DEBT	VAR	PERS
Accounting earnings (E)	1.00	0.281	0.2633	0.2320	0.2030	0.3496	0.3328	-0.3856
Multinationality (MULTY)		1.00	0.3588	0.3727	0.1652	0.2814	0.3685	-0.4813
Size (SIZE)			1.00	0.3670	0.3489	0.2051	0.2586	-0.4788
Growth opportunities (GROWTH)				1.00	0.0690	0.0067	0.3351	0.0103
Systematic risk (RISK)					1.00	0.1172	0.3417	0.0158
Leverage (DEBT)						1.00	0.1557	-0.0596
Earnings variability (VAR)							1.00	-0.2069
Earnings persistence (PERS)								1.00

Notes: Stock returns (R) are measured for the twelve-month period from nine months prior to the fiscal year-end through three months after the fiscal year-end, earnings (E) is the accounting earnings per share, multinationality (MULTY) is measured as foreign sales/total sales, size (SIZE) is measured as the company's market value of equity (in 000s), systematic risk (RISK) is measured by the market model beta, growth opportunities (GROWTH) are measured by the market-to-book ratio for common equity, leverage (DEBT) is measured by the ratio of total debt to total assets, earnings variability (VAR) is measured by the standard deviation of earnings for the twenty quarters 1994–1998, earnings persistence (PERS) is the first-order autocorrelation in earnings for the twenty quarters 1994–1998, and price (P) is the stock price at the beginning of the period. The sample size is 404 firm-year observations.

Table 2B.2
Summary Statistics for the Variation in Section 5

Panel A: Descriptive Statistics

Variable	Mean	Standard deviation	Median	First quartile	Third quartile
Absolute Abnormal Accrual (/AAC/)	0.0190	0.0110	0.0179	0.0120	0.0092
Multinationality (MULTY)	0.3492	0.142	0.3345	0.2360	0.4520
Size (SIZE)	8.782	0.9284	8.6983	8.1616	9.4140
Systematic risk (RISK)	0.090	0.131	0.044	0.016	0.124
Leverage (DEBT)	0.1583	0.1428	0.1384	0.0541	0.2277
Growth opportunities (GROWTH)	35.893	52.129	2.460	1.5881	4.2165
Earnings variability (VAR)	0.1673	0.0789	0.1374	0.1164	0.1930
Earnings persistence (PERS)	-0.1618	0.1316	-0.015	-0.023	-0.0097

106

Panel B: Pearson correlation matrix

Variable	MULTY	SIZE	RISK	DEBT	GROWTH	VAR	PERS
Multinationality (MULTY)	1.00	0.0136	0.1642	-0.1576	0.0544	0.2448	0.0326
Size (SIZE)		1.00	0.1083	-0.1312	-0.0613	0.3006	0.1590
Systematic risk (RISK)			1.00	-0.1341	-0.0704	0.1606	0.0818
Leverage (DEBT)				1.00	-0.2428	-0.2193	0.1183
Growth opportunities (GROWTH)					1.00	-0.1521	-0.0651
Earnings variability (VAR)						1.00	0.0808
Earnings persistence (PERS)							1.00

Notes: Abnormal accrual (AAC) is defined as the current-period accrual less the expected normal accrual, where the difference is standardized by the beginning period stock price. Absolute abnormal accrual (/AAC/) is measured as the absolute value of AAC. All other variables are as defined in Table 2B.1.

Table 2B.3
Relation between Earnings and Returns Depending on the Level of Multinationality

Level of Multinationality	Number of Firm-Period Observations	Correlation between Earnings and Returns	Earnings Coefficient
0–75	404	0.07	0.06
0–25	108	0.42	0.57
25–50	232	0.53	0.58
50–75	64	0.65	0.71

Notes: Stock returns are measured for the twelve-month period extending from nine months prior to the fiscal year-end through three months after the fiscal year-end, earnings per share is scaled by the beginning-of-period stock price per share, and multinationality is equal to foreign sales/total sales. The sample of annual earnings reports is drawn from the 5-year period corresponding to the 1994–1998 calendar years. All correlations (Pearson) between annual accounting earnings per share and stock returns, the earnings coefficients from the regression of stock returns, and the earnings coefficients from the regression of stock returns on accounting earnings per share are significant at the 0.01 level or better.

Table 2B.4
Regression in Stock Return on Both Earnings and Earnings-Multinationality Interaction

$(R_{i,t}) = \alpha_0 + \alpha_1 \cdot E_{i,t}/P_{i,t-1} + \alpha_2 E_{i,t} \, MULTY_i/P_{i,t-1} + \varepsilon_{i,t}$

Parameter estimates

α_0	α_1	α_2	Sample Size	Adjusted R^2%	F-value (sig. level)
0.077	0.575	0.865	404	7.47	17.30
(18.57)*	(5.882)*	(5.57)*			(0.001)

Notes: Stock returns (R) are measured for the twelve-month period extending from nine months prior to the fiscal year-end through three months after the fiscal year-end. Earnings (E) are the accounting earnings per share, multinationality (MULTY) is equal to foreign sales/total sales, and price (P) is the stock price per share. Parameter estimates and t-statistics (in parentheses) are presented for the regression. A * designates statistical significance at the 0.01 level. The sample comprises firm-year observations from the 1994–1998 calendar years.

$$R_{i,t} = \alpha_0 + \alpha_1 \cdot E_{i,t}/P_{i,t-1} + \alpha_2 E_{i,t} \, MULTY_i/P_{i,t-1} \tag{2}$$
$$+ \alpha_3 E_{i,t} \, SIZE_i/P_{i,t-1} + \alpha_4 E_{i,t} \, GROWTH_i/P_{i,t-1}$$
$$+ \alpha_5 E_{i,t} \, RISK_i/P_{i,t-1} + \alpha_6 E_{i,t} \, DEBT_i/P_{i,t-1}$$
$$+ \alpha_7 E_{i,t} \, VAR_i/P_{i,t-1} + \alpha_8 E_{i,t} \, PERS + \varepsilon_{i,t}$$

The new variables are defined as follows: SIZE is the natural logarithm of a firm's market value of equity, RISK is a firm's systematic risk,[3] DEBT is the firm's ratio of total debt to total assets, GROWTH is measured as the market value of equity scaled by book value, VAR is the variability of earnings for all of the quarters of the period of analysis, PERS is persistence of earnings as measured by the first-order autocorrelation in earnings for the same period.

The results, shown in Table 2B.5, verify again the relation between multinationality and earnings' informativeness after the inclusion of these additional considerations. As expected, the market reaction to earnings was negatively related to systematic risk (α_5 [−0.532], significant at the 0.01 level), and to variability of earnings (α_7 [−0.338], significant at the 0.01 level). It is also positively related to firm size (α_3 [0.08], significant at the 0.01 level), growth opportunities (α_4 [0.351], significant at the 0.01 level), leverage (α_6 [0.199], significant at the 0.01 level), and earnings persistence (α_8 [0.057], significant at the 0.01 level).[4]

EARNINGS MANAGEMENT CONDITIONAL ON MULTINATIONALITY

The second hypothesis states that the magnitude of adjustments in managers' accounting choices is systematically related to multinationality. The higher the level of multinationality, the higher is managers' reliance on discretionary accruals, as measured by the magnitude of discretionary accrual adjustments.

An abnormal accruals research design is used to test the hypothesis of managers' accounting choices conditional on multinationality.[5] Basically, the abnormal accounting accrual (AAC) is computed as the current period accrual (AC) minus the expected normal accrual (E[AC]), and then standardized by beginning-of-year stock price (P):

$$AAC_{i,t} = [AC_{i,t} - E(AC)_{i,t}]/P_{i,t-1} \tag{3}$$

The accounting accrual (AC) is defined as the change in noncash working capital (i.e., change in noncash current assets less current liabilities) less depreciation expense.[6]

An accruals prediction model, suggested by Jones (1991), is used to estimate normal accruals. It is specified as:

$$AC_{i,t} = \beta_0/P_{i,t-1} + \beta_1 \cdot \Delta REV_{i,t}/P_{i,t-1} + \beta_2 \cdot PPE_{i,t}/ + \varepsilon_{it} \tag{4}$$

Table 2B.5
Regression of Returns on Earnings, Earnings-Multinationality Interaction, and Earnings Interaction with Other Determinants of Earnings Explanatory Power

$$(R_{i,t}) = \alpha_0 + \alpha_1 \cdot E_{i,t}/P_{i,t-1} + \alpha_2 E_{i,t} \cdot MULTY_i/P_{i,t-1} + \alpha_3 E_{i,t} \cdot SIZE_i/P_{i,t-1} + \alpha_4 E_{i,t} \cdot GROWTH_i/P_{i,t-1} + \alpha_5 E_{i,t} \cdot RISK_i/P_{i,t-1} + \alpha_6 E_{i,t} \cdot DEBT_i/P_{i,t-1} + \alpha_7 E_{i,t} \cdot VAR_i/P_{i,t-1} + \alpha_8 E_{i,t} \cdot PERS + \varepsilon_{i,t} \quad (2)$$

Parameter estimates

α_0	α_1	α_2	α_3	α_4	α_5	α_6	α_7	α_8	Sample Size	Adjusted R^2%	F
0.024	0.139	0.019	0.08	0.351	−0.532	0.199	−0.338	0.057	3.91	23.52	248.70*
(9.84)*	(5.09)*	(5.18)*	(2.73)*	(15.77)*	(−3.39)*	(3.48)*	(17.07)*	(4.20)*			

Notes: Stock returns (R) are measured for the twelve-month period from nine months prior to the fiscal year-end through three months after the fiscal year-end, earnings (E) is the accounting earnings per share, multinationality (MULTY) is the foreign sales/total sales, size (SIZE) is measured as the company's natural logarithm of the market value of equity, systematic risk (RISK) is measured by the market model beta, growth opportunities (GROWTH) are measured by the market-to-book ratio for common equity, leverage (DEBT) is measured by the ratio total debt to total assets, earnings variability (VAR) is measured by the standard deviation of earnings, earnings persistence (PERS) is the first-order autocorrelation in earnings, and price (P) is the stock price at the beginning of the period. The sample size comprises firm-year observations drawn from the 1994–1998 calendar years.

where the new variables are defined as follows:

$\Delta REV_{i,t}$ = changes in revenues from year t to $t-1$ for firm i
$PPE_{i,t}$ = gross property, plant, and equipment in year t

A time-series regression using available prior year data for seven years generated firm-specific and time-period-specific predictions of $E(AC_{i,t})$, which are then used in equation (3) to generate an estimate of abnormal accruals ($AAC_{i,t}$).

Because the interest in this study is with the magnitude of the accrual adjustments, rather than the direction of the accrual, the absolute value of the abnormal accrual (i.e., $/AAC_{i,t}/$) is used as a department variable in the following model:[7]

$$/AAC_{i,t}/ = \delta_0 + \delta_1 \cdot MULTY_i + \delta_2 \cdot SIZE_i + \delta_3 \cdot GROWTH_i \quad (5)$$
$$+ \delta_4 \cdot RISK_i + \delta_5 \cdot DEBT_i + \delta_6 \cdot VAR_i + \delta_7 \cdot PERS_i + \varepsilon_{it}$$

Equation (5) is a multivariate-pooled cross-sectional regression model to be used to investigate the joint interaction of multinationality and the level of abnormal accounting accruals.

The model includes, in addition to the multinationality variable, other factors that have been shown in previous research to affect the magnitude of abnormal accruals (Warfield et al., 1997). These factors include size of the firm, growth, systematic risk, leverage, earnings variability, and earnings persistence. Consistent with the second hypothesis, a positive relation between the level of multinationality and the magnitude of abnormal accruals is predicted (i.e., $\delta_1 > 0$). The evidence in Table 2B.6 supports the hypothesis that the magnitude of abnormal accruals is positively related to the level of multinationality (i.e., δ_1 equals 0.00002, which is significantly greater than zero at the 0.01 level).[8]

SUMMARY AND CONCLUSIONS

This appendix presented two hypotheses linking the level of multinationality to both the informativeness of earnings and the magnitude of discretionary accounting accrual adjustments. The hypotheses draw on multinationality theories and exploits (1) the internalization and the international diversification opportunities provided by multinational firms and (2) managers' incentives in using discretionary accounting accrual adjustments. Based on both the internalization theory and the imperfect world capital markets theory, the first hypothesis postulates that the informativeness of earnings in explaining stock returns varies systematically with the level of multinationality in the corporation. Based on the managerial objectives theory, the second hypothesis postulates that the managers' accounting choices are systematically related to the level of multinationality. The results on a sample of U.S. multinational firms show a significantly greater

Table 2B.6
Regression of Absolute Abnormal Accruals on Multinationality and Other Determinants of the Magnitude of Discretionary Accruals

$$|AAC_{i,t}| = \delta_0 + \delta_1 \cdot MULTY_i + \delta_2 \cdot SIZE_i + \delta_3 \cdot GROWTH_i + \delta_4 \cdot RISK_i + \delta_5 \cdot DEBT_i + \delta_6 \cdot VAR_i + \delta_7 PERS_i + \varepsilon_{it}$$

Parameter estimates

δ_0	δ_1	δ_2	δ_3	δ_4	δ_5	δ_6	δ_7
-0.077	0.00002	0.0003	0.01	0.00001	0.08	0.008	-0.00001
(-1.13)	(8.52)*	(7.48)*	(7.39)*	(4.52)*	(5.62)*	(17.68)*	(0.51)*

Sample size	Adjusted	F-Value
368	28.55%	75.26*

Notes: Absolute abnormal accruals (/AAC$_{i,t}$/) is defined as the current-period accrual loss of the expected normal accruals, where the difference is standardized by the beginning-period stock price. All other variables are as defined in Table 2B.3. The sample comprises firm-year observations drawn from the 1994–1998 calendar years.

A * designates statistical significance at the 0.01 level, two-tailed tests.

earnings coefficient for firms with higher multinationality and a positive relation between the magnitude of discretionary accruals and the level of multinationality.

NOTES

1. The internalization theory is developed in Coase (1937), Caves (1974), Hymer (1976), Dunning (1980, 1988), Rugman (1980, 1981), Casson (1987), Buckley (1988), Morck and Yeung (1991, 1992), Mishra and Gobelli (1998).

2. See Agmon and Lessard (1977), Brewer (1981), Errunza and Senbet (1981), Adler and Dumas (1983), Fatemi (1984), Doukas and Travlos (1988), and others.

3. Systematic risk is measured by the market model beta using the most recent sixty months' stock returns prior to the test period.

4. To measure the degree of collinearity among the regression variables, condition indexes are calculated. The condition index shows that the regression was 23.6, considered by Belsley et al. (1980) as indicative of moderate to strong multicollinearity. Similarly, to assess the effect of cross-correlation in the residuals for the estimation of parameters, bootstrapping analysis was conducted. The results showed bootstrapping estimates qualitatively identical to the estimates reported in Table 2B.5.

5. The abnormal accruals research design was pioneered by Healey (1985), DeAngelo (1986, 1988), Liberty and Zimmerman (1986), and others.

6. Specifically, the accounting per share is calculated as follows (Compustat data item numbers are in parentheses):

$$AC_{i,t} = [\cap \text{ Accounts receivable}_{i,t} (2) + \cap \text{ Inventories}_{i,t} (3)$$
$$+ \cap \text{ Other Current Assets}_{i,t} (68)] - [\cap \text{ Current Liabilities}_{i,t} (5)]$$
$$- [\text{Depreciation and Amortization Expense}_{i,t}(14)]$$

where the change ($\cap$) is the difference between years (t and t$-$1). The Compustat data item numbers for stock price, $P_{i,t-1}$ is (24).

7. A similar methodology is used by Warfield et al. (1995).

8. Similar results were obtained when the Jones model (1991) was replaced by either the modified Jones model (Dechow et al., 1995) or the cross-sectional Jones model (Defond and Jiambalvo, 1994).

REFERENCES

Adler, M., and B. Dumas. 1983. International portfolio choice and corporation finance: A synthesis. *Journal of Finance* 38: 925–984.

Agmon, J., and D. Lessard. 1977. Investor recognition of corporate international diversification. *Journal of Finance* 32: 1049–1055.

Belsley, D.A., E. Kuh, and R.E. Welsh. 1980. *Regression Diagnostics: Identifying Influential Data and Sources of Collinearity*. New York: Wiley.

Bodnar, G.M., and J. Weintrop. 1997. The valuation of the foreign income of U.S. multinational firms: A growth opportunities perspective. *Journal of Accounting and Economics* 24: 69–97.

Brewer, H.L. 1981. Investor benefits from corporate international diversification. *Journal of Financial and Quantitative Analysis* 16: 113–126.

Buckley, P. 1988. The limits of explanation: Testing the internalization theory of the multinational enterprise. *Journal of International Business Studies* 19: 113–126.

Casson, M. 1987. *The Firm and the Market.* London: Basil Blackwell.

Caves, R.E. 1974. Causes of direct investment: Foreign firms' shares in Canadian and United Kingdom manufacturing industries. *Review of Economics and Statistics* 56: 273–293.

Coase, R.H. 1937. The nature of the firm. *Economica* 4: 386–405.

DeAngelo, L.E. 1986. Accounting numbers as market valuation substitutes: A study of management buyouts of public stockholders. *The Accounting Review* 41: 400–420.

———. 1988. Managerial competition, information costs, and corporate governance: The use of accounting performance measures in proxy contests. *Journal of Accounting and Economics* 10: 3–36.

Dechow, P.M., R.G. Sloan, and A.P. Sloan. 1995. Detecting earnings management. *The Accounting Review* 70: 193–225.

Defond, M.L., and J. Jiambalvo. 1994. Debt covenant violations and manipulation of accruals. *Journal of Accounting and Economics* 17: 145–176.

Doukas, J., and N.G. Travlos. 1988. The effect of corporate multinationalism on shareholders' wealth: Evidence from international acquisitions. *Journal of Finance* 43: 1161–1175.

Dunning, J.H. 1980. Toward an eclectic theory of international production: Some empirical tests. *Journal of International Business Studies* 11: 9–31.

———. 1988. The eclectic paradigm of international production: A restatement and some possible extensions. *Journal of International Business* 19: 1–31.

Errunza, V.R., and L.W. Senbet. 1981. The effects of international operations on the market values of the firm: Theory and evidence. *Journal of Finance* 36: 401–417.

Fatemi, A.M. 1984. Shareholders' benefits from corporate international diversification. *Journal of Finance* 39: 1325–1344.

Healey, P. 1985. The effects of bonus schemes on accounting decisions. *Journal of Accounting and Economics* 7: 85–107.

Hymer, S. 1976. *The International Operations of National Firms: A Study of Direct Foreign Investment.* Cambridge, MA: MIT Press.

Jones, J. 1991. Earnings management during import relief investigations. *Journal of Accounting Research* 29: 193–228.

Liberty, S.F., and J.I. Zimmerman. 1986. Labor union contract negotiations accounting choices. *The Accounting Review* 61: 692–712.

Mishra, C., and D.H. Gobelli. 1998. Managerial incentives, internalization, and market valuation of multinational firms. *Journal of International Business Studies* 29, 3: 583–598.

Morck, R., and B. Yeung. 1991. Why investors value multinationality. *Journal of Business* 64: 165–187.

Morck, R., and B. Yeung. 1992. Internationalization: An event study test. *Journal of International Economics* 33: 41–56.

Rugman, A.M. 1980. Internalization as a general theory of foreign direct investment: A reappraisal of the literature. *Journal of Economic Literature* 116: 365–375.

Rugman, A.M. 1981. *Inside the Multinationals: The Economics of Internal Markets.* New York: Columbia University Press.

Warfield, T.D., J.J. Wild, and K.L. Wild. 1997. Managerial ownership, accounting choices, and informativeness of earnings. *Journal of Accounting and Economics* 20, 61–91.

Appendix 2C. Growth Opportunities and Earnings Management

INTRODUCTION

This appendix develops and tests the hypothesis that managers of multinational firms with a high level of the investment opportunity set make accounting choices to reduce reported earnings compared to managers of multinational firms with a low level of the investment opportunity set. Unlike in other studies, we assume that earnings management is a present and continuous phenomenon rather than a behavior conditioned by an eventual crisis. While all firms potentially resort to earnings management, the level of growth opportunity, as measured by the level of the investment opportunity set, is assumed to affect the nature of earnings management for high-growth opportunities firms. These firms will then potentially resort to income-reducing accruals. We argue that a high level of the investment opportunity set causes higher actual and/or future profitability and thus higher reported accounting numbers. A result of the actual and/or potential higher reported accounting numbers is the possible perception of the accounting rates of return as "excessive" and indicative of monopolistic power on the part of the firm, thereby increasing both the political costs and the political risk. In such a case, managers' reporting of lower earnings may be expected to reduce both political costs and political risk.

Accrual analysis, similar to that of Jones (1991), is performed on a sample of high- and low-growth opportunities of multinational U.S. firms to determine the extent of earnings management. Our findings indicate that managers of high-growth opportunity multinational firms facing potentially high political costs and political risk report income-decreasing accruals compared to low-growth opportunity firms.

GROWTH OPPORTUNITIES AND EARNINGS MANAGEMENT

The firm is composed of the value of assets in place and the value of expected future investment options or growth opportunities. The lower the proportion of firm value represented by assets in place, the higher the growth opportunities for a given level of firm value. These potential investment opportunities are

Source: F. Alnajjar and A. Riahi-Belkaoui, "Growth Opportunities and Earnings Management," *Managerial Finance* 27, 2 (2001), pp. 72–81. Reprinted with the permission of the editor.

described by Myers (1977) as call options whose values depend on the likelihood that management will exercise them. Like call options, these growth opportunities represent real value to the firm (Kester, 1984). Growth options include such discretionary expenditures as capacity expansion prospects, product innovations, acquisitions of other firms, investment in brand name through advertising, and even maintenance and replacement of existing assets. A significant portion of the market value of equity is accounted for by growth opportunities (Pindyck, 1988). These benefits of growth opportunities are expected to result in higher profitability and realized growth (Kallapur and Trombley, 1999) and higher political risk (Monti-Belkaoui and Riahi-Belkaoui, 1999). Both increased profitability and political risk are expected to induce managers to resort to income-reducing accruals.

First, the increase in profitability of multinational firms with a high level of growth opportunities increases both their political visibility and political costs. The political cost hypothesis predicts that managers confronted with the possibility of politically imposed wealth transfers will resort to earnings management to reduce the likelihood and size of this transfer (Watts and Zimmerman, 1978). These multinational firms with high-growth opportunities, like high-income firms, which are particularly vulnerable to wealth-extorting political transfers in the form of legislation and/or regulation, have an incentive to resort to accruals or other means to reduce their reported income numbers compared to low-growth opportunity and low-income firms.

Second, political risk is a phenomenon that characterizes an unfriendly climate to multinational firms with visible profitability and high-growth opportunities (Monti-Belkaoui and Riahi-Belkaoui, 1999). It refers to the potential economic losses arising as a result of governmental measures or special situations that may limit or prohibit the operational and profitable activities of a multinational firm. One way to limit the potential emergence of political risk is to reduce the reported earnings number. Earnings management in high-growth-opportunities multinational firms may be a way of reducing the factors mitigating the emergence of political risk.

This study hypothesizes that high-growth-opportunities multinational firms make accounting choices to reduce income and net worth compared to low-growth-opportunities multinational firms.

RESEARCH DESIGN

The objective of the study is to examine the potential relationship between growth opportunities and the discretionary accruals of firms as those accruals reflect accounting choices made by management. The technique used by Jones (1991) and Cahan (1992) for the estimation of nondiscretionary accruals is adopted in this study. It estimates nondiscretionary accruals by regressing total accruals on the change in sales (a proxy for level of activity) and on the fixed asset balance. This approach leads to an estimate of discretionary accruals that is less biased and less noisy than earlier models as well as eliminates the assumption that accruals remain stationary over time. The basic model is as follows:

$$A_{it} = b_0 + b_1 CHSALES_{it} + b_2 FIXASSETS_{it} + e_{it} \tag{1}$$

where

A_{it} = total accruals in year t/total assets$_{it}$

$CHSALES_{it}$ = change in sales from year $t-1$ to year t, (Sales Revenues$_{it}$ − Sales Revenue$_{it-1}$) / Total Assets$_{it}$

$FIXASSETS_{it}$ = fixed assets at the end of year t (Fixed Assets$_{it}$ / Total Assets$_{it}$)

In the estimation process, Equation (1) is expanded to include an indicator variable to measure the discretionary accruals of high-growth firms. The expansion also includes total assets as a measure of size and dummy variables for each year of analysis.

The effect of multinationality is tested by estimating Equation (2).

$$A_{it} = B_0 + B_1 CHSALES_{it} + b_2 FIXASSETS_{it} + b_3 IOS_{it} \tag{2}$$
$$+ b_4 TA_{it} + b_5 YR_{it} \ldots + b_9 YR_{it} + e_{it}$$

where TA is total assets, YR is a dummy variable for a year of analysis, and IOS is the investment opportunity set.

The expected sign of the coefficient for CHSALES is positive. It is expected to be negative for all the other explanatory variables. The coefficient of IOS will be negative if managers lower accruals for high-growth firms.

As in Hall and Stammerjohan (1997), a two-step generalized least square error components model is used in this study, as it is more efficient than the within-group estimator, fixed effects covariance model used by Cahan (1992).

DATA

Sample and Method

The sample consisted of all the firms included in Forbes' "most international" 100 American manufacturing and service firms for the 1987–1990 period. Financial data were collected from both the *Forbes* articles and Compustat. Total accruals are calculated for each firm as follows:

$$A_{it} = \frac{-DEP_{it} + (AR_{it} - AR_{it-1}) + (INV_{it} - INV_{it-1}) - (AP_{it} - AP_{it-1}) - (TP_{it} - TP_{it-1}) - DT_{it}}{TA_{it}}$$

where

DEP_{it} = depreciation expense and the depletion charge for firm i in year t
AR_{it} = accounts receivable balance for firm i at the end of year t
INV_{it} = inventory balance for firm i at the end of year t
AP_{it} = accounts payable for firm i at the end of year t
TP_{it} = taxes payable balance for firm i at the end of year t
DT_{it} = deferred tax expense for firm i at the end of year t
TA_{it} = total asset balance for firm i at the end of year t

The data are pooled over time and across firms, resulting in a sample of 339 firm-years. To test the effect of the investment opportunity set on discretionary accruals, a dichotomous indicator variable, IOS, is added to model (1). IOS takes on the value of 1 for the group firms classified as high-growth-opportunity firms and zero for firms classified as low-growth-opportunity firms. Model (1) is also expanded to include YR_{it}, dummy-coded variable as 1 for year t (t = 1987–1990), and TA_{it} for the total assets of the firm. The YR variables measure the time effect for each of the four years. The TA variable is added as a result of the size hypothesis whereby large firms are expected to make income-decreasing choices relative to small firms (Christie, 1990). The effect of size is important given the evidence presented later about the significant difference in size between the high-growth and the low-growth firms.

Measuring the Investment Opportunity Set

Because the investment opportunity set is not observable, there is no consensus on an appropriate proxy variable (Kallapur and Trombley, 1999). Similar to Smith and Watts (1992) and Gaver and Gaver (1993), we used an ensemble of variables to measure the investment opportunity set. The three measures of the investment opportunity set used are market-to-book assets (MASS), market-to-book equity (MV), and the earnings/price ratio (EP). These variables are defined as follows:

MASS = [Assets − Total Common Equity + Shares Outstanding * Share Closing Price] / Assets
MV = [Shares Outstanding * Share Closing Price / Total Common Equity]
EP = [Primary EPS before Extraordinary Items] / Share Closing Price

The results of a factor analysis of these measures of the investment opportunity set are shown in Table 2C.1. One common factor appears to explain the intercorrelations among the three individual measures. Based on these factor

Table 2C.1
Selected Statistics Related to a Common Factor Analysis of Three Measures of the Investment Opportunity Set for *Forbes'* "Most International 100 U.S. Firms"

1. **Eigenvalues of the Correlation Matrix: Total = 3, Average = 1**

Eigenvalue	1	2	3
	1.0540	0.9868	0.9592

2. **Factor Pattern**

FACTOR 1	MASS	MQV	EP
	0.62821	0.66411	0.46722

3. **Final Communality Estimates: Total = 1.053994**

MASS	MQV	EP
0.394651	0.441045	0.218299

4. **Standardized Scoring Coefficients**

FACTOR 1	MASS	MQV	EP
	0.59603	0.63009	0.43329

5. **Descriptive Statistics of the Common Factor Extracted from the Three Measures of the Investment Opportunity**

Maximum	Third Quartile	Median	First Quartile	Minimum	Mean
9.3593	3.2200	2.0450	1.5085	2.5209	1.9812

scores, high-growth firms are chosen from the top 25 percent of the distribution scores, while low-growth firms are chosen from the bottom 25 percent of the distribution factor scores.

TESTS AND RESULTS

Descriptive statistics are presented in Table 2C.2. The results for the error-components estimation of model (1) are reported in Table 2C.3. As expected, both CHSALES and FIXASSETS are statistically significant. The overall model is also significant with an F value of 30.818 and an adjusted R^2 of 16.73

Table 2C.2
Descriptive Statistics

A. High-Growth Sample

Variables	Mean	Standard Deviation	Maximum	Median	Minimum
Total Revenues (thousands)	3,624.6	2,8012.2	138,954	246,842	7,682
Total Assets (thousands)	54,186.5	50,397.7	261,860	35,475	8,462
Net Profit	1,812	1,320.65	8,132	1,608	0.4587

B. Low-Growth Sample

Variables	Mean	Standard Deviation	Maximum	Median	Minimum
Total Revenues (thousands)	6,556.19	3,696.6	18,805	5,835	2,816
Total Assets (thousands)	9.559.85	16,833.05	128,260	5,556	2,864
Net Profit	384.85	368.27	1,925.35	382.3	−618.2

percent. It appears that a significant portion of the variation in accruals of multinational firms can be explained by changes in sales and the fixed asset balance.

The error-components regression results for model (2) are reported in Table 2C.4. The results support the view that the variation in accruals can be explained by the change in sales, the fixed asset balance, and time-dependent effects. In addition, the variable of interest, IOS, is significant at the 0.01 level, with a one-tailed test, and its sign is negative. Because high growth was coded as 1, the positive sign of IOS indicates that discretionary accruals of high-growth firms were higher than for low-growth firms, which supports the political cost and political risk hypothesis.

SUMMARY AND CONCLUSIONS

This study examines, on a longitudinal basis, whether managers of multinational firms respond to the political costs associated with a high level of growth opportunities by adjusting their discretionary accruals. Discretionary accruals for the 100 largest U.S. multinationals were examined over the 1987–1990 period, using the residuals of a fixed effects covariance model that regressed total ac-

Table 2C.3
Results of Regression Estimation—Model (1)
$(A_{it} = b_0 + b_1 CHSALES_{it} + b_2 FIXASSETS_{it} + e_{it})$

Interdependent Variables	Expected Sign	Coefficient	t-value	One-tailed Probability
Intercept		-0.0326	7.538	0.0001
CHSALES	+	0.0180	4.059	0.0001
FIXASSETS	-	-0.1532	-7.885	0.0001
$n=$	339			
R^2		0.1723	F Statistic	Probability
Adjusted R^2		0.1673	30.818	0.0001

Variable definitions:

$$A_{it} = \frac{-DEP_{it} + (AR_{it} - AR_{it-1}) + (INV_{it} - INV_{it-1}) - (AP_{it} - AP_{it-1}) - (TP_{it} - TP_{it-1}) - DT_{it}}{TA_{it}}$$

Where

DEP_{it} = depreciation expense and the depletion charge for firm i in year t
AR_{it} = accounts receivable balance for firm i at the end of year t
INV_{it} = inventory balance for firm i at the end of year t
AP_{it} = accounts payable for firm i at the end of year t
TP_{it} = taxes payable balance for firm i at the end of year t
DT_{it} = deferred tax expense for firm i at the end of year t
TA_{it} = total asset balance for firm i at the end of year t
$CHSALES_{it}$ = (net sales$_{it}$ − net sales$_{it-1}$) / TA_{it}
$FIXASSETS_{it}$ = fixed assets$_{it}$ / TA_{it}

cruals on the change in sales, the fixed assets balance, and a dummy variable for each year of the study. The hypothesis is tested using a test designed with a dummy variable, coded 1 for high growth, included in the accrual model. This growth variable was significant with a positive sign, which indicates that the discretionary accruals were higher for high-growth firms. The results support the political cost and political risk hypothesis associated with multinationality and are consistent with the view that managers adjust earnings in response to a high level of growth.

The results, however, cannot be generalized, as the sample includes only the most multinational U.S. firms. This appendix identifies this area for future research. The longitudinal approach could be extended to explore response to a wider range of growth.

Table 2C.4
Results of Regression Estimation—Model (2)
$(A_{it} = B_0B_1CHSALES_{it} + b_2FIXASSETS_{it} + b_3IOS_{it} + b_4TA_{it} + b_5YR_{it} \ldots\ldots + b_9YR_{it})$

Interdependent Variables	Expected Sign	Coefficient	t-value	One-tailed Probability
Intercept		-0.0158	-2.876	0.0156
CHSALES	+	0.0028	4.256	0.0001
FIXASSETS	-	-0.1818	-6.538	0.0002
IOS	+	0.0081	+2.656	0.0116
TA	-	-0.0000007	-2.588	0.0112
YR_1		-0.0031	-4.868	0.0001
YR_2		-0.0018	-4.062	0.0001
YR_3		-0.00132	-4.850	0.0001
R^2		0.3612	F Statistics	Probability
Adjusted R^2		0.3322	4.856	0.0001
n	166			

Variable definitions:

TA = Total Assets
TR = Year
IOS = 1 if growth opportunities are high; 0 if growth opportunities are low.

REFERENCES

Cahan, S. 1992. The effect of antitrust investigations on discretionary accruals: A refined test of the political-cost hypothesis. *The Accounting Review* 67 (January): 77–95.

Christie, A.A. 1990. Aggression of test statistics: An evaluation of the evidence on contracting and size hypotheses. *Journal of Accounting and Economics* 12 (January): 15–36.

Gaver, J.J., and K.M. Gaver. 1993. Additional evidence in the association between the investment opportunity set and corporate financing, dividend, and compensation policies. *Journal of Accounting and Economics* 16, 1/2/3: 125–140.

Hall, S.C., and W.W. Stammerjohan. 1997. Damage awards and earnings management in the oil industry. *The Accounting Review* (January): 47–65.

Jones, J. 1991. Earnings management during import relief investigations. *Journal of Accounting Research* 29 (Autumn): 193–228.

Kallapur, S., and M.A. Trombley. 1999. The association between investment opportunity set and realized growth. *Journal of Business, Finance, and Accounting* 96, 3 (December): 505–519.

Kester, W.C. 1984. Today's options for tomorrow's growth. *Harvard Business Review* 62, 2: 153–160.

Monti-Belkaoui, J., and A. Riahi-Belkaoui. 1999. *The Nature, Estimation, and Management of Political Risk.* Westport, CT: Greenwood.

Myers, S.C. 1977. Determinants of corporate borrowing. *Journal of Financial Economics* 5, 2: 147–175.

Pindyck, R.S. 1988. Irreversible investment, capacity choice and the value of the firm. *The American Economic Review* 78, 5: 969–985.

Smith, C.W., and R.L. Watts. 1992. The investment opportunity set and corporate financing, dividend, and compensation policies. *Journal of Financial Economics* 32, 3: 263–292.

Watts, R.L., and J.L. Zimmerman. 1978. Towards a positive theory of determination of accounting standards. *The Accounting Review* 53 (January): 112–134.

Appendix 2D. Contextual Accrual and Cash Flow Based Valuation Models: Impact of Multinationality and Reputation

INTRODUCTION

This appendix investigates the impact of the contextual factors of multinationality and reputation on accrual and cash flow based valuations. The nature and amount of information in cash flows and accruals were first examined by Wilson (1986) using stock behavior around the release of annual reports. He concluded that the market reacts more favorably the larger (smaller) are the cash flows (current accruals). Bernard and Stober (1989) were, however, unable to confirm Wilson's results over a longer period, and according to the state of the economy. This appendix extends the works of Wilson and Bernard and Stober in two ways. The first is to assess the generality and robustness of Wilson's results by using a total market value based valuation model rather than an excess-return based model. In situations where prices lead earnings, price level regressions are better specified than return/changes regressions for estimating the price earnings relation. The results confirm Wilson's results. The second is to examine two contextual models of the implications of cash and accruals. We argue that the preference of cash flows over accruals will arise under conditions of high multinationality and high reputation. Support for the hypotheses was found. In sum, we are able to identify the economic logic underlying how the market assimilates information about cash and accruals under the specific contextual environments of multinationality and corporate reputation.

Source: Reprinted from A. Riahi-Belkaoui, "Contextual Accrual and Cash Flow Based Valuation Models: Impact of Multinationality and Reputation," *Advances in Financial Planning and Forecasting* 2001, pp. 25–35. Copyright 2001. Reprinted with permission from Elsevier Science.

MARKET VALUATION MODELS

A Simplified Model

A simplified model relates market value of equity at the end of a period to the corresponding accruals and cash flows as follows:

$$MV_{it} = a_0 + A_{it} + a_{2i} CF_{it} + e_{it} \tag{1}$$

where

MV_{it} = Market value of equity of firm i at the end of year t

AT_{it} = Total accruals of firm i at the end of year t

CF_{it} = Cash flows of firm i at the end of year t

All variables are deflated by total assets at the end of year t.

Impact of Multinationality

Investors recognize the enhancement of firm value through internationalization. The evidence shows that investors recognize multinationality given that multinational firms show lower systematic risk and unsystematic risk compared to securities of purely domestic firms (Errunza and Senbet, 1981; Yang et al., 1985; Agmon and Lessard, 1977). To test the incremental association between market value of equity and multinationality, after controlling for accruals and cash flows, equation (1) is adjusted as follows:

$$MV_{it} = a_0 + a_{1i}A_{it} + a_{2i} CF_{it} + a_{3i} MULTY_{it} + e_{it}^1 \tag{2}$$

where

$MULTY_{it}$ = Level of multinationality of firm i at the end of year t

Impact of Reputation

To create the right impression or reputation, firms signal their key characteristics to constituents to maximize their social status (Spence, 1974). Basically, corporate audiences were found to construct reputation on the basis of accounting and market information or signals regarding firm performance (Fombrum and Shanley, 1990; Riahi-Belkaoui and Pavlik, 1991; Belkaoui, 1992). Then reputations have become established and constitute signals that may affect actions of firms' stakeholders, including their shareholders. Specifically, a good reputation can be construed as a competitive advantage within an industry (Fombrum and Shanley, 1990). This implies that investors use corporate reputation in determining firm value. To test for incremental association between the market value equity and reputation after controlling for accruals, cash flows, and multinationality, equation (2) is adjusted as follows:

$$MV_{it} = a_0 = a_1A_{it} + a_{2i}CF_{it} + a_{3i}MULTY_{it} + a_{4i}REP_{it} + e_{it}^2 \tag{3}$$

where

REP_{it} = Corporate reputation score for firm i at the end of year t

RESEARCH METHOD

In this study, incremental associations between market value and cash flow from operations, multinationality, and corporate reputation, after controlling for accruals, are presented as evidence of the relevance of the contextual environment of cash flow based valuation models. To describe and assess the significance of these relationships, we use three linear regression approaches (Equations 1–3) that relate market value of equity to the accounting and non-accounting variables mentioned earlier.

Data and Sample Selection

The population consists of firms included in both *Forbes'* most international 100 American manufacturing and service firms and *Fortune's* surveys of corporate reputation from 1987 to 1990. The security data are collected from the CSRP Return files. The accounting variables are collected from Compustat. Cash flows from operations are reported under SFAS No. 95 (Compustat item 308). The derivation of the total accruals, multinationality, and corporate reputation variables are explained later. The final sample included 360 firm-year observations that have all the accounting and nonaccounting variables.

Measuring Total Accruals

Total accruals are calculated for each firm as follows (Healy, 1985):

$$A_{it} = \frac{DEP_{it} + (AR_{it} - AR_{it-1}) + (INV_{it} - INV_{it-1}) - (AP_{it} - AP_{it-1}) - (TP_{it} - TP_{it-1}) - DT_{it}}{TA_{it}}$$

where

DEP_{it} = Depreciation expense and the depletion charge for firm i in year t
AR_{it} = Accounts receivable balance for firm i at the end of year t

INV_{it} = Inventory balance for firm i at the end of year t

AP_{it} = Accounts payable for firm i at the end of year t

TP_{it} = Taxes payable balance for firm i at the end of year t

DT_{it} = Deferred tax expense for firm i in year t

TA_{it} = Total asset balance for firm i at the end of year t

Measuring Multinationality

Previous research has attempted to measure three attributes of multinationality:

1. *Performance*—in terms of what goes on overseas (Dunning 1995).
2. *Structure*—in terms of how resources are used overseas (Stopford and Wells 1972).
3. *Attitude or Conduct*—in terms of what is top management orientation (Perlmutter, 1969).

Sullivan (1994) developed nine measures, of which five were shown to have a high reliability in the construction of a homogeneous measure of multinationality: (1) foreign sales as a percentage of total sales (FSTS), (2) foreign assets over total assets (FATA), (3) overseas subsidiaries as a percentage of total subsidiaries (OSTS), (4) top management's international experience (TMIE), and (5) psychic dispersion of international operations (PDIO).

In this study we follow a similar approach by measuring multinationality through three measures: (1) foreign sales/total sales (FSTS), (2) foreign profit/total profits (FPTP), and (3) foreign assets/total assets (FATA). As shown in Table 2D.1, one common factor appears to explain the intercorrelations among the three variables, as the first eigenvalue alone exceeds the sum of commonalities. The common factor is significantly and positively correlated with the three measures. The factor scores were used to measure the degree of multinationality of firms in the sample.

Measuring Corporate Reputation

A multiple-constituency view of effectiveness is used in this study, where organizational effectiveness measures the extent to which an organization meets the needs, expectations, and demands of important external constituencies beyond those directly associated with the company's products and markets (Riahi-Belkaoui and Pavlik, 1992). A good example of the multiple constituency view is the annual reputational index of corporations disclosed by *Fortune* magazine.

The *Fortune* survey covers every industry group comprising four or more companies. The industry groups are based on categories established by the U.S. Office of Management and Budget (OMB). The survey asked executives, directors, and analysts in particular to rate a company on the following eight key attributes of reputation:

Table 2D.1
Selected Statistics Related to a Common Factor Analysis of Three Measures of Multinationality for *Forbes'* "Most International 100 U.S. Firms" for the 1987–1990 Period

1.   Eigenvalues of the Correlation Matrix:

Eigenvalues	1	2	3
	1.8963	0.9169	0.1868

2.   Factor Pattern
FACTOR 1

FS/TS	0.93853
FP/TP	0.40913
FA/TA	0.92089

3.   Final Communality Estimates: Total = 1.389626

FS/TS	FP/TP	FA/TA
0.8808	0.16738	0.84804

4.   Standardized Scoring Coefficients
FACTOR 1

FS/TS	0.49494
FP/TP	0.21575
FA/TA	0.48563

5.   Descriptive Statistics of the Common Factor Extracted from the Three Measures of Multinationality

Maximum	201.051
Third Quartile	52.231
Median	41.501
First Quartile	30.648
Minimum	5.198
Mean	43.062

Variable definitions:
FS/TS: Foreign sales/ Total sales.
FP/TP: Foreign profits/Total profits.
FA/TA: Foreign assets/Total assets.

1. Quality of management

2. Quality of products/services offered

3. Innovativeness

4. Value as long-term investment

5. Soundness of financial position

6. Ability to attract/develop/keep talented people

7. Responsibility to the community/environment

8. Wise use of corporate assets

Table 2D.2

Selected Statistics Related to a Common Factor Analysis of Measures of Reputation

1.   Eigenvalues of the Correlation Matrix:
Eigenvalues

1	2	3	4	5	6	7	8
6.7805	0.5562	0.3835	0.1343	0.1808	0.0544	0.0476	0.0331

2.   Factor Pattern*
FACTOR 1

R_1 0.9537	R_4 0.9650	R_7 0.8080
R_2 0.9184	R_5 0.8987	R_8 0.9484
R_3 0.8796	R_6 0.9809	

3.   Final Communality Estimates: Total = 1.389626

R_1	R_2	R_3	R_4	R_5	R_6	R_7	R_8
0.9096	0.8435	0.7737	0.9312	0.8077	0.9621	0.6520	0.8996

4.   Standardized Scoring Coefficients
FACTOR 1

R_1 0.1406	R_4 0.1423	R_7 0.1191
R_2 0.1354	R_5 0.1325	R_8 0.1398
R_3 0.1279	R_6 0.1446	

Descriptive Statistics of the Common Factor Extracted from the Eight Measures of Reputation

Maximum	9.001
Third Quartile	7.274
Median	6.604
First Quartile	6.076
Minimum	3.154
Mean	6.592

* R_1 = Quality of management.
  R_2 = Quality of products/services.
  R_3 = Innovativeness.
  R_4 = Value as long-term investment.
  R_5 = Soundness of financial position.
  R_6 = Ability to attract, develop and keep talented people.
  R_7 = Responsibility to the community and environment.
  R_8 = Wise use of corporate assets.

Ratings were on a scale of 0 (poor) to 10 (excellent). The score met the multiple-constituency ecological model view of organizational effectiveness. For purposes of this study, the 1987 to 1990 *Fortune* magazine surveys were used. To obtain a unique configuration, a factor analysis is used to isolate the factor common to the eight measures of reputation. All the observations were subjected to factor analysis, and one common factor was found to explain the intercorrelations among the eight individual measures. Table 2D.2 reports the results of the common factor analysis. One common factor appears to explain the inter-correlations among the eight variables, as the first eigenvalue alone exceeds the sum of the commonalities. The common factor is significantly and positively correlated with the eight measures. As pointed out earlier, based on the factor scores, high-reputation firms were chosen from the top 24 percent of the distribution factor scores while low-reputation firms were chosen from the bottom 25 percent of the distribution factor scores.

RESULTS

Panel A of Table 2D.3 reports descriptive statistics for the variables used in our tests and panel B shows correlations among variables. The correlations reported in panel B of Table 2D.3 show that all correlations between MV_{it}, A_{it}, CF_{it}, $MULTY_{it}$, and REP_{it} are significant at the 0.01 level. The significant association among these variables indicates some degree of collinearity among the independent variables in the regression analyses. However, the maximum condition index in all subsequent regressions with earnings and both cash flow variables is only 4.45. As suggested by Belsey et al. (1980), mild collinearity is diagnosed for maximum condition indices between 5 and 10, and severe collinearity for an index over 30. Thus, collinearity does not seem to influence results.

For each of the multivariate regressions to be reported, we perform additional specification tests, including checks for normality and consideration of various scatter plots. A null hypothesis of normality could not be rejected at the 0.01 level in all cases, and the plots revealed some heteroskedasticity but no other obvious problems. Therefore, we calculated the t-statistics after correcting for heteroskedasticity.

Table 2D.3 presents the regression results for equations (1) to (3). Equation (1) relates the total market value deflated by total assets to the accruals and cash flows from operations, also deflated by total assets. As shown in Table 2D.4, the coefficient for total accruals is significantly negative, while the coefficient for cash flows is significantly positive. As expected, the total market value is negatively related to the total accruals and positively related to cash flows. As in Wilson (1986), these results show that the market reacts favorably the larger (smaller) are the cash flows (current accruals). At the same time, the results show that accruals and cash flows from operations provide incremental value-relevance beyond one another in explaining market value.

Equation (2) relates the total market value to multinationality in addition to accruals and cash flows from operations. As shown in Table 2D.4 the coefficient of multinationality is significantly positive at the 0.01 level. In addition, R^2 increased from 62.96 percent in equation (1) to 73.28 percent in equation (2). The evidence suggests that multinationality provides incremental value-relevance beyond accruals and cash flows in explaining market value.

Table 2D.3
Descriptive Statistics and Correlations

Panel A: Descriptive Correlations

Variables	Mean	Standard Deviation	Minimum	25%	Median	75%	Maximum
MV_{it}	0.894	0.791	0.018	0.381	0.665	1.132	5
A_t	0.047	0.024	0.010	0.031	0.047	0.062	0.175
CF_{it}	0.104	0.062	0.052	0.065	0.112	0.143	0.254
$MULTY_{it}$	43.062	19.682	5.198	30.648	41.503	52.231	201.059
REP_{it}	6.592	0.974	3.154	6.076	6.604	7.264	9.001

Panel B: Correlations

	MV_{it}	A_t	CF_I	$MULTY_{it}$	REP_{it}
MV_{it}	1.000				
A_t	0.061*	1.000			
CF_I	0.717*	0.454*	1.000		
$MULTY_{it}$	0.096*	0.023	-0.012	1.000	
REP_{it}	0.512*	0.070	0.495*	0.009	1.000

MV_{it} = Market value of equity for firm i in period t.
A_{it} = Total accruals for firm i in period t.
CF_{it} = Cash flows from operations for firm i in period t.
$MULTY_{it}$ = Index of multinationality for firm i in period t.
REP_{it} = Index of reputation for firm i in period t.
*Significant at $\alpha = 0.01$.

Equation (3) relates the market value to the accounting variables of accruals and cash flows and the nonaccounting variables of multinationality and corporate reputation. As shown in Table 2D.4, the coefficient for corporate reputation (0.0821) is significantly positive at the 0.01 level. This evidence suggests that corporate reputation provides incremental value relevance beyond accruals, cash flows, and multinationality in explaining market value.

To rule out the possibility that the total accruals and cash flows are proxying for cross-sectional differences in industry membership, the regressions were also run with a dummy variable representing twenty-two industries. The industry dummy variable was found to be insignificant.

Table 2D.4
Regression Results of Linear Models[1]

	Model 1	Model 2	Model 3
Intercept	0.1703 (2.737)*	-0.1082 (-1.36)	-0.6129 (-2.870)
A_{it}	-11.2791 (-9.521)*	-16.7071 (-14.621)*	-16.2253 (-12.406)*
CF_{it}	11.8366 (24.703)*	14.6982 (30.106)*	13.8484 (22.240)*
$MULTY_{it}$		0.0043 (3.3347)*	0.0047 (3.253)
REP_{it}			0.0821 (2.534)*
Adjusted R^2	0.6296	0.7328	0.7588
N	360		

Notes:
1. Model 1: $MV_{it} = a_0 + a_{1t} A_{it} + a_{2i} CF_{it} + e_{it}$.
Model 2: $MV_{it} = a_0 + a_{1t} A_{it} + a_{2i} CF_{it} + a_{3i} MULTY_{it} + e^1_{it}$.
Model 3: $MV_{it} = a_0 + a_{1t} A_{it} + a_{2i} CF_{it} + a_{3i} MULTY_{it} + REP_{it} + e^2_{it}$.
2. MV = Market value of equity of firm i at the end of year t.
A_{it} = Total accruals of firm i at the end of year t.
CF_{it} = Cash flows of firm i at the end of year t.
$MULTY_{it}$ = Level of multinationality of firm i at the end of year t.
REP_{it} = Corporate reputation score for firm i at the end of year t.
*Significant at 0.001 level.
**Significant at 0.05 level.

SUMMARY AND CONCLUSIONS

This appendix examined the generality and robustness of an accrual and cash flow based model that includes the contextual factors of multinationality and corporate reputation. The evidence confirms previous results presented by Wilson (1986) using total market value as a dependent variable and a price level rather than a return/changes regression. Basically, the larger (smaller) the market value, the larger (smaller) the cash flows (current accruals). In addition, the preference of cash flows over accruals arises under conditions of high multinationality and high corporate reputation. The results verify the economic logic underlying how the market assimilates information about cash and accruals under the specific contexts of multinationality and reputation. First, a price level regression seems to provide a better specification of this economic logic. Second, contextual factors play a fundamental role in the same economic logic. Future research needs to examine the role of other contextual factors in the determination of the relationship between the market value and accruals and cash flows.

REFERENCES

Agmon, T., and D. Lessard. (1977). Investor Recognition of Corporate International Diversification. *Journal of Finance* 32, 1049–1055.

Belkaoui, A. (1992). Organizational Effectiveness, Social Performance and Economic Performance. *Research in Corporate Social Performance and Policy* 12, 143–155.

Belsey, D., E. Kuh, and R. Welsch. (1980). *Regression Diagnostics*. New York: John Wiley & Sons.

Bernard, V., and T. Stober. (1989). The Nature and Amount of Information in Cash Flows and Accruals. *The Accounting Review* (October), 624–652.

Dunning, J.H. (1995). Reappraising the Eclectic Paradigm in an Age of Alliance Capitalism. *Journal of International Business Studies* 26, 461–492.

Errunza, V., and L. Senbet. (1981). The Effects of International Corporate Diversification, Market Valuation and Size Adjusted Evidence. *Journal of Finance* 11, 717–743.

Fombrum, C., and M. Shanley. (1990). What's in a Name? Reputational Building and Corporate Strategy. *Academy of Management Journal* 33, 233–258.

Healy, P.M. (1985). The Effect of Bonus Schemes on Accounting Decisions. *Journal of Accounting and Economics* 7, 85–107.

Perlmutter, H.V. (1969). The Tortuous Evaluation of the Multinational Corporation. *Columbia Journal of World Business* 7, 9–18.

Riahi-Belkaoui, A., and E. Pavlik. (1991). Asset Management Performance and Reputation Building for Large U.S. Firms. *British Journal of Management* 2, 231–238.

Riahi-Belkaoui, A., and E. Pavlik. (1992). *Accounting for Corporate Reputation*. Westport, CT: Quorum Books.

Spence, A.M. (1974). *Market Signaling: Information Transfer in Hiring and Related Screening Process*. Cambridge, MA: Harvard University Press.

Stopford, J.M., and L.T. Wells. (1972). *Managing the Multinational Enterprise*. New York: Basic Books.

Sullivan, D. (1994). Measuring the Degree of Internationalization of a Firm. *Journal of International Business Studies* 25, 325–342.

Wilson, P. (1986). The Relative Information Content of Accruals and Cash Flows: Combined Evidence at the Earnings Announcement and Annual Report Release Date. *Journal of Accounting Research* (September), 165–200.

Yang, H., J. Wansley, and W. Lane. (1985). Stock Market Recognition of Multinationality of a Firm and International Events. *Journal of Business, Finance, and Accounting* 2, 263–274.

Chapter 3

Creativity in Accounting

INTRODUCTION

Creativity in accounting implies a liberal interpretation of accounting rules, allowing choices that may result in a depiction of financial situations that are more or less optimistic than the real situations. The creativity in accounting may take different forms depending on the objectives of the preparers of the accounting reports. These forms of creativity in accounting are generally known in practice and in the literature as (1) the selective financial misrepresentation hypothesis, (2) big bath accounting, and (3) creative accounting. Each of these forms is explicated and illustrated in this chapter as evidence of this general thesis of "designed" versus "principle" accounting.

THE SELECTIVE FINANCIAL MISREPRESENTATION HYPOTHESIS

Accounting information is basically the accounting surrogate used by decision makers who can't rely on directly observed events. A manipulation of these surrogates provides decision makers with the opportunity of sending signals that shape people's perceptions of managerial performance, which is made possible by arbitrary, complicated, and misleading rules. The selective financial misrepresentation hypothesis as advanced by Revsine[1] maintains, "The problem is not accidental, but instead results from contrived and flexible reporting rules promulgated by standard setters who have been 'captured' by the intended regulatees and others involved in the financial reporting process."[2] The "capturing" refers to the process where the main objective of regulation, which is the protection of consumers, is reversed to make the regulatees the beneficiaries.[3] The selective financial representation hypothesis is assumed to be across both public and private sectors "since participation in both sectors is motivated to support standards that selectively misrepresent economic reality when it suits their purpose."[4] It applies to managers, shareholders, auditors, and standard setters.

1. Managers prefer "loose" reporting standards over tight standards because they allow (1) a shifting of income between years more favorable to bonus attainment, (2) impressing the shareholders, and (3) protecting their jobs by forestalling takeovers.[5]

2. Shareholders benefit also from the loose standards given that the smoothing of reporting earnings by managers lowers the volatility of reported earnings, lowering the market's perception of default risk and increasing firm value.

3. Auditors may prefer the same reporting rules that distort economic reality for client *harmony* or rigid rules when they present a convenient shield to hide behind.[6]

4. Standard setters may favor the self-misrepresentation hypothesis for both self-protection and altruism.

5. Academics may favor the selective misrepresentation hypothesis as it provides them with the opportunity of providing theories and proposals in exchange for more remuneration and prestige.

The situation calls for a change by insulating the standard-setting process from regulatory capture. Revsine suggests the following four-step process:

1. educating the public,
2. improving the process for selecting and monitoring standard setters,
3. establishing new funding arrangements, and
4. creating independence for the standard setters.[7]

SEC Chairman Levitt proposed a six-part action plan to address these issues and improve the "reliability and transparency" of financial statements:

- Public companies will be required to make detailed disclosures about the impact of changes in accounting assumptions so that the market can "better understand the nature and effects of the restructuring liabilities and other loss accruals."

- New SEC guidance will emphasize "the need to consider qualitative, not just quantitative factors" when judging materiality.

- The American Institute of Certified Public Accountants (AICPA) will clarify the rules for auditing purchased research and development and "argue for existing guidance on restructuring, large acquisition write-offs, and revenue recognition practices."

- Additional SEC guidance on revenue recognition may be published. This project will consider the applicability of recently adopted software revenue recognition standards to other industries.

- The FASB will accelerate certain projects that relate to the definition of constructive liability.

- The SEC's Divisions of Enforcement and Corporation Finance will review companies that announce "restructuring liability reserves, major write-offs, or other practices that appear to manage earnings."[8]

"BIG BATH" ACCOUNTING

"Big bath" accounting refers generally to the steps taken by management to drastically reduce current earnings per share in order to increase future earnings per share. The situation is akin to a choice of income-decreasing procedures that increase the probability of meeting future earnings' targets. As stated by Healy,

[I]f earnings are so low that no matter which accounting procedures are selected target earnings will not be met, managers have incentives to further reduce current earnings by deferring revenues on accelerating write-offs, a strategy known as "taking a bath."[9]

The big bath procedure may generally follow a change in the management, giving an opportunity to new managers to develop a lower income anchor against which they will be evaluated in the future, guaranteeing themselves an initial good performance.[10]

A good description of "big bath" follows:

Companies are most likely to take a big bath during particular periods. First, when new managers take over, they are tempted to write off the old projects and assets of their predecessors to show strong improvements during the coming years. Second, when a company has a large nonrecurring gain, it might search for expenses to charge against it. And third, when earnings are particularly weak, management sees an opportunity to shift additional expenses (which will most likely not even be noticed) to the current period. The benefit, naturally, is that the additional current changes mean fewer changes in the future.[11]

Another good definition of "big bath" follows:

The bath is described as a "clean up" of balance sheet accounts. Assets are written down or written off, and provisions are made for estimated losses and expenses which may be incurred in the future. These actions decrease income or increase losses for the current period while relieving future income of expenses, which it would otherwise have had to absorb. In simple terms taking a bath tends to inflate future income by depressing current income.[12]

Most of the evidence in "big bath" accounting is anecdotal and of a journalistic nature.

The following three stories give good examples of how "big bath" accounting is used.

1. In December 1990, the Financial Accounting Standards Board (FASB) issued Statement No. 106, "Employers' Accounting for Post Retirement Benefits

Other than Pensions" to account for health care and other welfare benefits provided to retirees, their spouses, dependents, and beneficiaries. These other welfare benefits refer to life insurance offered outside a pension plan, dental care as well as medical care, eye care, legal and tax services, tuition assistance, day care, and housing assistance. At the time of the adoption of FASB Statement No. 106, a transitional amount is computed. It is equal to the difference between (1) the accumulated postretirement benefit obligation (APBO) and (2) the fair value of the plan assets, plus any accrued obligation or less any prepaid cost (asset). Given that most plans were unfunded and most employees were accruing benefits costs for the first time, the transition amounts were material. The choices were either (1) an immediate charge to expense for unrecognized past costs as well as recognition of the total unrecognized liability, which will create a major drain on the reported earnings in the year of change, or (2) deferral and amortization of the expense, as well as the recognition of a rapidly increasing liability, which will create a major drain on the earnings for many years.[13] The choice of the first option will constitute a good example of a "big bath" choice. In fact, the adoption of FASB No. 106 led (1) IBM to declare a $2.3 billion change, resulting in IBM's first-ever quarterly loss in March 1991, (2) General Electric Co. to declare a $2.7 billion change, and (3) AT&T to absorb a $2.1 billion pretax hit for postretirement benefits in the fourth quarter of 1993.[14]

2. In March 2001, Procter & Gamble announced that it would take a $1.4 billion change to reduce its workforce by 9 percent or 9,600 employees. These changes followed a $2.1 billion restructuring effort that started in 1999. Then, in June 2001 the company announced that it would take another change of $900 million to write off underperforming assets. This is a good example of a "big bath" approach that seems unending, stretching the definition of onetime expense too liberally.

3. Nortel Networks, a company that stood in the year 2000 as a glamour stock, declared a $19.2 billion loss in the second quarter of the year 2001. The $19.2 billion loss exceeded the annual gross domestic product of El Salvador and approaches that of Bolivia. In a year the market value of the company shrank by one-quarter trillion dollars. Of this $19.2 billion loss, $12.3 billion was a write-off that Nortel was taking in goodwill on recent acquisitions. The story unfolds as follows. In the year 2000 Nortel went on an acquisition spree, acquiring eleven technology concerns at a time when its own tangible assets were just $167 million. This did not stop Nortel from paying an exorbitant $19.7 billion, mostly in shares for the acquisitions, which was equivalent to 118 times the value of these acquired companies. For example, in 2000 Nortel paid Xros $3.2 billion in stock at a time when Xros' tangible assets were $3 million. This "big bath" story is a good example of a management making blundering buys and then trying to start again from scratch.

CREATIVE ACCOUNTING

Creative accounting is a term generally used in the popular press to refer to what journalists suspect that accountants do to make financial results look much better than they should. This suspicion is prevalent in most countries. It is most acknowledged in the United States by Schilit,[15] in the United Kingdom by Griffiths,[16] in France by Stolowy,[17] and in Australia by Rennie[18] and Craig and Walsh.[19] As a result of this international evidence in the phenomenon, creative accounting has acquired various characterizations and definitions. Descriptions of creative accounting follow:

1. Creative accounting represents the means by which is achieved a deviation between accounts that are anything other than an approximation and that have their basis in the transactions and events of the year under review and the original starting point.[20]

2. Creative accounting involves manipulation, deceit, and misrepresentation.[21]

3. Creative accounting involves an accounting sleight of hand.[22]

4. Creative accounting include activities such as "fiddling the books," "cosmetic reporting," and "window dressing."[23]

5. Creative accounting is the "transformation of financial accounting figures from what they actually are to what preparers desire by taking advantage of the existing rules and/or ignoring some or all of them."[24] It involves both "window dressing" and "off-balance sheet financing." Window dressing is defined as the arrangement of affairs so that the financial statements give a misleading or unrepresentative impression of their financial position.[25] Off-balance sheet financing is defined as "the funding or refunding of a company's operations in such a way that, under legal requirements and existing accounting conventions, some or all of the finance may not be shown on its balance sheet."[26]

6. Creative accounting was also referred to as the use of accounting gimmicks to boost anemic earnings or to smooth out erratic earnings.[27] This is accomplished by the use of seven major shenanigans defined as follows:

   a. Recording revenue before it is earned

   b. Creating fictitious revenue

   c. Boosting profits with nonrecurring transactions

   d. Shifting current expenses to a later period

   e. Failing to record or disclose liabilities

   f. Shifting current income to a later period

   g. Shifting future expenses to an earlier period.[28]

Shenanigans are defined as follows:

Unlike obscenity, financial shenanigans are easy to define but more difficult to detect in practice. Financial shenanigans are actions or omissions intended to hide or distort the real financial performance or financial condition of an entity. They range from minor deceptions (such as failing to clearly segregate operating from non-operating gains and losses) to more serious misapplications of accounting principles (such as failing to write off worthless assets; they also include fraudulent behavior, such as the recording of fictitious revenue to overstate the real financial performance).[29]

EXAMPLES OF CREATIVE ACCOUNTING

Examples of creative accounting from different countries have been documented in the literature. In France, the titles of professional and academic articles give a clear appreciation of the magnitude and the gravity of the problem. The terms and/or titles include[30] (1) the "art of cooking the books,"[31] (2) "the art of computing its profits,"[32] (3) "the art of presenting a balance sheet,"[33] (4) "the provisions or the art of saving money,"[34] (5) "a fine art."[35] Like human beings, French accounts are "made up,"[36] with "their book unproved,"[37] getting a "face lift"[38] with "depreciation muscled and provisions plumped,"[39] "dressed,"[40] and "cleaned."[41] Stolowy[42] goes one step further by identifying the options available within French generally accepted accounting principles that can be used to generate creative accounting solutions; similar categories were also offered by Bonnet.[43]

Evidence for creative accounting was also noticed for Spain.[44] But, the United States and the United Kingdom seem to provide a more favorable terrain for the creative accounting process. The U.K. evidence on creative accounting is provided by Griffiths,[45] Naser,[46] and Smith.[47] Smith's book identifies specific cases of creative accounting in the use of accounting techniques on acquisition and disposal, extraordinary and exceptional items, off-balance-sheet finance, contingent liabilities, capitalization of costs, brand accounting, changes in depreciation policy, convertibles with put options, pension fund accounting, and currency mismatching.[48] The following clever explanation is provided for the choice of the title of the book:

The title *Accounting for Growth* was a deliberate pun. We feel that much of the apparent growth in profits which had occurred in the 1980's was the result of accounting sleight of hand rather than genuine economic growth, and we set out to expose the main techniques involved, and to give live examples of companies using those techniques.[49]

Naser defined creative accounting as

1) the process of manipulating accounting figures by taking advantage of the loopholes in accounting rules and the choices of measurement and disclosure practices in them to transform financial statements from what they should be, to what preparers would prefer to see reported, and 2) the process by which transactions are structured so as to produce the required accounting results rather than reporting transactions in a neutral and consistent way.[50]

From a review of the literature he identified the following factors that may motivate managers to adopt creative accounting schemes:

1. *Misinformation, signaling, and financial motives.* This argument is derived from Peasnell and Yaansah's[51] distinction between the misinformation and signaling motives and financial motives to establish creative accounting schemes.[52]

2. *The agency and the political cost incentives.* This argument is derived from the argument that the choice of accounting techniques depends on the political process of cash flow effects and contracting.

3. *Poor management.* This argument is derived from the thesis that poor management, by neglecting the system of accounting information and failing to respond to change, resorts to creative accounting to reduce the predictive nature of certain ratios.[53]

4. *Reducing the uncertainty and risk.* This is derived from an argument made by Goodfellow[54] that creative accounting schemes are used as a result of increased volatility in the related market elements, interest, inflation and exchange rates.

5. *The weakness of the current accounting concepts, particularly under inflation.* This is derived from arguments made that off-balance-sheet financing schemes are the result of the lack of authoritative accounting guidance in the subject,[55] and as a result of the failure of historical cost accounting to deal effectively with inflation.[56]

Naser[57] also illustrated schemes of creative accounting associated with short-term investment, accounting for stock, accounting for tangible fixed assets, accounting for intangible assets, accounting for long-term liabilities, and accounting for shareholders' contributed capital. Griffiths[58] illustrated similar schemes associated with income and expenses, foreign currencies, pensions, stock, current assets, share capital, fixed assets, cash and borrowings, off-balance-sheet financing, acquisitions and mergers, brands and goodwill, and deferred taxation. Despite the Accounting Standards Board's (ASB) effort to outflow the most flagrant abuses, creative accounting goes on in the United Kingdom. Griffiths offers the following explanation:

The biggest problem it [the ASB] faces is the unwitting conspiracy between the city and the industry which ensures that the black and white which so many appear to demand will be condemned always to a murky grey. While much is made of the tension between companies and their investors there is a remarkable overlap in their interests. Both would like to see a steady increase in a business's earnings growth profile. In reality it is rarely achievable. However, that does nothing to diminish the zealous pursuit of this elusive holy grail.[59]

In the U.S. context, various books presented flagrant cases of creative accounting.[60] The most recent example by Schilit identified seven so-called shenanigans. They are discussed as follows:

1. The first shenanigan consists of recording revenue too soon, either before the earnings process has been completed or before an exchange has occurred. It is generally done by

   a. shipping goods before a sale is finalized.

   b. Recording revenue when important uncertainties exist as in the cases where (1) the risks and the benefit of ownership have not been transferred to the buyer, (2) the buyer may return the goods, and (3) the buyer may not pay for the goods.

   c. Recording revenue when future services are still due, especially in the case of hasty recognition of franchise revenue.

2. The second shenanigan consists of recording bogus revenues. It is generally done by:

   a. Recording income on exchange of similar assets.

   b. Recording refunds from suppliers as revenue.

   c. Using bogus estimates of interim financial reports.[61]

3. The third shenanigan consists of boosting income with onetime gains. It is generally done by:

   a. Boosting profits by selling undervalued assets where the undervaluation was a result of one of the following situations:

     • "A Company acquired assets in a business combination that was accounted for as a pooling of interest.

     • A Company uses the LIFO [last in, first out] inventory method (especially with many inventory pools).

     • A Company acquired real estate (or other investments) years ago that has appreciated considerably in value."[62]

   b. Boosting profits by retiring debt.

   c. Failing to segregate unusual and nonrecurring gains or losses from recurring income.

   d. Burying losses under noncontinuing operations.

4. The fourth shenanigan consists of shifting current expenses to a later permit. It is generally done by:

   a. Improperly capitalizing costs, notably start-up costs.

   b. Depreciating or amortizing costs too slowly by choosing long amortization periods for intangibles and leasehold improvements and by increasing the depreciation or amortization period.

   c. Failing to write off worthless assets by not writing off bad loans and other uncollectibles and by keeping worthless investments on the books.[63]

5. The fifth shenanigan consists of failing to record or disclose all liabilities. It is generally done by:

   a. Reporting revenue rather than a liability when cash is received.

   b. Failing to accrue expected or contingent liabilities.

   c. Failing to disclose commitments and contingencies.

   d. Engaging in transactions to keep debt off the books.[64]

6. The sixth shenanigan consists of shifting current income to a later period by creating reserves to shift sales revenue to a later period.

7. The seventh shenanigan consists of shifting future expenses to the current period. It is done by:

a. Accelerating discretionary expenses into the current period by prepaying operating expenses or decreasing the depreciation or amortization period.

b. Writing off future years' depreciation or amortization.[65]

FLEXIBILITY AND CREATIVE ACCOUNTING

The U.S. generally accepted accounting principles have tended to shy away from rigid positions in accounting problems and provided flexibility allowing judgment and choices among various options. What resulted from this flexibility and the need to exercise judgment is a move toward creativity in the judgment, leading potentially to creative accounting schemes. In short, there is a continuum of thinking going from flexibility to creativity to creative accounting.

As stated by Jameson:

Creative accounting is not against the law. It operates within the letter both of the law and of accounting standards but it is quite clearly against the spirit of both. . . . It is essentially a process of using the rules, the flexibility provided by them and the omissions within them, to make financial statements look somewhat different from what was intended by the rule. It consists of rule-bending and loophole-seeking.[66]

In what follows, some of the options available under U.S. GAAP that may lead to creativity and creative accounting are presented.

The Balance Sheet

1. The balance sheet is supposed to be a reflection of the financial structure of the firm. Unfortunately, historical cost is the common valuation basis of most assets and liabilities. What's missing are the current values of the assets and liabilities as well as significant nonquantitative information. Basically, the historical cost basis is a "creative accounting" device used for the sake of practicality and verifiability to avoid showing the fair value of the firm.

2. The assets are segregated in current and noncurrent assets where the rule of thumb is that if an asset is to be turned into cash or to be used to pay a current liability within a year of the operating cycle, whichever is longer, that asset is considered a current asset. The classification scheme is arbitrary and can easily be used as a form of creative accounting classification.

3. Each type of assets and liabilities can be classified or measured according to different options and refinements available within generally accepted accounting principles and therefore is an ideal tool for creative accounting. They are illustrated in the next sections of this chapter.

4. The balance sheet is a stock concept, reflecting the so-called financial structure at one time, which is the end of the fiscal year. Between the end of the year and issuance of the balance sheet, subsequent events or post–balance sheet events need to be disclosed in the notes. These events generally provide

evidence about conditions that (1) either existed at the balance sheet, affect the estimates used in preparing financial statements, and call for additional adjustments or (2) existed after the balance sheet date and call for additional disclosure. Examples of subsequent events that require disclosure include:

a. Sale of bonds or capital stock; stock splits or stock dividends.

b. Business combination pending or effected.

c. Settlement of litigation when the event giving rise to the claim took place subsequent to the balance sheet date.

d. Loss of plant or inventories from fire or flood.

e. Losses on receivables resulting from conditions (such as customer's major casualty) arising subsequent to the balance sheet date.

f. Gains or losses on certain marketable securities.[67]

A form of creative accounting is the failure to adjust and/or disclose these events.

Income Statement

1. The bottom figure of net income for the year does not reveal the real picture. More useful insights are revealed from a segregation of results from regular continuing operations from the results of nonrecurring activities. For example, an $18.6 million income reported by National Patent Development, a maker of soft contact lenses, is a markup of (1) $7.5 million of income from gain on the sale of stock by a subsidiary, (2) $2.4 million gain in the exchange of stock, (3) $ 3.6 million from gain on the sale of stock in its investment portfolio, and (4) $3.2 million from the settlement of lawsuits related to patent infringements. These nonoperating or nonrecurring gains are not sustainable.[68]

2. The income figures are much affected by the type of accounting methods in general and allocation methods in particular. One can just imagine the surprise of those actors, writers, and producers who signed "net profit contracts" in highly successful movies to find out later that, thanks to big studios' ability to allocate overhead costs creatively, the movies declared a loss.

3. Revenues consist generally of sales, fees, interest, dividends, and rents while gains and losses consist of many types resulting from the sale of investments, sale of plant assets, settlement of liabilities, write-off of assets due to obsolescence or casualty, and theft; expenses consists of cost of goods sold, depreciation, interest, rent, salaries and wages, and taxes. Creative accounting blurs the distinction between revenues and gains and between expenses and losses to highlight a different performance[69] between operating activities and nonoperating activities. For example, loss-reporting Internet firms may want to highlight a positive gross margin by shifting some product costs to period costs or to unusual activities.

4. Most firms have adopted a "modified, all-inclusive concept" with irregular items classified in the following five general categories:

a. Discontinued operations
b. Extraordinary items
c. Unusual gains and losses
d. Changes in accounting principle
e. Changes in estimate

Each of these categories leads to good potential for creative accounting. Let's examine each:

Discontinued operation. The profession requires that the results of operations of a segment that will be disposed of be reported in conjunction with the gain and loss on disposal, separately from continuing operations. However, the disposal of a part of a business, the shifting of activities from one time of a business to another, and the phasing out of a product line and the changes due to technological improvement, which all contribute to disposal of assets, are not considered disposals of a segment or a business and are not classified as discontinued operations. In addition, if a loss is expected on disposal, the estimated loss is reported at the measurement date, while an expected gain is reported when realized, which is ordinarily the disposal date. The conservative position creates an opportunity for immediate recognition of losses and a deferring of gains until realized.

Extraordinary items. APB opinion No. 30 gives the following definitions:

"Extraordinary items are events and transactions that are distinguished by their unusual nature and by the infrequency of their occurrence." Both of the following criteria must be met to classify an event or transaction as an extraordinary item:

a. Unusual Nature. The underlying event or transaction should possess a high degree of abnormality and be of a type clearly unrelated to, or only incidentally related to, the ordinary and typical activities of the entity, taking into account the environment in which the entity operates.
b. Infrequency of Occurrence. The underlying event or transaction should be of a type that would not reasonably be expected to recur in the foreseeable future, taking into account the environment in which the entity operates.[70]

In addition, the APB indicated that the following gains and losses are not extraordinary items:

a. Write-down or write-off of receivables, inventories, equipment leased to others, deferred research and development costs, or other intangible assets.
b. Gains or losses from exchange or translation of foreign currencies, including those relating to major devaluations and revaluations.

c. Gains or losses on disposal of a segment of a business.

d. Other gains or losses from sale or abandonment of property, plant, or equipment used in the business.

e. Effects of strikes, including those against competitors and major suppliers.

f. Adjustment of accruals on long-term contracts.[71]

This definition makes it difficult to classify an item as extraordinary. At the same time it allows the exercise of a lot of judgment in determining whether an item should be reported as extraordinary. A firm may consider a write-down or write-off of receivables or inventory an extraordinary item if it can prove that they are the result of an "unusual" and "infrequent" event such as an earthquake. The creative accounting part resides in finding the good excuse of "unusual" and "infrequent" nature of the activity. This situation is helped by the inconsistent professional position that considers (1) the disposal of a business segment at a gain or loss not as an extraordinary item and (2) the material gains or losses from extinguishment of debt as an extraordinary item.

Unusual gains and losses. These are unusual or infrequent items that are disclosed separately from extraordinary items. The most frequent and abused item, a sign of creative accounting, is the well-known and well-used restructuring change relating to major reorganization of a company's affairs, such as costs incurred for employee layoffs, plant closings, write offs of assets, and so on. Some firms tend to exaggerate with this form of creative accounting, such as when restructuring changes were taken six years in a row between 1988 and 1993 by Citicorp, five out of six years in 1988–1994 by Eastman Kodak Co., and seven out of ten years from 1985 to 1994 by Westinghouse Electric. These known "first cousins" to extraordinary gains and losses are the most flagrant form of creative accounting in the income statement.

Changes in accounting principle. The adoption of an accounting principle different from the one previously used is recognized by the inclusion of the cumulative effect net of tax in the current year's income statement. The change of inventory method or depreciation method may be dictated by either economic circumstances or purely creative accounting purposes to affect the level of profit.

Changes in estimates. They are normal, nonrecurring corrections and adjustments, such as changes in the realizability of receivables and inventories, changes in estimated lives of equipment, intangible assets, changes in estimated liability for warranty costs, income taxes and salary payments that change the income statement only in the account affected. They provide ideal options for creative accounting.

5. While the income contains all the revenues, expenses, gains, and losses recognized during a period, many items bypass income and are "dumped" directly in the equity section as "comprehensive income." Examples of these items include gains and losses in available-for-sale securities.

Cash

1. Cash consists of coin, currency, available funds on deposits at the bank, and negotiable instruments such as money orders, certified checks, cashier's checks, personal checks, and bank drafts. Money market funds are generally classified as temporary investments. If they provide checking account privileges, they are classified as cash. Checking account privileges can increase cash and decrease temporary investments.

2. Lending institutions may require firms to maintain a minimum cash balance in checking or saving accounts, known as compensating balances. These legally restructured deposits need to be disclosed separately among the "cash and cash equivalent items" in current assets. Similarly, restricted cash for specific purposes such as petty cash, payroll, and dividend funds also deserves a separate classification. The separate classification applies also to bank overdraft.

3. Short-term paper needs to be classified as temporary investments. Similarly, postdated checks and IOUs should be classified as receivables, while postage in hand should be classified as prepaid expenses. Any misclassification of accounts cited in the previous paragraphs is merely an attempt at creative accounting.

Receivables

1. A distinction should be made between trade receivables and nontrade receivables. Examples of nontrade receivables include (1) advances to employees and subsidiaries, (2) dividends and interest receivable, (3) deposits to cover potential damages and losses, (4) deposits as guarantee of performance in payments, and (5) claims. These nontrade receivables may be classified as accounts receivable or notes receivable.

2. Short-term receivables are valued and reported at then net realizable value, which is what is expected to be received in cash. This requires the estimation of both uncollectible receivables and any returns and allowances to be granted. Recording the uncollectibles may be either through the direct write-off method or the allowance method. The allowance method allows either the use of percentage-of-sales (income statement) approach, the percentage-of-receivable (balance sheet) approach, or the aging schedule approach. While the percentage-of-receivable approach provides a more accurate valuation of receivables in the balance sheet, the percentage-of-sales approach provides better matching in the income statement.

3. More creative accounting is possible in the creation of two other contra accounts to the accounts receivable, namely, the allowance for sales returns and allowances and the allowance for collection expenses.

4. Accounts or notes receivables may be transferred to another company for cash. Depending on meeting specific conditions, the transfer may be accounted for as a secured borrowing or a sale of receivables, with a different impact in

the balance sheet. A sale occurs if these conditions are met: (1) the transferred assets are isolated from the transferer, (2) the transferee has the right to pledge or sell the assets, and (3) the transferer does not maintain control through a repurchase agreement. If the conditions are not met, it is accounted for as a secured borrowing.

5. Creative accounting is possible in the classification of receivables if there are "failures" in (1) the segregation of different types of receivables, (2) ensuring that the valuation accounts are appropriately offset against the proper receivable accounts, (3) the disclosure of any loss contingencies on receivables, (4) the disclosure of receivables pledged as collateral, and (5) the disclosure of significant concentration of risks arising from receivables.

6. Because the numerical guidelines exist for concentration risk, three items need to be disclosed: (1) information on the characteristic that determines the concentration, (2) amount of loss that could occur upon nonperformance, and (3) information on any collateral related to the receivable.

Inventory

1. For a manufacturing concern, inventories refer to finished goods inventory, goods-in-process inventories, and raw materials inventory. A separate manufacturing or factory supplies inventory may also be included. Proper segregation of the firm items would be more informative than the disclosure of a single amount for inventories.

2. Another useful segregation would include goods in transit, consigned goods, and special sales arrangements such as (1) sales with buyback agreement, (2) sales with high rates of return, and (3) sales on installment.

3. In sales with buyback arrangements, the firm may finance its inventory and not show an inventory or a liability on its balance sheet. Basically, it involves a product financing arrangement whereby Firm X sells an inventory to Firm Y and agrees at the same time to repurchase it later at a set price. Firm Y uses the inventory as a collateral to get a loan and to pay Firm X. Firm X eventually repurchases the inventory in the future, allowing Firm Y to use the proceeds to repay the loan. This allows Firm X to avoid personal property taxes in some states, remove current liability from its balance sheet, and affect its income.

4. In the case of sales with a high rate of return as in publishing, music, toys, and sporting goods, the firm may record the sales and estimate sales returns and allowance amount or wait until it has indications of the amount of inventory that will be returned. Creative accounting may be needed to determine when the inventory is sold and removed from the balance sheet.

5. In the case of sales in installment, the question is whether to withhold the legal title to the merchandise until all the payments have been made or record the sale after an estimation of the bad debt.

6. Product costs are "attached" to the inventory while the selling and administrative expenses are charged as period costs. While it is easy to consider

direct material and direct labor as product costs, the manufacturing overhead costs are allocated. Some of these costs may be "improperly" treated as period costs in an effort to "boost" the level of gross margin.

7. Interest costs related to assets constructed for internal use on assets produced as discrete projects (such as ships or real estate projects) for lease or sale are capitalized. Creative accounting may lead to the capitalization of interest costs for projects that are routine and repetitive.

8. The use of absorption costing for GAAP reporting and tax purposes leads to a profit that is more a function of production rather than sales strategy (i.e., it leads to the creation of "inventory" profits).

9. Costs such as bidding, warehousing, purchasing, officer salaries, and administrative and selling expenses may be capitalized for tax purposes. Creative accounting may lead to efforts to capitalize some of these costs for GAAP reporting.

10. Cost-flow assumptions include (1) the specific identification method, (2) the average cost method, (3) the first in, first out method (FIFO), and (4) the last in, first out method (LIFO). The cost-flow assumptions are not necessarily consistent with the flow of goods. While the choice of a cost-flow assumption should be to best reflect periodic income, other considerations may prevail.

11. Firms may use LIFO for tax and GAAP reporting and use other cost-flow techniques for internal reporting. As a result, a LIFO reserve is created and is equal to the difference between (1) inventory at the lower of LIFO cost or market and (2) inventory at replacement cost or at the lower of cost determined by some acceptable inventory accounting method or market. Either the LIFO reserve or the replacement cost of the inventory should be disclosed.

12. The use of LIFO has many benefits. However, LIFO liquidation, resulting from the erosion of LIFO inventory, can lead to distortions in net income and heavy tax payments.

13. Dollar-value FIFO techniques are generally used to protect LIFO layers from erosion. Subjectivity may enter in the selection of the items to be put in a pool. In addition, the firm may set up pools that are easy to liquidate, thereby increasing income by decreasing inventory and matching lower cost inventory to revenues. Creative accounting may become a matter of setting an adequate number of pools.

14. Inventories are valued on the basis of the lower of cost or market. The market is determined by the middle value of (1) net realizable value, (2) replacement cost, and (3) net realizable value less a normal profit margin and depends on judgments pertaining to (1) the sales price, (2) the normal profit margin, and (3) the replacement cost.

Property, Plant, and Equipment

1. Property, plant, and equipment or plant assets or fixed assets are valued at historical cost, which fails to account for changes in specific and general price levels.

2. Self-constructed assets either do not include fixed overhead or include an allocated portion. Creative accounting may enter into the allocation process. In addition, actual interest capitalized is a result of judgment in (1) the qualifying assets, (2) the capitalization period, and (3) the amount to capitalize.

3. Judgment and creativity may be required for the capitalization of costs subsequent to acquisition, such as additions, improvements and replacements, rearrangement and reinstallation, and repairs. As an example, if the judgment about repairs is that it is ordinary, the change is expensed; however, if the judgment is that it is major, it is capitalized.

Depreciation

1. Depreciation is a way of allocating the cost of a tangible asset over an estimated life of the asset. It requires a judgment on (1) the appropriate systematic and rational way of allocation and (2) an estimate of the useful life of the asset.

2. While the estimation of the useful life is supposed to consider physical factors (such as casualty or expiration of physical life) and economic factors (such as obsolescence), arbitraries in the estimation of the useful life may be a result of the use of creative accounting.

3. Depreciation techniques include the (1) activity method, the (2) straight line method, (3) decreasing change accelerated methods such as sum-of-the-year's digits and declining-balance method, and (4) special depreciation methods such as group and composite methods and hybrid combination methods. The selection of a technique is supposed to be based on securing the best matching of revenues and expenses. Other considerations such as practicality, lowering of taxes, and creative accounting may predominate.

4. In addition to the judgments about depreciation, firms may elect to make judgments about the need to recognize impairments of long-lived assets. Examples of events and circumstances that may lead to an impairment follow:

A significant decrease in the market value of an asset

A significant change in the extent or manner in which an asset is used

A significant adverse change in legal factors or in the business climate that affects the value of an asset

An accumulation of costs significantly in excess of the amount originally expected to acquire or construct an asset

A projection or forecast that demonstrates continuing losses associated with an asset.[72]

The impairment decision rests on a recoverability test comparing the sum of the expected future net cash flows (undiscounted) to carrying amount of the asset. The events and circumstances leading to impairment as well as the recoverability tests may rest on judgment based on creative accounting considerations.

5. Either the full cost concept or the successful efforts concept may be used for the accounting for exploration costs in the oil and gas industry. One may early guess that big oil companies will rely on the successful efforts method while small, exploration-oriented companies will rely on full cost accounting. A large oil company using full cost accounting will show a material increase in income.

6. Knowledgeable guesses, at best, are used for the estimation of recoverable reserves and disposal value.

Intangible Assets

1. Intangibles, such as patents, copyrights, franchises, goodwill, organization costs, and trademarks or trade means, are characterized by both the lack of physical evidence and the degree of uncertainty concerning future benefits. In the cases of both specifically identifiable intangibles and goodwill-type intangibles, they are capitalized if purchased and expensed if created internally. If capitalized, they are amortized over a period not exceeding forty years. The flexibility and the judgment entering into the determination of the useful life of the intangibles lead to possible creative accounting scenarios.

2. Both product patents and process patents are amortized over the legal life or the useful life, whichever is shorter. In addition, the legal fees are capitalized as part of the patents. Both the determination of the useful life and legal fees are left to judgments conducive to creative accounting solutions. For example, the value of a patent on a balance sheet may just increase because of the mounting costs in successfully defending a patent suit. The higher the legal fees, the higher the value of the patents.

3. The legal life of copyrights (life of the creator plus fifty years) is not a guarantee that the firm may choose a shorter period of time for the amortization of copyrights.

4. Even though the firm is allowed up to forty years to amortize a trademark or trade name, it may choose a shorter period.

5. A totally arbitrary period may also be chosen for the amortization of organization cost, even though the maximum period is forty years.

6. The operating losses incurred in the early years by a developing-stage firm can be capitalized by some firms, although expensing makes more sense.

7. Franchises with limited life are expenses, while franchises with an indefinite life or a perpetual franchise should be capitalized and amortized over a period not exceeding forty years. The definition of the life of the franchise is left to contractual arrangements that may be defined with creative accounting scenarios in mind.

8. Goodwill is the difference between the purchase price and the fair market value of the assets. It is generally amortized over a period not exceeding forty years. Both the valuation of assets and the choice of the amortization period

create various scenarios for creative accounting. The amortization of negative goodwill, or bad will, will create the unusual situation of increasing earnings.

9. Both specifically intangible and goodwill types of intangibles may be subject to loss or impairment if it is judged that the undiscounted sum of future net cash flows is less than the carrying value of the intangible.

10. The costs of research and development activities are expensed when incurred. The judgment of activities that are considered as R&D activities and the activities not considered R&D are a matter of judgment and therefore susceptible to creative accounting scenarios.

11. Software costs for software created internally are expensed until technological feasibility has been established. Then, they are capitalized and amortized over future periods. Software costs, if purchased to be sold, leased, or marketed to third parties, are capitalized and amortized over a future period.

Current Liabilities

1. Current liabilities are obligations whose liquidation is reasonably expected to require use of existing resources properly classified as current assets or the creation of other current liabilities and that have a maturity within one year of the operating cycle, whichever is longer. The account will not be comparable from one industry to another given the different operating cycles adopted.

2. Both the maturing portion of long-term debt and a liability that is due within a year (or operating cycle) should be classified as a current liability. Any other long-term debt classified as current liabilities is a form of creative accounting.

3. Property taxes payable can be changed in (1) the year in which paid, (2) the year ending on assessment (or lien) date, (3) the year beginning on assessment (or lien) date, (4) calendar or fiscal year of taxpayer including assessment (or lien) date, (5) calendar or fiscal year of taxpayer prior to the payment date, (6) fiscal year of governing body levying the tax, and (7) year appearing on the tax bill.

4. While gain contingencies are recognized only in the notes, loss contingencies are recognized by a charge to expense and a liability if the event is probable and the loss can be reasonably estimated. Whether an event is probable, reasonably probable, or remote is left to the exercise of judgment and hence creativity.

5. Both litigation, claims, and assessments as well as unfilled suits and unasserted claims whose outcomes can be predicted need to be recognized by a liability. Failure to do so is clearly a manifestation of creative accounting.

6. A contingent liability that is generally not recorded or infrequently recorded by a lot of firms is environmental liability in spite of the staggering costs that could be incurred for the cleaning of toxic waste sites. A range for the liability needs to be determined, and a best estimate within the range is to be

reported. Failure to find a best estimate results in the reporting of the lower end of the range and the disclosure of the higher end of the range.

Long-Term Debt

1. Long-term debt is issued with specific covenants and restrictions stated in the bond indenture or note agreement. To the extent that some of these stipulations are important, they should be disclosed in the notes. Failure to do so defeats the full disclosure principle.

2. Because of differences between the stated rate or coupon rate and the market or effective rate, bonds are issued at either a premium or a discount. The amortization of the discount or premium may be based on either the effective interest method or the straight-line method.

3. The debt issue costs are generally capitalized, then amortized.

4. While debt may be extinguished through cash payments, a lot of firms resort to in-substance defeasance, which requires the firm to set up an irrecoverable trust of securities whose principal and interest are pledged to pay off debt.

5. Firms may try to acquire debt and avoid recording the obligations on the balance sheet through various forms of off-balance-sheet financing. This may be easily accomplished by two entities, X and Y, forming a new entity, W, that borrows funds that are guaranteed by the firms X and Y. In this case X and Y have incurred more debt that does not appear on the balance sheets. The agreement with the new entity may include either a take-or-pay contract or a through-put agreement. These off-balance-sheet financing schemes are good examples of creative accounting schemes.

6. It is interesting to note that in case of trouble debt restructuring whose terms are modified, the official accounting positions that (1) the creditor's loss is based on cash flows discounted at the historical effective rate of interest and (2) the debtor's gain are computed on the basis of undiscounted amounts.

Stockholders' Equity

1. Subscriptions receivable, which indicate the amount yet to be collected before subscribed stock will be issued, may be accounted for as subscriptions receivable on the balance sheet (a current asset account) or a deduction from stockholders' equity (a contra equity account). The contra equity account is favored by the SEC.

2. Stock issued for services or property other than cash is valued at the more clearly determinable fair value of the stock issued or fair market value of the noncash considerations received. A choice of the fair market value of the noncash considerations received may lead to judgments that cause either an overvaluation of the assets, resulting in "watered stock," or an undervaluation of the assets, resulting in "secret reserves."

3. The costs of issuing stocks may be (1) debited to paid-in-capital in excess of par or stated value, as a reduction of the amounts paid-in, or (2) capitalized as an organization cost and expensed over an arbitrary time not exceeding forty years.

4. Although treasury stock is subtracted from the total common stock, some firms may find an "unusual" explanation for classifying it as an asset on the balance sheet.

5. Treasury stock may be accounted for at the cost method or the par value method or a method required by a state law.

6. In the case of "greenmail payments" to repurchase shares to avert a hostile takeover, the premium is debited to treasury stock rather than charged as an expense.

7. A separable disclosure is needed for redeemable preferred stock, nonredeemable preferred stock, and common stock. The SEC requires that redeemable preferred stock not be included in stockholders' equity.

8. Transient preferred, which is preferred stocks to be redeemed over short periods, is just "thinly" disguised debt.

Retained Earnings

1. Restrictions on payment of dividends and other distributions to owners may exist for (1) firms operating in states using the 1950 Model Business Corporation Acts, (2) firms operating in states using the 1984 Revised Model Business Corporation Act, and (3) firms using hybrid restrictions. Adequate disclosures about these restrictions and the legality of dividends are required.

2. Information on dividend policy warrants disclosure.

3. Property dividends should be based on the fair value of the property to be distributed, and gains or losses resulting from the reevaluation should be recognized.

4. Whenever appropriation of retained earnings takes place, the firm should offer an adequate explanation for the action taken.

Investments

1. Various classification schemes are needed to account for investments creating opportunities for creative accounting.

2. Debt securities can be classified as (1) held-to-maturity, (2) trading securities, or c) available-for-sale. The unrealized gains and losses are recognized in net income for trading securities and in other comprehensive income and as a separate component of stockholders' equity for available-for-sale securities. As such, the classification judgment has an impact on the level of income reported.

3. Equity securities for holding less than 20 percent are also classified as

either available-for-sale or trading securities. The unrealized gains and losses are also recognized in net income for trading equity securities and in other comprehensive income for available-for-sale securities.

4. Firms may elect to transfer securities from one classification group to another, thereby affecting the level of income or the level of comprehensive income.

Revenue Recognition

1. Revenue recognition means that the revenues have been both realized and earned. The timing of recognition is (1) the date of sale for the sale of product from an inventory, (2) services performed and billable for rendering a service, (3) as time passes or assets are used for the use of an asset, and (4) date of sale for the sale of asset other than inventory. However, departures from the sales basis are frequent and need to be justified.

2. For revenue recognized at a point of sales, creative accounting may take place in three cases of (1) sales with buyback agreements, (2) sales when right of return exists, and (3) trade loafing and channel surfing.

3. Is a sale with buyback agreements a sale or creative accounting?

4. When should sales with right of return be recorded? Should they be recorded when the return privileges have expired?

5. Are the techniques of trade loafing and channel surfing legitimate sales or a form of creative accounting? Offering deep discounts to generate "phony sales" is a form of profit distortion and creative accounting.

6. For long-term construction contracts, revenue is recognized before delivery using either (1) the percentage-of-completion method or (2) the completed-contract method. When using the percentage-of-completion method, the determination of the progress toward completion is based on judgmental techniques such as (1) cost-to-cost method, (2) the "efforts expended methods," and (3) "units of work performed method."

7. When revenue is deferred until cash is received, two techniques may be used, either (1) the installment sales method or (2) the cost recovery method.

Income Taxes

1. Deferred tax assets and deferred tax liabilities are recognized as a result of the differences between pretax, financial income and taxable income. Judgment is needed for the portion of deferred tax asset that will not be realized and that needs to be recognized by a valuation allowance.

2. The deferred tax accounts need to be classified as either net current amount or net noncurrent amount based on a judgment of the expected reversal date of the temporary difference (if not related to a specific asset or liability).

Leases

4. One or more of four criteria need to be met before a lease is recorded as a capital lease resulting in capitalization on the balance sheet. Not meeting any of the four criteria results in classifying and accounting for the lease as an operating lease. The lease contract may be written in such a way as to fail to meet any of the four criteria. This is a form of "creative contracting" resulting in "creative accounting."

CONCLUSIONS

Good evidence of designed or managed accounting is the amount of creativity in accounting practice. The creativity is generally a by-product of the flexibility and the variety of options available within GAAP as well as the result of very "liberal" reading of the accounting rules. This creativity is manifest in the inside use of (1) selective financial misrepresentation, (2) big bath accounting, and (3) creative accounting.

NOTES

1. L. Revsine, "The Selective Financial Misrepresentation Hypothesis," *Accounting Horizons* (December 1991), pp. 16–27.

2. Ibid., p. 16.

3. G.J. Stigler, "The Theory of Economic Regulation," *Bell Journal of Economics and Management Science* (Spring 1971), pp. 3–21.

4. Revsine, "The Selective Financial Misrepresentation Hypothesis," p. 17.

5. Ibid.

6. Ibid., p. 19.

7. Ibid., p. 24.

8. "SEC Chairman Discusses Earnings Management," *Deloitte & Touche Review* (October 12, 1998), p. 1.

9. P.N. Healy, "The Effect of Bonus Schemes on Accounting Decisions," *Journal of Accounting and Economics* 7 (1985), p. 86.

10. N.L. Moore, "Management Changes and Discretionary Accounting Decisions," *Journal of Accounting Research* (Spring 1973), pp. 100–107.

11. H.M. Schilit, *Financial Shenanigans* (New York: McGraw-Hill, 1993), p. 121.

12. R.M. Copeland and M.L. Moore, "The Financial Bath: Is It Common?" *MSU Business Topics* (Autumn 1972), p. 63.

13. R.E. Kieso and J.J. Weygandt, *Intermediate Accounting*, 9th ed. (New York: John Wiley & Sons, 1998), p. 1126.

14. Ibid., p. 1126.

15. Schilit, *Financial Shenanigans*.

16. I. Griffiths, *Creative Accounting* (London: Irwin, 1986); I. Griffiths, *New Creative Accounting* (London: Macmillan, 1995).

17. S. Herve, "Comptali Creative," in Bernard Colasse (ed.), *Encyclopedie de Comptabilite, Controle de bestion et audit* (Paris: Economica, 2000), pp. 157–158.

18. P. Revsine, "The Corporate AIDS—Funny Financing and Creative Accounting," *Rydges* (November 1989), pp. 18–20.

19. R. Craig and P. Walsh, "Adjustments for Extraordinary Items, in Smoothing Reported Profit of Listed Australian Companies: Some Empirical Evidence," *Journal of Business Finance and Accounting* (Spring 1989), pp. 229–245.

20. Griffiths, *New Creative Accounting*, pp. vii–viii.

21. M. Jameson, *A Practical Guide to Creative Accounting* (London: Kogan Page, 1988).

22. Pijper, T., *Creative Accounting: The Effectiveness of Financial Reporting in the U.K.* (London: Macmillan, 1994).

23. M.R. Mathews and M.H.B. Perera, *Accounting Theory and Development* (Melbourne: Nelson, 1996), p. 228.

24. K.H.M. Naser, *Creative Financial Accounting: Its Nature and Use* (New York: Prentice-Hall, 1993), p. 2.

25. Ibid., p. 2.

26. Ibid.

27. Schilit, *Financial Shenanigans*, p. ix.

28. Ibid., p. x.

29. Ibid., p. 1.

30. H. Stolowy and G. Breton, "A Framework for the Classification of Accounts Manipulations," Working paper, HEC, Paris, 2001.

31. J.J. Bertolus, "L' Art de Truquez Un Bilan," *Science & Vie Economie* (June 1988), pp. 17–23.

32. M. Lignor, "L'Art de Calculer Ses Benefices," *L'Enterprise* 50 (1989), pp. 17–18, 20.

33. I. Goumin, "L'Art de Presenter Un Bilan," *La Tribune* (March 28, 1991), p. 11.

34. D. Pourquery, "Les Provisions on L' Art de Mettre de l'Argent de Cote," *Science & Vie Economie* 73 (1991), pp. 72–75.

35. D. Le double, "La Creative en Comptabilite," *Semaine Juridique* 25 (1993), p. 224.

36. P. Agede, "Haliller Ses Comptes," *L'Enterprise* 106 (1994), pp. 82–85.

37. P. Lonliere, "Pour Embellir ses Comptes, Teromson Cede Ses Pnetes," *Liberation* (May 5, 1992), pp. 20–32.

38. Agede, "Haliller Ses Comptes," p. 83.

39. Ibid., p. 84.

40. J. Audas, "Le Window-Dressing un L' Halillage des Bilans," *Option Finance* (January 18, 1993), p. 29.

41. A. Feity, "La BIMP Innove pour Nettoyer son Bilan," *Option Finance* (May 30, 1994); N. Sibbert, "Club Mediterrannee—le Nettoyage des Computes," *La Vie Francaise* (February 1–7, 1994), p. 11; J.F. Polo, "Elf Toilette ses Computes avant la Privatisation," *Les Echos* (January 19, 1994), p. 11.

42. Stolowy, "Comptabilite Creative," pp. 157–178.

43. F. Bonnet, *Pieges (et Delices) de la Comptabilite (Creative)* (Paris: Economica, 1995).

44. J. Blake and O. Amat, "Creative Accounting Is Not Just an English Disease," *Management Accounting* (October 1996), p. 54.

45. Griffiths, *Creative Accounting*; Griffiths, *New Creative Accounting*.

46. Naser, *Creative Financial Accounting*.

47. T. Smith, *Accounting for Growth* (London: Century Business, 1996).

48. Ibid.

49. Ibid., p. 4.

50. Naser, *Creative Financial Accounting*, p. 59.

51. Ibid., p. 59.

52. K.V. Peasnell and R.A. Yaasnah, "Off-Balance Sheet Financing," *Certified Research Report 10* (London: Chartered Association of Certified Accountants, 1998).

53. J. Argenti, *Corporate Collapse: The Cause and Symptoms* (New York: McGraw-Hill, 1976).

54. J.M. Goodfellow, "Now You See Thru, Now You Don't," *CA Magazine* (December 1988), pp. 16–23.

55. R. Dieter and J. Watt, "Get off the Balance Sheet," *Financial Executive* (January 1980), pp. 42–49; J.E. Stewart and B.S. Neuhausen, "Financial Instruments and Transactions: The CPA's New Challenge," *Journal of Accounting* (August 1986), pp. 102–112; J. Samuels, C. Rickwood, and A. Piper, *Advanced Financial Accounting* (London: McGraw-Hill, 1989).

56. Argenti, *Corporate Collapse*.

57. Naser, *Creative Financial Accounting*.

58. Griffiths, *New Creative Accounting*.

59. Ibid., p. xi.

60. A.J. Briloff, *Unaccountable Accounting* (New York: Harper & Row, 1972); A.J. Briloff, *More Debits than Credits* (New York: Harper & Row, 1972); Schilit, *Financial Shenanigans*.

61. Ibid., pp. 43–45.

62. Ibid., p. 61.

63. Ibid., p. 79.

64. Ibid., p. 107.

65. Ibid., p. 119.

66. Jameson, *A Practical Guide to Creative Accounting*, p. 20.

67. Kieso and Weygandt, *Intermediate Accounting*, p. 219.

68. Ibid., p. 147.

69. Ibid.

70. "Reporting the Results of Operations," *Opinions of the Accounting Principles Board No. 30* (New York: AICPA, 1973).

71. Ibid.

72. Kieso and Weygandt, *Intermediate Accounting*, p. 557.

SELECTED REFERENCES

Griffiths, I. *Creative Accounting*. London: Irwin, 1986.

Griffiths, I. *New Creative Accounting*. London: Macmillan, 1995.

Jameson, M. *A Practical Guide to Creative Accounting*. London: Kogan Page, 1988.

Naser, K.H.M. *Creative Financial Accounting: Its Nature and Use*. New York: Prentice-Hall, 1993.

Pijper, T. *Creative Accounting: The Effectiveness of Financial Reporting in the U.K.* London: Macmillan, 1994.

Priloff, A.J. *Unaccountable Accounting*. New York: Harper & Row, 1972.

Priloff, A.J. *More Debits than Credits*. New York: Harper & Row, 1976.
Revsine, L. "The Selective Financial Misrepresentation Hypothesis." *Accounting Horizons* (December 1991), pp. 16–27.
Schilit, H.M. *Financial Shenanigans: How to Detect Accounting Criminals and Fraud in Financial Reports*. New York: McGraw-Hill, 1993.
Smith, T. *Accounting for Growth*. London: Century Business, 1996.

Appendix 3A. The Context of the Contemporary Accounting Profession

INTRODUCTION

Standard setting, the practice of the auditing and accounting craft, and accounting research are practiced in a shifting and conflictual terrain as new environmental conditions emerge. These environmental changes may be characterized by three new trends: (1) technical and ideological proletarianization of accountants in public and private practices, (2) the institutional capitalism of the new governing class, and (3) the assimilation of academic accountants into a flawed universal class. This defines a new social order where a diverse group of protagonists from different contradictory classes take, define, and defend their view and the scope of the discipline. This appendix describes the elements of this new order as it bears on conflict in the field of accounting and contributes to the malaise, inadequacies, issues, and unresolved problems facing the accounting world (Belkaoui, 1985b).

GENESIS OF EMERGING STRUCTURAL CHANGES

Most countries in the world are facing economic, social, political, and cultural crises, whether they are developing or developed countries. These crises, which defeat the idea of the stability of monopoly capitalism, emanate from the organization of production at the world level, not just within the U.S. economy. At the world level there is no monopoly capitalism, but there are a large number of firms competing in an overall, anarchistic situation of global production (Bergesen, 1983, p. 11). Despite the efforts to solve these crises, the prospects of immediate relief seem dim. In effect, regarding the most pressing problems of inflation, unemployment, inequality, imbalances in international trade, and Third World debt, governments have resorted to the politics of short-term situations without a clear vision of the desired evolution of societies and economies (Touraine, 1977, p. 3).

Source: Reprinted from A. Riahi-Belkaoui, "The Context of the Contemporary Accounting Profession," *Advances in Public Interest Accounting* 4, 1991, pp. 83–97. Copyright 1991. Reprinted with permission from Elsevier Science.

These crises persist, leaving a trail of failures in the economic and political relations of capitalist reproduction. This should not be surprising, as it is in the nature of capitalistic production to be constantly exposed to a variety of internally and externally generated disturbances setting off general crises.

A Marxist view of these crises stems from the position that "though capitalism is capable of self-expansion, the accumulation process deepens the internal contradictions on which it is based, until they erupt in a crisis: the limits to capitalism are *internal* to it" (Shaikh, 1978, p. 220). These contradictions originate in the needed class structure in which the continued existence of one dominating class requires the continued existence of a subordinate class. Societies are now constituted by groups of protagonists competing for economic and social power and political authority. Dominant modes of interaction, however, consistently favor one category of actors and result in the systematic exploitation of others (Offe, 1985, p. 2). At every societal level, groups of protagonists face each other over the contradictions that separate them. As an example, in the debt crises, financial capital and industrial capital find themselves in conflict; management and shareholders are in disagreement in management buyouts; and employees and management dispute each other's claims to pension funds.

Accounting is not immune to these contradictions. The management of certified public accountant (CPA) firms ally themselves with the managers of institutional capitalism, while the working accountants in CPA firms are proletarianized. Because of these contradictory interests within the profession, management attempts to create a "manufactured consciousness" of the users through a domination of information. Accounting academics strive to develop a consciousness that can help accountants to function as a universal class. Instead, they create a flawed universal class, motivated by self-interest and the need to monopolize their special brand of "cultural" capital.

The emerging structural changes in the accounting environment (i.e., contradictory classes in the accounting profession and academic accountants as a flawed universal class) are contradictions created by the global conflicts and the emergence of new protagonists in the accounting environment as well as in other environments. They lead to class differences and conflicts over the role and conduct of the discipline. They are examined next.

TECHNICAL AND IDEOLOGICAL PROLETARIANIZATION OF ACCOUNTANTS

The first element in the new era of conflict is the emergence of new class differences among accountants. Accountants as professional employees in accounting or nonaccounting organizations are considered members of the new class of salaried professionals. They are identified by Bell and other "postindustrial" theorists as major protagonists of the new coming postindustrial society or as members of the "new working class," "professional-managerial class," "new petty bourgeoisie," or "new class" and are identified by Marxist theorists as major new actors in contemporary capitalism (Bell, 1961; Ehrenreich and Ehrenreich, 1976; Poulantzas, 1975; Touraine, 1977).[1] There was a tremendous growth of accountants in the labor force from 22,916 in 1900 (0.08 percent of the labor force) to 1,047,000 in 1980 (1.08 percent of the labor force), a percentage increase from 1900 to 1980 of 4,468.86 percent (Derber, 1983). It is the highest increase among professionals, surpassing that of physicians (224.01 percent), lawyers (408.27 percent), architects (750.58 percent), dentists (371.94 percent), engineers (3,717.26 percent), and natural scientists (2,399.17 percent).[2] The U.S. Bureau of Labor Statistics reports that in 1986 there were 1.3 million accountants and auditors, up from 1.1 million in 1983 (Kleiman, 1987).

This growth of accountants followed the need for more advanced accounting technologies to deal with requirements of a more sophisticated production apparatus. The use of these advanced technologies requires accountants to pool their efforts in small and/or large CPA firms, leading to a decline in opportunities for self-employment in the field and to their dependence on the financial and institutional resources of corporations and the state.

Accountants were reluctant to abandon the idea of an independent economic position; however, increasingly, they joined accounting and nonaccounting firms, small and large, corporate or state bureaucracies. In the process they became subject to the authority and control of heteronomous management and suffered a slow degradation of status and reward.[3] What really resulted from these developments is a proletarianization of accountants, working according to a division of labor conceived and monitored by management, following procedural rules and repertoires created by administrative processes and/or fiat. While they still maintain control over their own knowledge base, which gives them some negotiating powers, their contractual employment totally subordinates them to a heteronomous management that appropriated the power over the total labor process.

The proletarianization of accountants reflected a shift of control toward employers or management and a loss of the creative freedom that accountants enjoyed as self-employed professionals. Thus, the change in accounting technology forced a change in the structure of the accounting labor process and put the accountants in a new form of "proletarian class," subordinated, like the craftspeople before them, to capitalist management. In the process, as theorized by Marx, they lost control of both the *means* and *ends* of labor, a phenomenon labeled *technical* proletarianization (Baran and Sweezy, 1966; Braverman, 1966). It has been speeded up and made easier by the higher degree of specialization and fragmentation imposed on accounting practice, a process of "deskilling," that is, of rationalizing previously professional tasks into a number of routinized functions requiring little training. An AICPA task force lists forty-one activities that describe the six general work categories performed by CPAs in public accounting practice: engagement management and administration, auditing, tax practice, management advisory services, other professional services, and office and firm administration (AICPA, 1983). A challenge facing accounting firms over the coming decade will be the need for even more *specialization* in auditing, tax, and consulting.

In addition to technical proletarianization, the emergence of the "new working class" or "professional managerial class" led also to an *ideological proletarianization*, which refers to the appropriation of control by management for capital, over the goals and social purposes to which work is put (Marglin, 1975). Ideological proletarianization may be more pronounced in accounting due to the general inability of accountants to control organizational policy and the specific goals and purposes of work. The accountant, bound by the specialized tasks, has lost control of the nature of the total product and may be indifferent to the outcome of the activities in which he or she was involved. This loss of vision of the total product and its use and disposition allows the direct management of labor (i.e., the technical proletarianization). In this way, technical and ideological proletarianization feed on each other.

The technical proletarianization of the accountant may lead to the accountant's losing the knowledge base as "capital" restructures through management the specification of the product and management restructures the organization of work.[4]

Proletarianization renders the accountant a mere technician of functionaries, separate from the major social, moral, and technological issues of his or her profession.[5] The end and social use of the accountant's labor is institutionally channeled with little provision made for his or her interest as a professional and the interest of the clients.[6] Marx discusses a similar transition from independent professional "craftsman" to de-skilled worker as the transition from formal subsumption to real subsumption.

These changes have led to the decrease in the number and quality of people going into accounting programs. The accounting profession lacks "glamour," and survey results suggest that accountants come from poorer socioeconomic backgrounds than do attorneys and physicians (Estes, 1984). The director of personnel at one of the Big Eight firms explains as follows: "Part of it is that a number of people find investment banking sexier, more exiting. You can make a big buck a lot quicker" (Kleiman, 1987). The lack of glamour may force the profession to offer high entry-level salaries. For now, in answer to the technical and ideological proletarianization, the accountant as well as other members of the "new working class" may respond by either *ideological desensitization*, a denial or separation of the self from the ideological control of the job, disclaiming either interest or responsibility for the social issues to which their work is put, or *ideological cooperation*, a redefinition of one's goals to make them consistent with institutional imperatives (Derber, 1983, p. 335).

In either case—ideological desensitization or ideological cooperation—there is high likelihood of alienation of accountants from their work, evidenced by the high level of turnover. About 85 percent of the accounting graduates joining the big CPA firms will leave within ten years for positions in government, industry, education, or smaller CPA firms (Kollaritsch, 1968). Benke and Rhode (1984) estimated the replacement cost of each entry-level staff accountant to exceed $20,000, and for one large CPA firm with a turnover of 10,000 employees over a recent ten-year period (Healy, 1976), that price would be $200 million in replacement costs. Other studies reported an increase in the level of turnover (Benke, 1978; Konstans and Ferris, 1981). Variables explaining this high turnover were found to be (1) the work environment in the audit department, (2) the coworkers and uncompensated overtime (in the tax department), and (3) professional challenge in the management services department (Benke and Rhode, 1984).

Alienation in the domain of work has a fourfold aspect: a person is alienated from the object that he or she produces, from the process of production, from himself or herself, and from the community of his or her fellows.

In their alienated condition, the mind-set of accountants, their consciousness, is to a large extent only the reflection of the conditions in which they find themselves and of the position in the process of production. This situation is particularly serious for female accountants. The percentage of female accounting graduates with bachelor's and master's degrees increased from 28 percent in 1976–1977 to 49 percent in 1985–1986. Yet, they feel that they do not have the same chance for promotion as men (Jayson and Williams, 1986) and that they do not earn as much (Olson and Frieze, 1986).

INSTITUTIONAL CAPITALISM AND CLASSWIDE RATIONALITY

The second element in the new conflictual order concerns the nature of the governing class in corporations and accounting firms. The social organization of the corporate community is composed of enduring informal and formal networks among large corporations, senior managers and directors of these companies, and the associations that represent them to the public (Useem, 1982, 1983). The policies espoused by business are the product of this social organization. While the results are not very conclusive, there is still the generally accepted notion that the corporate community is socially unified, cognizant of its classwide interest, and politically active. It is characterized by a socially cohesive national upper class, composed chiefly of corporate executives, primary owners, and their descendants, who constitute "the governing class of America" (Domhoff, 1974, p. 109). The same conclusion is drawn for Britain with the argument that

elite pluralism does not . . . prevent elites in capitalist society from constituting a dominant economic class, possessed of a high degree of cohesion and solidarity, with common interest and common purposes which far transcend their specific differences and disagreements. (Miliband, 1969, p. 47)

This governing class is composed of

those who own and those who control capital on a larger scale: whether top business executives or rentiers make no difference in this context. Whatever divergences of interest there may be among them on this score and others, latent as well as manifest, they have a common stake in one overriding cause: to keep the working rule of the society capitalist. (Westergaard and Resler, 1975, p. 346)

From this common cause stemmed the need for them to have common background and patterns of socialization, generally articulated in a new class awareness (Scott, 1979, pp. 125–126). This new class entered the political arena, with an unusual force and coherence, ensuring the success of the likes of Reagan and Thatcher and influencing their policies (Useem, 1983, p. 285). This situation precipitated the shift from "managerial capitalism" to "institutional capitalism." With managerial capitalism replacing family capitalism, managers and professional management found themselves in charge. Institutional capitalism, spurred by the rise of the new governing class, emerged to give to corporations a new power and class orientation. As stated by Useem,

[C]ompany management is now less than fully in charge; classwide issues intrude into company decisions; and competition is less pitched. Management decisions to underwrite political candidates, devote company resources to charitable causes, give advertising space to matters of public movement, and assume more socially responsible attitudes derive in part from company calculus, but also from a classwide calculus. (Useem, 1983, p. 305)

A *classwide rationality*, replacing the former assumption of *corporate rationality*, assumes that the corporate elite is largely capable of identifying and promoting its common political objectives. This classwide principle, replacing both the *upper class principle* and its successor, the corporate principle, and asserting that membership in the corporate elite is primarily determined in a set of interrelated networks transecting virtually all corporations, is also present in the accounting firms. Although corporate rationality still characterizes much of the internal organization of accounting firms, classwide rationality now characterizes its highest circles. Old school ties and kindred signs of proper breeding facilitate the access to the highest circles of the CPA firms.[7] The classwide principle espoused by the managerial elite of the CPA firms led them to espouse the broader need of big business and to oppose public regulation of their trade[8] (Previts, 1978; Arthur Andersen & Co., 1979; Elliott and Schultze, 1979; Chetkovich, 1980; Flegm, 1984). While not limited to the elite accounting firms, the political interest of the new corporate elite has been shown to transcend individual firms and to possess an internal cohesion that facilitates expression of those interests in the political process (Useem, 1982). In fact, challenges to the position of accounting firms, whether from Congress or the SEC, have further consolidated the political capacities of the new corporate elite of accounting

firms, as they were able to weather the storms of various congressional investigations, the findings of special task forces, and SEC interventions. The classwide rationality of the high circles of the CPA firms, the social cohesion of its
members, and their commitment to special interests have proven to be a formidable weapon to any attempts to regulate them (Olson, 1982, chap. 3; Belkaoui, 1989).

For example, in 1986 a bill was introduced in the House of Representatives
of the U.S. Congress requiring auditors to report immediately to federal authorities any suspicions of fraud that are detected in auditing a company's books.
It also called for the signing of the financial statements by the individual auditor,
not just the firm. As a result of the pressures put forth by the accounting profession, the bill did not pass.

In addition to their role in the profession, accountants and other financial
specialists are prominently represented in the managerial hierarchies of corporations (Armstrong, 1987, p. 415). In the United Kingdom company directors
with backgrounds in banking or accountancy outnumber those with any form of
technical training (BIM, 1972). An emphasis on financial as opposed to alternative means of control, especially at the higher level, was introduced by the
same accountants in key positions (Granick, 1971, p. 56). As a result of this
trend, Armstrong argued that organized professions are competitively engaged
in "collective mobility projects" (cf. Larson, 1977), aimed at securing access to
key positions of command in management hierarchies (Armstrong, 1985). Their
goal is seen as complete control by a competitive use of their techniques.

The means of competition is the monopolization of a body of knowledge and expertise
which offers, or appears to offer, a solution to a key problem within the functions of
capital. To the extent that professions succeed by these means in attaining command
positions, they are then in a position to sponsor characteristic means of controlling the
rest of the management hierarchy and, ultimately, the labor process itself (if indeed this
was not the crisis which enabled them to achieve dominance in the first place). (Armstrong, 1987, pp. 416–425)

ACADEMIC ACCOUNTANTS: A FLAWED UNIVERSAL
CLASS

The third element in the new conflictual order is a new class of academic
accountants. The proletariat as a universal class was best expressed by Marx
and Engels' theory of the "universal class of the proletariat" in the *Holy Family*
(Engels and Marx, [1844] 1975), refuting Bruno Bauer's criticisms and doubts
that the proletariat could develop consciousness that would be necessary to perform its function as a universal class (Engels and Marx, 1975, p. 86). Gouldner
joins the critical group, arguing that the lowliest class never came to power and
that throughout the world during the twentieth century, a new class of intellectuals emerged, looking like the universal class defined by Hegel (Hegel, 1942,

pp. 131–134, 197–200), but not representing a universal class (Gouldner, 1979). *The new class is thus a flawed universal class.*

Gouldner advanced two major propositions: first, the rise of a "new class" of humanistic intellectuals and technical intelligentsia, whose universalism is badly flawed; and second, the growing dominance of this class, as a cultural bourgeoisie having monopoly over cultural capital and professionalism from which it gains its power.

This new class includes both technical and human intellectuals. It forms one "speech community" sharing a "culture of critical discourse" (CCD). The CCD is a concept derived from the different linguistic repertoires identified in socio-linguistics (Berstein, 1974). Its definition is similar. The culture of critical discourse (CCD) is a historically evolved set of rules, a grammar of discourse, which (1) is conceived to justify its assertions, (2) whose mode of justification does not proceed by involving authorities and (3) prefers to elicit the *voluntary* consent of those addressed solely on the basis of arguments addressed. This is a culture of discourse in which there is nothing that speakers will on principle permanently refuse to discuss or make problematic; indeed, they are even willing to talk about the value of talk itself and its possible inferiority to silence or to practice.

This grammar is the deep structure of the common ideology shared by the new class. *The shared ideology of the intellectuals and intelligentsia is thus an ideology about discourse.* Apart from the underlying technical languages (or sociolects) spoken by specialized professions, intellectuals and intelligentsia are commonly committed to a culture of critical discourse. CCD is the latent but mobilizable infrastructure of modern "technical language" (Gouldner, 1978, pp. 176–177) as well as of modern intellectuals and their linguistic culture.

This new class is flawed because it is considered elitist and self-seeking and uses its special knowledge to advance its own interests and power.[9] It does not represent the universal interest. The new class is dominant because of its monopolistic access to cultural capital. Borrowing from Pierre Bourdieu's theory of cultural reproduction (Bourdieu, 1977), Gouldner suggests that the new class uses cultural reproduction to maintain its interest and power just as economic reproduction is used to serve the interests of the holders of economic capital. Therefore, members of the new class will develop within the process of "cultural capital accumulation" to further their particular interests and the interests of those who share their culture of critical discourse.

The new class relies on credentials in capitalizing culture and monitoring the supply of specifically trained labor.

Culture is transmitted through education and socialization. Generally, it is known that those with more formal education have life-time earnings in excess of those with less. This increased income reflects the capital value of increased education. (Gouldner, 1979, p. 26)

This gives them a privileged position in the labor market and the potential for a new dominant class position. The trend has started with the new class developing a high level of status consciousness to defend their privileges (e.g., academic freedom to publish, to review, to recruit, etc.).

Whether the supply of accounting research by academic accountants is in response to the demand for value-free knowledge (Peasnell and Williams, 1986), or to the demands of the markets for excuses (Watts and Zimmerman, 1979), academic accountants are also motivated by self-interest and the pressing need to publish (Orleans, 1962). They have gained a power associated with their monopoly over the cultural accounting capital. The research findings have given them consulting and policy-making powers to advance their own interests rather than the universal interest. For a culture of critical discourse, they have developed their linguistic repertoires, which differentiate them from other accounting speech communities (Belkaoui, 1978, 1980; Haried, 1980). As a new class, academic accountants also rely on credentials as criteria for membership, including Ph.D. degrees and publications in the "right" journals.[10]

According to Gouldner,

[P]rofessionalism is one of the public ideologies of the New Class. [P]rofessionalism is a tacit claim of the New Class to technical and moral superiority over the old class . . . professionalism tacitly deauthorized the old class. (Gouldner, 1979, p. 19)

Through the new professional role, the academic accountants claim their own cultural research domain and in the process receive a higher compensation from the market system for accepting the professional role (Lewis et al., 1984).

Intellectuals who are willing to behave like professionals are allowed to form a relatively autonomous stratum with particularistic interest. They can use the mechanisms of licensing and the professional associations to establish monopolies with their markets. (Szelenyi, 1982)

The fragmentation of the American Accounting Association with separate "cultural" sections evidences this phenomenon (Belkaoui and Chan, 1987).

The same fragmentation orients the accounting researcher more toward immediate political actions (policy) than toward "theoretical" formulations of problems with general significance. This new close relationship to the policymaker, whether it is the FASB, the SEC, the AAA, or any other institution, makes him or her a "bureaucratic" intellectual who exercises advisory and technical functions within a bureaucracy as opposed to those intellectuals who elect to stay unattached to a bureaucracy (Nettl, 1969, pp. 15–32; Merton, 1968, pp. 265–266).

The bureaucratic intellectual is reduced to being an "ideologue" because he or she subordinates or abandons the search for a universally comprehensive understanding of social, cultural, and physical reality in favor of an immediately instrumental arbitration of competing policies or courses of action (Barrow, 1987, p. 423). Such a role is unfortunate if one subscribes to the prevailing assumption that a "particularization" of intellectual activity that links or constrains academic inquiry to specific social interests or needs leads to a fall from the "sacred" and a descent into the dishonorable realm of "ideology" (Mannheim, 1971, pp. 116–131; 1986, pp. 265–266; Ashcraft, 1980).

In addition to the role of teachers involved in the process of creating formal knowledge as opposed to its mere transmission (Aron, 1962; Lipset and Dobson, 1972; Shils, 1972a, pp. 206–209; Berger, 1976, p. 5), the intellectuals moved to a role of "rationalization." As Shils suggests, in all modern societies (both liberal and totalitarian) "the trend of the present century" has been to increase pressures toward internal homogeneity due to the "incorporation of intellectuals in organized societies" (1972b, p. 191). Intellectuals serve to elaborate the underlying "laws" of national and social organization relevant to the routing development and application of scientific knowledge to economic production and its social organization (Machlup, 1962; Price, 1965; Bell, 1973, pp. 165–166; Galbraith, 1978, pp. 292–306). The call came mostly from the state to assist in reorienting the underlying mass population and in developing policies to ameliorate and prevent disturbances (Habermas, 1970, pp. 62–80; Galbraith, 1978, pp. 206–220; Gouldner, 1979, pp. 24–25).[11] As a result, intellectuals have typically labored under the patronage of ruling classes or in institutions controlled by them (Aron, 1962, p. 204; Parsons, 1970, p. 14]. The accounting intellectuals fit the described scenarios as they strive to provide the right excuses (Watts and Zimmerman, 1979) and create a new but flawed universal class.

CONCLUSIONS

A new order is appearing in the field of accounting in which a diverse group of protagonists from different contradictory classes define and defend their view of the scope and the conduct of the discipline. First, accountants as members of the new class of salaried professionals have lost control of the labor process, resulting in a technical and ideological proletarianization of the accountants. Second, a new governing class inbred by classwide rationality and internal cohesion has given rise to an institutional capitalism that supplants the interest of individual firms. Finally, the academic accountants, as part of the flawed universal class, are motivated by their subjectified interests and the need to monopolize their special brand of "cultural" capital. What results is a new class-based conflict in accounting characterized by the contradictions and antinomies inherent in the predicament of the new "socialized" accounting workforce.

NOTES

1. A Marxist definition includes this professional-managerial class of "salaried mental workers who do not own the means of production and whose major function in the

social division of labor may be described broadly as the reproduction of capitalist culture and capitalist class relations" (Ehrenreich and Ehrenreich, 1976, p. 13).

2. The data are taken from the Bureau of Labor Statistics and the Bureau of Census.

3. The starting salaries of accounting undergraduates joining the big CPA firms declined in real terms in the 1980s, hovering in 1987 around $22,000.

4. The growth of management advisory services activities, the increased specialization in the profession, the emerging conflict between professionalism and commercialism in accounting, and the call for non-CPA associate membership for non-CPAs point in that direction (Belkaoui, 1985b).

5. The *Report* of the National Commission on Fraudulent Financial Reporting (1987) noticed a breakdown in the financial reporting system and revealed that fraudulent financial reporting usually occurs as the result of certain environmental, institutional, or individual forces and opportunities.

6. The managing partner of the Grant Thornton accounting firm, who had a crucial role in the fraud at E.S.M. Government Securities Inc., gave this account of the same conflict: "I often wondered what I would do if somebody walked in and said, 'Look what I've found.' But it never happened. I gave them [his team of auditors] the same baloney answer that I had been given back in '78. It never dawned on them that it just didn't make sense" (Branningan, 1987, p. 29).

7. Marx refers to the opportunistic and pragmatic alliance described in *The Eighteenth Brumaire of Louis Napoleon* (1852), involving a conservative peasantry and Louis Napolean. Following Marx's analysis in the *Eighteenth Brumaire*, both corporations and accounting firms live under economic conditions of existence that separate their model of life, their interest, and their culture from those of other classes and puts them in hostile opposition to the latter; they form a class.

8. Arthur Andersen & Co., basing its computations on company-supplied data, estimated the annual cost of governmental regulation (1977 impact of six general regulatory agencies and programs on forty-eight large companies, all members of the Business Roundtable) at $2.6 billion. Throughout the report, Arthur Andersen did not bother to provide an estimate of the benefits of regulation (Comptroller General, 1977; DeFina, 1977; Weidenbaum, 1978; Arthur Andersen, 1979; Data Resources, 1979; Green and Waitzman, 1980).

9. Burnam saw the emergence of the new class as necessary to fulfill the basic functional requirements of modern society (Burnam, 1962, pp. 256–266).

10. Konrad and Szelenyi go one step further by arguing that the knowledge of the intellectuals reflects their own interests, and when they become a class, their knowledge is subordinated to those interests (Konrad and Szelenyi, 1979, p. 9).

11. As a result the legitimacy of contemporary universities is more and more dependent on their ability to adopt national economic and political goals as part of their traditional historical mission (Price, 1984/1985).

REFERENCES

American Institute of Certified Public Accountants (AICPA), Practice Analysis Task Force. *AICA Report of the Practice Analysis Task Force*. New York: AICPA, 1983, pp. 119–125.

Armstrong, P. "Changing Management Control Strategies: The Role of Competition between Accounting and Other Organizational Professions." *Accounting, Organizations and Society* (May 1985), pp. 129–148.

———. "The Rise of Accounting Controls in British Capitalist Enterprises." *Accounting, Organizations and Society* (October 1987), pp. 415–436.

Aron, R. *The Opinion of the Intellectuals*. New York: W.W. Norton, 1962.

Arthur Andersen & Co. *Cost of Government Regulation Study*. Washington, DC: Business Roundtable, 1979.

Ashcraft, R. "Political Theory and the Problem of Ideology." *Journal of Politics* (August 1980), pp. 687–705.

Baran, P., and P.M. Sweezy. *Monopoly Capital*. New York: Monthly Review Press, 1966.

Barrow, C.W. "Intellectuals in Contemporary Social Theory: A Radical Critique." *Sociological Inquiry* (Fall 1987), pp. 415–430.

Belkaoui, A. "Linguistic Relativity in Accounting." *Accounting, Organizations and Society* (October 1978), pp. 97–100.

———. "The Interprofessional Linguistic Communication of Accounting Concepts: An Experiment in Sociolinguistics." *Journal of Accounting Research* (Autumn 1980), pp. 362–374.

———. *Accounting Theory*. San Diego: Harcourt, 1985a.

———. *Public Policy and the Practice and Problems of Accounting*. Westport, CT: Quorum Books, 1985b.

———. *The Coming Crisis in Accounting*. Westport, CT: Quorum Books, 1989.

Belkaoui, A., and J. Chan. "Professional Value System of Academic Accountants." *Advances in Public Interest Accounting* 2 (1987).

Bell, D. *The End of Ideology*. New York: Free Press, 1973.

Benke, R.L. "A Multivariate Analysis of Job Satisfaction of Professional Employees in Big Eight Public Accounting Firms." Unpublished D.B.A. diss., Florida State University, 1978.

Benke, R.L., Jr., and J.G. Rhode. "Intent to Turnover among Higher Level Employees in Large CPA Firms." *Advances in Accounting* 1 (1984), pp. 157–174.

Berger, P.L. "The Socialist Myth." *Public Interest* 44 (Summer 1976), pp. 3–16.

Bergesen, A. *Crisis in the World Systems*. Beverly Hills, CA: Sage, 1983.

Berstein, S. "Social Class, Language and Socialization." In F.A. Sebeok (ed.), *Current Trends in Linguistics*. The Hague: Mouton, 1974.

BIM. "The Board of Directors: A Survey of Its Structure, Composition and Role." Management Survey Report No. 10. BIM, 1972.

Bourdieu, P. *Reproduction in Education, Society and Culture*. Beverly Hills, CA: Sage, 1977.

Branningan, M. "Auditor's Downfall Shows a Man Caught in Trap of His Own Making." *Wall Street Journal* (March 4, 1987), p. 29.

Braverman, H. *Labor and Monopoly Capital*. New York: Monthly Review Press, 1966.

Burnam, J. *The Managerial Revolution*. Bloomington: Indiana University Press, 1962.

Chetkovich, M.N. "The Accounting Profession Responds to the Challenge of Regulation." In J.W. Buckley and J.F. Weston (eds.), *Regulation and the Accounting Profession*. Belmont, CA: Lifetime Learning Publications, 1980.

Comptroller General, Government Regulatory Activity. *Justification, Processes, Impacts, and Alternatives*. Washington, DC: General Accounting Office, 1977.

Data Resources. *The Macroeconomic Impact of Federal Pollution Control Program, 1978 Assessment*. Washington, DC: Council on Environmental Quality, 1979.

Defina, R. *Public and Private Expenditures for Federal Regulation of Business*. St. Louis: Washington University, Center for the Study of American Business, 1977.

Derber, C. "Managing Professionals." *Theory and Society* 12 (1983), pp. 309–341.

Domhoff, G.W. *The Bohemian Grove and Other Retreats*. New York: Harper & Row, 1974.

Ehrenreich, B., and J. Ehrenreich. "The Professional Managerial Class." *Radical America* 11 (1976), pp. 7–31.

Elliott, R.X., and W. Schultze. "Regulation of Accounting: Practitioner's Viewpoint." In A.R. Abdel-Khalik (ed.), *Government Regulations of Accounting and Information*. Tallahassee: University Presses of Florida, 1979.

Engels, F., and K. Marx. *The Holy Family*. In F. Naun and F. Engels, *Collected Works*, Vol. 4. New York: International Publishers, 1975.

Estes, R. "An Intergenerational Comparison of Socioeconomic Status among CPAs, Attorneys, Engineers and Physicians." In B. Schwartz (ed.), *Advances in Accounting*, Vol. 1. Greenwich, CT: JAI Press, 1984, pp. 1–18.

Flegm, E.H. *Accounting: How to Meet the Challenges of Relevance and Regulation*. New York: John Wiley & Sons, 1984.

Galbraith, J.K. *The New Industrial State*. Boston: Houghton Mifflin, 1978.

Gouldner, A. "The New Class Project, I." *Theory and Society* 6 (1978), pp. 153–203.

Gouldner, A.W. *The Future of the Intellectuals and the New Class*. New York: Continuum Publishing, 1979.

Granick, D. *Managerial Comparisons of Four Developed Countries: France, Britain, the United States and Russia*. Cambridge, MA: MIT Press, 1971.

Green, M., and N. Waitzman. "Cost, Benefit and Class." *Working Payers for a New Society* 7 (May/June 1980), pp. 39–51.

Habermas, J. *Toward a Rational Society*. Boston: Beacon Press, 1970.

Haried, A.A. "The Semantic Dimensions of Financial Statements." *Journal of Accounting Research* (Autumn 1980), pp. 632–674.

Hegel, G.W.F. *Hegel's Philosophy of the Right*, translated by T.M. Knot. Oxford: Clarendon Press, 1942.

Healy, J. "The Drudge Is Dead." *MBA* (November 1976), pp. 48–56.

Jayson, S., and K. Williams. "Women in Management Accounting: Moving Up . . . Slowly." *Management Accounting* (July 1986), pp. 20–26.

Kleiman, C. "Scrutiny Hasn't Put Crimp in Auditing." *Chicago Tribune* (November 29, 1987), Section 8, p. 1.

Kollaritsch, F.P. "Job Migration Patterns of Accountancy." *Management Accounting* (September 1968), pp. 52–55.

Konrad, G., and I. Szelenyi. *The Intellectuals on the Road to Class Power*. New York: Harcourt Brace Jovanovich, 1979.

Konstans, C., and K. Ferris. "Female Turnover in Professional Accounting Firms: Some Preliminary Findings." *Michigan CPA* (Winter 1981), pp. 11–15.

Larson, M.S. *The Rise of Professionalism: A Sociological Analysis*. Berkeley: University of California Press, 1977.

Lewis, M.T., W.T. Lin, and D.Z. Williams. "The Economic Status of Accounting Educators: An Empirical Study." In B. Schwartz (ed.), *Advances in Accounting*, Vol. 1. Greenwich, CT: JAI Press, 1984, pp. 127–144.

Lipset, S.M., and R.B. Dobson. "The Intellectual as Critic and Rebel." *Daedalus* 101 (Summer 1972), pp. 137–198.

Machlup, F. *The Production and Distribution of Knowledge in the United States.* Princeton, NJ: Princeton University Press, 1962.

Mannheim, K. "The Ideological and Sociological Interpretation of Intellectual Phenomena." In K.H. Wolff (ed.), *From Karl Mannheim.* New York: Oxford University Press, 1971.

———. *Ideology and Utopia.* San Diego: Harcourt Brace Jovanovich, 1986.

Marglin, S. "What Do Bosses Do?" *Review of Radical and Political Economics* 6 (Summer 1975), pp. 60–112, and 7 (Spring 1975), pp. 20–37.

Marx, K. *Early Writings,* translated and edited by T.B. Bottomore. New York: McGraw-Hill, 1964.

Merton, R.K. *Social Theory and Social Structure.* New York: Free Press, 1968.

Miliband, R. *The State in Capitalist Society.* New York: Basic Books, 1969.

National Commission on Fradulent Financial Reporting. *Report of the National Commission on Fraudulent Reporting.* New York: AICPA, 1987.

Nettl, J.P. "Power and the Intellectuals." In C.C. O'Brien and W.D. Vanech (eds.), *Power and Consciousness.* New York: New York University Press, 1969, pp. 53–124.

Offe, C. *Disorganized Capitalism.* Cambridge, MA: MIT Press, 1985.

Olson, J., and L. Friez. "Women Accountants—Do They Earn As Much As Men?" *Management Accounting* (July 1986), pp. 27–31.

Olson, W.E. *The Accounting Profession, Years of Trial—1969–1980.* New York: AICPA, 1982.

Orleans, H. *The Effects of Federal Programs on Higher Education.* Washington, DC: Brookings Institution, 1962.

Parsons, T. "The Intellectual: A Social Role Category." In P. Reiff (ed.), *On Intellectuals.* New York: Doubleday, 1970.

Peasnell, K.V., and D.J. Williams. "Ersatz Academics and Scholar-Saints: The Supply of Financial Accounting Research." *Abacus* (September 1986), pp. 121–135.

Poulantzas, N. *Classes in Contemporary Capitalism.* London: Verso, 1975.

Previts, G.J. "The SEC and Its Chief Accountants: Historical Impressions." *The Journal of Accountancy* (August 1978), pp. 13–22.

Price, D.K. *The Scientific Estate.* Cambridge, MA: Harvard University Press, 1965.

Price, G. "Universities Today: Between the Corporate State and the Market." *Culture, Education and Society* 39 (Winter 1984/1985), pp. 43–58.

Scott, J. *Corporations, Classes and Capitalism.* London: Hutchinson, 1979.

Shaikh, A. "An Introduction to the History of Crisis Theories." In *U.S. Capitalism in Crisis.* New York: Union for Radical Political Economists, 1978, pp. 219–241.

Shils, E. *The Constitution of Society.* Chicago: University of Chicago Press, 1972a.

———. *The Intellectuals and the Powers.* Chicago: University of Chicago Press, 1972b.

Szelenyi, I. "Gouldner's Theory of Intellectuals as a Flawed Universal Class." *Theory and Society* 11 (1982), pp. 779–798.

Touraine, A. "An Introduction." In N. Brisbaum (ed.), *Beyond the Crisis.* New York: Oxford University Press, 1977, pp. 3–13.

Useem, M. "Classwide Rationality in the Politics of Managers and Directors of Large Corporations in the United States and Great Britain." *Administrative Science Quarterly* 27 (1982), pp. 199–226.

———. "Business and Politics in the United States and United Kingdom." *Theory and Society* (1983), pp. 281–307.

Watts, R.L., and J.L. Zimmerman. "The Demand for and Supply of Accounting Theories: The Market for Excuses." *The Accounting Review* (April 1979), pp. 273–305.

Weidenbaum, M.L. *Business, Government and the Public*. Englewood Cliffs, NJ: Prentice-Hall, 1978.

Westergaard, J., and H. Resler. *Class in a Capitalist Society*. London: Heinemann, 1975.

Williams, P.F. "The Legitimate Concern with Fairness." *Accounting, Organizations and Society* (March 1987), pp. 169–192.

Chapter 4

Fraud in Accounting

Fraud in the accounting environment is on the increase, causing enormous losses to firms, individuals, and society and creating a morale problem in the workplace. It takes place as corporate fraud, fraudulent financial reporting, white-collar crime, or audit failures. This chapter explicates the nature of fraud in the accounting environment, provides some theoretical explanations of the phenomenon from the field of criminology, and explores some outcome situations arising from corporate fraud.

NATURE OF FRAUD IN THE ACCOUNTING ENVIRONMENT

Fraud has many definitions. It is a crime. The Michigan criminal law states:

Fraud is a generic term, and embraces all the multifarious means which human ingenuity can devise, which are resorted to by one individual to get advantage over another by false representations. No definite and invariable rule can be laid down as a general proposition in defining fraud, as it includes surprise, trick, cunning and unfair ways by which another is cheated. The only boundaries defining it are those that limit human knavery.[1]

Fraud is the intentional deception of another person by lying and cheating for the purpose of deriving an unjust, personal, social, political, or economic advantage over that person.[2] It is definitively immoral.

Within a business organization fraud can be perpetrated for or against the firm. It is then *corporate fraud*. Management or a person in a position of trust can perpetrate it. It is then *management fraud* or *white-collar crime*. It may involve the use of an accounting system to portray a false image of the firm. It is then a form of *fraudulent financial reporting*. It may also involve a failure of the auditor to detect errors or misstatements. It is then an *audit failure*. In all these cases—corporate fraud, management fraud, white-collar crime, fraudulent financial reporting, audit failure—the accountant as preparer, auditor, or user stands to suffer heavy losses.

Corporate Fraud

Corporate fraud or economic crimes are perpetrated generally by officers, executives, and/or profit center managers of public companies to satisfy their short-term economic needs. In fact, the short term-oriented management style may create the need for corporate fraud, given the pressure to increase current profitability in the face of few opportunities and the need to take unwise risks with the firm's resources. As confirmed by Jack Bologna:

Rarely is compensation based on the longer term growth and development of the firm. As a consequence of this myopic view of performance criteria, the executives and officers of many public companies have a built-in incentive or motivation to play fast and loose with their firm's assets and financial data.[3]

In fact, more than the pressure for short-term profitability, economic greed and avarice blot social values and lead to corporate fraud. Evidence from the Federal Bureau of Investigation shows that arrests from two categories of corporate fraud have climbed: fraud jumped 75 percent between 1976 and 1986, and embezzlement rose 26 percent.[4] In fact, corporate fraud goes beyond mere fraud and embezzlement. The situation points to a myriad of activities that may result in corporate fraud. The increase in corporate fraud in the United States and elsewhere is the result of the erosion in business ethics.

Fraudulent Financial Reporting

Fraudulent financial reporting is so rampant that a special commission was created to investigate it: the National Commission on Fraudulent Financial Reporting. The commission defined fraudulent financial reporting as "intentional or reckless conduct, whether act or omission, that results in materially misleading financial statements." Such reporting undermines the integrity of financial information and can affect a range of victims: shareholders, creditors, employees, auditors, and even competitors. It is used by firms that are facing economic crises as well as by those motivated by misguided opportunism.

Common types of fraudulent financial reporting include

1. the manipulation, falsification, or altering of records or documents
2. the suppression or omission of the effects of completed transactions from records or documents

3. the recording of transactions without substance

4. the misapplication of accounting policies, and

5. the failure to disclose significant information

There is a deliberate strategy to deceive by distorting the information and the information records. This results from a number of documented dysfunctional behaviors: smoothing, biasing, focusing, gaming, filtering, and illegal acts. Such behaviors generally occur when managers have a low belief both in the analyzability of information and in the measurability and verifiability of data.[5] Of all these documented dysfunctional behaviors, the one most likely to result in fraudulent financial reporting is the occurrence of illegal acts by violation of a private or public law through various types of fraud. One type of fraud is within the accounting system. Examples include the following:

1. False input scams (creating fake debits)

   a. False or inflated claims from vendors, suppliers, benefits claimants, and employees or false refund or allowance claims by customers

   b. Lagging on receivable payments or customer bank deposits

   c. Check kiting

   d. Inventory manipulation and reclassification

      (1) Arbitrary write-ups and write-downs

      (2) Reclassification to lower value-obsolete, damaged, or "sample" status

   e. Intentional misclassification of expenditures

      (1) Operational expense versus capital expenditures

      (2) Personal expense versus business expense

   f. Fabrication of sales and cost of sales data

   g. Misapplication and misappropriation of funds and other corporate assets (theft and embezzlement)

   h. Computerized input and fraudulent access scams

      (1) Data diddling and manipulation

      (2) Impersonation and impostor terminal

      (3) Scavenging

      (4) Piggybacking

      (5) Wiretapping

      (6) Interception and destruction of input and source documents

      (7) Fabrication of batch or hash totals

      (8) Simulation and modeling fraud (fraudulent parallel systems)

   i. Forgery, counterfeiting, or altering of source documents, authorizations, computer program documentation, or loan collateral

   j. Overstating revenues and assets

   k. Understating expenses and liabilities

l. Creating off-line reserves

m. Related party transactions

n. Spurious assets and hidden liabilities

o. "Smoothing" profits

p. Destruction, obliteration, and alteration of supporting documents

q. Exceeding limits of authority

2. False throughput scams

a. Salami slicing, trapdoors, Trojan horse, logic

b. Designed random error during processing cycle

3. Output scams

a. Scavenging through output

b. Output destruction, obliteration

c. Theft of output reports and logs

d. Theft of programs, data files, and systems programming and operations documentation[6]

Fraud does not always start with an illegal act. Managers are known to choose accounting methods in terms of their economic consequences. Various studies have argued that managerial preferences for accounting methods and procedures may vary, depending on the expected economic consequences of those methods and procedures. It has been well established that the manager's choice of accounting methods may depend on the effect on reported income,[7] the degree of owner versus manager control of the company,[8] and methods of determining managerial bonuses.[9] This effort to use accounting methods to show a good picture of the company becomes more pressing on managers who are facing some form of financial distress and are in need of showing the economic events in the most optimistic way. This may lead to suppressing or delaying the dissemination of negative information.[10] The next natural step for these managers is to use fraudulent financial reporting. To hide difficulties and to deceive investors, declining and failing companies have resorted to the following fraudulent reporting practices: (1) prematurely recognizing income, (2) improperly treated operating leases as sales, (3) inflating inventory by improper application of the last in, first out (LIFO) inventory method, (4) fictitious amounts in inventories, (5) failure to recognize losses through write-offs and allowances, (6) improperly capitalized or deferred costs and expenses, (7) unusual gains in operating income, (8) overvalued marketable securities, (9) "sham" year-end transactions to boost reported earnings and (10) changing their accounting practices to increase earnings without disclosing the changes.[11]

One factor in the increase of fraudulent financial reporting that has escaped scrutiny is the failure of accounting educational institutions to teach ways of detecting fraud and the importance of its detection to the entire financial reporting system. The emphasis in the university and the CPA examinations is with financial auditing rather than with forensic, fraud, or investigative reporting. J.C. Threadway Jr., chairman of the National Commission on Fraudulent Financial Reporting, sees it this way:

If you go back to the accounting literature of the 1920s or earlier, you'll find the detection of fraud mentioned as the objective of an audit much more prominently. Our work to date in looking at the way accounting and auditing are taught today in colleges and business schools indicates that fraud detection is largely ignored. In fact, there are texts currently in use that do not even talk about the detection of fraud.[12]

Because the Securities and Exchange Commission is dedicated to the protection of the interests of investors and the integrity of capital markets, it is concerned that adequate disclosures are provided for the public to allow a better judgment of the situation. One financial disclosure fraud enforcement program called for disclosures in four areas:

1. Liquidity problems, such as (1) decreased inflow of collections from sales to customers, (2) the lack of availability of credit from suppliers, bankers, and others, and (3) the inability to meet maturing obligations when they fall due.
2. Operating trends and factors affecting profits and losses, such as (1) curtailment of operations, (2) decline of orders, (3) increased competition, or (4) cost overruns on major contracts.
3. Material increases in problem loans must be reported by financial institutions.
4. Corporations cannot avoid their disclosure obligations when they approach business decline or failure.

Corporations need to adopt measures to reduce exposure on causes of fraudulent and questionable financial reporting practices. Examples of suggestions for the reduction of exposure include:

1. The formulation of desired behavior
2. The maintenance of effective system of internal control
3. The maintenance of effective financial organization with acknowledged responsibility for maintaining good financial reporting practices
4. The maintenance of effective internal audit function
5. Having the board of directors play an active role in reviewing financial reporting policies and practices
6. The monitoring of capabilities and circumstances of individuals in positions affecting the financial reporting
7. The promise and use of strong penalties for the violation of guidelines
8. Making sure that the performance targets are realistic
9. Being aware of high emphasis on short-term financial performance[13]

White-Collar Crime

White-collar crime was a concern for Durkheim, who was convinced that the "anomie state" of "occupational ethics" was the cause "of the incessant recurrent conflicts, and the multifarious disorders of which the economic world exhibits so sad a spectacle."[14] At the same time, Ross noticed the rise in vulnerability created by the increasingly complex forms of interdependence in society and the exploitations of these vulnerabilities by a new class that he called "criminaloid."[15] He argued that a new criminal was at large, one

who picks pockets with a railway rebate, murders with an adulterant instead of a bludgeon, burglarizes with a "rake-off" instead of a jimmy, cheats with a company prospectus instead of a deck of cards, or scuttles his town instead of his ship.[16]

The phrase "white-collar crime" was originated in Edwin Sutherland's presidential address to the American Sociological Society in December 1939.[17] He defined it as "a crime committed by a person of respectability and high social status in the course of his occupation."[18] A debate followed, with Clinard and Reier's defining white-collar crime as restricted only to "illegal activities among business and professional men,"[19] and Harting's defining it as "a violation of law regulating business, which is committed for a firm by the firm or its agents in the conduct of its business."[20] Basically, one view of white-collar crime focused on occupation, and the other focused on the organization, but in fact the world of both occupation and organization is the world of white-collar crime and constitutes what the knife and gun are to street crime.[21] White-collar crimes have not been condemned as vehemently as other common crimes. One reason is that their crime is not to cause physical injury but to further organizational goals. In fact, individuals were found to consider organizational crimes far less serious than those with physical impact.[22] Another reason for the indifference to white-collar crime may be the possibility that members of the general public are themselves committing white-collar crimes on a smaller scale.[23] In addition, the white-collar criminal generally finds support for his or her behavior in group norms, which place him or her in a different position from the common criminal. As Aubert explains:

But what distinguishes the white-collar criminal in this aspect is that his group often has an elaborate and widely accepted ideological rationalization for the offenses, and is a group of great social significance outside the sphere of criminal activity—usually a group with considerable economic and political power.[24]

The white-collar criminal is motivated by social norms, accepted and enforced by groups that indirectly give support to the illegal activity. In many cases the organization itself is committing the white-collar crime, sometimes because it may be the only response to economic demands.

White-collar crime may be characterized by five principal components: (1) intent to commit the crime, (2) disguise of purpose, (3) reliance on the naïveté of the victim(s), (4) voluntary victim action to assist the offender, and (5) concealment of the violation.[25] Unlike traditional crime, its objective is to steal kingly sums rather than small sums of money, and its modus operandi is to use technology and mass communications rather than brute force and crude tools. In addition, white-collar crime relies on the ignorance and greed of its victim.[26] It inflicts economic harm and physical harm and damages the social fabric.

Audit Failure

Auditors are expected to detect and correct or reveal any material omissions or misstatements of financial information. When auditors fail to meet these expectations, an audit failure is the inevitable result. The level of audit quality can avoid the incurrence of audit failures. Audit quality has been defined as the probability that financial statements contain no material omission or misstatements.[27] It has also been defined in terms of audit risk, with high-quality services reflecting lower audit risk.[28] Audit risk was defined as the risk that "the auditor may unknowingly fail to appropriately modify his opinion on financial statements that are materially misstated."[29]

Audit failures do, however, occur and, as a consequence, bring audit firms face-to-face with costly litigation and loss of reputation, not to mention court-imposed judgments and out-of-court settlements. The client's or user's losses lead to the litigation situation and the potential of payments to the plaintiff. Litigation can be used as an indirect measure of audit quality using an inverse relation—auditors with relatively low (high) litigation offer higher- (lower-) quality audits. This relation was verified in a study that indicated, as expected, that non-Big Eight firms as a group had higher litigation occurrence rates than the Big Eight and that supported the Big Eight as quality-differentiated auditors.[30]

But not all litigations follow directly from audit failures. In a study that described the role of business failures and management fraud in both legal actions brought against auditors and the settlement of such actions, Palmrose found that (1) nearly half of the cases that alleged audit failures involved business failures or clients with severe financial difficulties, and (2) most lawsuits that involved bankrupt clients also involved management fraud.[31] These findings point to the fact that business failures and management fraud play a great role in the occurrence of audit failures, which calls for the auditor to take a responsible attitude in the detection of fraud, as it may affect the audit quality, the audit risk, and the potential for costly litigations. As stated by Connor:

Establishing the requirement to identify the conditions underlying fraudulent reporting as an independent objective of the audit process would help to clarify auditor responsibility and increase auditor awareness of this responsibility. Performance of the recommended procedures of management control review and evaluation and fraud risk evaluation would improve the probability of detecting conditions leading to misstated financial statements. The required focus on financial condition would help identify more effectively those entities that would qualify as business failure candidates in the near term.[32]

Although management fraud and business failure may play a great role in audit failures, there are other reasons for such failures. For example, St. Pierre and Anderson's extended analysis of documented audit failures identified three other reasons: (1) error centering on the auditor's interpretation of generally accepted accounting principles; (2) error centering on the auditor's interpretation of generally accepted auditing standards or implementation of generally accepted auditing standards; and (3) error centering on fraud of the auditor.[33]

FRAMEWORK FOR FRAUD IN THE ACCOUNTING ENVIRONMENT

We have established that fraud is rampant in the accounting environment, taking the shape of corporate fraud, fraudulent financial reporting, white-collar crime, and audit failures. The main issue is to determine the causes and, above all, provide an explanation for the situation. Descriptive characteristics of the person or the situation that may lead to fraud in the accounting environment abound. For example, there is a need to watch for "red flags," which do not necessarily prove management fraud, but when enough of them exist, there is the potential for corporate fraud. Red flag characteristics to be wary of in the course of an audit include the following:

- A person who is a wheeler-dealer
- A person without a well-defined code of ethics
- A person who is neurotic, manic-depressive, or emotionally unstable
- A person who is arrogant or egocentric
- A person with a psychopathic personality

Financial pressures lead to the following possible red flags within the industry

1. Unfavorable economic conditions within that industry
2. Heavy investments or losses
3. Lack of sufficient working capital
4. Success of the company dependent on one or two products, customers, or transactions
5. Excess capacity
6. Severe obsolescence
7. Extremely high debt

8. Extremely rapid expansion through new business or product lines

9. Tight credit, high interest rates, and reduced ability to acquire credit

10. Pressure to finance expansion through current earnings rather than through debt or equity

11. Profit squeeze (costs and expenses rising higher and faster than sales and revenues)

12. Difficulty in collecting receivables

13. Unusually heavy competition (including low-priced imports)

14. Existing loan agreements with little flexibility and tough restrictions

15. Progressive deterioration in quality earnings

16. Significant tax adjustments by the IRS

17. Long-term financial losses

18. Unusually high profits with a cash shortage

19. Urgent need for favorable earnings to support high price of stock, meet earnings forecast, and so on

20. Need to gloss over a temporary bad situation and maintain management position and prestige

21. Significant litigation, especially between stockholders and management

22. Unmarketable collateral

23. Significant reduction in sales backlog indicating future sales decline

24. Long business cycle

25. Existence of revocable and possibly imperiled licenses necessary for continuation of business

26. Suspension or delisting from a stock exchange[34]

27. Fear of a merger

Merchant cites as causes of fraudulent financial reporting organizational factors and personal circumstances:

By providing incentives for deception, by failing to persuade managers and employees that chances of detection are higher and penalties severe, and by failing to provide adequate moral guidance and leadership, corporations increase the use of illegal and unethical practices.[35]

Although these descriptive characteristics may be useful for detecting the potential for fraud in the corporate environment, they do not provide an adequate normative explanation of why fraud happens. The field of criminology offers various models and theories that are very much applicable to fraud in the accounting environment and may offer alternative explanations for the phenomenon.

The Conflict Approach

The consensus approach and the conflict approach are two major views that hypothesize about law and society.[36] Influenced by anthropological and sociological studies of primitive law, the consensus approach sees laws developing out of public opinion as a reflection of popular will. The conflict approach sees laws as originating in a political context in which influential interest groups pass laws that are beneficial to them. A third view argues for an integrated approach that focuses on the different functions of the consensus and conflict approaches, with the conflict approach ideal to explain the creation of criminal law and the consensus perspective, the operation of the law.

In the case of the accountant and fraud it can be argued, using the conflict approach, that accounting interest groups presented a favorable picture of their problematic situation by insisting that they can control for fraud and worked to get their view of the situation more widely recognized. The process led to less stringent regulation enacted for fraudulent reporting cases and white-collar crime. Basically, it fits with the notion that the criminal law that emerges after the creation of the state is designed to protect the interests of those who control the machinery of the state, including the accounting profession.

The consensus approach refers instead to the widespread consensus about the community's reaction to accounting fraud and to the legislation enacted. The consensus approach to accounting fraud may have resulted from either the ignorance or the indifference of the general public to the situation. Another explanation is the idea of differential consensus related to the support of criminal laws.[37] While serious crimes receive strong support for vigorous actions, crimes relating to the conduct of business and professional activities generate an apathetic response.

If one adopts a conflict model of crime, then the origin of the fraudulent practices in accounting may be linked to a society's political and economic development. As society's political and economic development reaches higher stages, institutions are created to accommodate new needs and to check aggressive impulses. In the process these restraining institutions create a system of inequality and spur the aggressive and acquisitive impulses that the consensus model of crime mistakes for part of human nature. The powerful elites rather than the general will arise to label the fraudulent practices in accounting as criminal because these crimes affect these elites as they are related to property and its possession and control. At the same time, members of that same elite constitute a major component of those participating in the fraudulent practices in accounting. Their motivation to engage in the practices remains the question. The conflict model of crime would attribute the practices to a system of inequality that values certain kinds of aggressive behavior. Basically, those engaging in fraudulent practices in accounting are reacting to the life conditions of their own social class: acquisitive behavior of the powerful, on the hand, and the high-risk property crimes of the powerless, on the other. One would conclude that the focus of the attack on the fraudulent practices should be toward the societal institutions that led to the isolation of the individuals. It implies a reorganization of these institutions to eliminate the illegal possession of rights, privileges, and position.[38]

The Ecological Theory

An examination of some of the notorious accounting frauds, white-collar crimes, and audit failures may suggest that some criminal types are attracted to business in general and to accounting in particular. Therefore, the criminal cases are not indicative of a general phenomenon in the field but the result of the criminal actions of the minority of criminal types that have been attracted to the discipline of accounting. This approach is known as the "Lombrosian" view of criminology. But with the Lombrosian theory of a physical "criminal type" losing its appeal, the ecological theory appears as a more viable and better alternative to an explanation of the fraud phenomenon in accounting. It adopts as a basis of explanation of corporate fraud the concept of social disorganization, which is generally defined as the decrease in influence of existing rules of behavior on individual members of the group. Criminal behavior in the accounting field is to be taken as an indicator of a basic social disorganization. First, weak social organization of the discipline of accounting leads to criminal behavior. Second, with the social control of the discipline waning because of the general public indifference, some accountants are freed from moral sensitivities and are predisposed to corporate fraud, white-collar crime, and audit failure. Then the general public's failure to function effectively as an agency of social control is the immediate cause of corporate fraud, white-collar crime, fraudulent financial reporting, and audit failure. Basically, some accountants are freed from moral sensitivities when social control breaks down or fails to function properly.

The Cultural Transmission Theory

Unlike the ecological theory, which assumes that criminal behavior is a product of common values incapable of realization because of social disorganization, the cultural transmission theory attempts to identify the mechanisms that relate social structure to criminal behavior. One mechanism is the conception of differential association, which maintains that a person commits a crime because he or she perceives more favorable than unfavorable definitions of law violation. A person learns to become a criminal. As explained by Sutherland:

As part of the process of learning practical business, a young man with idealism and thoughtfulness for others is inducted into white-collar crime. In many cases he is ordered by a manager to do things, which he regards as unethical or illegal, while in other cases he learns from those who have the same rank as his own how they make a success. He learns specific techniques for violating the law, together with definitions of situations in which those techniques may be used. Also he develops a general ideology.[39]

This mechanism assumes, then, that delinquents have different values from those of nondelinquents. Criminal behavior is the result of values that condone crime. Criminals have been socialized into the values that condone crime. They were transmitted into a culture of crime. Their behavior is an expression of specific values.[40]

Basically, what is implied is that fraudulent behavior in accounting is learned; it is learned indirectly or by indirect association with those who practice the illegal behavior. An accountant engages in fraud because of the intimacy of his or her contact with fraudulent behavior. This is called the process of "differential association." Sutherland explains:

It is a genetic explanation of both white-collar criminals and lower-class criminality. Those who become white-collar criminals generally start their careers in good neighborhoods and good homes, graduate from colleges with some idealism, and with little selection on their part, get into particular business situations in which criminality is practically a folk way. The lower-class criminals generally start their careers in deteriorated neighborhoods and families, find delinquents at hand from whom they acquire the attitudes toward, and the techniques of, crime through association with delinquents and through partial segregation from law-abiding people. The essentials of the process are the same for the two classes of criminals.[41]

Anomie Theories

Anomie, as introduced by Durkheim, is a state of normlessness or lack of regulation, a disordered relation between the individual and the social order, which can explain various forms of deviant behavior.[42] Merton's formulation of anomie focuses not on the discontinuity in the life experiences of an individual but on the lack of fit between values and norms that confuses the individual.[43] As an example in achieving the American Dream, a person may find himself or herself in a dilemma between cultural goals and the means specified to achieve them. The ways adopted include conformity, innovation, ritualism, retreatism, and rebellion.[44]

Conformity to the norms and use of legitimate means to attain success do not lead to deviance. Innovation refers to the use of illicit means to attain success and may explain white-collar crime in general and fraudulent accounting and auditing practices in particular. Merton states: "On the top economic levels, the pressures toward innovation not infrequently erase the distinction between business-like stirrings this side of the mores and sharp practices beyond the mores."[45]

Ritualism refers to an abandoning of the success goal. "Though one draws in one's horizons, one continues to abide almost compulsively by institutional norms."[46] Retreatism is basically a tacit withdrawal from the race, a way of escaping from it all.

Finally, rebellion is a revolutionary rejection of the goals of success and the means of reaching it. Those adaptations are a result of the emphasis in our society on economic success and on the difficulty of achieving it.

Only when a system of cultural values extols, virtually above all else, certain common success-goals for the population at large while the social structure rigorously restricts or completely closes access to approved modes of reaching these goals *for a considerable part of the same population* does deviant behavior ensue on a large scale.[47] Interestingly enough, Merton goes as far as suggesting that deviance develops among scientists because of the emphasis on originality. Given limited opportunity and short supply, scientists would resort to devices such as reporting only data that support one's hypothesis, secrecy, stealing ideas, and fabricating data.[48]

Unlike Durkheim, Merton believes that anomie is a permanent feature of all modern industrial societies. Their emphasis on achievement and the pressures that result lead to deviance. The anomie thesis is further explored in the work of Cohen[49] and Cloward and Ohlin.[50] Cohen attributes the origins of criminal behavior to the impact of ambition across those social positions for which the possibilities of achievement are limited. What results is a nonutilitarian delinquent subculture.[51] Individuals placed in low social positions accept societal values of ambition but are unable to realize them because of lack of legitimate opportunities to do so. Cloward and Ohlin suggest that the resulting delinquent behavior is, however, conditioned by the presence or absence of appropriate illegitimate means.[52]

Corporate fraud, fraudulent reporting practices, white-collar crime, and audit failures are a result of anomie in modern societies. Basically, delinquent accountants emerge among those whose status, power, and security of income are relatively low but whose level of aspiration is high, so that they strive to emerge from the bottom using even illegal ways. Fraudulent behavior among accountants is then the solution to status anxiety. It results from the discrepancy between the generally accepted values of ambition and achievement and the inability to realize them and the availability of appropriate illegitimate means.

A Framework for Fraud in Accounting

The various theories from the field of criminology offer alternative explanations for corporate fraud, white-collar crime, fraudulent financial reporting, and audit failures. They can be integrated in a framework to be used for identifying the situations most conducive to those phenomena (see Figure 4.1). Basically, the framework postulates that corporate fraud, white-collar crime, fraudulent financial reporting, and audit failures occur most often in the following situations:

In which accounting and business groups have presented a favorable picture

Figure 4.1
A Framework for Fraud in Accounting

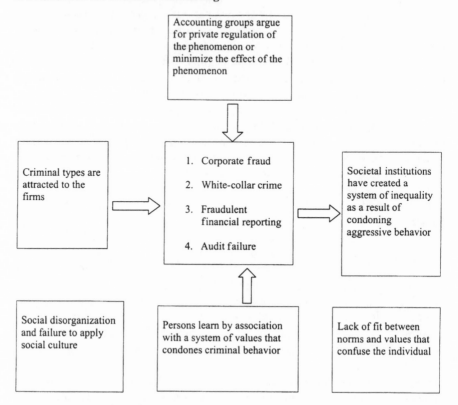

of their problematic situation by insisting that they can control for fraud and worked to get their view of the situation more widely recognized. What may exist is a situation in which the accountants and/or businessmen have stated that they are taking private actions to avoid public regulation of the phenomena, whereas in fact their actions were mere cosmetic changes or camouflage of serious problems in the profession. There have been many examples of situations in which the accounting profession has argued for private regulation of various problems that affect the profession, the discipline, and standard setting and has thwarted the actions of legislators who were trying to put a stop to the abuses. One has only to recall the failure of various congressional committees investigating the profession to enact any fundamental regulations to change the nature, character, structure, and behaviors of the profession to illustrate the point. From a conflict approach, this is clearly a situation in which the interests of those who control the machinery of the state, including the power of the accounting profession, are protected from stringent regulation.

In which societal institutions have accumulated power, privileges, and posi-

tion, creating a perception of inequality in those who are not members of these institutions. Basically, the situation may lead to an isolation of individuals in a situation in which the acquisitive behavior of the powerful is evident in their daily lives. The lower-level accountant may react to this situation of powerlessness, inferiority, and exclusion by resorting to the various types of illegal activities covered in this chapter. It would be a mere reaction to a system of inequality that values aggressive behavior as explained by the conflict model.

In which firms in general have attracted some criminal types. This Lombrosian view of the phenomenon applies to various accounting frauds.

In which social disorganization in general and failure to apply social control exist. Basically, weak social organization of the discipline and failure of the general public to be concerned creates a climate conducive to fraud.

In which people are placed in a system of values that condones corporate fraud, white-collar crime, fraudulent financial reporting, and audit failures.

In which there is a lack of fit between values and norms that compose the person.

OUTCOME SITUATIONS THAT ARISE FROM CORPORATE FRAUD

Away from RICO to ADR

There is definitely a dramatic increase in the number of claims against certified public accountants (CPAs) and in the amounts sought by claimants as a result of the expanding scope of accountants' liability and the Racketeer-Influenced and Corrupt Organization (RICO) Act liability. RICO, originally used by people victimized by a "pattern of racketeering activity" to sue for treble damages and attorney fees, has been used more and more in commercial litigation growing out of fraudulent securities offerings, corporate failures, and investment disappointments. A situation in which codefendent auditors (sometimes in alleged conspiracy with their client and its management) had violated the federal mail and securities fraud statutes by improperly auditing and issuing audit opinions on their client's financial statements on two or more specified occasions and by employing in the operations of their firms (in or affecting interstate commerce) the fees received for those audits, by reason of which plaintiffs were injured in their business or property, is claimed to allege a violation of statutory provisions of RICO.[53] Efforts were made in 1987 to reform the civil provisions of RICO. In fact, a Senate bill introduced by Senator Howard Metzenbaum continues to permit plaintiffs to seek multiple damages in cases otherwise punishable under the securities laws if the plaintiffs are small investors. The definition of small investor includes more than 50 percent of the more than 45 million investors in securities in the United States. This spells bad news for the accounting profession. Witness the following statement made by B.Z. Lee, the AICPA's choice for testifying to the need to reform RICO:

Of greatest concern to the accounting profession . . . is the fact that RICO continues to be used to evade the standards of the securities laws and to raise the stakes in ordinary litigation arising from securities transactions.[54]

For now, fraudulent cases that involve auditors will continue to be prosecuted with RICO liability in mind. In these fraudulent cases accountants have found themselves named as codefendants. The rationale behind the courts' proneness to hold auditors liable for losses associated with business failures results from the belief that auditors "(1) can best prevent the losses associated with business failures and (2) are able to spread their liability through insurance."[55] What auditors face is a dangerous gamble that is trial by jury, especially with the risk of RICO-treble damage judgments. Not only may the average juror not understand the complexities of the cases, but the CPA may face the situation of claims without merit because his or her factual and legal positions may be misunderstood or rejected by the same jurors. The trial by jury may also be an expensive alternative even if the CPA's position prevailed. Witness the following assessment of the situation:

Even if the accountant ultimately prevails at trial, the costs of protracted litigation, including attorneys' fees and deposition costs, can be prohibitively high. Thus, even a win before a jury often translates into great pecuniary loss. Litigation costs and exposure aside, an additional substantial burden is placed on an accountant defendant who is called away from practice—losing both time and fees—and required to produce and review records, study claimants' documents and testimony, appear as a witness on deposition, attend depositions of others and be in attendance at trials.[56]

The trial by jury can also be detrimental to accountants because of the several often repeated arguments that are increasingly persuasive in courts. These arguments include the perceptions (1) that auditors are equipped to prevent the losses associated with business failures, (b) that accountants have deep pockets that can use their insurance to spread the losses, and (c) that equity calls for placing the blame for losses resulting from business failures on auditors.[57] What appear to be more beneficial options for resolving claims against CPAs are the alternative dispute resolution (ADR) methods: arbitration, court-assessed arbitration, mediation, and mistrial.

The AICPA's special committee on accountants' legal liability prepared in 1987 a paper on ADR as a flexible approach to resolving litigation with a client by transforming the typical confrontational position into one of cooperation to reach a mutually advantageous solution.[58] One suggestion made is for the accountant and his or her client to agree on some element of an engagement letter or on a separate agreement that any disputes between them will be determined by ADR procedures. The following two model paragraphs are offered for an engagement letter, one specifically for arbitration and the other for general procedure:

Model Arbitration Paragraph

Any controversy or claim arising out of or relating to our engagement to [describe service, e.g., audit the company's financial statements] shall be resolved by arbitration in accordance with the Commercial Arbitration Rules of the American Arbitration Association, and judgment on the award rendered by the Arbitrator(s) may be rendered in any Court having proper jurisdiction.

Model General ADR Paragraph

In the event of any dispute between us relating to our engagement to [describe engagement, e.g., audit the company's financial statements; prepare the company's tax returns], we mutually agree to try in good faith to resolve the dispute through negotiation or alternative dispute resolution techniques before pursuing full-scale litigation.[59]

Arbitration is now appearing as the more viable option. The pros for arbitration include (1) its informal nature, (2) the choice of knowledgeable professionals as arbitrators, (3) its low cost, (4) its avoidance of the wrong judgments by an unsophisticated jury, (5) the neutralizing of the hostility factor to professionals and sympathy factor to alleged victims prevalent in a jury trial, and (6) the elimination of the risk of a runaway jury's returning a verdict that far exceeds actual losses. These features are summed up as follows.

In arbitration, extensive and time-consuming discovery, which has become standard practice in litigation, is generally not permitted. During the preparatory stages of arbitration, lengthy depositions usually aren't allowed, and limited documentation is exchanged on an informal basis. At arbitration hearings, the rules of evidence are more relaxed. Because of the expertise of the members of the panel, the need for experts to make detailed explanations to unsophisticated jurors is substantially reduced. Fewer witnesses need to be called to testify, fewer technical requirements need to be met, and fewer technical evidentiary objections and arguments need to be made.[60]

Naturally, there are limitations to arbitration. The major limitations are the absence of judicial review and the loss of the court's requirement that evidence be legally admissible and weighed in accordance with legal principles. Other limitations are expressed as follows.

While the American Institute of CPAs' accountants' legal liability special committee has submitted proposed alternative dispute resolution and arbitration clauses, the inclusion of these clauses in the initial engagement letter may subject a member to a coverage defense in any subsequent litigation. . . . Arbitration includes numerous negative points such as limited discovery, limited appeal and a difficulty in confining the arbitrators' decision to case and statutory law. This is particularly true when a defense may involve a question of privity. These negative points severely affect the insurer's ability to defend an insured in a malpractice claim. It seems to me that a CPA may subject himself to an insurance coverage dispute by including an arbitration clause in the initial engagement letter, since the clause binds the CPA and his insurer to submit to future arbitration.[61]

The Liability Exposure Expands

With the number of lawsuits filed in 1987 reaching one private lawsuit for every fifteen Americans, accountants were not immune to the epidemic of lawsuits. The consequences include escalating judgments and legal costs and astronomical increases in the premiums for professional liability. Even the AICPA professional liability insurance plan increased the premium to 200 percent by the end of 1985, along with a coupling of deductibles and reduction in the maximum coverage available from $20 million in 1984 to $5 million in 1985. The situation is explained as follows: As a result of the premium increase, some medium-sized firms previously paying about $3,400 for $5 million in coverage saw their bills jump to $10,250. In addition, the deductible per claim doubled from $3,500 to $7,000.[62]

To make things worse, megasuits are now being filed against the eight largest accounting firms. Examples include (1) the $260 million damage suit filed in 1985 by the British government for alleged negligence against the auditors of the Delorean Motor Co. in Northern Ireland and (2) the $100 million judgment brought against an Australian accounting partnership in *Cambridge Credit Corporation Ltd. v. Hutcheson.*[63]

The nature of accounting liability has changed since the first English lawsuit against an auditor in 1887.[64] Two major suits had a profound effect: Judge (later Justice) Benjamin N. Cardozo's opinion in *Ultramares Corp. v. Touche* in 1931[65] and the McKesson & Robbins business fraud and settlement with accountants in 1938.[66] The *Ultramares Corp. v. Touche* decision was that accountants are liable for negligence to their clients and to those who they know will be using their work product. More precisely, Judge Cardozo held that accountants could not be held liable to third parties because it might

expose accountants to a liability in an indeterminate amount for an indeterminate time to an indeterminate class. The hazards of business conducted on these terms are so extreme as to enkindle doubt whether a flaw may not exist in the implication of a duty that exposes to these consequences.[67]

The doctrine known as the "privity defense" has recently been eroded with a dramatic expansion in the scope of an auditor's availability for negligence. As Minow states: "The new theory seems to be that the accountant should be held responsible for a business that doesn't function properly."[68] The new *doctrine of indeterminate liability* extends the accountants' liability to any investor or creditor who can convince the court or a jury that the accountant, in hindsight, could have prevented a business failure or fraud by disclosing it. Another new doctrine known as the *fraud-on-the-market theory* allows investors to recover from defendants for alleged misrepresentations of which the investors were completely unaware as long as reliance on the statements by the market affected the price of the security bought or sold by the plaintiff. An example of the new doctrines came in 1983, when the New Jersey Supreme Court, in *Rosenblaum v. Adler*, held that the accountants can be held of negligence to any reasonable "third parties" relying on that information, especially that which the accountants are able to use and misuse:

Independent auditors have apparently been able to obtain liability insurance covering these risks or otherwise to satisfy their financial obligation. We have no reason to believe they may not purchase malpractice insurance policies that cover their negligence leading to misstatements relied upon by persons who received the audit from the company pursuant to a proper business purpose. Much of the additional costs incurred either because of more thorough auditing review or increased insurance premiums would be borne by the business entity and its stockholders or its customers.[69]

There is definitely a misperception of the accounting profession and its work product. Victor Earle, general counsel of Peat, Marwick, Main & Co., stated this misperception with prescience a decade ago:

The misconceptions in the public mind are at least fivefold: first, as to scope—that auditors make a 100% examination of the company's records, which can be depended upon to recover all errors or misconduct; second, as to evaluation—that auditors test the wisdom and legality of a company's multitudinous business decisions; third, as to precision—that the numbers set forth in a company's audited financial statements are immutable absolutes; fourth, as to reducibility—that the audited results of a company's operations for a year can be synthesized into a single number; and fifth, as to approval—that by expressing an option on a company's financial statement, the auditors "certify" its health and attractiveness for investment purposes.[70]

The liability exposure of U.S. accounting firms doing audits of overseas subsidiaries of American companies also increased tremendously in March 1988, when a federal judge ruled that United States-based accounting firms can be sued in U.S. courts for allegedly shoddy audits in other nations. The decision came after the Court denied a motion by Arthur Andersen & Co. to throw out a $260 million suit against it by the British government for allegedly negligent audits after the collapse of Delorean Motor Co.'s Irish unit. That the U.S. courts will have jurisdiction in such cases spells more trouble for American accounting firms, as U.S. courts are known to be far tougher on accountants than are English and European courts.[71]

In March 1988 the liability exposure took a different dimension when the Supreme Court made it easier for shareholders to file class-action lawsuits against companies that issue misleading information. In its ruling the Supreme Court endorsed the efficient market hypothesis, which maintains that all publicly available information is reflected in the market price. Therefore, shareholders who allege misleading information and security fraud don't have to prove that they have relied on the misleading information. Basically, nobody can hide anymore behind a white collar.[72]

Those developments put the accounting profession in a dangerous situation, as all business failures could be blamed on the accountant and as the normal risks of investment may be shifted from the investor to the accountant. Frivolous litigation may arise, leading the accounting profession to avoid serving riskier industries and to avoid innovations in its own practice. A case in point is the review of earnings forecasts. Minow explains:

Accountants would be discouraged from innovations within their own practice, such as review of earnings forecasts, which, though potentially highly useful to the investing public, are necessarily speculative and, in the current climate, pose obvious litigation risks to accountants.[73]

Fraud Engagement: The Issues

Fraud as the intentional deception, misappropriation of resources, or distortion of data to the advantage of the perpetrator may involve either a manager or an employee. Management fraud is the most difficult to detect and can cause irreparable damage. The conduct of an audit in accordance with generally accepted accounting principles does not anticipate deceit and may fail to detect fraud. The key to fraud prevention could be effective and functioning internal controls. However, some fraud schemes may be effectively designed to work within the framework of an effective internal control system. The level of assurance of these controls becomes the key, even though fraud is most associated with a problem of integrity and, therefore, not easily quantifiable. What may be needed besides the audit is a fraud engagement. This is different from an audit based on a generally accepted auditing standard in the following way:

In short, the fraud engagement requires a specialized program that is singularly designed for discovery. It is ideally concerned with what lies behind transactions, with regard to materiality, and is not concerned with the application of generally accepted accounting principles unless misapplication has led to fraudulent statements. In its purest form, therefore, it is a hybrid of auditing and management advisory services. And the individual searching for fraud must have a detection mentality that is tempered with a high level of innovation and skepticism.[74]

Fraud engagement should be looking for specifically recurring fraud schemes and watch for specific indicators of fraud. Recurring fraudulent schemes include the following:

• Petty cash embezzlement, generally camouflaged by false or inadequate documentation
• Accounts payable fraud involving the formation of a dummy corporation to invoice the payer and receive the funds

- Cash inventory schemes in which inventory is purchased with cash or its equivalent, rather than by check, and is not placed on the books
- False payroll schemes involving the creation of a fictitious employee, with management cashing his or her spurious payroll checks
- Lapping schemes in which employees steal from one customer's account and attempt to cover the theft by applying to that account later collections from another customer
- Kickback schemes[75]

All of these schemes involve some diversion of assets or information followed by the prevention or deferral of the activities' disclosure. They can be detected if certain indicators or indicia are carefully watched, especially those indicators or indicia that are present time and again when fraud occurs. The following irregularities deserve closer scrutiny:

1. High rates of employee turnover, particularly in the accounting or bookkeeping departments
2. Refusal to use serially numbered documents or the undocumented destruction of missing numbers
3. Excessive and unjustified cash transactions
4. Excessive and unjustified use of exchange items, such as cashier's checks, traveler's checks, and money orders
5. Failure to reconcile checking accounts
6. Excessive number of checking accounts with a true business purpose
7. The existence of liens and other financial encumbrances before a bankruptcy, which may indicate that the bankruptcy was planned
8. Photocopies of invoices in files
9. A manager or employee who falls in debt
10. Excessive number of unexplained corporate checks bearing second endorsements
11. Excessive or material changes in bad-debt write-off
12. Inappropriate freight expenses in relation to historical sales or industry norms
13. Inappropriate ratio of inventory components
14. Business dealings with no apparent economic purpose
15. Assets apparently sold but possession maintained
16. Assets sold for much less than they are worth
17. Continuous rollover of loans to management or loans to employees not normally included in the loans accounts
18. Questionable changes in financial ratios, such as net income and inventory
19. Questionable leave practices, such as the failure or refusal of an employee to take leave[76]

It follows that auditors have to expand their role to that of police officers and engage in detecting and reporting fraud and financial weaknesses in the firms that they audit. The three-year examination of the auditing profession by the House Subcommittee on Oversight and Investigations that ended in 1988 had a nonnegotiable item for the profession, which is to be the voluntary protector of the investor or face legislation that will make this role mandatory.[77] For that, Congress will use the Treadway findings as a basis for the legislation and increase the SEC power to impose sanctions and push for criminal prosecution. One would not blame Congress, as the typical situation now shows a failure of auditing standards when they allow auditors to wait until a company has failed before notifying the SEC of possible fraud. A case in point is the ZZZZ Best One, in which Ernst and Whinney had good reason to believe long before ZZZZ Best collapsed that many of the statements made by the carpet cleaning company were fraudulent. It was over and of no use to anyone when Ernst and Whinney decided to make its knowledge of fraud public. Only after the bankruptcy did Ernst and Whinney file documents with the SEC indicating that it had been tipped off that ZZZZ Best really was little more than a giant Ponzi scheme, costing investors more than $70 million.

Fraud auditing is then one solution to the problem of fraudulent financial reporting and fraud in general. It was referred to as the creation of an environment that encourages the detection and prevention of fraud in commercial transactions.[78] The advent of federal, criminal, and regulatory statutes involving business calls for some form of fraud auditing. When fraud auditing fails to connect the problems and frauds do happen, is there a role for forensic and investigative accounting? Forensic auditing deals with the relation and application of financial facts to legal problems.[79] What, then, is the difference between forensic accounting, fraud auditing, investigative auditing, and financial auditing? The answer to a survey among the staff members of Peat Marwick Lindquist Holmes, a Toronto-based firm of chartered accountants, is illustrative of the difference:

Forensic accounting is a general term used to describe any investigation of a financial nature that can result in some matter that has legal consequence.

Fraud auditing is a specialized discipline within forensic accounting, which involves the investigation of a particular criminal activity, namely fraud.

Investigative auditing involves the review of financial documentation for a specific purpose, which could relate to litigation support and insurance claims as well as criminal matters.[80]

Forensic accounting goes beyond routine auditing. It specializes in uncovering fraud in the ledger of business contracts and bank statements. Forensic auditors prepare a written profile of every key person involved with the company, including corporate officers, employees, and vendors. Keeping track of everything is the objective. The following comment by Douglas Carmichael illustrates the extent of the investigation under forensic auditing:

When the death of a company [occurs] under mysterious circumstances, forensic accountants are essential. . . . Other accountants may look at the charts. But forensic accountants actually dig into the body.[81]

THE POSITION OF THE ACCOUNTANTS IN THE COURTS

Do CPAs, because of their credentials as professionals, have special privileges in the legal system? The answer is that both as witnesses in the conduct of legal inquiry and as defendants in the law of torts, the accountants face a difficult and awkward situation.

Loss of Technical Privilege

The court requires of all witnesses that all relevant information be brought to court on pain of a charge of contempt. The best-known exception is the lawyer–client privilege. The general rule of privilege of Federal Rule of Evidence 503 reads as follows:

A client has a privilege to refuse to disclose and to prevent any other person from disclosing confidential communications made for the purpose of facilitating the rendition of professional [*sic*] legal services to the client, (1) between himself or his representative and his lawyer or his lawyer's representative, or (2) between his lawyer and the lawyer's representative, or (3) by him or his lawyer to a lawyer representing another in a matter of common interest, or (4) between representatives of the client or between the client and a representative of the client, or (5) between lawyers representing the client.

The same privilege has also been given to the psychologist and the physician (Supreme Court Standard 504) and the clergyman (Supreme Court Standard 506). How about accountants? Do they function or rate sufficiently high to overweigh the value of requiring them to reveal their secrets to the court? The official decision of the courts is that accountants cannot join the privileged few.

As part of the audit process, accountants review *contingencies* that could affect a company's financial conditions as reflected in its financial statements. They are guided in their analysis by Statement of Financial Accounting Standards (SFAS) No. 5, "Accounting for Contingencies." One of the important contingencies examined is that the Internal Revenue Service (IRS) will audit the company's tax return and make material adjustments to it. The auditor is assumed to estimate the probabilities of such adjustments and their magnitude. In the process the auditor prepares a number of papers, including an audit program, reports to management, and tax accrual work papers. The tax accrual papers, which are the subject of a controversy, usually consist of (1) a summary analysis of the transactions recorded in the taxpayer's income tax accounts, (2) a computation of the tax provision for the current year, and (3) a memorandum that discusses items reflected in the financial statements as income or expense, when the ultimate tax treatment is unclear.

The controversy is that the IRS policy states that its agents may seek access to both audit and tax work papers of independent accountants. Section 7602 of the Internal Revenue Code gives the commissioner of internal revenue sweeping authority to summons relevant documents in an investigation of income tax liability. In fact, the section gives the IRS the power to (1) examine any books, papers, records, or other data that may be relevant or material to such inquiry; (2) summon people to produce such books, papers, records, or other data; and (3) give such testimony, under oath, as may be relevant or material to such inquiry.

Would the access of the IRS to the tax accrual papers threaten an accountant's ability to perform an effective audit of a company's financial statements? Most concerned accountants would view the IRS review of their work papers as a fishing expedition and a mind-scam. Most would expect the courts to give them the same treatment as attorneys and reject the mind-scam of accountants. In effect, in *Hickman v. Taylor* (1947) the Supreme Court rejected a mind-scam of attorneys because it destroys the mental privacy that a professional needs to work effectively. The accountants used the mind-scam argument to argue against the IRS' use of the auditor's work papers. The Court's decisions, for some cases, were favorable to the accounting profession. This was true in *United States v. Humble Oil* (1974), *United States v. Powell* (1964), *SEC v. Arthur Young & Co.* (1979), *United States v. Matras* (1973), and *United States v. Coopers & Lybrand* (1977). Not all of the Court's decisions were favorable to accountants. This was true in *United States v. Arthur Young & Co.* (1981) and *United States v. Coopers & Lybrand* (1975). In fact, the Supreme Court, in March 1984, overruled the Second Circuit of Appeals and said that the IRS was entitled to see the tax accrual work papers of Arthur Young & Co. in the IRS' probe of Amerada Hess Corp. for 1972 through 1974. The company was accused of setting up a slush fund for political contributions and payments to foreign officials. Arthur Young and Amerada Hess argued that the work papers were irrelevant to any IRS investigation because they were not used in preparing the tax returns. Moreover, they argued that accountants and clients are protected by the same privilege of confidentiality as lawyers. Both arguments were rejected. The Court maintained, first, that the papers were relevant and, second, that lawyers are "advocates" and "advisers" for their clients, but accountants play a "public watchdog" role as auditors. Chief Justice Burger wrote:

By certifying the public reports that collectively depict a corporation's financial status, the independent auditor assumes a public responsibility transcending any employment relationship with the client. The independent public accountant performing this special function owes ultimate allegiance to the corporations' creditors and stockholders, as well as to the investing public.

The decision is not a cause for joy in the accounting profession despite assurance from the IRS that it will seek work papers only in unusual cases and when it cannot get the information from the taxpayer. But will the IRS stick to the policy in the future? The decision raises many questions:

1. Will the decision lead companies to be less candid with their outside auditors about their tax pictures?
2. Should not the accountants be protected from disclosure by the privilege of confidentiality that applies to work done by accountants in much the same way that it applies to lawyers' work?
3. Are the outside auditors "watchdogs" or "advocates and advisers" to their clients?
4. Will the relationship between the auditors and their clients change toward less communication and more distortion?
5. Will the companies continue to self-disclose if they know that the CPA may have to give the contents of the disclosure to the IRS? Will it lead to less forthright disclosure?
6. Will the discovery of tax accrual work papers provide the IRS with a road map to the corporation's most aggressive interpretations of the Revenue Code?
7. Is the auditor's work-product privilege analogous to the attorney's work-product doctrine?
8. If candid communications between the taxpayer and the auditor are essential to ensure adequate reserves for tax contingencies, would it not be more appropriate that records of communications stating why a tax position was taken by the taxpayer and the settlement posture on that position should seldom, if ever, be discovered by the IRS?
9. Is the full disclosure of questionable positions required for effective revenue collection?
10. Why should corporations provide the IRS with the substance of the case against them?
11. Is the IRS at a disadvantage in its examination of tax returns because the taxpayer, or his or her agent, possesses the sources of information that the IRS needs to audit the return?
12. Without client cooperation and self-disclosure, can the auditor review contingencies as required by SFAS No. 5 and be able to give an unqualified opinion, or is the auditor limited now to give only a qualified or adverse opinion or a disclaimer?

The Accountant as Defendant in the Law of Torts

The U.S. society is a litigious society. The price tag is enormous, with evidence showing that many civil cases that go to trial—with or without a jury—can easily cost the taxpayers more money than is at stake for any of the litigants. In a speech to the American Bar Association on February 12, 1984, Chief Justice Warren Burger observed: "Our system is too costly, too painful, too destructive, too inefficient for a truly civilized people." As a result, accountants find themselves affected in many ways by the litigation explosion.

What is affecting accountants started with prudent liability and the notion of strict liability, whereby "strict liability means that whenever a particular product emerges from an assembly line in a defective condition, the manufacturer will be liable for any injury that the defect causes."[82] The notion of strict product liability was later expanded to the area of professional liability affecting, in the process, architects, doctors, lawyers, accountants, and so on. In the case of the accountants, it meant that they should be held responsible for a business that does not function properly. This action has generated a flood of lawsuits against accountants. Each time a company fails, its independent auditors become one of the few potential defendants that are solvent and, therefore, likely targets for a suit. Given this situation, the first step is to identify the five potential sources of legal liability of accountants.

The first source of legal liability is the common liability to clients. This involves contractual liability, negligence liability, and problems of independence.

With respect to contractual liability, the auditor is bound by a contract with the client and an engagement letter specifying the scope of the audit, that his or her audit examination is to be performed with due care and in accordance with professional standards, and that an opinion is to be issued regarding the quality of the client's financial statement. Without this, the accountant would be subjected to legal liability.

With respect to negligence liability, it would arise not only from a breach of contract but also from a failure to observe professional standards and from lapses such as the following: (1) inadequate preparation by failing to prepare or revise the audit program for a client to take into account internal or external changes; (2) lapses in examination by omission or misapplication of a procedure required by the generally accepted standards; (3) inadequate supervision, review, and training of the audit staff; (4) shortcomings of evaluation and judgment; and (5) failure in reporting the right opinion. The accountant can avoid negligent liability if he or she can prove that (1) the client's own negligence contributed to the problem in the company; (2) the client failed to supervise the company's personnel, which contributed to the accountant's failure to fulfill his or her contract and to report the truth; (3) the client disregarded the auditor's recommendations; and (4) the client knew that reliance on the auditor's opinion is unjustified and that such reliance is a form of contributory negligence.

Problems of independence arise when the auditor issues an opinion on the financial statements while acting as an advocate for the client or as unjustifiably deferential to the client management's judgment. This usually happens when the accountant is also performing nonaudit accounting services for the client.

The second source of liability for accountants is the common liability to third parties. For a long time accountants were liable at common law for negligence in the performance of their professional engagements only to their clients. This is known as the *privity of contract doctrine*. The test of the privity of contract doctrine involving auditors came in *Ultramares Corp. v. Touche*.[83] In that case the defendant certified the accounts of a firm, knowing that banks and other lenders were guilty of negligence and fraudulent misrepresentation in not detecting fictitious amounts included in accounts receivable and accounts payable. In his opinion Justice Cardozo drew a sharp distinction between fraudulent conduct and merely negligent conduct, holding that the auditor would not be liable to third parties for the latter:

If liability for negligence exists, a thoughtless slip or blunder, the failure to detect a theft or forgery beneath the cover of deceptive entries, may expose accountants to a liability in an indeterminate amount for an indeterminate time to an indeterminate class. The hazards of a business conducted on these terms are so extreme as to rekindle doubt whether a flaw may not exist in an implication of a duty that espouses to these consequences. The court also stated, however, that if the degree of negligence is so gross as to amount to "constructive fraud," accountants' liability extends to third parties.

Then the defense of lack of privity eroded as the work of the auditors became more and more the subject of lawsuits by nonclient plaintiffs.

An accountant may be liable for ordinary negligence to third parties for whom the accountant knows the client has specifically engaged him or her to produce the accounting product. This type of third party is known as the *primary beneficiary*. An accountant may also be liable for ordinary negligence to third parties, those known or reasonably foreseen by the accountant, as well as those who the accountant knows will rely on his or her work product in making a particular business decision. This type of third party is known as the *foreseen party*. This liability may extend to all third parties, including merely foreseeable third parties. In other words, users of financial statements beyond those actually foreseen could hold a CPA liable.

In addition, accountants may be found liable to third parties for actual or constructive fraud that is inferred from evidence of gross negligence. The plaintiff is required, in this case, to prove that the auditor knew the falsity (or its equivalent) of a representation. This knowledge is known as the *scienter*, and the requirement of its proof is the *scienter requirement*. In any case, fraud consists of the following elements: (1) false representation, (2) knowledge of a wrong and acting with the intent to deceive, (3) intent to induce action in reliance, (4) justifiable reliance, and (5) resulting damage.

The third source of liability for accountants arises under the federal securities laws. Everybody relies on accountants to play a role in producing accurate information. This main responsibility lies in making an independent verification of a company's financial statements. The Securities and Exchange Commission (SEC) perceives the purpose of an audit as a public accountant's examination intended to be an independent check on management's accounting of its stewardships. Thus, the accountant has a direct and unavoidable responsibility, particularly where his or her engagement relates to a company that makes filings with the commission or where there is a substantial public interest. That audit responsibility is exactly the reason for the potential legal liability of a CPA under the federal securities laws, specifically under Section 11 of the Securities Act of 1933; Section 10(b) of the Securities Exchange Act of 1934 and related Rule 10b-5; Section 12(2) of the 1933 act; Sections 9 and 18 of the 1934 act; Section 17(a) of the 1933 act; and Section 14 of the 1934 act.

Section 11 of the 1933 act defines the rights of third parties and auditors as follows:

In case any part of the registration statement . . . contained an untrue statement of a material fact or omitted to state a material fact required to be stated therein or necessary to make the statements therein not misleading, any person acquiring such security . . . may . . . sue . . . every accountant . . . who has with his consent been named as having . . . certified any part of the registration statement . . . with respect to the statement in such registration . . . which purports to have been . . . certified by him.

Section 11 lists among potential defendants every accountant who helps to prepare any part of the registration statement or any financial statement used in it. It imposes a civil inability on accountants for misrepresentations or omissions of material facts in a registration statement. The leading Section 11 case, *Escott v. Barchris Construction Corp.*,[84] was a class action against a bowling alley construction corporation that had issued debentures and subsequently declared bankruptcy. The court ruled that the accountants were liable for not meeting the minimum standard of "due diligence" in their review of subsequent events occurring to the effective date of the registration statement.

Section 10(b) of the 1934 act states:

It shall be unlawful for any person directly or indirectly, by the use of any means or instrumentality of interstate commerce, or of the mails or of any facility of any national securities exchange, a) to employ any device, scheme, or artifice to defraud, b) to make any untrue statement of a material fact or omit to state a material fact necessary in order to make the statements made, in the light of the circumstances under which they are made, not misleading, or c) to engage in any act, practice, or course of business which operates or would operate as a fraud or deceit upon any person in connection with the purchase or sale of any security.[85]

The elements of Section 10(b) violations are, therefore, (1) a manipulative or deceptive practice, (2) in connection with a purchase or sale, (3) which results in a loss to the plaintiff. Unlike the case in Section 11 of the 1933 act, here the plaintiff carries the burden of proof under Section 10(b). For a while the courts disagreed on the standard of performance to enforce against an accountant under

Rule 10b-5. Then in 1976 the Supreme Court resolved the controversy in *Ernst & Ernst v. Hochfelder*[86] by ruling that some knowledge and intent to deceive are required before accountants can be held liable for violation of Rule 10b-5. In other words, the private suit must require the allegation of a scienter. Most lower courts have held that "recklessness" by a defendant is sufficient to satisfy the scienter requirement of Section 10(b), although mere negligence is not.

Section 12(2) of the 1933 act provides that any person who offers or sells a security by means of a prospectus or by oral statements that contain untrue statements or misleading opinions shall be liable to the purchaser for the damages sustained. Some courts have taken a broad view by implicating accountants as liable for aiding and abetting Section 12(2) violations.

Section 18(a) of the 1934 act imposes civil liability on accountants for filing a false or misleading statement. To escape liability, the defendant must prove that "he acted in good faith and had no knowledge that such statement was false or misleading."

Section 17(a) of the 1933 act states that it should be unlawful for any person in the offer or sale of securities (1) to defraud, (2) to obtain money or property by means of an untrue statement or misleading omission, or (3) to engage in any transaction, practice, or course of business that deceives a purchaser. This section does not state, however, whether a party violating the law is liable. The issue remains to be solved by the Supreme Court.

Section 14 of the 1934 act sets forth a comprehensive scheme governing solicitation of proxies. Rule 14a-9 outlaws proxy solicitation by use of false statements or misleading omissions.

The fourth source of liability for accountants arises under the Foreign Corrupt Practices Act (FCPA) of 1977. This act makes it illegal to offer a bribe to an official of a foreign country. It also requires SEC registrants under the 1934 act to maintain reasonably complete and accurate records and an adequate system of internal control to prevent bribery. Until now the SEC has refused to take any action against perceived violations of the accounting provisions of the FCPA unless those violations are linked to breaches of other securities.

The fifth source of liability is the criminal liability under both federal and state laws. The criminal provisions are in the Uniform Mail Fraud Statute and the Federal False Statements Statute. All of these statutes make it a criminal offense to defraud another person through knowingly being involved with false financial statements. Four of the most widely publicized criminal prosecutions were the *Continental Vending, Four Seasons, National Student Marketing*, and *Equity Funding* cases, in which errors of judgment on the part of the auditors resulted in criminal liabilities. The SEC position on bringing criminal charges against auditors was once stated as follows:

While virtually all Commission cases are civil in character, on rare occasions it is concluded that a case is sufficiently serious that it should be referred to the Department of

Justice for consideration of criminal prosecution. Referrals in regard to accountants have only been made when the Commission and the staff believed that the evidence indicated that a professional accountant certified financial statements that he knew to be false when he reported on them. The Commission does not make criminal references in cases that it believes are simply matters of professional judgment even if the judgments appear to be bad ones.[87]

CONCLUSIONS

The increase of fraud in the accounting environment is definitely an emerging problem for the accounting profession. The credibility of the profession and the field as a guarantor of the integrity of the financial recording system will suffer more unless drastic measures are taken to make the accountant and the auditor face the fraud problem as a major concern. The immorality of the phenomenon should be accentuated in special courses in the ethical problems of the profession. The education community should take the lead in sensitizing students to the existence, the gravity, the immorality, and the consequences of the problem. The short term-oriented management style that may account for a large proportion of corporate fraud needs to be de-emphasized because of its myopic view of the environment.

NOTES

1. *Michigan Law Review*, chap. 66, sect. 1529.
2. J. Bologna, *Corporate Fraud: The Basics of Prevention and Detection* (Boston: Butterworth Publishers, 1984).
3. Ibid., 10.
4. "Ethics 101," *U.S. News and World Report*, March 14, 1988, p. 76.
5. National Commission on Fraudulent Financial Reporting, *Report of the National Commission on Fraudulent Financial Reporting* (Washington, DC, April 1987), p. 2.
6. Bologna, *Corporate Fraud*, p. 63.
7. S. Lilien and V. Pastena, "Intermethod Comparability: The Case of the Oil and Gas Industry," *The Accounting Review* (July 1981), pp. 690–703.
8. D.S. Dhaliwal, G.L. Salamon, and E.D. Smith, "The Effect of Owner versus Management Control on the Choice of Accounting Methods," *Journal of Accounting and Economics* 1 (1982), pp. 41–53.
9. P.M. Healy, "The Effect of Bonus Schemes on Accounting Decisions," *Journal of Accounting and Economics* 1–3 (1985), pp. 85–107.
10. K.B. Schwartz, "Accounting Changes by Corporations Facing Possible Insolvency," *Journal of Accounting, Auditing and Finance* (Fall 1982), pp. 32–43; K.A. Merchant, *Fraudulent and Questionable Financial Reporting: A Corporate Perspective* (Morristown, NJ: Financial Executives Research Foundation, 1987), p. 105.
11. J.M. Fedders and L.G. Perry, "Policing Financial Disclosure Fraud: The SEC's Top Priority," *Journal of Accountancy* (July 1984), p. 59.
12. B. Lietbag, "Profile: James C. Treadway, Jr.," *Journal of Accountancy* (September 1986), p. 80.
13. Merchant, *Fraudulent and Questionable Financial Reporting*, p. 38.

14. E. Durkheim, *The Division of Labor in Society*, translated by George Simpson (New York: Free Press, 1964), p. 2.

15. E.A. Ross, *Sins and Society* (Boston: Houghton Mifflin, 1907).

16. Ibid., p. 7.

17. E. Sutherland, "White-Collar Criminality," *American Sociological Review* 5 (February 1940), pp. 110–123.

18. E. Sutherland, *White Collar Crime* (New York: Dryden Press, 1949), p. 9.

19. M.B. Clinard and R.F. Reier, *Sociology of Deviant Behavior* (New York: Holt, Rinehart, and Winston, 1979), p. viii.

20. F.E. Hartung, "White Collar Offenses in the Wholesale Meat Industry in Detroit," *American Journal of Sociology* 56 (1950), p. 25.

21. S. Wheeler and M.L. Rothman, "The Organization as Weapon in White-Collar Crime," *Michigan Law Review* (June 1982), pp. 1403–1476.

22. L.S. Shrager and O.F. Short Jr., "How Serious a Crime? Perceptions of Organizational and Common Crimes," in G. Geis and E. Stotland (eds.), *White-Collar Crime: Theory and Research* (London: Sage, 1980), p. 26.

23. V. Aubert, "White Collar Crime and Social Structure," *American Journal of Sociology* (November 1952), p. 265.

24. Ibid., p. 266.

25. H. Edelhertz, E. Stotland, M. Walsh, and J. Weimberg, *The Investigation of White Collar Crime: A Manual for Law Enforcement Agencies* (Washington, DC: U.S. Government Printing Office, 1970).

26. A. Bequai, *White-Collar Crime: A 20th Century Crisis* (Lexington, MA: Lexington Books, 1978), p. 13.

27. Z.V. Palmrose, "An Analysis of Auditor Litigation and Audit Service Quality," *The Accounting Review* (January 1988), p. 56.

28. L.E. DeAngelo, "Auditor Size and Audit Quality," *Journal of Accounting and Economics* (December 1981), pp. 183–199.

29. American Institute of Certified Public Accountants, *Professional Standards*, Vol. 1 (New York: AICPA, 1985), SAS no. 47.

30. Palmrose, "Analysis of Auditor Litigation," p. 72.

31. Z.-V. Palmrose, "Litigation and Independent Auditors: The Role of Business Failures and Management Fraud," *Auditing: A Journal of Practice and Theory* (Spring 1987), pp. 90–103.

32. J.E. Connor, "Enhancing Public Confidence in the Accounting Profession," *Journal of Accountancy* (July 1986), p. 83.

33. K. St. Pierre and J. Anderson, "An Analysis of Audit Failures Based on Documented Legal Cases," *Journal of Accounting, Auditing and Finance* (Spring 1988), pp. 229–247.

34. R.K. Elliott and J.J. Willingham, *Management Fraud: Detection and Deterrence* (New York: Petrocelli Books, 1980), p. 10.

35. K.A. Merchant, *Fraudulent and Questionable Financial Reporting* (New York: Financial Executives Research Foundation, 1987), p. 12.

36. J.T. Carey, *Introduction to Criminology* (Englewood Cliffs, NJ: Prentice-Hall, 1978), p. 8.

37. D.L. Gibbons, "Crime and Punishment: A Study in Social Attitudes," *Social Forces* (June 1969), pp. 391–397.

38. Carey, *Introduction to Criminology*, pp. 36–41.

39. Sutherland, *White Collar Crime*, p. 240.

40. W.B. Miller, "Lower Class Culture as a Generating Milieu of Gang Delinquency," *Journal of Social Issues* 14, 3 (1958), pp. 5–19.

41. Sutherland, "White Collar Criminality," p. 12.

42. Durkheim, *The Division of Labor in Society*.

43. R.K. Merton, "Social Structure and Anomie," *American Sociological Review* (October 1938), pp. 672–682.

44. R.K. Merton, *Social Theory and Social Structure* (New York: Free Press, 1957), pp. 31–60.

45. Ibid., p. 144.

46. Ibid., p. 150.

47. Ibid., p. 146.

48. R.K. Merton, "Priorities in Scientific Discovery: A Chapter in the Sociology of Science," *American Sociological Review* (December 1957), pp. 635–659.

49. A.K. Cohen, *Delinquent Boys: The Culture of the Gang* (New York: Free Press, 1955).

50. R.A. Cloward and L.E. Ohlin, *Delinquency and Opportunity* (New York: Free Press, 1960).

51. A.K. Cohen, "The Study of Social Disorganization and Deviant Behavior," in R.K. Merton, L. Boorm, and L.S. Cottrell Jr. (eds.), *Sociology Today: Problems and Prospects* (New York: Harper & Bros., 1959).

52. Cloward and Ohlin, *Delinquency and Opportunity*, p. 72.

53. R.J. Gomley, "RICO and the Professional Accountant," *Journal of Accounting, Auditing and Finance* (Fall 1982), pp. 51–60.

54. "AICPA Testifies at RICO Hearings: Support Boucher Proposal," *Journal of Accountancy* (January 1988), p. 82.

55. R.S. Banick and D.C. Broeker, "Arbitration: An Option for Resolving Claims Against CPAs," *Journal of Accountancy* (October 1987), p. 124.

56. Ibid., p. 126.

57. S.H. Collins, "Professional Liability: The Situation Worsens," *Journal of Accountancy* (November 1985), p. 66.

58. American Institute of Certified Public Accountants, Special Committee on Accountants' Legal Liability, *Alternative Dispute Resolution* (New York: AICPA, 1987).

59. Ibid., pp. 2, 8.

60. Ibid., p. 726.

61. J.D. Steward, "Arbitration," *Journal of Accountancy* (February 1988), p. 1213.

62. Collins, "Professional Liability," p. 57.

63. Ibid., p. 57.

64. *Leeds Estate, Building & Investment Co. v. Shepherd*, 36, Ch. D. 787 (18F7).

65. *Ultramares Corp. v. Torche*, 225 N.Y. 170, 174 N.E. 441 (1931).

66. See D.Y. Causey Jr., *Duties and Liabilities of Public Accountants* (Homewood, IL: Dow Jones–Irwin, 1982), pp. 16–17.

67. *Ultramares Corp. v. Torche*, 225 N.Y. 170, 179–180, 174 N.E. 441, 444 (1931).

68. N.N. Minow, "Accountants' Liability and the Litigation Explosion," *Journal of Accountancy* (September 1984), p. 72.

69. *Rosenblaum v. Adler*, Slip Op. A-39/85 (N.J., June 9, 1983), 21.

70. V. Earle, "Accountants on Trial in a Theater of the Absurd," *Fortune* (May 1972), p. 227.

71. L. Berton, "Accounting Firms Can Be Sued in U.S. over Audits Done Abroad, Judge Rules," *Wall Street Journal* (March 10, 1988), p. 2.

72. L.J. Tell, "Giliam's Legacy: Nobody Can Hide behind a White Collar," *Business Week* (February 8, 1988), p. 69.

73. Minow, "Accountants' Liability and the Litigation Explosion," p. 80.

74. M.M. Levy, "Financial Fraud: Schemes and Indicia," *Journal of Accountancy* (August 1985), p. 79.

75. Ibid., pp. 79–86.

76. Ibid., pp. 86–87.

77. S. Gaines, "From Balance Sheet to Fraud Beat," *Chicago Tribune* (February 28, 1988), sect. 7, p. 5.

78. J.G. Bologna and R.J. Lindquist, *Fraud Auditing and Forensic Accounting* (New York: John Wiley & Sons, 1987), p. 22.

79. Ibid., p. 85.

80. Ibid., p. 91.

81. D. Akst and L. Berton, "Accountants Who Specialize in Detecting Fraud Find Themselves in Great Demand," *Wall Street Journal* (February 26, 1988), sect. 2, p. 17.

82. J. Weberman, *The Litigious Society* (New York: Basic Books, 1981), p. 42.

83. *Ultramares Corp. v. Touche*, 255 N.Y. 170, 174, N.E. 441 (1931).

84. *Escott v. Barchis Construction Corp.* 283 F.Supp. 643 (S.D.N.Y. 1968).

85. Securities Act 1934, 17 C.F.R. Section 240. 10b-5 (1971).

86. *Ernst & Ernst v. Hochfelder*, 425 U.S. 185, 965 Ct. 1375, 47 L. Ed. 2d 668 (2nd ed.).

87. J.C. Burtow, "SEC Enforcement and Professional Accountants: Philosophy, Objectives and Approaches." *Vanderbilt Law Review* 78 (January 1975), p. 88.

SELECTED REFERENCES

"AICPA Testifies at RICO Hearings: Support Boucher Proposal." *Journal of Accountancy* (January 1988), p. 82.

Akst, D., and L. Berton. "Accountants Who Specialize in Detecting Fraud Find Themselves in Great Demand." *Wall Street Journal* (February 26, 1988), sect. 2, p. 17.

American Institute of Certified Public Accountants. *Professional Standards*, Vol. 1. New York: AICPA, 1985, SAS no. 47.

American Institute of Certified Public Accountants, Special Committee on Accountants' Legal Liability. *Alternative Dispute Resolution*. New York: AICPA, 1987.

Aubert, V. "White Collar Crime and Social Structure." *American Journal of Sociology* (November 1952), p. 265.

Banick, R.S., and D.C. Broeker. "Arbitration: An Option for Resolving Claims against CPAs." *Journal of Accountancy* (October 1987), p. 124.

Bequai, A. *White-Collar Crime: A 20th Century Crisis*. Lexington, MA: Lexington Books, 1978, p. 13.

Berton, L. "Accounting Firms Can Be Sued in U.S. over Audits Done Abroad, Judge Rules." *Wall Street Journal* (March 10, 1988), p. 2.

Bologna, J. *Corporate Fraud: The Basics of Prevention and Detection*. Boston: Butterworth Publishers, 1984, p. 39.

Bologna, J., and R.J. Lindquist. *Fraud Auditing and Forensic Accounting*. New York: John Wiley & Sons, 1987, pp. 22, 91.

Carey, J.T. *Introduction to Criminology*. Englewood Cliffs, NJ: Prentice-Hall, 1978, pp. 8, 36–41.

Causey, D.Y., Jr. *Duties and Liabilities of Public Accountants*. Homewood, IL: Dow Jones–Irwin, 1982, pp. 16–17.

Clinard, M.B., and R.F. Reier. *Sociology of Deviant Behavior*. New York: Holt, Rinehart, and Winston, 1979.

Cloward, R.A., and L.E. Ohlin. *Delinquency and Opportunity*. New York: Free Press, 1960.

Cohen, A.K. *Delinquent Boys: The Culture of the Gang*. New York: Free Press, 1955, pp. 77–82.

———. "The Study of Social Disorganization and Deviant Behavior." In Robert K. Merton, Leonard Boorm, and Leonard S. Cottrell Jr. (eds.), *Sociology Today: Problems and Prospects*. New York: Harper & Bros., 1959.

Collins, S.H. "Professional Liability: The Situation Worsens." *Journal of Accountancy* (November 1985), pp. 57, 66.

Connor, J.E. "Enhancing Public Confidence in the Accounting Profession." *Journal of Accountancy* (July 1986), p. 83.

Durkheim, E. *The Division of Labor in Society*, translated by George Simpson. New York: Free Press, 1964, p. 2.

Earle, V. "Accountants on Trial in a Theater of the Absurd." *Fortune* (May 1972), p. 227.

Edelhertz, H., E. Stotland, M. Walsh, and J. Weimberg. *The Investigation of White Collar Crime: A Manual for Law Enforcement Agencies*. U.S. Department of Justice, LEAH. Washington, DC: Government Printing Office, 1970.

"Ethics 101." *U.S. News and World Report* (March 14, 1988), p. 76.

Fedders, J.M., and L.G. Perry. "Policing Financial Disclosure Fraud: The SEC's Top Priority." *Journal of Accountancy* (July 1984), p. 59.

Gaines, S. "From Balance Sheet to Fraud Beat." *Chicago Tribune* (February 28, 1988), sect. 7, p. 5.

Gibbons, D.L. "Crime and Punishment: A Study in Social Attitudes." *Social Forces* (June 1969), pp. 391–397.

Gomley, R.J. "RICO and the Professional Accountant." *Journal of Accounting, Auditing and Finance* (Fall 1982), pp. 51–60.

Hartung, F.E. "White Collar Offenses in the Wholesale Meat Industry in Detroit." *American Journal of Sociology* 56 (1950), p. 25.

Leeds Estate, Building & Investment Co. v. Shepherd, 36, Ch. D. 787 (1887).

Levy, M.M. "Financial Fraud: Schemes and Indicia." *Journal of Accountancy* (August 1985), p. 79.

Lietbag, B. "Profile: James C. Treadway, Jr." *Journal of Accountancy* (September 1986), p. 80.

Merchant, K.A. *Fraudulent and Questionable Financial Reporting*. New York: Financial Executives Research Foundation, 1987, p. 12.

Merton, R.K. "Social Structure and Anomie." *American Sociological Review* (October 1938), pp. 672–682.

———. "Priorities in Scientific Discovery: A Chapter in the Sociology of Science." *American Sociological Review* (December 1957), pp. 635–659.

———. *Social Theory and Social Structure*. New York: Free Press, 1957, pp. 131–60.

Michigan Law Review, ch. 66, sect. 1529.

Miller, W.B. "Lower Class Culture as a Generating Milieu of Gang Delinquency." *Journal of Social Issues* 14, 3 (1958), pp. 5–19.

Minow, N.N. "Accountants' Liability and the Litigation Explosion." *Journal of Accountancy* (September 1984), pp. 72, 80.

National Commission on Fraudulent Financial Reporting. *Report of the National Commission on Fraudulent Financial Reporting.* Washington, DC: Author, April 1987, p. 2.

Palmrose, Z.-V. "Litigation and Independent Auditors: The Role of Business Failures and Management Fraud." *Auditing: A Journal of Practice and Theory* (Spring 1987), pp. 90–103.

———. "An Analysis of Auditor Litigation and Audit Service Quality." *The Accounting Review* (January 1988), pp. 56, 72.

Rosenblaum v. Adler, Slip Op. A-39/85. N.J. June 9, 1983, 21.

Ross, E.A. *Sins and Society.* Boston: Houghton Mifflin, 1907.

Russell, H.F. *Foozles and Fraud.* Altamonte Springs, FL: Institute of Internal Auditors, 1977.

Schwartz, K.B. *White Collar Crime.* New York: Dryden Press, 1949, p. 240.

———. "Accounting Changes by Corporations Facing Possible Insolvency." *Journal of Accounting, Auditing and Finance* (Fall 1982), pp. 32–43.

Schwartz, K.B., and K. Merton. "Auditor Switches by Failure Firms." *The Accounting Review* (April 1985), pp. 248–261.

Shrager, L.S., and O.F. Short Jr. "How Serious a Crime? Perceptions of Organizational and Common Crimes." In G. Geis and E. Stotland (eds.), *White-Collar Crime: Theory and Research.* London: Sage, 1980, p. 26.

Steward, J.D. "Arbitration." *Journal of Accountancy* (February 1988), pp. 12–13.

St. Pierre, K., and J. Anderson. "An Analysis of Audit Failures Based on Documented Legal Cases." *Journal of Accounting, Auditing and Finance* (Spring 1982), pp. 229–247.

Sutherland, E. "White-Collar Criminality." *American Sociological Review* (February 1940), pp. 210–231.

———. *White Collar Crime.* New York: Dryden Press, 1949, p. 9.

Tell, L. "Giliam's Legacy: Nobody Can Hide behind a White Collar." *Business Week* (February 8, 1988), p. 69.

Uecker, W.C., A.P. Brief, and W.R. Kinney Jr. "Perception of the Internal and External Auditor as a Deterrent to Corporate Irregularities." *The Accounting Review* (July 1981), pp. 465–478.

Ultramares Corp. v. Torche, 225 N.Y. 170, 179–180, 174 N.E. 441, 444 (1931).

Wheeler, S., and M.L. Rothman. "The Organization as Weapon in White-Collar Crime." *Michigan Law Review* (June 1982), pp. 1403–1476.

Chapter 5

Slack in Accounting

INTRODUCTION

Rational principles of management and accounting would dictate the planning and use of company resources in a manner emphasizing truth and accuracy in planning and optional efficiency in use. In reality, the prevailing principles of "designed" management and accounting favor the creation of organizational slack in the use of resources[1] and information distortion through slack budgeting in the planning and budgeting for the same resources.[2] Accordingly, this chapter reviews the research of this opportunistic behavior in management and accounting known as slack by differentiating between organizational slack and budgetary slack.

SLACK BEHAVIOR

Slack behavior refers to the tendency to deviate from principled management and accounting to designed management and accounting. It is a clear manifestation of opportunistic behavior by organizations and individuals.

Slack arises from the tendency of organizations and individuals to refrain from using all the resources available to them. It describes a tendency not to operate at peak efficiency. In general, two types of slack have been identified in the literature, organizational slack and budgetary slack. Organizational slack basically refers to an unused capacity, in the sense that the demands put on the resources of the organization are less than the supply of these resources. Budgetary slack is found in the budgetary process and refers to the intentional distortion of information that results from an understatement of budgeted sales and an overstatement of budgeted costs.

The concepts of organizational slack and budgetary slack appear in other literature under different labels. Economists refer to an X-inefficiency in instances where resources are either not used to their full capacity or effectiveness or are used in an extremely wasteful manner, as well as in instances where managers fail to make costless improvements. X-inefficiency is to be differentiated from allocative inefficiency, which refers to whether or not prices in a market are of the right kind, that is, whether they allocate input and output to those users who are willing to pay for them.[3] Categories of inefficiency of a nonallocative nature, or X-inefficiency, include inefficiency in (1) labor utilization, (2) capital utilization, (3) time sequence, (4) extent of employee cooperation, (5) information flow, (6) bargaining effectiveness, (7) credit availability utilization, and (8) heuristic procedures.[4]

Agency theory also refers to slack behavior. The problem addressed by the agency theory literature is how to design an incentive contract such that the total gains can be maximized, given (1) information asymmetry between principal and agent, (2) pursuit of self-interest by the agent, and (3) environmental uncertainty affecting the outcome of the agent's decisions.[5] Slack can occur when managers dwell in an "excess consumption of perquisites" or in a "tendency to shrink." Basically, slack is the possible "shrinking" behavior of an agent.[6]

The literature in organizational behavior refers to slack in terms of defensive, tactical responses and deceptive behavior. By viewing organizations as political environments, the deceptive aspects of individual power-acquisition behavior become evident.[7] A variety of unobtrusive tactics in the operation of power,[8] covert intents and means of those exhibiting power-acquisition behaviors,[9] and a "wolf in sheep's clothing"[10] phenomenon, whereby individuals profess a mission or goal strategy while practicing an individual-maximization strategy, characterize these deceptive behaviors, which are desired to present an illusionary or false impression. V.E. Schein has provided the following examples of deceptive behaviors in communication, decision making, and presentation of self.

Communication. With regard to written or oral communications, there may be an illusion that these communications include all the information or that these communications are true, which masks the reality either of their consisting of only partial information or of their actually distorting the information.

Decision making. A manager may present the illusion that he or she is actually compromising or giving in with regard to a decision, whereas in reality he or she is planning to lose this particular battle with the long-range objective of winning the war. Or a manager or a subunit may initiate a particular action and then work on plans and activities for implementing a program. This intensive planning and studying, however, may in reality be nothing more than a delaying tactic, during which the actual program will die or be forgotten. Underlying this illusion that one is selecting subordinates, members of boards of directors, or successors on the basis of their competence may be the reality that these individuals are selected for loyalty, compliance, or conformity to the superior's image.

Presentation of self. Many managers exude an apparent confidence, when in reality they are quite uncertain. Still other managers are skilled in organizing participatory group decision-making sessions, which in reality have been set up to produce a controlled outcome.[11]

Schein then hypothesized that the degree to which these behaviors are deceptive seems to be a function of both the nature of the organization and of the kinds of power exhibited (work-related or personal).[12] She relied on Cyert and March's dichotomization of organizations as either low- or high-slack systems.[13]

Low-slack systems are characterized by a highly competitive environment that requires rapid and nonroutine decision making on the part of its members and a high level of productive energy and work outcomes to secure an effective performance. High-slack systems are characterized by a reasonably stable environment that requires routine decision making to secure an effective performance.

Given these dichotomizations, Schein suggested that:

1. The predominant form of power acquisition behavior is personal in a high-slack organization and work-related in a low-slack organization.

2. The underlying basis of deception is the inherently overt nature of personal power acquisition behaviors in a high-slack organization and an organization's illusion as to how work gets done in a low-slack organization.

3. The benefits of deception to members are the provisions of excitement and personal rewards in a high-slack organization and the facilitation of work accomplishment and organizational rewards in a low-slack organization.

4. The benefits of deception to organization are to foster [the] illusion of a fast-paced, competitive environment in a high-slack organization and to maintain an illusion of workability of the formal structure in a low-slack organization.[14]

ORGANIZATIONAL SLACK

Nature of Organizational Slack

There is no lack of definitions for organizational slack, as can be seen from the definitions provided by Cyert and March,[15] Child,[16] Cohen, March, and Olsen,[17] March and Olsen,[18] Dimmick and Murray,[19] Litschert and Bonham,[20] and March.[21]

What appears from these definitions is that organizational slack is a buffer created by management in its use of available resources to deal with internal as well as external events that may arise and threaten an established coalition. Slack, therefore, is used by management as an agent of change in response to changes in both the internal and external environments.

Cyert and March's model explains slack in terms of cognitive and structural factors.[22] It provides the rationale for the unintended creation of slack. Individuals are assumed to "satisfice," in the sense that they set aspiration levels for performance rather than a maximization goal. These aspirations adjust upward or downward, depending on actual performance, and in a slower fashion than actual changes in performance. This lag in adjustment allows excess resources from superior performance to accumulate in the form of an organizational stabilizing force to absorb excess resources in good times without requiring a revision of aspirations and intentions regarding the use of these excess resources. "By absorbing excess resources it retards upward adjustment of aspirations during relatively good times . . . by providing a pool of emergency resources, it permits aspirations to be maintained during relatively bad times."[23]

Oliver E. Williamson has proposed a model of slack based on managerial incentives.[24] This model provides the rationale for managers' motivation and desire for slack resources. Under conditions where managers are able to pursue their own objectives, the model predicts that the excess resources available after target levels of profit have been reached are not allocated according to profit-maximization rules. Organizational slack becomes the means by which a manager achieves his or her personal goals, as characterized by four motives: income, job security, status, and discretionary control over resources.

Williamson makes the assumption that the manager is motivated to maximize his or her personal goals subject to satisfying organizational objectives and that the manager achieves this by maximizing slack resources under his or her control.

Williamson has suggested that there are four levels of profits: (1) a maximizing profit equal to the profit that the firm would achieve when marginal revenue equals marginal cost, (2) actual profit equal to the true profit achieved by the firm, (3) reported profit equal to the accounting profit reported in the annual report, and (4) minimum profit equal to the profit needed to maintain the organizational coalition. If the market is noncompetitive, various forms of slack emerge: (1) *slack absorbed as staff* equal to the difference between maximum and actual profit, (2) *slack in the form of cost* equal to the difference between reported and minimum profits, and (3) *discretionary spending for investment* equal to the difference between reported and minimum profits.

Income smoothing can be used to substantiate the efforts of management to neutralize environmental uncertainty and to create organizational slack by means of an accounting manipulation of the level of earnings. J.Y. Kamin and J. Ronen have related organizational slack to income smoothing by reasoning that what often results in slack accumulation is aimed at smoothing earnings.[25]

They hypothesized that management-controlled firms were more likely to be engaged in smoothing as a manifestation of managerial discretion and slack. "Accounting" and "real" smoothing were tested by observing the behavior of discretionary expenses vis-à-vis the behavior of income numbers. Their results showed (1) that a majority of the firms behaved as if they were income smoothers and (2) that a particularly strong majority was found among management-controlled firms with high barriers to entry. This line of reasoning was pursued by Ahmed Belkaoui and R.D. Picur.[26] Their study tested the effects of the dual economy on income-smoothing behavior. It was hypothesized that a higher degree of smoothing of income numbers would be exhibited by firms in the periphery sector than by firms in the core sector in reaction to different opportunity structures and experiences. Their results indicated that a majority of the firms may have been resorting to income smoothing. A higher number were found among firms in the periphery sector.

Lewin and Wolf proposed the following statements as a theoretical framework for understanding the concept of slack:

1. Organizational slack depends on the availability of excess resources.
2. Excess resources occur when an organization generates or has the potential to generate resources in excess of what is necessary to maintain the organizational coalition.
3. Slack occurs unintentionally as a result of the imperfection of the resource allocation decision-making process.
4. Slack is created intentionally because managers are motivated to maximize slack resources under their control to ensure achievement of personal goals subject to the achievement of organizational goals.
5. The disposition of slack resources is a function of a manager's expense preference function.
6. The distribution of slack resources is an outcome of the bargaining process-setting organization and reflects the discretionary power of organization members in allocating resources.
7. Slack can be present in a distributed or concentrated form.
8. The aspiration of organizational participants for slack adjusts upward as resources become available. The downward adjustment of aspirations for slack resources, when resources become scarce, is resisted by organizational participants.
9. Slack can stabilize short-term fluctuations in the firm's performance.
10. Beyond the short term, the reallocation of slack requires a change in organizational goals.
11. Slack is directly related to organizational size, maturity, and stability of the external environment.[27]

Functions of Organizational Slack

Because the definition of slack is often intertwined with a description of the functions that slack serves, L.J. Bourgeois discussed these functions as a means of making palpable the ways of measuring slack.[28] From a review of the administrative theory literature, he identified organizational slack as an independent variable that either "causes" or serves four primary functions: "(1) as an inducement for organizational actors to remain in the system, (2) as a resource for conflict resolution, (3) as a buffering mechanism in the work flow process, or (4) as a facilitator of certain types of strategic or creative behavior within the organization."[29]

The concept of slack as an inducement to maintain the coalition was first introduced by C.I. Barnard in his treatment of the inducement/contribution ratio (VC) as a way of attracting organizational participants and sustaining their membership.[30] March and H.A. Simon later described slack resources as the source of inducements through which the inducement/contribution ratio might exceed a value of 1, which is equivalent to paying an employee more than would be required to retain his or her services.[31] This concept of slack was then explicitly introduced by Cyert and March as consisting of payments to members of the coalition in excess of what is required to maintain the organization.[32]

Slack as a resource for conflict resolution was introduced in L.R. Pondy's goal model.[33] In this model subunit goal conflicts are resolved partly by sequential attention to goals and partly by adopting a decentralized organizational structure. A decentralized structure is made possible by the presence of organizational slack.

A notion of slack as a technical buffer from the variances and discontinuities caused by environmental uncertainty was proposed by J.D. Thompson.[34] It was also acknowledged in Pondy's system model, which described conflict as a result of the lack of buffers between interdependent parts of an organization.[35] Jay Galbraith saw buffering as an information-processing problem:

Slack resources are an additional cost to the organization or the customer. . . . The creation of slack resources, through reduced performance levels, reduces the amount of information that must be processed during task execution and prevents the overloading of hierarchical channels.[36]

According to Bourgeois, slack facilitates three types of strategic or creative behavior within the organization: (1) providing resources for innovative behavior, (2) providing opportunities for a satisficing behavior, and (3) affecting political behavior.[37]

First, as a facilitator of innovative behavior, slack tends to create conditions that allow the organization to experiment with new strategies[38] and introduce innovation.[39] Second, as a facilitator of suboptimal behavior, slack defines the threshold of acceptability of a choice, or "bounded search,"[40] by people whose bounded rationality leads them to satisfice.[41] Third, the notion that slack affects political activity was advanced by Cyert and March, who argued that slack reduces both political activity and the need for bargaining and coalition-forming activity.[42] Furthermore, W.G. Astley has argued that slack created by success results in self-aggrandizing behavior by managers who engage in political behavior to capture more than their fair share of the surplus.[43]

W. Richard Scott argued that lowered standards create slack—unused resources—that can be used to create ease in the system.[44] Notice the following comment:

Of course, some slack in the handling of resources is not only inevitable but essential to smooth operations. All operations require a margin of error to allow for mistakes, waste, spoilage, and similar unavoidable accompaniments of work.[45]

But the inevitability of slack is not without consequences:

The question is not whether there is to be slack but how much slack is permitted. Excessive slack resources increase costs for the organization that are likely to be passed on to the consumer. Since creating slack resources is a relatively easy and painless solution available to organizations, whether or not it is employed is likely to be determined by the amount of competition confronting the organization in its task environment.[46]

Measurement of Organizational Slack

One problem in investing empirically in the presence of organizational slack relates to the difficulty of securing an adequate measurement of the phenomenon. Various methods have been suggested. In addition to these methods, eight variables that appear in public data, whether they are created by managerial actions or made available by environment, may explain a change in slack.[47] The model, suggested by Bourgeois, is as follows:

$$\text{Slack} = f(\text{RE, DP, G\&A, WC/S, D/E, CR, I/P, P/E})$$

where

RE = Retained earnings

DP = Dividend payout

G&A = General and administrative expense

WC/S = Working capital as a percentage of sales

D/E = Debt as a percentage of equity

CR = Credit rating

I/P = Short-term loan interest compared to prime rate

P/E = Price/earnings ratio

Here RE, G&A, WC/S, and CR are assumed to have a positive effect on changes and DP, D/E, P/E, and I/P are assumed to have a negative effect on changes in slack.

Some of these measures have also been suggested by other researchers. For example, Martin M. Rosner used profit and excess capacity as slack measures,[48] and Lewin and Wolf used selling, general, and administrative expenses as surrogates for slack.[49] Bourgeois and Jitendra V. Singh refined these measures by suggesting that slack could be differentiated on an "ease-of-recovery" dimension.[50] Basically, they considered excess liquidity to be available slack, not yet earmarked for particular uses. Overhead costs were termed recoverable slack, in the sense that they are absorbed by various organizational functions but can be recovered when needed elsewhere. In addition, the ability of a firm to generate resources from the environment, such as the ability to raise additional debt or equity capital, was considered potential slack. All of these measures were divided by sales to control for company size.

Building on Bourgeois and Singh's suggestions, Theresa K. Lant opted for the four following measures:

1. Administrative Slack = (General and Administrative Expenses)/Cost of Goods Sold
2. Available Liquidity = (Cash + Marketable Securities − Current Liabilities)/Sales
3. Recoverable Liquidity = (Accounts Receivable + Inventory)/Sales
4. Retained Earnings = (Net Profit − Dividends)/Sales[51]

Lant used these measures to show empirically (1) that available liquidity and general and administrative expenses have significantly higher variance than profit across firms and across time and (2) that the mean change in slack is significantly greater than the mean change in profit. She concluded as follows:

These results are logically consistent with the theory that slack absorbs variance in actual profit. They also suggest that the measures used are reasonable measures for slack. Thus, it supports prior work which has used these measures and implies that further large sample models using slack as a variable are feasible since financial information is readily available for a large number of firms. Before these results can be generalized however, the tests conducted here should be replicated using different samples of firms from a variety of industries.[52]

Organizational Slack and Competition

The line of research studying the impact of market competition on internal efficiency of firms suggested results about competition reducing slack. Hart[53] and Scharfstein[54] use a hidden information model with a common shock transmitted via the market price to show that the (informational) effect of an increase in competition by entrepreneurial (profit-maximizing) firms on the internal efficiency of managerial firms depends on the specification of managers' preferences. This informational effect of competition was also confined in a hidden action model.[55] Similarly, when the strategic value of incentive contracts under much different market conditions is examined, it will appear that the increase in the intensity of completion leads to more X-inefficiency.[56] A similar negative relation between the intensity of completion and the degree of internal efficiency was observed in a Cournot principal-agent model, where the principal's managerial benefit of including the agent to minimize cost becomes smaller when competition increases.[57] In the case of multinational firms with multiple plants in different locations, the in-home competition may have an impact on slack under different economic conditions. For example, Kerschbamer and Tournas evaluated the impact of variations of product demand on the amount of internal slack in multiplant firms in a model in which facilities can produce output at a privately known cost up to a previously determined capacity level.[58] Their model shows the amount of slack to be pro-cyclical in the sense that as capacity constraints become tighter in booms, slack increases in booms, because the power of in-house competition is reduced, while the opposite is true in downturns.

BUDGETARY SLACK

Nature of Budgetary Slack

The literature on organizational slack shows that managers have the motives necessary to desire to operate in a slack environment. The literature on budgetary slack considers the budget as the embodiment of that environment and, therefore, assumes that managers will use the budgeting process to bargain for slack budgets. As stated by Michael Schiff and Lewin, "managers will create slack in budgets through a process of understating revenues and overstating costs."[59] The general definition of budgetary slack, then, is the understatement of revenues and the overstatement of costs in the budgeting process. A detailed description of the creation of budgetary slack by managers was reported by Schiff and Lewin in their study of the budget process of three divisions of multidivision companies.[60] They found evidence of budgetary slack through underestimation of gross revenue, inclusion of discretionary increases in personnel requirements, establishment of marketing and sales budgets with internal limits on funds to be spent, use of manufacturing costs based on standard costs that do not reflect process improvements operationally available at the plant, and inclusion of discretionary "special projects."

Evidence of budgetary slack has also been reported by others. A.E. Lowe and R.W. Shaw found a downward bias, introduced through sales forecasts by line managers, which assumed good performance where rewards were related to forecasts.[61] M. Dalton reported various examples of department managers' allocating resources to what they considered justifiable purposes, even though such purposes were not authorized in their budgets.[62] G. Shillinglaw noted the extreme vulnerability of budgets used to measure divisional performance given the great control exercised by divisional management in budget preparation and the reporting of results.[63]

Slack creation is a generalized organizational phenomenon. Many different organizational factors have been used to explain slack creation, in particular, organizational structure, goal congruence, control system, and managerial behavior. Slack creation is assumed to occur in cases where a Tayloristic organizational structure exists,[64] and it is also assumed to occur in a participative organizational structure.[65] It may be due to conflicts that arise between the individual and organizational goals, leading managers intentionally to create slack.

It may also be due to the attitudes of management toward the budget and to worst views of the budgets as a device used by management to manipulate them.[66] Finally, the creation of slack may occur whether or not the organization is based on a centralized or decentralized structure.[67] With regard to this last issue, Schiff and Lewin have reported that the divisional controller appears to have undertaken the tasks of creating and managing divisional slack and is most influential in the internal allocation of slack.

Using agency theory, budgetary slack can be attributed to four conditions: "1) information asymmetry between the superior (the principal) and the subordinate's effort or output potential, 2) uncertainty in the relation between effort and output, 3) conflicting goals between the superior and the subordinate, and 4) opportunism or self-interest on the part of the subordinate."[68]

Budgeting and the Propensity to Create Budgetary Slack

The budgeting system has been assumed to affect a manager's propensity to create budgetary slack, in the sense that this propensity can be increased or decreased by the way in which the budgeting system is designed or complemented. Mohamed Onsi was the first to investigate empirically the connections between the type of budgeting system and the propensity to create budgetary slack.[69] From a review of the literature, he stated the following four assumptions:

1. Managers influence the budget process through bargaining for slack by understating revenues and overstating costs.
2. Managers build up slack in "good years" and reconvert slack into profit in "bad years."
3. Top management is at a "disadvantage" in determining the magnitude of slack.
4. The divisional controller in decentralized organizations participates in the task of creating and managing divisional slack.[70]

Personal interviews of thirty-two managers of five large national and international companies and statistical analysis of a questionnaire were used to identify the important behavioral variables that influence slack buildup and utilization. The questionnaire's variables were grouped into the following eight dimensions:

1. Slack attitude, described by the variables indicating a manager's attitude to slack.
2. Slack manipulation, described by the variables indicating how a manager builds up and uses slack.
3. Slack institutionalization, described by the variables that make a manager less inclined to reduce his or her slack.
4. Slack detection, described by the variables indicating the superior's ability to detect slack based on the amount of information that he receives.

5. Attitude toward the top management control system, described by the variables indicating an authoritarian philosophy toward budgeting being attributed to top management by divisional managers.

6. Attitudes toward the divisional control system, described by variables on attitudes toward subordinates, sources of pressure, budget autonomy, budget participation, and supervisory uses of budgets.

7. Attitudes toward the budget, described by variables on attitude toward the level of standards, attitude toward the relevancy of budget attainment to valuation of performance, and the manager's attitude (positive or negative) toward the budgetary system in general, as a managerial tool.

8. Budget relevancy, described by variables indicating a manager's attitudes toward the relevancy of standards for his department's operation.[71]

Factor analysis reduced these dimensions to seven factors and showed a relationship between budgetary slack and what Onsi called "an authoritarian top management budgetary control system." Thus, he stated:

Budgetary slack is created as a result of pressure and the use of budgeted profit attainment as a basic criterion in evaluating performance. Positive participation could encourage less need for building up slack. However, the middle managers' perception of pressure was an overriding concern. The positive correlation between managers' attitudes and attainable level of standards is a reflection of this pressure.[72]

Cortland Cammann explored the moderating effects of subordinates' participation in decision making and the difficulty of subordinates' jobs based on their responses to different uses of control systems by their superiors.[73] His results showed that the use of control systems for contingent reward allocation produced defensive responses by subordinates under all conditions, which included the creation of budgetary slack. Basically, when superiors used budgeting information as a basis for allocating organizational rewards, their subordinates' responses were defensive. Allowing participation in the budget processes reduced this defensiveness.

Finally, Kenneth A. Merchant conducted a field study designed to investigate how managers' propensities to create budgetary slack are affected by the budgeting system and the technical context.[74] He hypothesized that the propensity to create budgetary slack is positively related to the importance placed on meeting budget targets and negatively related to the extent of participation allowed in budgeting processes, the degree of predictability in the production process, and the superiors' abilities to create slack. Unlike earlier studies drawn across functional areas, 170 manufacturing managers responded to a questionnaire measuring the propensity to create slack, the importance of meeting the budget, budget participation, the nature of technology in terms of work-flow integration and product standardization, and the ability of superiors to detect slack. The results suggested that managers' propensities to create slack (1) do vary with the setting and with how the budgeting system is implemented; (2) are lower where managers actively participate in budgeting, particularly when technologies are relatively predictable; and (3) are higher when a tight budget requires frequent tactical responses to avoid overruns.

The three studies by Onsi, Cammann, and Merchant provide evidence that participation may lead to positive communication between managers so that subordinates feel less pressure to create slack. This result is, in fact, contingent on the amount of information asymmetry existing between the principals (superiors) and the agents (the subordinates). Although participation in budgeting leads subordinates to communicate or reveal some of their private information, agents may still misrepresent or withhold some of their private information, leading to budgetary slack. Accordingly, Alan S. Dunk proposed a link between participation and budgetary slack through two variables: superiors' budget emphasis in their evaluation of subordinate performance and the degree of information asymmetry between superiors and subordinates:[75] "When participation, budget emphasis, and information asymmetry are high (low), slack will be high (low)."[76] The results, however, showed that low (high) slack is related to high (low) participation, budget emphasis, and information asymmetry. The results are stated as follows:

The results of this study show that the relation between participation and slack is contingent upon budget emphasis and information asymmetry, but in a direction contrary to expectations. The results provide evidence for the utility of participative budgeting, and little support for the view that high participation may result in increased slack when the other two predictors are high. Although participation may induce subordinates to incorporate slack in budgets, the results suggest that participation alone may not be sufficient. The findings suggest that slack reduction results from participation, except when budget emphasis is low.[77]

Budgetary Slack, Information Distortion, and Truth-Inducing Incentive Schemes

Budgetary slack involves a deliberate distortion of input information. Distortion of input information in a budget setting arises, in particular, from the need of managers to accommodate their expectations about the kinds of payoffs associated with different possible outcomes. Several experiments have provided evidence of such distortion of input information. Cyert, March, and W.H. Starbuck showed in a laboratory experiment that subjects adjusted the information that they transmitted in a complex decision-making system to control their payoffs.[78] Similarly, Lowe and Shaw have shown that in cases where rewards were linked to forecasts, sales managers tended to distort the input information and to induce biases in their sales forecast.[79] Dalton also provided some rich situational descriptions of information distortion in which lower-level managers distorted the budget information and allocated resources to what were perceived to be justifiable objectives.[80] Finally, a payoff structure can induce a forecaster to bias intentionally his or her forecast. R.M. Barefield provided a model of forecast behavior that showed a "rough" formulation of a possible link between a forecaster's biasing and the quality of the forecaster as a source of data for an accounting system.[81]

Taken together, these studies suggest that budgetary slack, through systematic distortion of input information, can be used to accommodate the subjects' expectations about the payoffs associated with various possible outcomes. They fail, however, to provide a convincing rationalization of the link between distortion of input information and the subjects' accommodation of their expectations. Agency theory and issues related to risk aversion may provide such a link. Hence, given the existence of divergent incentives and information asymmetry between the controller (or employer) and the controlee (or employee) and the high cost of observing employee skill or effort, a budget-based employment contract (i.e., where employee compensation is contingent on meeting the performance standard) can be Pareto-superior to fixed pay or linear sharing rules (where the employer and employee split the output).[82] However, these budget-based schemes impose a risk on the employee, as job performance can be affected by a host of uncontrollable factors. Consequently, risk-averse individuals may resort to slack budgeting through systematic distortion of input information. In practice, moreover, any enhanced (increased) risk aversion would lead the employee to resort to budgetary slack. One might hypothesize that, without proper incentives for truthful communication, the slack budgeting behavior could be reduced. One suggested avenue is the use of truth-inducing, budget-based schemes.[83] These schemes, assuming risk neutrality, motivate a worker to reveal truthfully private information about future performance and to maximize performance regardless of the budget.

Accordingly, Mark S. Young conducted an experiment to test the effects of risk aversion and asymmetric information on slack budgeting.[84] Five hypotheses related to budgetary slack were developed and tested using a laboratory experiment. The hypotheses were as follows:

Hypothesis 1: A subordinate who participates in the budgeting process will build slack into the budget.

Hypothesis 2: A risk-averse subordinate will build in more budget slack than a non-risk-averse subordinate.

Hypothesis 3: Social pressure not to misrepresent productive capability will be greater for a subordinate whose information is known by management than for a subordinate having private information.

Hypothesis 4: As social pressure increases for the subordinate, there is a lower degree of budgetary slack.

Hypothesis 5: A subordinate who has private information builds more slack into the budget than a subordinate whose information is known by management.[85]

The results of the experiment confirmed the hypotheses that a subordinate who participates builds in budgetary slack and that slack is, in part, attributable to a subordinate's risk preferences. Given state uncertainty and a worker-manager information asymmetry about performance capability, the subjects in the experiment created slack even in the presence of a truth-inducing scheme. In addition, risk-averse workers created more slack than non-risk-averse workers did. Similarly, C. Chow, J. Cooper, and W. Waller provided evidence that, given a worker-manager information asymmetry about performance capability, slack is lower under a truth-inducing scheme than under a budget-based scheme with an incentive to create slack.[86]

Both Young's and Chow, Cooper, and Waller's studies were found to have limitations.[87] With regard to Young's study, William S. Waller found three limitations:

First, unlike the schemes examined in the analytical research, the one used in his study penalized outperforming the budget, which limits its general usefulness. Second, there was no manipulation of incentives, so variation in slack due to incentives was not examined. Third, risk preferences were measured using the conventional lottery technique of which the validity and reliability are suspect.[88]

With regard to Chow, Cooper, and Waller's study, Waller found the limitations to be the assumption of state certainty and the failure to take risk preference into account. Accordingly, Waller conducted an experiment under which subjects participatively set budgets under either a scheme with an incentive for creating slack or a truth-incentive scheme like those examined in the analytical research. In addition, risk neutrality was induced for one-half of the subjects, and constant, absolute risk aversion for the rest, using a technique discussed by J. Berg, L. Daley, J. Dickhaut, and T. O'Brien that allows the experimenter to induce (derived) utility functions with any shape.[89] The results of the experiment show that when a conventional truth-inducing scheme is introduced, slack decreases for risk-neutral subjects but not for risk-averse subjects. Added to the evidence provided by the other studies, this study indicates that risk preference is an important determinant of slack, especially in the presence of a truth-inducing scheme.

Basically, there is preliminary evidence that risk-averse workers create more budgetary slack than risk-neutral ones. In addition, "truth-inducing incentive schemes" reduce budgetary slack for risk-neutral subjects but not for risk-averse subjects. It seems that resource allocations within organizations are mediated by perceptions of risk, where risk is a stable personal trait. Accordingly, D.C. Kim tested whether risk preferences are domain-specific, that is, whether latent risk preferences translate into differing manifest risk preferences according to the context.[90] He relied on an experiment simulating the public accountants' budgeting of billable bonus to test the hypothesis that subject preference for tight or safe budget behavior depends on the performance of coworkers and domain-specific risk preferences. The results supported the view that subordinates' risk preferences are influenced by a situation-dependent variable. As stated by Kim:

The reversal of risk preferences around a neutral reference point is statistically significant for both dispositionally risk-averse and dispositionally risk-seeking subjects. The dispositional variable also contributes to the explanation of variations in subjects' manifest risk preferences. Thus the propensity to induce budgetary slack seems to be a joint function of situations and dispositions.[91]

Budgetary Slack and Self-Esteem

The enhancement of risk aversion and the resulting distortion of input information can be more pronounced when self-esteem is threatened. It was found that persons who have low opinions of themselves are more likely to cheat than persons with higher self-esteem.[92] A situation of dissonance was created in an experimental group by giving out positive feedback about a personality test to some participants and negative feedback to others. All of the participants were then asked to take part in a competitive game of cards. The participants who received a blow to their self-esteem cheated more often than those who had received positive feedback about themselves. Could it also be concluded that budgetary slack through information distortion may be a form of dishonest behavior, arising from the enhancement of risk aversion caused by a negative feedback on self-esteem? A person's expectations can be an important determinant of his or her behavior. A negative impact on self-esteem can lead an individual to develop an expectation of poor performance. At the same time, the individual who is given negative feedback about his or her self-esteem would be more risk-averse than others and would be ready to resort to any behavior to cover the situation. Consequently, the person may attempt to distort the input information in order to have an attainable budget. Belkaoui accordingly tested the hypothesis that individuals given negative feedback about their self-esteem would introduce more bias into estimates than individuals given positive or neutral feedback about their self-esteem.[93] One week after taking a self-esteem test, subjects were provided with false feedback (either positive or negative) and neutral feedback about their self-esteem score.

They were then asked to make two budgeting decisions, first one cost estimate and then one sales estimates for a fictional budgeting decision. The results showed that, in general, the individuals who were provided with information that temporarily caused them to lower their self-esteem were more apt to distort input information than those who were made to raise their self-esteem. It was concluded that, whereas slack budgeting may be consistent with generally low self-esteem feedback, it is inconsistent with generally high or neutral self-esteem feedback.

Toward a Theoretical Framework for Budgeting

A theoretical framework aimed at structuring knowledge about biasing behavior was proposed by Kari Lukka.[94] It contains an explanatory model for budgetary biasing and a model for budgetary biasing at the organizational level.

The explanatory model of budgetary biasing at the individual level draws from the management accounting and organizational behavior literature and related behavioral research to suggest a set of intentions and determinants of budgetary biasing. Budgetary biasing is at the center of many interrelated and sometimes contradictory factors with the actor's intentions as the synthetic core of his or her behavior.

The model for budgetary biasing at the organizational level shows that the "bias contained in the final budget is not the result of one actor's intentional behavior, but rather the result of the dialectics of the negotiations."[95] Whereas budgetary biases 1 and 2 are the original biases created in the budget by the controlling unit and the controlled unit, biases 3 and 4 are the final biases to end up in the budget after the budgetary negotiations, which are characterized by potential conflicts and power factors. The results of semistructured interviews at different levels of management of a large decentralized company verified the theoretical framework. The usefulness of this theoretical framework rests on further refinements and empirical testing.

Positive versus Negative Slack

Although the previous sections have focused on budgetary, or positive, slack, budgetary bias is, in fact, composed of both budgetary slack and an upward bias, or a negative slack. Whereas budgetary slack refers to bias in which the budget is designed intentionally so as to make it easier to achieve the forecast, upward bias refers to overstatement of expected performance in the budget. David T. Otley has described the difference as follows: "Managers are therefore likely to be conservative in making forecasts when future benefits are sought (positive slack) but optimistic when their need for obtaining current approval dominates (negative slack)."[96]

Evidence for negative slack was first provided by W.H. Read, who showed that managers distort information to prove to their superiors that all is well.[97] He cited several empirical studies of budgetary control that indicated that managers put a lot of effort and ingenuity into assuring that messages conveyed by budgetary information serve their own interests.[98] Following earlier research by Barefield, Otley argued that forecasts may be the mode, rather than the means, of people's intuitive probability distributions.[99] Given that the distribution of cost and revenue is negatively skewed, there will be a tendency for budget forecasts to become unintentionally biased in the form of negative slack. Data collected from two organizations verified the presence of negative slack.

REDUCING BUDGETARY SLACK: A BONUS-BASED TECHNIQUE

In general, firms use budgeting and bonus techniques to overcome slack budgeting. One such approach consists of paying higher rewards when budgets are set high and achieved and lower rewards when budgets are either set high but not met or set low and achieved. G.S. Mann presented a bonus system that gave incentives for managers to set budget estimates as close to achievable levels as possible.[100] The following two formulas were proposed:

Formula 1 applies for bonus if actual performance is equal to or greater than budget.

(multiplier no. 2 × budget goal) + [multiplier no. 1 × (actual level achieved − budget goal)]

Formula 2 applies for bonus if actual performance is less than budget.

(multiplier no. 2 × budget goal) + [multiplier no. 3 × (actual level achieved − budget goal)]

The three multipliers set by management served as factors in calculating different components of bonuses. They were defined as follows:

Multiplier no. 1 (which must be less than multiplier no. 2, and which in turn must be less than multiplier no. 3) is used when actual performance is greater than budget. It provides a smaller bonus per unit for the part of actual performance that exceeds the budgeted amount.

Multiplier no. 2 is the rate per unit used to determine the basic bonus component. It is based on the budgeted level of activity which equals multiplier no. 2 times the budgeted level.

Multiplier no. 3 is the rate used to reduce the bonus when the achieved level is less than the budget (multiplier no. 3 times work of units by which actual performance fell short of budget).[101]

Figure 5.1 shows an illustration of the application of the method and the effect of variations in multipliers or bonuses. As the figure shows, the manager will be rewarded for accurate estimation of the level of rates. In addition, the multipliers can be set with greater flexibility for controlling the manager's estimates.

CONCLUSION

Organizational slack and budgetary slack are two hypothetical constructs to explain organizational phenomena that are prevalent in all forms of organiza-

Figure 5.1
Reducing Slack through a Bonus System

(1)	(2)	(3)	(4) Bonus I	(5) Bonus II
Budget Slacks	Actual Slacks	State of Nature	Multiple No. 1 = $.05 Multiple No. 2 = $.10 Multiple No. 3 = $.15	Multiple No. 1 = $.01 Multiple No. 2 = $.10 Multiple No. 3 = $.30
200,000	180,000	Overestimation	$17,000	$14,000
200,000	200,000	Actual = Budget	20,000	20,000
200,000	220,000	Underestimation	21,000	22,000

tions. Evidence linking both constructs to organizational, individual, and contextual factors is growing and in the future may contribute to an emerging theoretical framework for an understanding of slack. Further investigation into the potential determinants of organizational and budgetary slack remains to be done. This effort is an important one because the behavior of slack is highly relevant to the achievement of internal economic efficiency in organizations. Witness the following comment:

The effective organization has more rewards at its disposal, or more organizational slack to play with, and thus can allow all members to exercise more discretion, obtain more rewards, and feel that their influence is higher.[102]

NOTES

1. R.M. Cyert and J.G. March (eds.), *A Behavioral Theory of the Firm* (Englewood Cliffs, NJ: Prentice-Hall, 1963).

2. A.Y. Lewin and C. Wolf, "The Theory of Organizational Slack: A Critical Review," *Proceedings: Twentieth International Meeting of TIMS* (1976), pp. 648–654.

3. H. Leibenstein, "Allocative Efficiency vs. X-Efficiency," *American Economic Review* (June 1966), pp. 392–415.

4. H. Leibenstein, "X-Efficiency: From Concept to Theory," *Challenge* (September–October 1979), pp. 13–22.

5. N. Choudhury, "Incentives for the Divisional Manager," *Accounting and Business Research* (Winter 1985), pp. 11–21.

6. S. Baiman, "Agency Research in Managerial Accounting: A Survey," *Journal of Accounting Literature* (Spring 1982), pp. 154–213.

7. D. Packard, *The Pyramid Climber* (New York: McGraw-Hill, 1962); E.A. Butler, "Corporate Politics-Monster or Friend?" *Generation* 3 (1971), pp. 54–58, 74; A.N. Schoomaker, *Executive Career Strategies* (New York: American Management Association, 1971).

8. J. Pfeffer, "Power and Resource Allocation in Organizations," in B.M. Shaw and G.R. Salancik (eds.), *New Directions in Organizational Behavior* (Chicago: St. Clair Press, 1977).

9. V.E. Schein, "Individual Power and Political Behaviors in Organizations: An Inadequately Explored Reality," *Academy of Management Review* (January 1977), pp. 64–72.

10. B. Bowman and W. Malpive, "Goals and Bureaucratic Decision-Making: An Experiment," *Human Relations* (June 1977), pp. 417–429.

11. V.E. Schein, "Examining an Illusion: The Role of Deceptive Behaviors in Organizations," *Human Relations* (October 1979), pp. 288–289.

12. Ibid., p. 290.

13. Cyert and March, *A Behavioral Theory of the Firm*.

14. Schein, "Examining an Illusion," p. 293.

15. Cyert and March, *A Behavioral Theory of the Firm*.

16. J. Child, "Organizational Structure, Environment, and Performance: The Role of Strategic Choice," *Sociology* 6, 1 (1972), pp. 2–22.

17. M.D. Cohen, J.G. March, and J.P. Olsen, "A Garbage Can Model of Organizational Choice," *Administrative Science Quarterly* 17, 1 (1972), pp. 1–25.

18. J.G. March and J.P. Olsen, *Ambiguity and Choice* (Bergen: Universitetsforlagt, 1976).

19. D.E. Dimmick and V.V. Murray, "Correlates of Substantive Policy Decisions in Organizations: The Case of Human Resource Management," *Academy of Management Journal* 21, 4 (1978), pp. 611–623.

20. R.J. Litschert and T.W. Bonham, "A Conceptual Model of Strategy Formation," *Academy of Management Review* 3, 2 (1978), pp. 211–219.

21. J.G. March, interview by Stanford Business School Alumni Association, *Stanford GSB* 47, 3 (1978–1979), pp. 16–19.

22. Cyert and March, *A Behavioral Theory of the Firm*.

23. Ibid., p. 38.

24. O.E. Williamson, "A Model of Rational Managerial Behavior," in Cyert and March, *A Behavioral Theory of the Firm*; O.E. Williamson, *The Economics of Discretionary Behavior: Managerial Objectives in a Theory of the Firm* (Englewood Cliffs, NJ: Prentice-Hall, 1964).

25. J.Y. Kamin and J. Ronen, "The Smoothing of Income Numbers: Some Empirical Evidence on Systematic Differences among Management-Controlled and Owner-Controlled Firms," *Accounting, Organizations and Society* (October 1978), pp. 141–157.

26. A. Belkaoui and R.D. Picur, "The Smoothing of Income Numbers: Some Empirical Evidence on Systematic Differences between Core and Periphery Industrial Sector," *Journal of Business Finance and Accounting* (Winter 1984), pp. 527–545.

27. Lewin and Wolf, "The Theory of Organizational Slack," p. 653.

28. L.J. Bourgeois, "On the Measurement of Organizational Slack," *Academy of Management Review* 6, 1 (1981), pp. 29–39.

29. Ibid., p. 31.

30. C.I. Barnard, *Functions of the Executive* (Cambridge, MA: Harvard University Press, 1938).

31. J.G. March and H.A. Simon, *Organizations* (New York: John Wiley and Sons, 1958).

32. Cyert and March, *A Behavioral Theory of the Firm*, p. 36.

33. L.R. Pondy, "Organizational Conflict: Concepts and Models," *Administrative Science Quarterly* 12, 2 (1967), pp. 296–320.

34. J.D. Thompson, *Organizations in Action* (New York: McGraw-Hill, 1967).

35. Pondy, "Organizational Conflict."

36. J. Galbraith, *Designing Complex Organizations* (Reading, MA: Addison-Wesley, 1973), p. 15.

37. Bourgeois, "On the Measurement of Organizational Slack," p. 34.

38. D.C. Hambrick and C.C. Snow, "A Contextual Model of Strategic Decision Making in Organizations," in R.L. Taylor, J.J. O'Connell, R.A. Zawaki, and D.D. Warrick (eds.), *Academy of Management Proceedings* (1977), pp. 109–112.

39. Cyert and March, *A Behavioral Theory of the Firm.*

40. March and Simon, *Organizations.*

41. H.A. Simon, *Administrative Behavior* (New York: Free Press, 1957).

42. Cyert and March, *A Behavioral Theory of the Firm.*

43. W.G. Astley, "Sources of Power in Organizational Life" (Ph.D. diss., University of Washington, 1978).

44. W.R. Scott, *Organizations: Rational, Natural and Open Systems* (Englewood Cliffs, NJ: Prentice-Hall, 1981), p. 216.

45. Ibid.

46. Ibid.

47. Bourgeois, "On the Measurement of Organizational Slack," p. 38.

48. M.M. Rosner, "Economic Determinant of Organizational Innovation," *Administrative Science Quarterly* 12 (1968), pp. 614–625.

49. A.Y. Lewin and C. Wolf, "Organizational Slack: A Test of the General Theory," *Journal of Management Studies* (forthcoming).

50. L.J. Bourgeois and J.V. Singh, "Organizational Slack and Political Behavior within Top Management Teams," Working paper, Graduate School of Business, Stanford University, 1983.

51. T.K. Lant, "Modeling Organizational Slack: An Empirical Investigation," Stanford University Research Paper no. 856, July 1986.

52. Ibid., p. 14.

53. O. Hart, "The Market Mechanism as an Incentive Scheme," *Bell Journal of Economics* 14 (1983), pp. 366–382.

54. D. Scharfstein, "Product Market Competition and Managerial Slack," *Rand Journal of Economics* 14 (1988), pp. 147–153.

55. B. Hermalin, "The Effects of Competition on Executive Behavior," *Rand Journal of Economics* 23 (1992), pp. 350–365.

56. H. Horn, H. Lang, and S. Lundgren, "Competition, Long Run Contracts and Inefficiencies in Firms," *European Economic Review* 38 (1994), pp. 213–233.

57. S. Martin, "Endogenous Firm Efficiency in a Cournot Principal-Agent Model," *Journal of Economic Theory* 59 (1993), pp. 445–450.

58. R. Kerschbamer and Y. Tournas, "In-House Competition, Organizational Slack and the Business Cycle," Working paper, Department of Economics, University of Vienna, July 2000.

59. M. Schiff and A.Y. Lewin, "The Impact of People on Budgets," *Accounting Review* (April 1970), pp. 259–268.

60. M. Schiff and A.Y. Lewin, "Where Traditional Budgeting Fails," *Financial Executive* (May 1968), pp. 51–62.

61. A.E. Lowe and R.W. Shaw, "An Analysis of Managerial Biasing: Evidence from a Company's Budgeting Process," *Journal of Management Studies* (October 1968), pp. 304–315.

62. M. Dalton, *Men Who Manage* (New York: John Wiley and Sons, 1961), pp. 36–38.

63. G. Shillinglaw, "Divisional Performance Review: An Extension of Budgetary Control," in C.P. Bonini, R.K. Jaedicke, and H.M. Wagner (eds.), *Management Controls: New Directors in Basic Research* (New York: McGraw-Hill, 1964), pp. 149–163.

64. C. Argyris, *The Impact of Budgets on People* (New York: Controllership Foundation, 1952), p. 25.

65. E.H. Caplan, *Management Accounting and Behavioral Sciences* (Reading, MA: Addison-Wesley, 1971).

66. Argyris, *The Impact of Budgets on People*.

67. Schiff and Lewin, "Where Traditional Budgeting Fails," pp. 51–62.

68. Stevens, D.E. "Determinants of Budgetary Slack in the Laboratory: An Investigation of Contracts for Self-Interested Behavior." Working paper, Syracuse University, March 2000, p. 1.

69. M. Onsi, "Factor Analysis of Behavioral Variables Affecting Budgetary Slack," *Accounting Review* (July 1973), pp. 535–548.

70. Ibid., p. 536.

71. Ibid., p. 539.

72. Ibid., p. 546.

73. C. Cammann, "Effects of the Use of Control Systems," *Accounting, Organizations and Society* (January 1976), pp. 301–313.

74. K.A. Merchant, "Budgeting and the Propensity to Create Budgetary Slack," *Accounting, Organizations and Society* (May 1985), pp. 201–210.

75. A.S. Dunk, "The Effect of Budget Emphasis and Information Asymmetry on the Relation between Budgetary Participation and Slack," *The Accounting Review* (April 1993), pp. 400–410.

76. Ibid., p. 400.

77. Ibid., pp. 408–409.

78. R.M. Cyert, J.G. March, and W.H. Starbuck, "Two Experiments on Bias and Conflict in Organizational Estimation," *Management Science* (April 1961), pp. 254–264.

79. Lowe and Shaw, "An Analysis of Managerial Biasing."

80. Dalton, *Men Who Manage*.

81. R.M. Barefield, "A Model of Forecast Biasing Behavior," *Accounting Review* (July 1970), pp. 490–501.

82. J.S. Demski and G.A. Feltham, "Economic Incentives in Budgetary Control Systems," *Accounting Review* (April 1978), pp. 336–359.

83. Y. Ijiri, J. Kinard, and F. Putney, "An Integrated Evaluation System for Budget Forecasting and Operating Performance with a Classified Budgeting Bibliography," *Journal of Accounting Research* (Spring 1968), pp. 1–28; M. Loeb and W. Magat, "Soviet Success Indicators and the Evaluation of Divisional Performance," *Journal of Accounting Research* (Spring 1978), pp. 103–121; P. Jennergren, "On the Design of Incentives in Business Firms—A Survey of Some Research," *Management Science* (February 1980), pp. 180–201; M. Weitzman, "The New Soviet Incentive Model," *Bell Journal of Economics* (Spring 1976), pp. 251–257.

84. M.S. Young, "Participative Budgeting: The Effects of Risk Aversion and Asymmetric Information on Budgetary Slack," *Journal of Accounting Research* (Autumn 1985), pp. 829–842.

85. Ibid., pp. 831–832.

86. C. Chow, J. Cooper, and W. Waller, "Participative Budgeting: Effects of a Truth-Inducing Pay Scheme and Information Asymmetry on Slack and Performance," Working paper, University of Arizona, Tucson, 1986.

87. W.S. Waller, "Slack in Participative Budgeting: The Joint Effect of a Truth-Inducing Pay Scheme and Risk Preferences," *Accounting, Organizations and Society* (December 1987), pp. 87–98.

88. Ibid., p. 88.

89. J. Berg, L. Daley, J. Dickhaut, and J. O'Brien, "Controlling Preferences for Lotteries on Units of Experimental Exchange," *Quarterly Journal of Economics* (May 1986), pp. 281–306.

90. D.C. Kim, "Risk Preferences in Participative Budgeting," *The Accounting Review* (April 1992), pp. 303–318.

91. Ibid., p. 304.

92. E. Aronson and D.R. Mettee, "Dishonest Behavior as a Function of Differential Levels of Induced Self-Esteem," *Journal of Personality and Social Psychology* (January 1968), pp. 121–127.

93. A. Belkaoui, "Slack Budgeting, Information Distortion and Self-Esteem," *Contemporary Accounting Research* (Fall 1985), pp. 111–123.

94. K. Lukka, "Budgetary Biasing in Organizations: Theoretical Framework and Empirical Evidence," *Accounting, Organizations and Society* (February 1988), pp. 281–301.

95. Ibid., p. 292.

96. D.T. Otley, "The Accuracy of Budgetary Estimates: Some Statistical Evidence," *Journal of Business Finance and Accounting* (Fall 1985), p. 416.

97. W.H. Read, "Upward Communication in Industrial Hierarchies," *Human Relations* (1962), pp. 3–16.

98. G.H. Hofstede, *The Game of Budget Control* (London: Tavistock, 1968); A.G. Hopwood, "An Empirical Study of the Role of Accounting Data in Performance Evaluation," *Journal of Accounting Research* (Supplement, 1972), pp. 156–182; D.T. Otley, "Budget Use and Managerial Performance," *Journal of Accounting Research* (Spring 1978), pp. 122–149.

99. R.M. Barefield, "Comments on a Measure of Forecasting Performance," *Journal of Accounting Research* (Autumn 1969), pp. 324–327; Otley, "The Accuracy of Budgetary Estimates."

100. G.S. Mann, "Reducing Budget Slack," *Journal of Accountancy* (August 1988), pp. 118–122.

101. Ibid., p. 119.

102. C. Perrow, *Complex Organizations: A Critical Essay* (Glenview, IL: Scott, Foreman, and Company, 1972), p. 140.

SELECTED REFERENCES

Antle, R., and G. Eppen. "Capital Rationing and Organizational Slack in Capital Budgeting." *Management Science* (February 1985), pp. 163–174.

Argyris, C. *The Impact of Budgets on People.* New York: Controllership Foundation, 1952.

Aronson, E., and D.R. Mettee. "Dishonest Behavior as a Function of Differential Levels of Induced Self-Esteem." *Journal of Personality and Social Psychology* (January 1968), pp. 121–127.

Barefield, R.M. "A Model of Forecast Biasing Behavior." *Accounting Review* (July 1970), pp. 490–501.

Barnea, A., J. Ronen, and S. Sadan. "Classifactory Smoothing of Income with Extraordinary Items." *Accounting Review* (January 1976), pp. 110–122.

Belkaoui, A. *Conceptual Foundations of Management Accounting.* Reading, MA: Addison-Wesley, 1980.

———. "The Relationships between Self-Disclosure Style and Attitudes to Responsibility Accounting." *Accounting, Organizations and Society* (December 1981), pp. 281–289.

———. *Cost Accounting: A Multidimensional Emphasis.* Hinsdale, IL: Dryden Press, 1983.

———. "Slack Budgeting, Information Distortion and Self-Esteem." *Contemporary Accounting Research* (Fall 1985), pp. 111–123.

Belkaoui, A., and R.D. Picur. "The Smoothing of Income Numbers: Some Empirical Evidence of Systematic Differences between Core and Periphery Industrial Sectors." *Journal of Business Finance and Accounting* (Winter 1984), pp. 527–545.

Bourgeois, L.J. "On the Measurement of Organizational Slack." *Academy of Management Review* 6, no. 1 (1981), pp. 29–39.

Bourgeois, L.J., and J.V. Singh. "Organizational Slack and Political Behavior within Top Management Teams." *Academy of Management Proceedings* (1983), pp. 43–47.

———. "Organizational Slack and Political Behavior within Top Management Teams." Working paper, Graduate School of Business, Stanford University, 1983.

Bourgeois, L.J., and W.G. Astley. "A Strategic Model of Organizational Conduct and Performance." *International Studies of Management and Organization* 9, 3 (1979), pp. 40–66.

Brownell, P. "Participation in the Budgeting Process—When It Works and When It Doesn't." *Journal of Accounting Literature* (Spring 1982), pp. 124–153.

Caplan, E.H. *Management Accounting and Behavioral Sciences.* Reading, MA: Addison-Wesley, 1971.

Carter, E. "The Behavioral Theory of the Firm and Top-Level Corporate Decisions." *Administrative Science Quarterly* 16, 4 (1971), pp. 413–428.

Child, J. "Organizational Structure, Environment, and Performance: The Role of Strategic Choice." *Sociology* 6, 1 (1972), pp. 2–22.

Chow, D. "The Effects of Job Standard Tightness and Compensation Scheme on Performance: An Exploration of Linkages." *Accounting Review* (October 1983), pp. 667–685.

Christensen, J. "The Determination of Performance Standards and Participation." *Journal of Accounting Research* (Autumn 1982), pp. 589–603.

Cohen, M.D., J.G. March, and J.P. Olsen. "A Garbage Can Model of Organizational Choice." *Administrative Science Quarterly* 17, 1 (1972), pp. 1–25.

Collins, F. "Managerial Accounting Systems and Organizational Control: A Role Perspective." *Accounting, Organizations and Society* (May 1982), pp. 107–122.

Conn, D. "A Comparison of Alternative Incentive Structures for Centrally Planned Economic Systems." *Journal of Comparative Economics* (September 1979), pp. 261–278.

Cyert, R.M., and J.G. March. "Organizational Factors in the Theory of Oligopoly." *Quarterly Journal of Economics* (April 1956), pp. 44–66.

———— (eds.). *A Behavioral Theory of the Firm.* Englewood Cliffs, NJ: Prentice-Hall, 1963.

Cyert, R.M., J.G. March, and W.H. Starbuck. "Two Experiments on Bias and Conflict in Organizational Estimation." *Management Science* (April 1961), pp. 254–264.

Dalton, M. *Men Who Manage.* New York: John Wiley and Sons, 1961.

Demski, J.S., and G.A. Feltham. "Economic Incentives in Budgetary Control Systems." *Accounting Review* (April 1978), pp. 336–359.

Dunk, A.S. "The Effect of Budget Emphasis and Information Asymmetry on the Relation between Budgetary Participation and Slack." *The Accounting Review* (April 1993), pp. 400–410.

Gonik, J. "Tie Salesmen's Bonuses to Their Forecasts." *Harvard Business Review* (May–June 1978), pp. 116–123.

Hopwood, A.G. "An Empirical Study of the Role of Accounting Data in Performance Evaluation." *Journal of Accounting Research* (Supplement, 1972), pp. 156–182.

Irjiri, Y., J. Kinard, and F. Putney. "An Integrated Evaluation System for Budget Forecasting and Operating Performance with a Classified Budgeting Bibliography." *Journal of Accounting Research* (Spring 1968), pp. 1–28.

Itami, H. "Evaluation Measures and Goal Congruence under Uncertainty." *Journal of Accounting Research* (Spring 1975), pp. 163–180.

Jennergren, P. "On the Design of Incentives in Business Firms—A Survey of Some Research." *Management Science* (February 1980), pp. 180–201.

Karpik, P., and A. Riahi-Belkaoui. "A Comparison of the Financial Characteristics of Companies in the Core and Periphery Economies." *Advances in Quantitative Analysis in Finance and Accounting* 2 (1993), pp. 105–139.

Kerr, S., and W. Slocum Jr. "Controlling the Performances of People in Organizations." In W. Starbuck and P. Nystrom (eds.), *Handbook of Organizational Design*, Vol. 2. New York: Oxford University Press, 1981, pp. 116–134.

Kim, D.C. "Risk Preferences in Participative Budgeting." *The Accounting Review* (April 1992), pp. 303–319.

Lecky, P. *Self-Consistency.* New York: Island Press, 1945.

Leibenstein, H. "Allocative Efficiency vs. X-Efficiency." *American Economic Review* (June 1966), pp. 392–415.

————. "X-Efficiency: From Concept to Theory." *Challenge* (September–October 1979), pp. 13–22.

Levinthal, D., and J.G. March. "A Model of Adaptive Organizational Search." *Journal of Economic Behavior and Organization* (May 1981), pp. 307–333.

Lewin, A.Y., and C. Wolf. "The Theory of Organizational Slack: A Critical Review." *Proceedings: Twentieth International Meeting of TIMS* (1976), pp. 648–654.

Litschert, R.J., and T.W. Bonham. "A Conceptual Model of Strategy Formation." *Academy of Management Review* 3, 2 (1978), pp. 211–219.

Locke, E., and D. Schweiger. "Participation in Decision Making: One More Look." In B. Staw (ed.), *Research in Organizational Behavior.* Greenwich, CT: JAI Press, 1979, pp. 265–339.

Loeb, M., and W. Magat. "Soviet Success Indicators and the Evaluation of Divisional Performance." *Journal of Accounting Research* (Spring 1978), pp. 103–121.

Lowe, A.E., and R.W. Shaw. "An Analysis of Managerial Biasing: Evidence from a Company's Budgeting Process." *Journal of Management Studies* (October 1968), pp. 304–315.

March, J.G., and H.A. Simon. *Organizations.* New York: John Wiley and Sons, 1958.

Mezias, S.J. "Some Analytics of Organizational Slack." Working paper, Graduate School of Business, Stanford University, November 1985.

Miller, J., and J. Thornton. "Effort, Uncertainty, and the New Soviet Incentive System." *Southern Economic Journal* (October 1978), pp. 432–446.

Mitroff, I.I., and J.R. Emshoff. "On Strategic Assumption-Making: A Dialectical Approach to Policy and Planning." *Academy of Management Review* 4, 1 (1979), pp. 1–12.

Moch, M.K., and L.R. Pondy. "The Structure of Chaos: Organized Anarchy as a Response to Ambiguity." *Administrative Science Quarterly* 22, 2 (1977), pp. 351–362.

Parker, L.D. "Goal Congruence: A Misguided Accounting Concept." *Abacus* (June 1976), pp. 3–13.

Riahi-Belkaoui, A. *The New Foundations of Management Accounting.* Westport, CT: Quorum Books, 1992.

Schein, V.E. "Examining an Illusion: The Role of Deceptive Behaviors in Organizations." *Human Relations* (October 1979), pp. 287–295.

Schiff, M. "Accounting Tactics and the Theory of the Firm." *Journal of Accounting Research* (Spring 1966), pp. 62–67.

Schiff, M., and A.Y. Levin. "Where Traditional Budgeting Fails." *Financial Executive* (May 1968), pp. 51–62.

———. "The Impact of People on Budgets." *Accounting Review* (April 1970), pp. 259–268.

———. *Behavioral Aspects of Accounting.* Englewood Cliffs, NJ: Prentice-Hall, 1974.

Simon, H.A. *Administrative Behavior.* New York: Free Press, 1957.

Singh, J.V. "Performance, Slack and Risk Taking in Strategic Decisions: Test of a Structural Equation Model." Ph.D. diss., Stanford Graduate School of Business, 1983.

———. "Performance, Slack, and Risk Taking in Organizational Decision Making." *Academy of Management Journal* (September 1986), pp. 562–585.

Stolzenberg, R.M. "Bringing the Boss Back In: Employer Size, Employee Schooling, and Socioeconomic Achievement." *American Sociological Review* 43 (1978), pp. 42–53.

Swieringa, R.J., and R.H. Moncur. "The Relationship between Managers' Budget Oriented Behavior and Selected Attitudes, Position, Size and Performance Measures." *Journal of Accounting Research* (Supplement, 1972), p. 19.

Thompson, J.D. *Organizations in Action.* New York: McGraw-Hill, 1967.

Waller, W.S., and C. Chow. "The Self-Selection and Effort of Standard-Based Employment Contracts: A Framework and Some Empirical Evidence." *Accounting Review* (July 1985), pp. 458–476.

Watchel, H.M. "The Impact of Labor Market Conditions on Hard-Core Unemployment." *Poverty and Human Resources* (July–August 1970), pp. 5–13.

Weitzman, M. "The New Soviet Incentive Model." *Bell Journal of Economics* (Spring 1976), pp. 251–257.

Williamson, O.E. "A Model of Rational Managerial Behavior." In Richard M. Cyert and James G. March (eds.), *A Behavioral Theory of the Firm.* Englewood Cliffs, NJ: Prentice-Hall, 1963, pp. 113–128.

———. *The Economics of Discretionary Behavior: Managerial Objectives in a Theory of the Firm.* Englewood Cliffs, NJ: Prentice-Hall, 1964.

Winter, S.G. "Satisficing, Selection, and the Innovating Remnant." *Quarterly Journal of Economics* 85 (1971), pp. 237–257.
Young, M.S. "Participative Budgeting: The Effects of Risk Aversion and Asymmetric Information on Budgetary Slack." *Journal of Accounting Research* (Autumn 1985), pp. 829–842.

Appendix 5A. Slack Budgeting, Information Distortion and Self-Esteem

INTRODUCTION

Psychological variables are very helpful in explaining some of the accountant's behavioral patterns and can contribute to the development of better management accounting systems (Belkaoui, 1980; Collins, 1982). Personality traits and behavioral factors may be indicative of different accounting behavior and effectiveness. For example, self-disclosure was found to be positively related to attitudes to responsibility accounting (Belkaoui, 1981), and Gordon's Personality Profile and the Ohio State Leadership Behavior Description Questionnaire were found to be a predictor of budgeting behavior (Hopwood, 1972; Swieringa and Moncur, 1972). Slack creation is another important managerial behavior in need of explanation, correction, and/or control. An evaluation of the effectiveness of a firm's control system requires, among other things, the identification of the behavioral factors that lead to slack creation (Onsi, 1973, p. 535). Accordingly, this appendix reports on research designed to provide insights into the relationships between individual characteristics and slack creation. More specifically, it examines slack budgeting as a case of information distortion and investigates empirically the effects of self-esteem feedback on information distortion.

THEORY

Slack Budgeting and Information Distortion

The literature on the behavioral implications of budgets as instruments of planning and control has found its way into most cost accounting textbooks (Belkaoui, 1983). It is suggested that the budget in its dual role of being a planning tool and a control device may give rise to slack. Cyert and March (1963) defined organizational slack as the difference between "the total resources available to the firm and the total necessary to maintain the organizational coalition" (p. 36). Slack arises from imperfections in the organizational process of resource allocation. Slack may be distributed in the form of additional dividends and excessive wages beyond the minimum required to obtain a healthy coalition

Source: A. Riahi-Belkaoui, "Slack Budgeting, Information Distortion and Self-Esteem," *Contemporary Accounting Research* (Fall, 1985), pp. 11–123. Reprinted with permission.

of all the participants in the organization or be undistributed as idle cash and securities. In examining the relationships between the controller and the controlled within the organization, Schiff and Lewin (1970) argued that these relationships revolved around the budget process and that the "controlled" exercise significant influence on the outcome of the budgets by the incorporation of slack into their budgets.[1] In brief, since the budget is an expression of the performance criteria and because managers bargain and participate in its formation, the budget process may become the vehicle for slack. Thus, organizational slack is a general organizational phenomenon that may be reflected in slack budgeting behavior. In an accounting framework, slack budgeting is, in general, operationally defined as the process of understating revenues and overstating costs. Lowe and Shaw (1968) report also on downward and upward bias introduced in sales forecasts by line managers that may indicate the existence of negative slack in some cases.

Slack creation is a generalized organizational phenomenon. Various organizational factors have been used to explain slack creation, namely, organizational structure, goal congruence, control system, and managerial behavior. Basically (1) it is assumed to occur in cases where a Tayloristic organizational structure exists (Argyris, 1952, p. 25), although it is also assumed to occur in a participative organization structure (Caplan, 1971, p. 85); (2) it may be due to conflicts arising between the individual and organizational goals leading managers to intentionally create slack (March and Simon, 1958, p. 84; Williamson, 1964; Parker, 1976, p. 12); (3) it may be due to the attitudes of management toward the budget and to the workers' views of budgets as devices used by management to manipulate them (Argyris, 1952); and (4) it may occur whether or not the organization is based on a centralized or decentralized structure (Schiff and Lewin, 1970, p. 264).

Whatever the sources or causes of slack creation, slack involves a deliberate distortion of input information. Distortion of input information in a budget setting in particular arises from a need by managers to accommodate their expectations about the kinds of payoff associated with different possible outcomes. For example, Cyert, March, and Starbuck (1961) (hereafter referred to as CMS) showed in a laboratory experiment that subjects adjusted the information that they transmitted in a complex decision-making system to control their payoffs. Similarly, Lowe and Shaw (1968) have shown that in cases where rewards were related to forecast, sales managers tended to distort the input information and to induce biases in their sales forecasts. Dalton (1961) also provided some rich situational descriptions of information distortion in which lower-level managers distorted the budget information and allocated resources to what were perceived to be justifiable objectives. Finally, given the existence of a payoff structure that may induce a forecaster to intentionally bias his or her forecast, Barefield (1970) provides a model of forecast behavior that shows a "rough" formulation of a possible link between a forecaster's biasing and the quality of the forecaster as a source of data for an accounting system. All these studies seem to suggest that slack budgeting through systematic distortion of input information may be used to accommodate the subject's expectations about the payoffs associated with various possible outcomes. They fail, however, to provide a better rationalization of the link between distortion of input information and the subject's accommodation of expectations. Agency theory- and risk aversion-related issues may provide such a link. Hence, given the existence of divergent incentives and information asymmetry between controller (or employer) and controllee (or employee) and the high cost of observing employee skill or effort, a budget-based employment contract (i.e., employee compensation is contingent on meeting the performance standard) can be Pareto-superior to fixed pay or linear sharing rules (where the employer and employee split the output) (Demski and Feltham, 1978). However, these budget-based schemes impose a risk on the employee (since job performance may be affected by a host of uncontrollable factors). Consequently, risk-averse individuals may resort to slack budgeting through systematic distortion of input information. Moreover, any enhanced (increased) risk aversion would, in practice, lead the employee to resort to slack budgeting.

Self-Esteem

The enhancement of risk aversion and the resulting distortion of input information may be more pronounced when self-esteem is threatened. It was found that persons who have low opinions of themselves are more likely to cheat than persons with high self-esteem (Aronson and Mettee, 1968). A situation of dissonance was created in an experimental group by giving out positive feedback about a personality test to some participants and negative feedback to others. Then, all the participants were asked to take part in a competitive game of cards. The participants who received a blow to their self-esteem cheated more than those who had received positive feedback about themselves. Could it also be concluded that slack budgeting through information distortion may be a form of dishonest behavior arising from enhancement of risk aversion caused by negative feedback on self-esteem? A person's expectations may be an important determinant of his or her behavior. Negative feedback on self-esteem may lead an individual to develop an expectation of poor performance. At the same time the individual who is given negative feedback about his or her self-esteem would be more risk-averse than others and would be ready to resort to any behavior to cover the situation. Consequently, he or she may attempt to distort the input information in order to have an attainable budget. Accordingly, one hypothesis may be stated as follows: *Individuals given negative feedback about their self-esteem will introduce more bias into estimates than individuals given positive or neutral feedback about their self-esteem.*

METHOD

A laboratory experiment was used to investigate the impact of self-esteem feedback on input information distortion in a budgeting task. The subjects were sixty male and female students drawn from the fourth-year undergraduate accounting theory class, the second-year graduate managerial accounting class, and the introductory undergraduate accounting class in the Faculty of Administration at the University of Ottawa who agreed to cooperate and participate in the experiment. Students rather than managers were used in order to better isolate the impact of self-esteem on input information distortion, given that managers may be influenced by a host of other organizational factors to create slack. The subjects were told that they were participating in a study concerned with the correlation between self-esteem scores and "estimation aptitudes." They were told that the Tennessee Self-Concept Scale (TSCS) would be used to measure their self-esteem, and the "estimation aptitudes" would be ascertained upon the completion of a budgeting test (Fitts, 1965).

All subjects were given the TSCS and were informed of its nature and intent. The test belongs to a wide variety of instruments that have been employed to measure the self-concept. The instrument is simple for the subject to understand, which explains its popularity as a means of studying and understanding human behavior. Sociologists, psychiatrists, theologians, philosophers, educators, and psychologists have increasingly come to view the self-concept as a central construct for the understanding of people and their behavior. Consequently, a whole theoretical school, known as self-theory, has evolved, as evidenced by works of people like Rogers (1951), Snygg and Combs (1949), Lecky (1945), Wylie (1961), and others. Self-theory is strongly phenomenological in nature and is based on the general principle that people react to their phenomenal world in terms of the way that they perceive this world. Self-theory holds that people's behavior is always meaningful and that we understand each person's behavior only if we can perceive his or her phenomenal world as he or she does. The TSCS was devised for the purpose of measuring the self-concept. Although subject to the limitations of any verbal or pencil-and-paper type of scale, the TSCS is nevertheless applicable to a broad range of people and situations (Fitts and Hammer, 1969; Fitts, 1970, 1972a, 1972b, 1972c; Fitts et al., 1971; Thompson, 1972). It yields a number of measures and scores and is well standardized. Among these scores are:

The self-criticism score (SC): High scores indicate a normal, healthy openness and capacity for self-criticism.

The positive score (P): Scores on ninety items are summed to provide a total *P* score, which reflects general esteem. In general, people with high scores tend to like themselves, feel that they are persons of value and worth, have confidence in themselves, and act accordingly. People with low scores are doubtful about their own worth and unhappy and have little faith or confidence in themselves (Fitts, 1965, p. 1).

Other scores are provided by the TSCS. To avoid any confusion, only the positive score is used in this study. The subjects were provided with sufficient information about the TSCS and the positive score to consider it relevant and important.

A week after the administration of the TSCS and before participating in a budgeting paper-and-pencil test, subjects were assigned to one of three experimental conditions: positive, neutral, and negative feedback on self-esteem scores. This manipulation of self-esteem was done by disclosing the highest, lowest, and average scores in the class and by either (1) communicating the right score, (2) having the subject's score equal to the highest score in the class, or (3) having the subject's score equal to the lowest score in the class. In general, the first alternative was communicated to those whose right score was around the average score in the class, the second alternative to those with low scores, and the third alternative to those with high scores. The last two alternatives were aimed at temporarily inducing either an increase in self-esteem or a decrease in self-esteem. *The first alternative, where no change in self-esteem was sought, was intended for control purposes.*[2]

The highest scores were 405 for the positive score and 46 for the self-criticism score. The lowest scores were 261 for the positive score and 23 for the self-criticism score. The average scores were 310 for the positive score and 32 for the self-criticism score. The provision of such a range of scores for the false feedback groups was assumed to be high enough to generate a blow to the self-esteem of the subject.[3] To avoid any confusion, the subjects were provided with only the positive scores.

The experimental material included four pages: one page for instructions; one page for the positive, neutral, or negative feedback on their self-esteem scores; and the last two pages for a paper-and-pencil test requiring the subject to make cost and sales estimates.

The instructions stated:

The purpose of this experiment is to correlate the estimation ability with self-esteem characteristics. In order to get a true measure of a person's estimation ability, it is necessary to keep in mind the estimation's objective function which is first, to insure that the budget is attainable and, second, that the budget is accurate. In order to accomplish this, I am having you engage in the estimation of both cost and sales for a fictional situation. It is important that you keep the estimation's objective function in mind when making your decision. The second page gives your self-esteem score. The last two pages constitute the budgeting situation.

The second page for the feedback on the self-esteem scores stated:

In the middle of the semester, you were asked to complete the Tennessee Self-Concept Scale. The test belongs to a wide variety of instruments which have been employed to measure the self-concept. The test gives a measure of self-esteem. Persons with high scores tend to like themselves, feel that they are persons of value and worth, have confidence in themselves, and act accordingly. Your score was _____. The highest, the lowest, and the average scores in your class were respectively _____, _____, _____.

The last two pages of the experimental material included a paper-and-pencil budgeting test requiring each subject to make ten estimates on the basis of the estimates of others. Two versions of the budgeting test were presented: a cost version and a sales version. The cost version reads as follows:

Assume that you are the controller of a manufacturing company considering the production of a new product. You are required to submit your estimate of the unit cost of the product if 500,000 units are produced. Your two assistants A and B, in whom you have equal confidence, presented you with preliminary estimates. For each of the cases below, indicate your estimate of costs you would submit.

The sales version reads as follows:

Assume that you are the marketing manager of a manufacturing concern considering the production of a new product. You are required to submit your estimate of the sales volume of the product if the price is set at $10.80. Your two assistants A and B, in whom you have equal confidence, presented you with preliminary estimates. For each of the cases below, indicate what estimates of sales you would submit.

Each question was followed by a list of ten pairs of numbers, representing the ten pairs of estimates by the two subordinates. The experiment involved in each case the choice between two estimates of cost and two estimates of sales. The cost estimates are indicated below:

Cost Estimates Presented to Participants

Cases	A's Estimate	B's Estimate	Your Estimate
(1)	$1.54	$6.75	$____
(2)	$8.42	$4.56	$____
(3)	$3.25	$7.52	$____
(4)	$1.25	$4.35	$____
(5)	$6.54	$4.70	$____
(6)	$1.80	$7.30	$____
(7)	$6.89	$1.65	$____
(8)	$3.25	$7.52	$____
(9)	$4.74	$1.54	$____
(10)	$3.20	$5.35	$____

The sales estimates were similar in value except that the cost estimates are expressed in dollars, and those for sales in units. However, the sales estimates were presented in various different orders to obscure the similarities in values. One such order of sales estimates is indicated below:

Sales Estimates Presented to Participants

Cases	A's Estimate	B's Estimate	Your Estimate
(1)	320,000 units	535,000 units	____ units
(2)	474,000	154,000	____
(3)	325,000	752,000	____
(4)	689,000	165,000	____
(5)	180,000	730,000	____
(6)	654,000	470,000	____
(7)	125,000	435,000	____
(8)	325,000	752,000	____
(9)	842,000	456,000	____
(10)	154,000	675,000	____

The three types of feedback on self-esteem scores (negative, neutral, and positive) and the two types of budgeting decisions (cost and sales estimates) resulted in the $2 \times 3 \times N$ factorial design in Table 5A.1. The group receiving the correct and hence neutral feedback was intended to be the control group in this experiment.

The nature of the task is assumed to lead the subjects to build in slack. First, it asks for an attainable budget. Second, the courses being taken by the subjects and taught by the experimenter emphasize the notion of a biased payoff schedule within an organization. Therefore, following the argumentation provided by CMS (1961, p. 254), if the payoffs are perceived to be biased or if they are perceived to depend on considerations other than the relations between the estimate and the true value, the tactical decision on biasing the estimate becomes important to the estimator.

RESULTS

Each subject's cost and sales estimates, E, were transformed into a summary statistic, x, which represented the weight assigned to the larger of the two given numbers in the pair presented to the subject such that

$$E = xU + (1 - x)L$$

where U is the upper number, and L the lower number.

Upper and lower limits of the ten pairs ranged from 125 to 842 and included two pairs in which the difference was approximately 200; two pairs in which the difference was approximately 300: two pairs in which the difference was approximately 400; two pairs in which the difference was approximately 550; one pair in which the difference was 521; and one pair in which the difference was 386.

Table 5A.1
Diagram of the Two-Factor Sample Experiment

		Types of feedback sample experiment		
		Negative	Correct	Positive
Types of budgeting	Cost	n = 20	n = 20	n = 20
decisions	Sales	n = 20	n = 20	n = 20

The use of a linear combination of the two estimates was considered superior to a single reliance on the mean. In effect, the summary statistic, x, highlights the bias brought by the subject to his or her estimates better than a single use of the mean estimate. It is used in the study as the database for the analysis of variance. The mean estimate does not highlight the bias because it gives equal weight to the observations.

The analysis of variance is summarized in Table 5A.2. The main effects were significant. The nature of the feedback on self-esteem had an impact on the weight assigned to the largest estimate ($F_{obs} = 6.71 > F_{.95}$ (2, 54) = 3.20), and the nature of the budgeting decision had an impact on the weight assigned by the subject to the highest estimate ($F_{obs} = 5.71 > F_{.95}$ (1, 54) = 4.00). The interaction effects were also significant ($F_{obs} = 5.44 = F_{.95}$ (1, 54) = 3.20). The nature of the interaction effects is indicated by an inspection of the cell means. These means are shown in Table 5A.3. A geometric representation of these means is also given in Figure 5A.1. This figure presents the profiles corresponding to the simple main effects of the type of feedback on self-esteem for each of the budgeting decisions. A response of 0.5 is unbiased, and responses of > 0.5 for cost estimates and < .05 for sales estimates represent slack creation. The profiles for the cost and sales decisions appear to have different slopes indicating that an analysis of the simple effects is warranted. Only one simple effect is significant. Given negative feedback on self-esteem, the impact of the budgeting decision on the weights assigned to the highest estimate is different ($F_{obs} = 14.2 > F_{.95}$ (1, 54) = 4.00). In fact, in the case of negative feedback, thirteen of the cost response points were superior to 0.5, and fourteen of the sales response points were inferior to 0.5.

However, the experimental data do not indicate a difference in the weights assigned given a neutral ($F_{obs} = 0.9$) or positive ($F_{obs} = 1.01$) feedback on self-esteem. Although the results are not significant, the positive feedback caused slack to be incorporated with cost estimation. If the positive feedback were significant, the evidence in this study would have been consistent with a curvilinear hypothesis that invalid feedback on self-esteem causes the incorporation of slack. Given the results of this study, however, the evidence seems more

Table 5A.2
Summary ANOVA for Gain and Simple Effects

Source of variation	SS	Y	MS	F
A (Budgeting decision)	0.68	1	0.68	5.71*
A for b_1 (negative feedback)	$(1.690)^1$	(1)	(1.690)	(14.2)*
A for b_2 (neutral feedback)	(0.115)	(1)	(0.115)	(0.9)
A for b_3 (positive feedback)	(0.221)	(1)	(.0221)	(1.01)
B (feedback on self-esteem)	1.6	2	0.8	6.71*
B for a_1 (cost decision)	(0.546)	(2)	(0.273)	(2.29)
B for a_2 (sales decision)	(0.955)	(2)	(0.473)	(3.9)
AB	1.336	2	0.668	5.44*
Within cell	6.474	54	0.119	
Total	10.090	59		

Notes:
*significant at .05 level.
^{1}data for simple effects are in parentheses.
Legend: SS = Sum of squares; Y = Degrees of freedom; MS = Mean square; F = F statistic.

Table 5A.3
Mean of Cells Summary Table

	Negative Feedback	Neutral Feedback	Positive Feedback
Cost	0.81	0.50	0.75
Sales	0.23	0.65	0.54

consistent with the linear hypothesis that negative feedback on self-esteem causes the incorporation of slack.

DISCUSSION

The above results suggest that inaccurate but neutral or positive feedback on self-esteem may not result in observed differences in the cost of sales budgeting decisions. An inaccurate but favorable feedback on self-esteem does not seem to lead to a slack budgeting behavior and distortion of input information. Similarly, negative but inaccurate feedback does lead to a difference in the type of budgeting decision, cost or sales. The inaccurate and negative feedback of self-esteem seems to result in the distortion of input information. An examination

Figure 5A.1
Profiles of Simple Effects of Feedback on Self-Esteem (Mean Weight Assigned to the Highest Estimate)

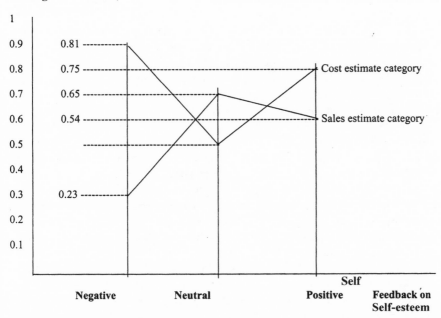

of Figure 5A.1 shows that given negative feedback on self-esteem, subjects tend to overestimate cost and underestimate sales.

These results seem to support the findings of CMS in part. They support the same idea that "cost and sales would tend to be estimated with a bias even though the bias might be in a different direction for each type of estimate." They also support their main proposition that "estimates within a complex decision making system involve attempts by the estimators to control their payoffs." Two differences arise, however, when comparing the scope of both results. First, the differences in the cost and sales estimation decisions result, in our study, in the creation of slack. Our subjects tend to overestimate cost and underestimate sales. Second, our results show that the bias introduced by the estimators is caused by the inaccurate and negative feedback on self-esteem.

One possible interpretation consistent with the observed effect may be related to the cognitive dissonance theory. Inaccurate and negative feedback on self-esteem may lead to enhanced risk aversion and increased dissonance, and since dissonance and risk aversion lead to an effort to reduce them, and since the only means of reduction in this experiment is the budget, slack budgeting behavior is expected.[4]

Another possible interpretation is that slack budgeting behavior occurs as a result of being consistent with an enhanced risk aversion due to a negative self-concept. The inaccurate and negative feedback on self-esteem apparently accentuates the risk aversion, leading to a distortion of input information. In other words, a shock to one's self-esteem will cause one to be willing to be a party to cheating to achieve success. Given the nature of the task, the behavior is similar to that which would be exhibited by an increase in one's risk aversion. Two words of caution to qualify this conclusion are necessary. First, this study did not assess risk aversion directly, and, therefore, one cannot infer from the analysis that individuals with negative feedback on self-esteem are indeed risk averters. Second, future research should incorporate an incentive scheme; otherwise, the effects in the negative case may be overstated.

To be consistent with the work of Rogers (1951), the slack budgeting behavior may be altered by first changing the self-concept in a positive direction and thereby reducing the risk aversion. Clearly, any planning or control system within a firm must take into account the predisposition and biases created in the planner by the nature of the feedback on his or her performance and consequently on his or her self-esteem: an inaccurate and negative feedback on self-esteem may induce slack. So, the control of slack during the budget-setting period should be emphasized in the case of those employees who had previously received invalid feedback on their performance and self-esteem. In short, if an individual in an organization is tempted to use slack budgeting, it may be easier for him or her to yield to this temptation if his or her self-esteem has been lowered by inaccurate negative feedback. It is, however, appropriate to caution that the suggestions derived from the findings are tentative pending replication and further demonstrations of the external validity of this experiment.

One possible improvement would be to investigate whether the results of this study are due solely to the effects of negative and positive feedback on the subjects or are due to their perceived level of self-esteem. A second possible improvement would be to investigate the effects on estimation of accurate information concerning high and low self-esteem. To do so, the experiment should include individuals with high and low levels of self-esteem who either receive no feedback concerning their self-esteem levels (additional control group) or who receive accurate feedback concerning their self-esteem (additional experimental group). Another possible improvement would be to design an experiment dealing with more than the two budgetary items examined in this experiment, namely, cost and sales volume.

CONCLUSION

Certain hypotheses on slack budgeting were deduced from an examination of the nature of the feedback of self-esteem on the distortion of input information. Three main results appear. First, it can be said that the nature of the feedback on self-esteem has an impact on organizational estimation decisions. Second, the experiment also indicates that the nature of the budgeting decision leads to a different estimation figure. Finally, the negative and inaccurate feedback of self-esteem appears to accentuate the distortion of input information and the creation of slack. Until the impact of accurate feedback of self-esteem is investigated, this study's findings indicate that negative feedback should not be released before it has been categorically proven to be accurate.

NOTES

1. Various organizational processes grounded in the development and maintenance of coalitions as well as a variety of group and political behaviors may constitute other cases in which these relationships may be either successfully resolved or not.

2. Parametric and nonparametric tests ($\alpha = .10$) failed to reject the hypothesis of no differences in the TSCS scores of the three types of subjects (fourth-year undergraduate, first-year undergraduate, and second-year graduate).

3. At the end of the experiment the subjects were debriefed and given their correct TSCS scores.

4. In other words, to reduce the risk aversion and to reach more consonance, subjects reverted to a slack budgeting behavior.

REFERENCES

Argyris, C. *The Impact of Budgets on People*. New York: The Controllership Foundation, 1952.

Aronson, E., and D.R. Mettee. "Dishonest Behavior as a Function of Differential Levels of Induced Self-Esteem." *Journal of Personality and Social Psychology* (January 1968), pp. 121–127.

Barefield, R.M. "A Model of Forecast Biasing Behavior." *The Accounting Review* (July 1970), pp. 490–501.

Belkaoui, A. *Conceptual Foundations of Management Accounting*. Reading, MA: Addison-Wesley, 1980.

———. "The Relationships between Self-Disclosure Style and Attitudes to Responsibility Accounting." *Accounting, Organizations and Society* (December 1981), pp. 281–289.

———. *Cost Accounting: A Multidimensional Emphasis*. Hinsdale, IL: Dryden Press, 1983.

Caplan, E.H. *Management Accounting and Behavioral Sciences*. Reading, MA: Addison-Wesley, 1971.

Collins, F. "Managerial Accounting Systems and Organizational Control: A Role Perspective." *Accounting, Organizations and Society* (May 1982), pp. 107–122.

Cyert, R.M., and J.G. March. *A Behavioral Theory of the Firm*. Englewood Cliffs, NJ: Prentice-Hall, 1963.

Cyert, R.M., J.G. March, and W.H. Starbuck. "Two Experiments on Bias and Conflict in Organizational Estimation." *Management Science* (April 1961), pp. 254–264.

Dalton, M. *Men Who Manage*. New York: John Wiley, 1961.

Demski, J.S., and G.A. Feltham. "Economic Incentives in Budgetary Control Systems." *The Accounting Review* (April 1978), pp. 336–359.

Fitts, W.F. *Manual for the Tennessee Self-Concept Scale.* Nashville, TN: Counselor Recording and Tests, 1965.

———. *Interpersonal Competence: The Wheel Model.* Nashville, TN: Counselor Recording and Tests, 1970.

———. *The Self-Concept and Behavior: Overview and Supplement.* Nashville, TN: Counselor Recording and Tests, 1972a.

———. *The Self-Concept and Performance.* Nashville, TN: Counselor Recording and Tests, 1972b.

———. *The Self-Concept and Psychopathology.* Nashville, TN: Counselor Recording and Tests, 1972c.

Fitts, W.F., J.L. Adams, G. Radford, W.C. Richard, B.K. Thomas, M.M. Thomas, and W. Thompson. *The Self-Concept and Self-Actualization.* Nashville, TN: Counselor Recording and Tests, 1971.

Fitts, W.F., and W.T. Hammer. *The Self-Concept and Delinquency.* Nashville, TN: Counselor Recording and Tests, 1969.

Hopwood, A.G. "An Empirical Study of the Role of Accounting Data in Performance Evaluation." *Empirical Research in Accounting: Selected Studies*, suppl. to *Journal of Accounting Research* 10 (1972), pp. 194–209.

Lecky, P. *Self-Consistency.* New York: Island Press, 1945.

Lowe, A.E., and R.W. Shaw. "An Analysis of Managerial Biasing: Evidence from a Company's Budgeting Process." *The Journal of Management Studies* (October 1968), pp. 304–315.

March, J.G., and H.A. Simon. *Organizations.* New York: John Wiley, 1958.

Onsi, M. "Factor Analysis of Behavioral Variables Affecting Budgetary Slack." *The Accounting Review* (July 1973), pp. 535–548.

Parker, L.D. "Goal Congruence: A Misguided Accounting Concept." *Abacus* (June 1976), pp. 3–13.

Rogers, C.R. *Client Centered Therapy.* Boston: Houghton Miffin, 1951.

Schiff, M., and A.Y. Lewin. "The Impact of People on Budgets." *The Accounting Review* (April 1970), pp. 259–268.

Snygg, D., and A.W. Combs. *Individual Behavior.* New York: Harper and Row, 1949.

Swieringa, R.J., and R.H. Moncur. "The Relationship between Managers' Budget Oriented Behavior and Selected Attitudes, Position, Size and Performance Measures." *Empirical Research in Accounting: Selected Studies*, suppl. to *Journal of Accounting Research* 10 (1972), p. 19.

Thompson, W. *Correlates of the Self-Concept.* Nashville, TN: Counselor Recording and Tests, 1972.

Williamson, O.E. *The Economy of Discretionary Behavior: Managerial Objectives in the Theory of the Firm.* Englewood Cliffs, NJ: Prentice-Hall, 1964.

Wylie, R.C. *The Self-Concept: A Critical Survey of Pertinent Research Literature.* Lincoln: University of Nebraska Press, 1961.

Appendix 5.B. The Association between Performance Plan Adoption and Organizational Slack

INTRODUCTION

Recent accounting research has argued that managerial compensation contracts influence managerial decision making (Watts and Zimmerman, 1978; Hagerman and Zmijewski, 1979; Dukes et al., 1981; Horwitz and Kolodny, 1981) and motivate executives to improve firm performance by working harder, lengthening their decision horizons, and becoming less risk-averse in their investment decisions (Smith and Watts, 1982; Larcker, 1983; Baril, 1988). The evidence shows that performance plan adoption was associated with an increase in capital expenditures (Larcker, 1983; Gaver, Gaver, and Furze, 1989).[1] The resources used for the increased capital expenditures are derived from organizational slack.

Organizational slack is a cushion of actual resources used by organizations to adapt successfully either to internal pressures for adjustments or to external pressures for change in policy (March, 1979; Bourgeois, 1981).[2] A review of the concept of organizational slack and its use in theory indicates that there are two measures (Bourgeois, 1978; Singh, 1983, pp. 37–49). Organizational slack is conceptualized as *unabsorbed slack*, which corresponds to the excess, uncommitted resources in organizations. It is also conceptualized as *absorbed slack*, which corresponds to excess costs in organizations (Williamson, 1964). This distinction raises the following question: How does performance plan adoption affect changes in absorbed and unabsorbed slack? The question is investigated here. The empirical results indicate that firms adopting performance plans (relative to similar nonadopting firms) decreased the amount of unabsorbed slack that they were holding.

These results make a significant contribution to research for two reasons. First, they demonstrate a relationship between performance plan adoption and unabsorbed slack. It suggests that some of the resources needed for investment following the adoption of performance plans, as shown by Larcker (1983), come from the organization's unabsorbed slack. Second, they show that the adoption of performance plan is not sufficient to reduce absorbed slack. This means that managers have incentives to invest unused resources but that the plan is insufficient to get them to give up perks.

The remainder of this appendix consists of four sections. First is the introduction of the concept of organizational slack, followed by discussion of the theoretical linkages between performance plan adoption and organizational slack and description of the methodology used. The next section presents the empirical results. Finally, the research findings are discussed and summarized.

Source: A. Riahi-Belkaoui, "The Association between Performance Plan Adoption and Organizational Slack," *Indian Accounting Review* (December 1999): 13–27. Reprinted with permission.

ORGANIZATIONAL SLACK

Slack arises from the tendency of organizations and individuals to refrain from using all the resources available to them. It describes a tendency not to operate at peak efficiency. In general, two types of slack have been identified in the literature: organizational slack and budgetary slack. Organizational slack refers to an unused capacity, in the sense that the demands put on the resources of the organization are less than the supply of these resources. Budgetary slack is found in the budgetary process and refers to the intentional distortion of information that results from an understatement of budgeted sales and overstatement of budgeted costs. The interest in this study is with organizational slack. It is a buffer created by management in its use of available resources to deal with internal as well as external events that may arise and threaten an established coalition. Organizational slack, therefore, is used by management as an agent of change in response to changes in both the internal and external environments.

Cyert and March (1963) explain organizational slack in terms of cognitive and structural factors. They provide a rationale for the unintended creation of organizational slack. Individuals are assumed to "satisfice," in the sense that they set aspiration levels for performance rather than a maximization goal. The aspirations adjust upward or downward, depending on actual performance, and in a slower fashion than actual changes in performance. This lag in adjustment allows excess resources from superior performance to accumulate in the form of organizational slack. This form is then used as a stabilization force to absorb excess resources in good times without requiring a revision of aspiration and intentions regarding the use of these excess resources.

O.E. Williamson (1964) proposed a model of slack based on managerial incentives. This model provides the rationale for managers' motivation and desire for slack resources. Under conditions in which managers are able to pursue their own objectives, the model predicts that excess resources available after target levels of profit have been reached are not allocated according to profit maximization rules. Organizational slack becomes the means by which a manager achieves his or her personal goals, as characterized by four motives: income, job security, status, and discretionary control over resources. Williamson makes the assumption that the manager is motivated to maximize his or her personal goals subject to satisfying organizational objectives and that the manager achieves this by maximizing slack resources under his or her control.

The slack, as identified by Cyert and March and/or Williamson, can be conceptualized as unabsorbed, corresponding to the excess uncommitted resources, or absorbed, corresponding to the excess costs in the organization (Bourgeois, 1981). They are assumed in this study to be affected by the adoption of performance plans. A rationale for this thesis follows.

PERFORMANCE PLANS AND ORGANIZATIONAL SLACK

In essence, organizational slack is the difference between resources available to management and the resources used by management. Management uses it as a buffer to deal with internal as well as external events that may arise and/ or threaten an established coalition (Cyert and March, 1963, p. 36). The performance plan adoptions motivate management to improve firm performance as evidenced by the increase in capital expenditures reported by Larcker (1983). The resources needed by management for such endeavors can be easily provided by the excess resources of organizational slack. The use of organizational slack may, however, depend on whether the slack is absorbed or unabsorbed.

First, performance plans are based on accounting measures of corporate performance. The adoption of performance plans will encourage managers to allocate their efforts to the improvement of the short-term accounting performance measure through reduction of costs. Accordingly, absorbed slack, also labeled administrative slack, is expected to decrease following the adoption of the performance plan.

Second, the adoption of the performance plan will encourage the managers to allocate their efforts to the improvement of long-term accounting performance measures by searching, and spending for, new investment opportunities. Some of the resources needed for the new investment may come from unabsorbed slack. Accordingly, unabsorbed slack is expected to decrease following the adoption of a performance plan.

The following research hypotheses are examined in the subsequent empirical study.

H1: The adoption of a performance plan is associated with a decrease in absorbed slack.

H2: The adoption of a performance plan is associated with a decrease in unabsorbed slack.

METHODS

This study uses a longitudinal design because the relationship between performance plan adoption and organizational slack occurs over time.

Sample and Data Collection

A list of corporate incentive plans was obtained from previous research (Larcker, 1983) and through independent historical research. Each experimental firm was required to satisfy two criteria. First, the performance plan adoption must have occurred during the 1971–1982 period. Second, a firm passing the criterion must have a matching control firm.

Seventy experimental firms were identified. The control firms were required to satisfy the following criteria:

1. same industry as the experimental firms.[3]
2. similar size as the experimental firm measured by corporate sales in the year prior to performance plan adoption by the experimental firm.
3. similar fiscal year as the experimental firm.

The sample of companies is shown in Table 5B.1. The plans were all long-term plans consisting of forty-four performance unit plans and twenty-six performance share plans. To measure the effect of the performance plan, organizational slack is analyzed before and after the change while controlling for one categorical variable and two covariates.

Independent Variables

Financial statement data for years -5 to $+5$ (relative to the year of adoption of the performance plan by the experimental company) for each firm were collected from Compustat. Year 0, the year of adoption of the performance plan, was excluded from the analysis to avoid confounding the slack measures with outcomes during the transition. The data collected were on absorbed slack and unabsorbed slack. Various measures of slack have been used. Rosner (1968) used profit and excess capacity as slack measures. Lewin and Wolf (1976) suggested selling, general, and administrative expenses as surrogates for slack.

A case for financially derived measures of slack was made by Bourgeois (1981) and Bourgeois and Singh (1983). A two-component concept of slack was proposed that made the distinction between absorbed slack, referring to slack absorbed as costs in organizations, and unabsorbed slack, referring to uncommitted resources. Analogously, absorbed slack was measured by (1) the ratio of selling, general, and administrative expenses to cost of goods sold in order to capture slack absorbed in salaries, overhead expenses, and various administrative costs and (2) the ratio of working capital to sales in order to capture the absorption of slack related to capital utilization. Unabsorbed slack was computed as (cash plus marketable securities minus current liabilities) divided by sales, in order to capture the amount of liquid resources uncommitted to liabilities in the near future (Singh, 1986).

Control Variable and Covariates

One control variable and two covariates were used to control for possible intervening effects. First, to control for size and profitability, total assets and

Table 5B.1
Sample of Companies

Experimental Firm	Year	Control Firm	Experimental Firm	Year	Control Firm
A.E. Staley	1980	Hormel	Intl. Harvester	1975	Borg Warne
Akzona	1971	Lowenstein	Koopers	1979	Phelps Dodge
Allied Corp.	1980	Halliburton	Manville	1978	U.S. Gypsum
AMF	1980	General Tire	Merck	1982	Sterling Drug
Armstrong Rubber	1982	Cooper Tire	Minnesota Mining & Mfg. Co.	1981	TRW
Ashland Oil	1979	Standard Oil (Ohio)	Monsanto	1974	Dow Chemical
Atlantic Richfield	1976	Cities Service Co.	Nabisco	1976	Campbell Taggert
Baxter Travenol	1982	Schering-Plough	Nalco	1977	Schering-Plough
Beatrice Foods	1978	Quaker Oats	Nashua	1981	Dennison
Bemis	1974	Great Northern Nekoosa	NCR	1982	Deere
Bendix	1974	Fruehauf	NL Industries	1978	Schlumberger
Black & Decker	1980	Baker Intl.	Outboard Marine	1982	Briggs & Stratton
Bristol Myers	1978	Avon Products	Owens-Corning	1980	Libby Owens Food
Burroughs	1982	Digital Equipment	Owens-Illinois	1975	Owens-Corning
Cabot	1972	Handy & Harman	Phillips Petroleum	1978	Cities Service Co.
Celanese	1980	Hercules	Pillsbury	1975	Intl. Multifoods
Central Soya	1981	Anderson Clayton	Ralston-Purina	1975	Carnation
Cincinnati Milacron	1979	Ametek	Rexnord	1982	Smith Intl.
Combustion Eng.	1978	Gillette	Roblin	1977	Midland-Ross
Cooper Labs	1978	ICN Pharm.	Rockwell Intl.	1977	General Dynamics
Corning Glass	1979	Norton	Sanders Associates	1980	Tracor
Crown Zellerbach	1973	Diamond Intl.	Sealed Power	1978	Compugraphic
Datapoint	1979	Storage Technology	Shell	1979	Standard Oil (Indiana)
Diamond Shamrock	1980	Sherwin Williams	Singer	1981	Martin Marietta
Dover	1974	Harsichfeger	Squibb	1975	Pfizer
Eaton	1974	Lockheed	Sun Co.	1972	Royal Dutch Petroleum–N.Y.
Emerson Electronic	1977	Whirlpool	Sybron	1981	Becton Dickinson
Ferro	1982	Syntex	Texas Instruments	1980	Raytheon
FMC	1973	DuPont	Textron	1982	Dresser Inc.
General Mills	1980	Carnation	Toro	1976	Hesston
General Motors	1982	Ford Motor Co.	Union Oil of California	1975	Conoco
Hershey Foods	1978	Intl. Multifoods	United Technologies	1979	Boeing
Hobart	1977	Scott & Fetzer	Vulcan Materials	1973	Anchor Hocking
Honeywell	1978	Litton	Warner Lambert	1982	American Home Products
Illinois Toolwork	1980	Hornsichfeger	Westinghouse	1979	RCA

Note: *Year in which the experimental firm adopted a performance plan.

rate of return on assets were used as covariates. Second, an influence on the use of slack may have advantages or disadvantages resulting from early or late adoption of performance plans with a set of competitors. Another argument is that imitators may learn from first adopters' mistakes and can benefit from the adoption of performance plans. To control for innovation effects, the experimental firms were coded into two groups, with the first thirty early adopters of performance plans classified as early adopters and the rest as late adopters.

Data Analysis

Analysis of covariance was used to test the overall relationship between (1) slack and firm effect, (2) slack and performance plan adoption, and (3) the interaction of firm effect and performance plan adoption on slack. The model's control variable was early/late adoption, and covariates included assets and rate of return on assets.

RESULTS

Tables 5B.2–5B.4 present overall results for the two measures of absorbed slack and the measure of unabsorbed slack. Table 5B.5 presents the means and standard deviations of each of the slack measures before and after the adoption of the performance plan for both the experimental and control groups of firms.

The first measure of absorbed slack is the ratio of selling, general, and administrative expenses as a percentage of cost of goods sold. It captures slack absorbed in salaries, overhead expenses, and various administrative costs. The results for this measure of absorbed slack are reported in Table 5B.2 and show that the main firm effects and performance plan adoption as well as the interactive effects on slack are both insignificant. The same result is found in Table 5B.5 for this measure. The second measure of absorbed slack is the ratio of working capital of sales, which is used to capture the absorption of slack related to capital utilization. Results regarding this second measure of absorbed slack are summarized in Table 5B.3 and show that the main effects of firm effects and performance plan adoption as well as the interaction effects on slack are all insignificant. The same result is found in Table 5B.5 for this measure.

The measure of unabsorbed slack is the ratio of cash plus marketable securities minus current liabilities to sales. This measure is used to capture the amount of liquid resources uncommitted to liabilities in the near future. Results regarding this measure of unabsorbed slack are summarized in Table 5B.4 and show that the following relationships are all significant at $\alpha = 0.05$: (1) between slack and firm effect, (2) between slack and performance plan adoption, and (3) between firm effect-performance plan adoption interactions and slack. An ex-

Table 5B.2
Results of Overall Analysis of Covariance for Absorbed Slack Computed as Selling, General, and Administrative Expenses/Cost of Goods Sold*

Sources	F	P
A: Firm effect (experimental control)	1.53	0.2170
B: Performance plan adoption (before/after)	0.92	0.3382
A x B interaction	0.89	0.3462
Control variables		
Early/late adoption	21.79	0.0001
Covariates		
Size	28.27	0.0001
Rate of return on assets	71.87	0.0001

Notes:
*$R^2 = 0.1607$.
Overall $F = 20.88$ ($p = 0.0001$).

Table 5B.3
Results of Overall Analysis of Covariance for Absorbed Slack Computed as Working Capital/Sales*

Sources	F	P
A: Firm effect (experimental control)	0.13	0.7152
B: Performance plan adoption (before/after)	3.19	0.0748
A x B interaction	0.06	0.8093
Control variables		
Early/late adoption	1.58	0.2094
Covariates		
Size	35.52	0.0001
Rate of return on assets	136.79	0.0001

Notes:
*$R^2 = 0.2084$.
Overall $F = 29.54$ ($p = 0.0001$).

amination of the mean results on absorbed slack in Table 5B.5 shows a significant reduction in unabsorbed slack taking place subsequent to the adoption of the performance plan. This result is consistent with hypothesis 2. That is, unabsorbed slack declines following the adoption of the performance plan. It suggests that following the implementation of compensation plans managers do seek

Table 5B.4
Results of Overall Analysis of Covariance for Unabsorbed Slack Computed as Cash + Marketable Securities − Current Liabilities/Sales*

Sources	F	P
A: Firm effect (experimental control)	5.09	0.0245
B: Performance plan adoption (before/after)	14.13	0.0002
A x B interaction	4.38	0.0368
Control variables		
Early/late adoption	0.01	0.9217
Covariates		
Size	7.11	0.0079
Rate of return on assets	165.10	0.0001

Notes:
*R^2 = 0.2255.
Overall F = 32.67 (p = 0.0001).

Table 5B.5
T-Tests and Slack Means by Firm Group before and after Performance Plan Adoption

	Before Adoption	After Adoption	T
Slack 1			
Experimental Group—Mean	0.2571	0.30571	1.4962
Control Group—Mean	0.3216	0.3215	0.0021
Slack 2			
Experimental Group—Mean	0.1928	0.21166	1.3015
Control Group—Mean	0.1992	0.2135	0.9486
Slack 3			
Experimental Group—Mean	−0.1881	−0.1236	−2.1209
Control Group—Mean	−0.0713	−0.1252	−2.9442

new investment opportunities, as shown in Larcker (1983). It also suggests that some of the resources needed for the new investment come from the unabsorbed slack existing in the firms. The amount of liquid resources uncommitted to liabilities in the near future appears as the first resources to be invested by managers following the adoption of performance plans.

DISCUSSION AND SUMMARY

The hypothesis that changes in executive compensation contracts are associated with changes in managerial decisions is important to the incentive research taking place in management, accounting, and economics. One incentive question investigated in this study concerns the association between performance plan adoption and organizational slack. A differentiation was made between absorbed slack and unabsorbed slack. The results on absorbed slack were insignificant. However, the empirical results indicate that, when compared to similar non-adopting firms, those firms that adopt performance plans exhibit a significant reduction in unabsorbed slack following plan adoption. A logical interpretation is that the performance plan encourages managers to allocate their efforts toward improving accounting-based, long-term performance measures by increasing capital investment. That investment leads to a reduction of the unabsorbed slack. The unabsorbed slack is used to fund some of the increase in capital investment. Before these results can be generalized, future research should investigate the impact of the use of different measures of organizational slack, different firms, and different periods.

NOTES

1. Other related evidence indicates that the adoption of a performance plan was associated with (1) a decrease in corporate risk (Gaver, Gaver, and Furze, 1989), (2) mixed evidence on the stock market reaction to the announcement of performance plan adoption (Larcker, 1983; Brickley, Bhagat, and Lease, 1985; Gaver, Gaver, and Battistel, 1992; Kumar and Sopariwala, 1991), and (3) significant positive excess returns on announcements of earnings (Tehranian, Travlos, and Waegelein, 1987a, 1987b).

2. There is a clear differentiation between organizational slack, which refers to the difference between the available and used resources, and budgetary slack, which refers to the use of the budget process for the creation of attainable budgets.

3. For the seventy matched pairs, forty-six had the same two-digit SIC code, five had the same five-digit SIC code and nineteen had the same four-digit SIC code.

REFERENCES

Baril, C.P. 1988. "Long Term Incentive Compensation, Ownership and the Decision Horizon Problem." Working Paper, McIntyre School of Commerce, University of Virginia, Charlottesville.

Bourgeois, L.J. 1981. "Oil the Measurement of Organizational Slack." *Academy of Management Review* 6 (October): 29–39.

Bourgeois, L.J., and J.V. Singh. 1983. "Organizational Slack and Political Behavior within Top Management Teams." *Academy of Management Proceedings*: 43–47.

Brickley, J.A., S. Bhagat, and R.C. Lease. 1985. "The Impact of Long-Range Managerial Compensation Plans on Shareholder Wealth." *Journal of Accounting and Economics* 7 (April): 115–129.

Cyert, R.M., and J.G. March. 1963. *A Behavioral Theory of the Firm.* Englewood Cliffs, NJ: Prentice-Hall.

Dukes, R., T.R. Dyckman, and J. Elliot. 1981. "Accounting for Research and Development Costs: The Impact on Research and Development Expenditures." *Journal of Accounting Research* 18, Supplement: 1–26.

Gaver, J.J., K.M. Gaver, and G.P. Battistel. 1992. "The Stock Market Reaction to Performance Plan Adoptions." *The Accounting Review* 1 (January): 172–182.

Gaver, J.J., K.M. Gaver, and S. Furze. 1989. "The Association between Performance Plan Adoption and Corporate Investment Decisions." Working Paper, University of Oregon.

Hagerman, R.L., and M.E. Zmijewski. 1979. "Some Economic Determinants of Accounting Policy Choice." *Journal of Accounting and Economics* 1: 141–161.

Horwitz, B., and R. Kolodny. 1981. "The Economic Effects of Involuntary Uniformity in the Financial Reporting of R&D Expenditures." *Journal of Accounting Research* 18, Supplement: 38–74.

Kumar, R., and P.R. Sopariwala. 1991. "The Effect of Adoption of Long-Term Performance Plans on Stock Prices and Accounting Numbers." Working Paper, Virginia Polytechnic Institute and State University.

Larcker, D.F. 1983. "The Association between Performance Plan Adoption and Corporate Capital Investment." *Journal of Accounting and Economics* 5 (April): 9–30.

Lewin, A.Y., and C. Wolf. 1976. "The Theory of Organizational Slack: A Critical Review." *Proceedings: Twentieth International Meeting of ITMS*: 648–654.

March, J.G. 1978. "Bounded Rationality, Ambiguity and the Engineering of Choice." *Bell Journal of Economics* 9: 587–608.

Rosner, M.M. 1968. "Economic Determination of Organizational Innovation." *Administrative Science Quarterly* 12: 614–625.

Singh, J.V. 1983. "Performance, Slack and Risk Taking in Strategic. Decisions: Test of a Structural Equation Model." Unpublished doctoral diss., Graduate School of Business, Stanford University, Palo Alto, CA.

Singh, J.V. 1986. "Performance, Slack and Risk Taking in Organizational Decision Making." *Academy of Management Journal* 3 (September): 562–585.

Smith, C.W., and R.L. Watts. 1982. "Incentive and Tax Effects of U.S. Executive Compensation Plans." *Australian Journal of Management* 7 (December): 39–157.

Tehranian, H., T. Travlos, and J.F. Waegelein. 1985. "Market Reaction to Short-Term Executive Compensation Plan Adoption." *Journal of Accounting and Economics* 7 (April): 131–144.

Watts, R.L., and J.L. Zimmerman. 1978. "Towards a Positive Theory of the Determination of Accounting Standards." *The Accounting Review* (January): 112–134.

Williamson, O.E. 1964. *The Economics of Discretionary Behavior: Managerial Objectives in a Theory of the Firm.* Englewood Cliffs, NJ: Prentice-Hall.

Appendix 5.C. The Impact of the Multi-Divisional Structure on Organizational Slack: The Contingency of Diversification Strategy

INTRODUCTION

American corporations have been experimenting with various forms of organizational structure. The M-form or multi-divisional structure has evolved as the more popular solution to the problems of managing growth and diversity within a centralized structure. It is generally presented as providing information-processing advantages, as well as better performance in large multi-product firms (Teece, 1981). As a result the relationship between corporate diversification and firm performance has been at the forefront of issues relating to corporate strategy (Hoskisson, 1987). However, although implied by Williamson (1970) and Ezzamel (1985), the impact of the M-form implementation on organizational slack remains unexplored. This study examines the proposition that the impact of the implementation of such structure on organizational slack should vary with the diversification strategy adopted.[1] More specifically, given the trade-offs between control-system emphasis in various diversification strategies, certain controls are better suited to reducing certain types of slacks in certain strategies. The next sections cover the M-form hypothesis and organizational slack. Diversification strategy is then discussed, before a presentation of the central proposition. The next two sections set out the empirical results, and the appendix ends with a final discussion.

THE MULTI-DIVISIONAL FORM HYPOTHESIS

The multi-divisional form structure was adopted as a response to the increasingly complex administrative problems encountered within a centralized functional structure as firm size and diversity increased (Chandler, 1962). Building on Chandler's analysis, Williamson (1970) suggested that because of two problems encountered by expanding multi-product firms—cumulative control loss and confounding of strategic and operating decision making—there is the risk of failure to achieve least-cost profit maximization behavior. Basically, he maintained that as size increases, people reach their limits of control as a result of bounded rationality and start resorting to opportunism, thereby threatening efficiency and profitability. The M-form is presented as a unique structural framework that overcomes these difficulties and favors goal pursuits and least-cost behavior more nearly associated with the neoclassical profit-maximizing hypothesis.

Source: A. Riahi-Belkaoui, "The Impact of the Multi-Divisional Structure on Organizational Slack: The Contingency of Diversification Strategy." *British Journal of Management* 9, 1998, pp. 211–217. Reprinted with permission of Blackwell Publishing.

Based on the transaction-cost analysis, researchers investigated a hypothesis of links between the M-form structure and better performance.[2] Results to date provide either a support of the proposition that M-form implementation affects performance in large corporations regardless of other contingencies or mixed results (Cable and Dirrheimer, 1983; Ezzamel, 1985). These studies did not differentiate between the firms on the basis of their diversification strategy. Two studies provide evidence in support of a contingency view of the relationship between either performance (Hoskisson, 1987) or productivity (Riahi-Belkaoui, 1997) and implementation of the M-form structure. These studies examined considerations of return and risk, but not organizational slack.

ORGANIZATIONAL SLACK

Because the definition of slack is often intertwined with a description of the functions that slack serves, Bourgeois (1981) discussed these functions as a means of making palpable the ways of measuring slack.[3] From a review of administrative theory literature, he identified organizational slack as an independent variable that either "causes" or serves four primary functions:

1. as an instrument for organizational actors to remain in the system, a form of inducement (Barnard, 1938; March and Simon, 1958; Cyert and March, 1963);
2. as a resource for conflict resolution (Pondy, 1967);
3. as a technical buffer from the variances and discontinuities created by environmental uncertainty (Thompson, 1967; Galbraith, 1973);
4. as a facilitator of certain types of strategic or creative behavior, providing opportunities for a satisfying behavior and promoting political behavior (Hambrick and Snow, 1977).

One of the problems of empirically investigating the presence of organizational slack related to the difficulties of securing adequate measurement for the phenomenon. Various ad hoc measures based on questionnaires, interviews, or archival measures were proposed (Rosner, 1968; Bourgeois; 1981). Bourgeois and Singh (1983) refined these measures by suggesting that slack can be differentiated on an "ease of recovery dimension." A distinction is made between absorbed slack, slack that has been absorbed as cost in the organization, and unabsorbed slack, referring to excess liquidity not yet earmarked for particular uses.

Absorbed slack was measured by the level of general and administrative expenses divided by the cost of goods sold. This concept of absorbed slack, also referred to as administrative slack, captures slack absorbed as costs. It follows from Williamson's notion of slack as extra staff that can be reduced in difficult times (Williamson, 1970).

Unabsorbed slack was measured by the sum of cash and marketable securities minus current liabilities divided by sales. It follows the notion of slack as readily accessible resources not absorbed by costs, thus giving the amount of liquid resources uncommitted to liabilities in the near future.

DIVERSIFICATION STRATEGY AND CONTROL

Galbraith and Nathanson (1979) traced the growth of firms to three major categories of corporate diversification strategy: vertical integration, related business diversification, and unrelated business diversification.

Vertical integration offers the firm economics owing to control of its supply/output markets. The firm's value-added margin for a chain of processing is increased because of increased control over raw materials and/or outlets (Pfeffer and Salancik, 1978; Scherer, 1980; Harrigan, 1985). Furthermore, market transaction costs—such as opportunistic actions by traders or the drafting and monitoring of contingent claims contracts to ensure harmonious trading relationships—can be either eliminated or reduced (Hill and Hoskisson, 1987).

Firms pursuing a strategy of related diversification can realize synergistic economies of scope through the joint use of inputs (Teece, 1981). Exploitation of this energy is achieved through both tangible and intangible interrelationships (Porter, 1985). Tangible interrelationships are created by such devices as joint procurement of raw materials, joint development of shared technologies or production process, joint sales force, and joint physical distribution systems. Intangible interrelationships arise from the sharing of know-how and capabilities.

An unrelated diversification strategy is assumed to yield financial economies. The risk of pooling of imperfectly correlated income streams created by unrelated diversification is, in principle, assumed to produce an asset with a superior risk/return relationship (Lewellen, 1971).

The differences in economic characteristics between the three types of strategies create situations that will call for different types of control. It is suggested that control arrangements within a basic M-form framework must be consistent with a firm's corporate diversification strategy if the firm is to realize the economic benefits associated with that strategy. Similarly, based on a review of a large body of research on strategy implementation, Baysingh and Hoskisson (1989) concluded that firms pursuing a dominant or vertical strategy place a higher emphasis on strategic control than related and unrelated diversification, in that order, and a lower emphasis on financial controls than related and unrelated diversifiers, in that order.

THEORY AND HYPOTHESES

The M-form hypothesis predicts that under the U-form structure, a fair degree of managerial slack would develop within each department, causing the creation of discretionary investment projects to justify the extra staff (Ezzamel, 1985; Williamson, 1996). The implementation of the M-form structure is expected to reduce this managerial slack and channel the operation of the firm toward goal pursuit and least-cost behavior more nearly associated with the neoclassical profit maximization hypothesis (Williamson, 1970).

The reduction of slack following the implementation of the M-form differs, however, depending on whether slack refers to absorbed or unabsorbed slack and on the diversification strategy adopted.

If the diversification strategy adopted is a vertical integration or related diversification, a greater emphasis is placed on strategic control than on financial control. It eliminates the need for extra staff and discretionary investment projects, and the formulation of investment opportunities occurs at the top of the organization or at the level of strategic business units (Ackerman, 1976). Absorbed slack or administrative slack should therefore be expected to decrease following the implementation of the M-form by firms using either vertical integration or related diversification. The reduction of unabsorbed slack may be more difficult given the moderate or low reliance on financial controls.

If the diversification strategy adopted is an unrelated diversification, a higher emphasis is placed on financial control than on strategic control. It reduces the level of unabsorbed slack as cash flows are not automatically returned to their sources but, instead, are exposed to internal competition, and investment projects are evaluated on strict objective criteria. The reduction of absorbed slack may be more difficult because of the extra staff needed to manage the large accountability for divisional profits. This suggests the following two hypotheses:

H1: Implementation of the M-form structure in vertically integrated and in related diversified firms leads to a decrease in absorbed slack.

H2: Implementation of the M-form structure in unrelated diversified firms leads to a decrease in unabsorbed slack.

METHODS

Sample and Data Collection

Previous research has identified sixty-two firms that adopted the M-form during the period 1950–1978 (Armour and Teece, 1978). The sample used in this study consists of these firms. Each firm was diversified at the time of the restructuring and is classified by Rumelt's (1974) method as having been in one of three diversification classes: unrelated (sixteen firms), related (twenty-two firms), or vertical (twenty-four firms).

A longitudinal design is used to capture the effects over time of the implementation of the M-form.[4] Data for two measures of slack were collected for year −5 through year +5 (relative to the year of restructuring). In addition, three covariables (growth in gross national product [GNP], growth in total assets, and firm size) and two control variables (early/late adoption of the M-form and industry classification) are used.

Dependent Variable

Financial statement data for years -5 to $+5$ (relative to the year of restructuring) for each firm were collected from Compustat. Year 0, relative to the year of restructuring, was excluded from the analysis to avoid the potential confounding of slack measures with events during the transition. The data collected were absorbed slack—computed as general and administrative costs divided by cost of goods sold—and unabsorbed slack—computed as cash plus marketable securities minus current liabilities divided by sales.

Control Variables and Covariables

The two control factors (early/late adoption of the M-form and industry classification) and three covariates (growth in GNP, growth in total assets, and firm size) are included to control for possible intervening effects.

The early/late adopter control factor is motivated by the belief that late adopters learn from the experience of early adopters and are thus able to restructure faster and more efficiently (Mansfield, 1985). Early/late adoption is measured by the year of restructuring relative to the sample median. Hence, firms adopting the M-form structure prior to 1967 are classified as early movers, and those adopting in 1967 or later are classified as late movers. The industry control factor is included to control for industry effects. Firm size, asset growth rate, and GNP growth rate are included as covariates. Their use is motivated by the suggestion that firms may sacrifice profitability in periods of growth and by the need to control for changes in organizational slack related to major external shifts in aggregate demands. Firm size is measured as the proportional change in total assets, and GNP growth is measured as the proportional change in GNP. Each of the covariates is measured for the same period as the dependent variable.

DATA ANALYSIS

To test the overall relationship between organizational structure and organizational slack, between diversification strategy and organizational slack, and between the interactive effect of organizational structure and diversification strategy on organizational slack, an analysis of covariance is used. Tables 5C.1 and 5C.2 present the results of the analysis of covariance for absorbed and unabsorbed slack for the sixty-two firms in the sample. The results of the overall analysis of the covariance in both exhibits are highly significant and suggest that organizational structure and organizational slack as well as diversification strategy and organizational slack are related. The significant interaction effect in both figures between strategic type and the implementation of the M-form

Table 5C.1
Results of Overall Analysis of Variance for the Absorbed Slack

Sources	F	P
Diversification strategy	760.32	0.0001*
M-form implementation (before/after)	432.25	0.0001*
M-form* diversification interaction	851.26	0.0001*
Control variable		
Early/late adopter	2.85	0.094**
Covariates		
Size	0.00	0.947
Total asset growth	0.16	0.685
Total growth in GNP	1.08	0.295
Industry	684.19	0.001*

Notes: *Significant at $\alpha = 0.01$; **Significant at $\alpha = 0.10$.

suggests that the M-form implementation had a differential impact on organizational slack, depending on the diversification strategy adopted.

The impact of the M-form implementation on organizational slack is further investigated by performing mean comparisons of absorbed and unabsorbed slack before and after the M-form by strategic type. Table 5C.3 presents the results. It indicates that following the implementation of the M-form, vertically integrated and related diversified firms decreased their absorbed slack while unrelated diversified firms decreased their unabsorbed slack, which is consistent with both H1 and H2.

DISCUSSION

The objective of this study was to show that the implementation of the M-form structure creates differences in organizational slack measures in firms that employ different diversification strategies. The slack measures used were absorbed or administrative slack, and unabsorbed slack or available liquidity. The diversification strategies were related diversification, vertical integration, and unrelated diversification. The results show that the implementation of the M-form structure was supported for both absorbed and unabsorbed slack.

H1 was confirmed, suggesting that the implementation of a multidivisional

Table 5C.2
Results of Overall Analysis of Variance for the Unabsorbed Slack

Sources	F	P
Diversification strategy	5.76	0.0061*
M-form implementation (before/after)	7.06	0.0110**
M-form* diversification interaction	2.33	0.0032*
Control variable		
Early/late adopter	2.87	0.094**
Covariates		
Size	0.00	0.945
Total asset growth	0.17	0.683
Total growth in GNP	1.09	0.299
Industry	2.29	0.0033*

Notes: *Significant at $\alpha = 0.01$; **Significant at $\alpha = 0.10$.

structure leads to a reduction of absorbed slack or administrative slack in both vertically integrated and related diversified firms. This result follows from the general thesis that the M-form reduces the organizational slack developed within each department under the U-form and from the particular thesis that vertically integrated and related diversified firms rely most on strategic controls that are most effective in monitoring expenditures on excess staff and discretionary expenses.

H2 was also confirmed, suggesting that the implementation of a multidivisional structure leads to reduction of unabsorbed slack or available liquidity in unrelated diversified firms. This result follows again from the slack reduction thesis of the M-form hypothesis and from the particular thesis that unrelated diversified firms rely mostly on financial controls that are most effective in monitoring cash flows within the firm.

The results suggest that the M-form implementation increases the firm's capacity to manage absorbed slack in the cases of vertically integrated and related diversified firms and unabsorbed slack in the case of unrelated diversified firms. It points to additional benefits of the M-form, when coupled with the appropriate control system, strategic controls for the vertically integrated and related diver-

Table 5C.3
T-Tests and Slack Measures, Means, and Standard Deviations by Strategy Types
before and after M-form Implementation

Measures	Before M-form		After M-form		
	Mean	s.d.	Mean	s.d.	t
Vertically integrated firms					
Absorbed slack	0.16744	0.086100	0.14860	0.0674	0.8260
Unabsorbed slack	-0.05838	0.007711	-0.10210	0.0689	2.1339*
Related diversified firms					
Absorbed slack	0.28156	0.187870	0.29270	0.20022	-0.1859
Unabsorbed slack	-0.07611	0.147400	-0.14080	0.11942	1.5627**
Unrelated diversified firms					
Absorbed slack	2.66570	7.487400	0.20720	0.14642	1.2715**
Unabsorbed slack	-0.16067	0.108448	-0.14640	0.06373	-0.4394

Notes: *Significant at $\alpha = 0.05$; **Significant at $\alpha = 0.10$.

sified firms, and financial controls for the unrelated diversified firms. The efficient use of control systems is contingent on the nature of the diversification strategy. In general, benefits would result from an increase in the use of financial controls by the related diversified and vertically integrated firms and in the use of strategic controls by the unrelated diversified firms. In this particular case, a reduction in absorbed slack is possible through the implementation of strategic controls for vertically integrated and related diversified firms, and a reduction in unabsorbed slack is possible through the implementation of financial controls for the unrelated diversified firms. Obviously, more research is needed to verify these results using different measures of slack, and/or using different companies from different periods and from different countries.

NOTES

1. It follows from other studies showing the contingency of diversification strategy on the relationship between multi-divisional structure and performance (Hoskisson, 1987; Riahi-Belkaoui, 1997) and between multi-divisional structure and capital structure (Riahi-Belkaoui and Bannister, 1994).

2. Fligstein (1985) proposed five theories that may be used to explain the genesis of the multidivisional structure: (1) strategy-structure thesis (Chandler, 1962), (2) transaction-cost analysis (Williamson, 1970), (3) population-ecology theory (Hannan and Freeman, 1977, 1984), (4) control theory based on power (Pfeffer and Salancik, 1978; Pfeffer, 1981, 1982), and (5) organizational homogeneity theory (DiMaggio and Powell, 1983).

3. While this study examines the concept of organizational slack, most of the related accounting studies examined the concept of budgetary slack. The literature on organizational slack shows that managers have the motives necessary to operate in a slack environment. The literature on budgetary slack considers the budget as the embodiment of that environment and, therefore, assumes that managers will use the budgeting process to bargain for slack budgets (Schiff and Lewin, 1968; Merchant, 1985).

4. Various studies have evaluated various proxies of performance over several years following a major corporate policy (Healy and Palepu, 1988; Lakonishok and Vermaelen, 1990; Agrawal, Jaffee, and Mandelken, 1992; Cornett and Tehranian, 1992; Healy, Palepu, and Ruback, 1992; John, Lang, and Netter, 1992; Smith, 1990).

REFERENCES

Ackerman, R.W. (1976). "Influences of Integration and Diversity in the Investment Process." *Administrative Science Quarterly* 15, pp. 341–351.

Agrawal, A., F. Jaffe, and G. Mandelker. (1992). "The Post Merger Performance of Acquiring Firms: A Re-Examination of an Anomaly." *Journal of Finance* 47, pp. 1605–1622.

Armour, R.A., and D.J. Teece. (1978). "Organizational Structure and Economic Performance: A Test of the Multi Divisional Hypothesis." *Journal of Economics* 9, pp. 106–122.

Barnard, C.I. (1938) *Functions of the Executive.* Cambridge, MA: Harvard University Press.

Baysingh, B., and R.E. Hoskisson. (1989). "Diversification Strategy and R&D Intensity in Multi-Product Firms." *Academy of Management Journal* 12, pp. 310–322.

Bourgeois, L.J. (1981). "On the Measurement of Organizational Slack." *Academy of Management Review* 6, pp. 29–39.

Bourgeois, L.J., and J.V. Singh. (1983). "Organizational Slack and Political Behavior within Top Management." *Academy of Management Proceedings* 2(2), pp. 43–47.

Cable, J., and M.J. Dirrheimer. (1983). "Hierarchies and Markets: An Empirical Test of the Multidimensional Hypothesis in West Germany." *International Journal of Industrial Organization* 1, pp. 43–62.

Chandler, A.D., Jr. (1962). *Strategy and Structure: Chapters in the History of the American Industrial Enterprise.* Cambridge, MA: MIT Press.

Cornett, M.M., and H. Tehranian. (1992). "Change in Corporate Performance Associated with Bank Acquisitions." *Journal of Financial Economics* 31, pp. 211–234.

Cyert, R.M., and J.G. March. (1963). *A Behavioral Theory of the Firm.* Englewood Cliffs, NJ: Prentice-Hall.

DiMaggio, P., and W. Powell. (1983). "Institutional Isomorphism." *American Sociological Review* 48, pp. 142–160.

Ezzamel, M.A. (1985). "On the Assessment of the Performance Effects of Multidivisional Structures: A Synthesis." *Accounting and Business Research* 61, pp. 23–34.

Fligstein, N. (1985). "The Spread of the Multi Divisional Form among Large Firms, 1919–1979." *American Sociological Review* 3, pp. 377–391.

Galbraith, J.R. (1973). *Designing Complex Organizations*. Reading, MA: Addison-Wesley.

Galbraith, J.R., and D.A. Nathanson. (1979). "Role of Organizational Structure and Process." In D. Schendel and S. Hofer (eds.), *Strategic Management: A New View of Business Policy and Planning*. Boston: Little, Brown.

Hambrick, D.C., and C.C. Snow. (1977). "A Contextual Model of Strategic Decision Making in Organizations." *Academy of Management Proceedings* 3, pp. 109–112.

Hannan, M., and J. Freeman. (1977). "The Population Ecology of Organizations." *American Journal of Sociology* 92, pp. 929–964.

Hannan, M., and J. Freeman. (1984). "Structural Inertia and Organizational Change." *American Sociological Review* 49, pp. 149–164.

Harrigan, K.R. (1985). "Vertical Integration and Corporate Strategy." *Academy of Management Journal* 28, pp. 397–425.

Healy, P.M., and K.G. Palepu. (1988). "Earnings Information Conveyed by Dividend Initiations and Omissions." *Journal of Financial Economics* 21(2), pp. 149–175.

Healy, P.M., K.G. Palepu, and R.S. Ruback. (1992). "Does Corporate Performance Improve after Mergers?" *Journal of Financial Economics* 31(2), pp. 135–175.

Hill, C.W.L., and R.E. Hoskisson. (1987). "Strategy and Structure in the Multi Product Firm." *Academy of Management Review* 4, pp. 331–334.

Hoskisson, R.E. (1987). "Multi Divisional Structure and Performance: The Contingency of Diversification Strategy." *Academy of Management Journal* 3, pp. 625–644.

John, K., L.H.E. Lang, and J. Netter. (1992). "The Voluntary Restructuring of Large Firms in Response to Performance Decline." *Journal of Finance* 47(3), pp. 891–916.

Lakonishok, J., and T. Vermaelen. (1990). "Anomalous Price Behavior around Repurchase Tender Offers." *Journal of Finance* 45(2), pp. 455–477.

Lewellen, W. (1971). "A Pure Financial Rationale for the Conglomerate Merger." *Journal of Finance* 26, pp. 521–545.

Mansfield, E. (1985). "How Rapidly Does New Industrial Technology Leak Out?" *Journal of Industrial Economics* 34, pp. 217–255.

March, J.C., and H.A. Simon. (1958). *Organizations*. New York: John Wiley.

Merchant, K.A. (1985). "Budgeting and the Propensity to Create Budgetary Slack." *Accounting Organizations and Society* 10, pp. 201–210.

Pfeffer, J. (1981). *Power in Organizations*. Marshfield, MA: Pilman.

Pfeffer, J. (1982). *Organizations and Organizational Theory*. Marshfield, MA: Pilman.

Pfeffer, J., and G. Salancik. (1978). *The External Control of Organizations: A Resource Dependency Perspective*. New York: Harper and Row.

Pondy L.R. (1967). "Organizational Conflict: Concepts and Models." *Administrative Science Quarterly* 12(2), pp. 296–320.

Porter, L.R. (1985). *Competitive Advantage: Creating and Sustaining Superior Performance*. New York: Free Press.

Riahi-Belkaoui, A. (1997). "Multidivisional Structure and Productivity: The Contingency of Diversification Strategy." *Journal of Business Finance and Accountancy* 24, pp. 615–627.

Riahi-Belkaoui, A., and J. Bannister. (1994). "Multidivisional Structure and Capital

Structure: The Contingency of Diversification Strategy." *Managerial and Decision Economics* 15, pp. 267–276.

Rosner, M.M. (1968). "Economic Determinants of Organizational Innovation." *Administrative Science Quarterly* 12, pp. 614–625.

Rumelt, R.P. (1974). *Strategy, Structure and Economic Performance*. Cambridge, MA: Harvard University Press.

Scherer, F.M. (1980). *Industrial Market Structure and Economic Performance*. Chicago: Rand McNally.

Schiff, M., and A.Y. Lewin. (1968). "Where Traditional Budgeting Fails." *Financial Executive* (May), pp. 50–62.

Smith, A. (1990). "Corporate Ownership Structure and Performance: The Case of Management Buyouts." *Journal of Financial Economics* 27(1), pp. 143–164.

Teece, D.J. (1981). "Internal Organization and Economic Performance: An Empirical Analysis of the Profitability of Principal Firms." *Journal of Industrial Economics* 30, pp. 173–199.

Thompson, J.D. (1967). *Organizations in Action*. New York: McGraw-Hill.

Williamson, O.E. (1970). *Corporate Control and Business Behavior*. Englewood Cliffs, NJ: Prentice-Hall.

Williamson, O.E. (1996). *Mechanisms of Governance*. Oxford: Oxford University Press.

Index

About the Author

AHMED RIAHI-BELKAOUI is CBA Distinguished Professor of Accounting in the College of Business Administration, University of Illinois, Chicago. Author and coauthor of more than 40 Quorum books, he is an equally prolific contributor to the scholarly and professional journals of his field and has served on various editorial boards that oversee them. He is the editor of *Review of Accounting and Finance.*